ENTREPRENEURS IN CULTURAL CONTEXT, ed. by Sidney M. Greenfield, Arnold Strickon, and Robert T. Aubey. New Mexico, 1979. 373p (School of American Research, advanced seminar series) bibl index 78-21433. 22.50 ISBN 0-8263-0504-0. C.I.P.

Interest in the entrepreneur as a social institution continues to increase, and this collection of studies expands the investigation into anthropology. The concept of entrepreneurship may be too inclusive since the subjects range from 17th-century Portuguese officials to 20th-century state enterprise administrators in Mexico. Three of the ten cases studied were done in Mexico and in the US with one in the Seychelles and three in South America. A variety of businesses are examined in these countries at different stages of their development. Using interesting and extensive field research or historical documents, the ten authors also draw on previous studies they have made. There is little recognition of economic or business analysis of entrepreneurship other than Schumpeter's contribution of the entrepreneur as the innovator in society. The introduction and conclusion by the editors emphasize the importance of family and kinship for entrepreneurial activity and urge further research on these relationships. An interesting aspect is the crucial importance of information to these entrepreneurs, possibly because of the less developed economies in which they functioned. There is an impressive listing of references instead of a bibliography. Adequate index. Useful as a social analysis and reference on entrepreneurship for comparative research.

School of American Research
Advanced Seminar Series

DOUGLAS W. SCHWARTZ, GENERAL EDITOR

SCHOOL OF AMERICAN RESEARCH
ADVANCED SEMINAR SERIES

Entrepreneurs in Cultural Context

This Advanced Seminar
was made possible
by a generous gift from
the Weyerhaeuser Foundation, Inc.

ENTREPRENEURS IN CULTURAL CONTEXT

EDITED BY
SIDNEY M. GREENFIELD,
ARNOLD STRICKON,
AND ROBERT T. AUBEY

A SCHOOL OF AMERICAN RESEARCH BOOK
UNIVERSITY OF NEW MEXICO PRESS • Albuquerque

Library of Congress Cataloging in Publication Data
Main entry under title:

Entrepreneurs in cultural context.

(School of American Research advanced seminar series)
"A School of American Research book."
Bibliography: p. 351.
Includes index.
1. Entrepreneur—Addresses, essays, lectures.
I. Greenfield, Sidney M.   II. Strickon, Arnold.
III. Aubey, Robert T.   IV. Title.   V. Series: Santa
Fe, N.M. School of American Research. Advanced
seminar series.
HB615.E6   301.18'32   78-21433
ISBN 0-8263-0504-0

Foreword

Cultures are ultimately transformed by the actions and decisions of individuals. Perhaps in no area of social science research is this process more dramatically illustrated than in the study of the entrepreneur. This volume focuses on individuals who play this role, their social and cultural context, and the elements of a model elucidating their activity. Entrepreneurs operate on a common principle, orchestrating networks of trust and placing themselves in positions to obtain information, resources, and opportunities for investment. But for the process to operate, the individual involved must have a rare combination of traits: high physical energy, confidence to act on new opportunities, adaptability to altered conditions, and the ability to inspire others to follow new cultural paths. The entrepreneur is also able to work within the cultural system while consciously upsetting its state of equilibrium to his advantage. If successful, entrepreneurs may at least change the economy of a region and at most found an economic empire. In many ways, then, the entrepreneurs are the movers and shakers of any society.

Not all cultures equally encourage entrepreneurs, as evidenced by the contrast in economic growth between industrialized and Third World countries. So the interdisciplinary and cross-cultural perspectives of the advanced seminar on which this volume is based were ideal for examining the social base of entrepreneurial activity. Ten case studies present comprehensive descriptions and analyses of entrepreneurs in several cultural settings and reinforce one another, since each highlights specific aspects of the pattern.

A brief mention of the ten cases presented can only begin to indicate the insights provided in the volume. A seventeenth-century Brazilian entrepreneur is seen integrating several components of the sugarcane industry and illustrates the importance of family in developing a network of loyalty. The rise and decay of an elite Southern American planter in the nineteenth century illustrates the social basis of an information network. The founding and growth of the Life Insurance Company of Georgia explores the advantage taken of a new market situation. The bold innovations of a small-scale entrepreneur in the rural highlands of central Peru illustrate how social networks can act both as a support and as a constraint to the mobilization of resources as an enterprise diversifies. Entrepreneurs in rural Wisconsin show the operation of ethnic ties in the generation of business support. Successful decision making emerging from access to assorted networks of information in the public sector exemplifies how the entrepreneurial process was used in one phase of the Mexican bureaucracy. The capital mobilization process during the changing period of economic growth from the family firm to the investment group is illustrated from Mexican data. The dynamics of investment groups are shown as they operate in the industrial modernization of Nicaragua. A strategy of developing kin-type loyalty outside the family for the acquisition of trust relationships is illustrated by fiesta groups in rural Mexico. The effect of cultural values and social pressures on the success or failure of entrepreneurial activity is taken from a case in the Seychelles Islands comparing the results of African Creole, East Indian, and Chinese businessmen.

Following these detailed cases a final chapter utilizing the contributors' insights to examine the impact of individuals like entrepreneurs on changes in the cultural system produces an elegant theory of social change. Clearly this volume makes several important contributions to the social sciences in this case study documentation, its cross-cultural analysis of the entrepreneur, and the use of this material to create an exciting view of cultural alteration. It is certainly a distinguished addition to the School of American Research Advanced Seminar Series.

Douglas W. Schwartz

School of American Research

Preface

Although its genesis goes back to 1968, this book resulted directly from a seminar sponsored by the School of American Research in Santa Fe, New Mexico, in 1975, entitled "The Economic Anthropology of Investment Behavior in the Americas." The composition of the seminar—five anthropologists, three economists, and two historians—reflected the interdisciplinary framework that had characterized our approach to the project from its earliest, informal beginnings. The idea of bringing together a group of scholars from different disciplines to focus on entrepreneurial investment in the Americas emerged from panel discussions held at the 1970 and 1971 annual conventions of the American Anthropological Association on that topic. The basis of these, in turn, was an early draft of a paper by Robert T. Aubey, John Kyle, and Arnold Strickon, which was published in 1974 under the title, "Investment Behavior and Elite Social Structure in Latin America." That article was used by the participants of the School of American Research seminar, from which this volume grows, as the point of departure.

The original concept of using an interdisciplinary (specifically anthropology and economics) approach to the study of investment behavior arose from a series of discussions between Strickon and Aubey which began in 1968. At the time we both were working on similar socioeconomic phenomena albeit from different disciplinary approaches. In retrospect, our collaboration was probably inevitable given our general interests, areas of research, and association with the Ibero-American Studies Program at the University of Wisconsin-Madison. In point of fact, however, we were brought together by a colleague who, knowing what each of us was interested in, brought our work to each other's attention.

At that time Aubey was in the early stages of his work on investment groups in Latin America, and was rather frustrated in his attempts to assess more thoroughly the role and influence of extraeconomic variables such as family relationships and friendship on these investment groups. Although it was obvious that there was a high degree of interrelationship between families and certain groups of business firms, he felt that his lack of formal training in anthropology and sociology hindered an analysis of family influences. In a similar way, Strickon also expressed a feeling of frustration, but from the other side. He had recently returned from Argentina, where he had conducted research that had included a number of wealthy extended families which played rather important roles in regional and/or national society. It was obvious that in some way the very kinship structure of these units was related to the fact that they were business management groups as well. And Strickon was not professionally equipped to deal with this facet of family activities.

It was soon obvious to both of us that the complexity of the phenomena we were investigating required an approach that was not restricted to our respective disciplines. We set upon our new enterprise with a high degree of excitement and expectation until we were jolted back to the reality that our different conceptual frameworks and jargons made communication difficult in spite of our common fascination with the topic. Thus we had to spend the first months of our joint venture in learning basic concepts in the other's area of specialization, agreeing on a common jargon (at least between ourselves), and agreeing upon a level of analysis and approach to the materials that would be consistent with our respective professional orientations and yet would be significant within the conceptual framework of the other. We were immensely aided in this by the fact that about this time Burton Benedict's seminal article "Family Firms and Economic Development" (1968) appeared in the *Southwest Journal of Anthropology*.

During this period we decided that the material and approach we were developing would be ideal as the focal point for an Inter-departmental Seminar sponsored by the Ibero-American Studies Program on the Madison campus of the University of Wisconsin. The seminar permitted us to draw on the knowledge, and labor, of a number of advanced graduate students from a variety of disciplines. One of these students, John Kyle, who was then writing his doctoral dissertation, joined the two of us at the end of the seminar as a coauthor of the final article.

By this time, after trying out the investment paper on a number of faculty colleagues, we began to think of going public. It was at this point that Greenfield entered the picture. Sidney Greenfield had been working with Strickon on the papers from another confer-ence held at the School of American Research (Strickon and Green-field 1972). It was, of course, natural that Strickon should discuss our project with Greenfield, especially since each of the topics had some relevance for the other. Greenfield also could see the signifi-cance of the model we were developing for his own interests in Latin America and the European expansion. Greenfield urged that the Aubey, Kyle, and Strickon paper be presented at the next meet-ing of the American Anthropological Association, which was to be held in San Diego. The presentation there, in November 1970, was extremely successful both in leading us to further work on the manuscript and in generating discussion and interest. We decided to expand it still further at the following year's convention in New York. The participants in both these panels, and, of equal impor-tance, the lively discussion from the floor at both of the sessions, led us to begin exploring the possibilities of arranging a more intensive interchange than was possible at a national convention.

Our thoughts turned first to the School of American Research. Greenfield had been one of the organizers of the conference on patronage, the publication of which he and Strickon had edited. That volume had only recently appeared when we, with some trepi-dation (had we outworn our welcome?), approached the School's Board of Directors with the proposal for a conference on investment decision making. To our great pleasure the proposal was accepted and the conference scheduled.

The facilities provided by the School of American Research for scientific conferences are close to ideal. The director, Dr. Douglas Schwartz, and his staff provide facilities, a setting, staff, and services that permit the participants to devote themselves wholly and without distraction to their subject for five or six days, eighteen hours a day, if they so wish. And usually we did. Some of the participants had been directly or indirectly involved in the development of the conference almost from the beginning. William Glade, for example, had been the broker between Strickon and Aubey. Burt Benedict, in addition to authoring the stimulating work on family firms which had proven so important to us early in our work, had been a participant at both convention panels. Others came to our attention later, like Gerry Gold, who was an extremely active participant from the audience in the stimulating discussion following the formal presentation at the New York AAA convention panel. Still others, like Morton Rothstein and Norman Long, were known to the organizers only on the basis of their earlier work on related topics.

Each of the participants was instructed to prepare a paper which would be oriented primarily to substantive rather than theoretical issues. Earlier experience with conferences of this kind had indicated to us that to begin with theoretical issues increases the probability that people will align themselves along disciplinary, theoretical, ideological, and political lines, alignments which often hinder rather than enhance communication. We expected, rather, that the conceptual and theoretical issues would develop out of the discussion of the papers, as indeed they did. This sort of process required that all papers be distributed well in advance of the conference and that all be read by all participants in advance. And indeed they were. The discussions that resulted as each paper was brought in turn before the group were often hard and called the author to task in terms of problems and areas which were ignored, theoretical issues, and the like. We were not gentle with each other, yet we believe that in spite of the differences among the group in age, experience, academic rank, and so forth, there were no prima donnas, no ego trips, and no goats.

For those of us who were involved in this, the whole process—from our first discussion of a topic of common interest over a cup of coffee, through the intense personal interactions of the conference, to this volume—represents all that academia ought to be and too rarely is.

Robert T. Aubey
Arnold Strickon

Contents

PART 3 RESULTS AND OUTCOMES: SOCIAL PATTERNS
AND GROUPS

PART 4 NEW DIRECTIONS

PART 1

Introduction

1

Studies in Entrepreneurial Behavior: A Review and an Introduction

SIDNEY M. GREENFIELD

Department of Anthropology
University of Wisconsin–Milwaukee

ARNOLD STRICKON

Department of Anthropology
University of Wisconsin–Madison

ROBERT T. AUBEY

School of Business
University of Wisconsin–Madison

MORTON ROTHSTEIN

Department of History
University of Wisconsin–Madison

This book is about entrepreneurship and entrepreneurial behavior, but it did not start that way. Instead, the contributors were invited to prepare working papers for an advanced seminar on "The Economic Anthropology of Investment Behavior in Latin America." Not until we were discussing our papers at the School of American Research did we realize not only that we were discussing issues central to the study of entrepreneurship but that our interdisciplinary approach to investment decision making had added fresh insights and a new perspective to entrepreneurial studies. The authors revised their papers in the light of what we had learned during the

3

seminar so that in their published form the chapters to follow focus on entrepreneurship and the decision making it involves. The geographical coverage also has been expanded so that it no longer is restricted to Latin America. Instead, we now present a range of cases representing frontier situations in the expansion and complex growth of Western civilization.

In this introduction to the conference papers we shall (1) review briefly the history of entrepreneurial studies; (2) relate studies of investment decision making to the main issues and problems of entrepreneurial studies; (3) introduce the case studies that are the core of this volume; (4) summarize the major substantive findings of the case studies on the importance of social relationships of confidence and trust in the conduct of enterprise; and (5) introduce the new theoretical and conceptual directions in which we believe our approach will take entrepreneurial studies specifically and social science theory in general.

ENTREPRENEURIAL STUDIES: A REVIEW

Interdisciplinary interest in entrepreneurship and the behavior patterns associated with it is relatively recent. Since the end of the Second World War heightened concern with problems of economic development has contributed significantly to the spread of interest in the subject. Originally a concern of economists, historians, and the students of business (and their critics), entrepreneurship was taken up by psychologists, sociologists, and anthropologists after earlier scholars had grappled with it in a less than systematic way for about two generations.

Until the 1920s, for example, most economists were more interested in the institutional processes and arrangements that produced and sustained states of equilibrium in the "market" than they were either in the dynamics that changed the equilibrium or in adjustments to such change. Hence their theoretical and conceptual formulations of the behavior of individual participants in the market stressed the "rationally motivated" decisions that resulted in the maintenance of equilibrium. Individual behavior that disturbed the balance, or created a new one, consequently was neglected both in

4

theory and in practice. The conceptualization of entrepreneurship as an independent rather than a dependent variable was not an issue of importance to neoclassical economics. It was to become one, however, as economists began to revise their thinking in response to the events of the decades following the 1920s, the accelerated growth of the developed nations after 1945, and the absence of growth in the so-called Third World.

Modern scholarly interest in entrepreneurship derives from two overlapping lines of inquiry: (1) the efforts by theoretical economists to separate profits and other related elements conceptually from other returns to management in the market system; and (2) the work of economic institutionalists and business scholars interested in celebrating the achievements of, or criticizing, businessmen, firms, and even sectors of the economy. In the work of the theoretical economists the entrepreneur was an abstract figure, operating within the neoclassical framework and unaffected by influences external to the rational operation of the firm he directed. Out of this tradition, however, came *The Theory of Economic Development*, Joseph A. Schumpeter's major contribution to the reconceptualization of economic growth and the study of entrepreneurship. This work first appeared in German in 1912. After several revisions it was published in English in 1934 (a revised edition appeared in 1949). Schumpeter's thinking then was modified and elaborated in his two-volume study of *Business Cycles* (1939) and his "popular" wartime book, *Capitalism, Socialism, and Democracy* (1942), and was given final summation in his posthumous *A History of Economic Analysis* (1954). Several of his other writings also present aspects of his reasonably consistent views.

Schumpeter postulated his theory as an alternative to what he referred to as "equilibrium theories" of economic process. His basic point was that the ultimate explanation of economic conduct was to be found in noneconomic factors, and that these were brought into play through the actions of individuals operating in the market.

As the title of his book indicates, Schumpeter was interested primarily in economic growth. His analysis, however, rested upon a series of implicit assumptions rooted in those lines of eighteenth- and nineteenth-century European social thought that viewed society as an evolving organism that inevitably developed in a progressive direction (Nisbet 1969). Schumpeter therefore believed, like such thinkers as Adam Smith, Adam Ferguson, Auguste Comte, Herbert Spencer, Lewis Henry Morgan, Karl Marx, and Frederick Engels, that progress was inherent in nature and that the task of the scholar was to discover the pattern of its unfolding and recommend policies that would hasten its inevitable attainment. Following the course set by Adam Smith, which had been followed by most economists since Smith's time, Schumpeter accepted the equating of economic growth and progress. Therefore, in his view, the topic that should have been of primary concern for the discipline was economic growth and development. Furthermore, the task of the economist, as he saw it, was to ascertain and establish theoretical models to demonstrate how growth—i.e., progress—was to be attained.

Schumpeter took the social process to be a single, indivisible whole out of which the investigator extracted distinctive types of facts—economic, political, social, and so forth. "The designation of fact as economic," Schumpeter (1949:3) tells us, "already involves an abstraction, the first of many forced upon us by the technical conditions of mentally copying reality." Therefore, although interested in economic development, he sees the process as a part of total social reality.

Schumpeter (1949:66) defines development as "the carrying out of new combinations." He contrasts the normal flow of economic activities, upon which classical economics focused, with development, which he sees as a distinct process. Development, he writes (1949:64), "is spontaneous and discontinuous change in the channels of the flow, disturbance of equilibrium, which forever alters and displaces the equilibrium state previously existing." "Our theory of development," he continues (1949:64), is nothing but a treatment of this phenomenon and the processes incident to it."

Development, then, is the creation of new combinations of materials and forces that disturb previous equilibrium states and result in new ones that, *a priori*, are assumed to be better. The question for Schumpeter, then, is how the new combinations are brought about.

His answer to the question is entrepreneurship. "The carrying out of new combinations," he writes (1949:74), "we call 'enterprise'; the individuals whose function is to carry them out we call 'entrepreneurs' . . . " Entrepreneurship and the entrepreneur, then, are instruments in the Schumpeterian view—the means by which the economy (and society) is transformed and improved.

Schumpeter saw entrepreneurs as decision makers. But since he saw social reality as an integrated whole, individuals were seen as making choices and decisions in a variety of social contests and situations. The relevant ones, however, for the purpose of Schumpeter's analysis of economic growth, were those made in the economic arena, since only they could result in new economic combinations and hence development. But since he had made the individual a key to the growth process, and had chosen to view individuals as decision makers operating in a multiplicity of social situations, noneconomic aspects of their behavior and activities became part and parcel of the process of economic development. The point is that the ultimate explanation of economic growth and of societal advancement in the Schumpeterian model is to be found in noneconomic factors brought into play through the actions of entrepreneurs. The concepts of "innovation" (large-scale investment by entrepreneurs in methods of producing goods and services) and "creative destruction" (the displacement of old methods of combining materials and labor for production) are part of Schumpeter's enduring legacy to the understanding of the economic process.

By defining the entrepreneur as an innovator, Schumpeter had answered the question of how new combinations that disturb a system in equilibrium are brought about. The entrepreneurs of interest to him, however, were but a small minority: those whose innovations improved society through its transformation. They were the innovators of progressive change. Unfortunately, however, he could not pursue the other questions that followed logically from his definition of the entrepreneur as the innovator of progressive change. Who, for example, are entrepreneurs? Is it possible to differentiate between their functions and their characteristics as individuals? How can they be recognized and studied with greater precision? How are they, and the characteristics they may have in common, distributed within a given population? Which groups within a society are most likely to produce entrepreneurs, and why? What is the nature of the intersection between the behavior of the social group and the larger social order within which it functions? Such lines of inquiry clearly lay beyond the conventional bounds of economic scholarship. Prior to Schumpeter, among those trained in economics, only an eclectic and idiosyncratic thinker such as Veblen could examine the social and institutional framework within which entrepreneurs functioned.

The second line of inquiry into entrepreneurship developed from the writings of scholars such as A. P. Usher and N. S. B. Gras who were willing to abandon, at least temporarily, the theoretical rigor of classical economics in order to examine the lives of individual businessmen, firms, and even sectors of the economy. Much of their work drew its inspiration from ideas discussed at Harvard University in the 1920s and 1930s—the period during which Schumpeter was active there. Although for the most part composed of rather simplistic apologia for a firm, business leader, or industry, the number of studies generated was substantial, as is shown in the profusion of studies listed, for example, in Henrietta Larson's *Guide to Business History* (1964). These studies were intended to provide case histories that would serve students of management for their own purposes and provide friendly critics or defenders of the status quo in Europe and North America with data. The founding of the Business History Society and of a *Business History Review* were among the more enduring achievements of this line of inquiry (Parker 1973:27–31).

The Schumpeterian and business-history traditions merged to some extent in the mid 1940s with the establishment of the Center for Entrepreneurial Research at Harvard University by Arthur H. Cole, who had worked with Gras, Larson, and the Gidys at the Harvard Business School. Schumpeter, although not a part of the Center, provided intellectual support and encouragement to the venture. The founders of the Center defined "entrepreneurial history" as a new field with its own core of interests, its own practitioners, and even its own scholarly journal. Some of the best examples of their efforts are included in Hugh Aitken (ed.), *Explorations in Enterprise* (1967).

Through the initiative of Cole, Leland Jenks, Thomas C. Cochran, and others associated with the Center, the study of entrepreneurship became not only increasingly historical, but also psychological and sociological in its concerns. Interdisciplinary approaches were encouraged and other scholars stimulated to carry the study of entrepreneurship yet further from the disciplinary framework of economics. Nevertheless, the field still focused on industrial management in advanced societies.

At the end of the World War II, however, the attention of scholars engaged in entrepreneurial studies shifted gradually away from the functions of entrepreneurship in economic growth to the

8

psychological, social, and cultural characteristics of entrepreneurs. The writings of Thomas C. Cochran, for example, demonstrate progressively greater incursions into the social and cultural settings of business behavior and the attitudes and values of business leaders. By the late 1950s he was studying entrepreneurship in Puerto Rico and Argentina in an effort to make comparisons with the American business system (Cochran 1964:110–43).

The new dimensions in Cochran's work typify the directions studies in entrepreneurship were taking in the postwar era. They focused on discovering: (1) how entrepreneurs are influenced by the society in which they live; (2) how they contribute (if at all) to the economic growth and development of that society; and (3) how they may come to be included in programs of development and growth.

In the period following the war, for political and other reasons, the underdeveloped nations of the world were to replace the United States and Western Europe as the subjects of studies by economists and other scholars working in the area of development. Instead of continuing to focus almost exclusively on the industrialized societies moving toward new equilibrium states in a steady march toward progress, a new generation of scholars came to be interested in the so-called underdeveloped nations of the world, and tried to help them to "catch up," so to speak, with the presumably "advanced" nations of the West. The new interest in development and growth, therefore, was not concerned with the shape of the future states of the West, but rather with the transformation, or "modernization," of the underdeveloped nations of what came to be called the Third World.

Now the practical question asked by academics and governmental leaders alike was, How could development best be brought about? It was assumed, of course, that, as part of the change, behavior and social institutions would become more like those already present in the developed nations. But given this assumption, the analytical and research skills required were more historical, psychological, and sociological in character than economic. It was obvious, furthermore, that no matter what strategies of development a new nation's leaders might select, they would need an indigenous group of entrepreneurs and managers with the appropriate training and attitudes to bring into being and administer the new institutions and agencies that would come with modernization.

9

Most scholars engaging in research on entrepreneurship following the Second World War came to emphasize the psychological and social characteristics of the individual entrepreneur and the socialization process that formed him. Attention gradually shifted, therefore, from the functions of entrepreneurship in economic growth to the psychological traits of persons designated as entrepreneurs and to the social conditions that produced them.

One of the more influential studies in the early 1960s was the social psychologist David McClelland's *The Achieving Society* (1961). McClelland attempted to apply rigorous research procedures, using comparative analysis, to answer the question, Why do some societies produce outstanding individuals—i.e., entrepreneurs—while others do not? This line of thinking is based on the conclusions reached by Max Weber (1930) in his classic analysis of the presumed relationship between the "Spirit of Capitalism" and the "Protestant Ethic." McClelland accepted Weber's formulation and tried to carry it further by examining the elements that motivate individuals to behave in ways that promote economic growth. Phrasing his conclusions as a directive to heads of state and planners of traditional (underdeveloped) societies, he emphasized the need to break institutional constraints and create "other-directedness" in order to produce more high achievers who would pursue entrepreneurial careers.

At about the same time McClelland was pursuing his studies of achievement motivation, the economist Everett Hagen (1962) directed attention to the study of group behavior and social networks as essential for a more penetrating analysis of business activity in a larger social framework. Hagen focused on the highly visible minority groups that had produced disproportionately large numbers of entrepreneurs who had often played a strategic role in the development process. Such groups as dissenters in England from the sixteenth century onward, Protestants in France, samurai in Japan, and Jews in several countries were among the notable examples of minorities that had succeeded in business. Hagen found what he believed to be a common factor among them: a sense of separateness from the rest of the society in which they lived, combined with a feeling of being discriminated against by members of the larger society. They found compensation for this sense of diminished status, he maintained, in entrepreneurial achievement.

10

TRANSACTIONAL STUDIES OF INVESTMENT
DECISION MAKING

In 1968, quite independently of studies of entrepreneurship, Burton Benedict published a seminal anthropological paper examining the role of the family firm in the development process. Unlike most social scientists at the time, Benedict maintained that the family firm in some societies was a positive factor in development, not an obstacle. His argument rested on the fact that a firm composed of family members could make greater claims on the loyalty of its members and their labor than it could from employees hired in the marketplace. What Benedict had done, of course, was to look at the family firm in a new way. Instead of seeing it as an instance in a typology of firms, he viewed it as the outcome of the forces that gave it form. Consequently, he emphasized the loyalty and respect for the person or persons in authority inherent in kinship systems as the means by which the energies of its membership could be mobilized. Instead of examining a firm or a family, Benedict was looking at the choices and decisions of individuals made against the background of specifiable values and beliefs, constraints and incentives.

Independently, Robert Aubey and Arnold Strickon, working on the investment decisions and activities of Latin American elites, saw the possibility of applying Benedict's insights to the behavior of large-scale commercial groupings. Students of investment groups and business firms in Latin America had for some time sensed a relationship between these groups' activities in the economic sphere and the kinship and other social identities of their owners and top-level managers. But no attempt had been made to relate the obligations and constraints of kinship to the organization and conduct of business.

Following Benedict's line of thought, Aubey and Strickon, assisted by John Kyle, argued that investment was a process of resource acquisition; in the process, they maintained, the investor mobilized whatever resources were at his disposal (Aubey, Kyle, and Strickon 1974). One result of the resource acquisition process was the formation of social groups, which might be firms, investment groups, or extended families. Another was the refocusing of economic analysis away from the groups—corporations, family firms, and others—and

11

onto the individuals, and relations among them, who were behaving within a specific social and cultural matrix.

William P. Glade (1967), meanwhile, in an earlier paper criticizing the direction entrepreneurial studies had been taking, had provided the link between that body of literature and the decision-making, transactional studies of investment activity being undertaken by Benedict, Aubey, Kyle, and Strickon. Glade noted that entrepreneurial studies were embedded in a set of developmental assumptions that implied the movement of economies and societies from one stage or type to another. He realized further that studies to that time, or at least those summarized in Alec P. Alexander's (1967) survey, had isolated factors that could be grouped in the form of two contrasting models, one of a society that is traditional and stagnant, and another of a society that is modern and developed. What was still missing in the literature on entrepreneurship, according to Glade (1967:246), was "a theory of change which explains the transition from the state of affairs depicted by the 'undeveloped economy' model to that represented by the 'developed economy' model."

Glade then suggested what he called a "situational approach" to entrepreneurial decision making as the basis for a theory of social change. What he proposed was that at the micro level society be viewed as composed of individuals making decisions and choices within specific social and cultural settings. By doing this Glade had taken the first step toward reformulating the study of entrepreneurship. Previous studies had focused on the entrepreneur himself, on his psychological characteristics, his personality formation, or on his creative activity. The situational approach, in contrast, focuses not on the entrepreneur per se, but on entrepreneurial behavior and on the circumstances and situations within which choices and decisions are made. These circumstances, called the *opportunity structure* (the general economic, social, technological, political conditions) were viewed by Glade as a second level of analysis produced by exogenous factors. As these changed, however, they provided new opportunities for the individual members of society, some of whom might take advantage of them while others might not.

What emerges for Glade (1967:251), then, "as integral features of any given situation are both an 'objective' structure of economic opportunity and a structure of differential advantage in the capacity of the system's participants to perceive and act upon such opportunities." Those who act upon the opportunities, of course, are the entrepreneurs who move economy and society to new stages or equilibriums in the march toward progress.

Glade's micro-level imagery was the same as that being used in another context by Benedict, Aubey, Kyle, and Strickon. In fact, the 1974 paper by Aubey, Kyle, and Strickon can be seen in retrospect as an effort at the theoretical level to articulate the implications of the new perspective suggested by Glade.

At the seminar in Santa Fe, Glade was able to show the participants that by considering the social and cultural contexts of investment decision making they were in fact discussing entrepreneurship. Furthermore, their papers provided empirical support for the developing conceptual and theoretical reformulation.

THE PAPERS

The chapters to follow represent a range of cases in time and space. All, however, are related to the global expansion of Europe and its enduring consequences. They span a period of some three centuries and extend halfway around the world. Each paper describes efforts by individual entrepreneurs to obtain and secure new resources and new status. While some of the individuals may be thought of as copying behavioral patterns that had proven successful elsewhere, others were responding to new situations in new ways.

We have grouped the chapters in three parts. In the first, which includes the chapters by Greenfield, Rothstein, Blicksilver, Long, Strickon, and Glade, the emphasis is on the choices and decisions of individuals, either in specific situations or over the course of what may be thought of as their careers. In the second, which includes the papers by Aubey, Strachan, Gold, and Benedict, the emphasis is on the outcomes of the decisions, which is to say on the patterns and groupings that result from the change process. The contributions of anthropologists, economists, and historians are to be found in both groups.

In the first paper in part 2, Sidney M. Greenfield uses the biography of the seventeenth-century Luso-Brazilian figure Salvador Correia de Sá e Benavides to examine the opening up by the Portuguese of the central and southern coastal regions of Brazil. Salvador's forays from there into West Africa, Paraguay, and the Río de la Plata enable the author to explore decision making that spans the Atlantic Basin and articulates life in these far-flung regions. He examines Salvador's decisions and choices within the imperial framework and also points out the constraints within which other entrepreneurs of the period had to operate.

In chapter 3 Morton Rothstein examines the behavior of a group of planter-entrepreneurs in the American South in the early and middle years of the nineteenth century. The author shows us how the subjects he studied rose to leadership positions, only to lose their local political influence to rivals before the Civil War. His emphasis is on the relationships developed through kinship, inheritance, church affiliations and by other means with key figures in the national and international business community.

In chapter 4 Jack Blicksilver examines the actors and their decision-making behavior that resulted in the founding and growth of the Life Insurance Company of Georgia. As the author points out, the new situation was the market opportunity in the population of former slaves in the early twentieth-century American South. Blicksilver follows the development of the company and the decision-making activities of its leaders as it moves away from this specialized clientele and attempts to enter the larger situation of the southern insurance industry.

In chapter 5 Norman Long examines the career of Romero, a contemporary, lower-class, semirural Peruvian. Professor Long stresses the significance of personal social networks as resources in entrepreneurial activities and as constraints on the directions in which an entrepreneur may move. This point also is developed in the other papers in this section. It is noteworthy that Señor Romero's networks did not enable him to mobilize resources of the scale and significance organized by those individuals discussed in the other papers. Consequently he appears as the least successful of the individuals described in this section of the volume.

In the next chapter Arnold Strickon discusses three individual enterpreneurs in a Wisconsin county at three different points in time. Making explicit a theme already alluded to in the previous chapters, he develops for us the importance of relationships of confidence and trust in the mobilization of resources, a theme to which we shall

14

return in a moment. He then uses the analysis to delineate the populations present in the multicultural, complex society of the American Midwest.

In the final paper in part 2, William Glade addresses the question of entrepreneurial behavior in state-owned industries, using the careers of the several persons who have headed the Mexican firm CONASUPO. It is interesting that the behaviors described by Professor Glade as having been selected by the several entrepreneurs in this new state-owned enterprise are not dissimilar to those described in some of the preceding papers. The conclusion to be drawn is that the success of the state-owned enterprise depends to a considerable degree on the selection by its managers of the same behaviors that have proven successful in the private sector, a point that is reinforced by the descriptive materials presented in the papers by Aubey and Strachan in part 3.

Part 3, as previously noted, emphasizes the outcomes of decision making; the chapters focus on the groups and social patterns that are statistically preponderant in given populations at particular points in time. In chapters 8 and 9 Robert T. Aubey and Harry W. Strachan describe investment groups in Mexico and Nicaragua respectively. These groups, it appears, have emerged in Latin America and elsewhere independently or through diffusion in response to similar selective pressures. Their organizers and participants appear to be responding to similar sets of incentives and constraints. Faced with growing markets for an increasing variety of products, they find themselves short of the capital needed to organize production. On the one hand, their personal or kin-based networks are not able to supply the required amounts; on the other hand, impersonal capital markets are only weakly developed in their national economies. The solution to the apparent dilemma is the creation of the investment groups examined.

In chapter 10 Gerald L. Gold examines formalized fiesta groups of rancheros in the province of Hidalgo, Mexico. Operating within a series of constraints that limit their economic and political opportunities, the actors have selected behaviors that intensify their being part of, in their own perceptions at least, a distinctive populational segment. The dominant theme in their relationships is the importance of confidence and trust in maintaining their group membership.

In the final paper of part 3 Burton Benedict discusses the dominant patterns found in three diverse cultural segments in a recently independent island nation in the Indian Ocean. Specifically, he asks, Why is it that, with a high degree of probability, Chinese and Indians in Seychelles are successful shopkeepers, merchants, and entrepreneurs, while Creoles are not? He illustrates his presentation with examples of decision-making behavior. His analysis points up the differences in the patterned regularities in values, in role expectations and obligations, and in family and kinship patterns among the Chinese, Indian, and Creole populations.

The primary theme in Benedict's paper is the importance of social relationships that lead to trust and confidence among individuals. The importance of such relationships is that only where they prevail is it possible for an innovative, entrepreneurial individual to mobilize others and the resources to which they give him access in the attainment of his goals. This theme emerges as a substantive thread in all of the papers to follow.

RELATIONS OF CONFIDENCE AND TRUST IN ENTERPRISE

A pervasive theme in all the cases examined in this book is the importance of relationships of confidence and trust to the individuals whose lives and careers have been examined. Each seems to have a characteristic group or network of persons on whom he can depend and whom he can trust. From the members of this unit he is able to mobilize the kinds and quantities of resources needed to carry out the new combinations. Just who constitutes this trusted coterie in any particular case varies widely. For Glade's managers of public enterprises, for example, they are political and economic clients and political patrons; for Salvador Correia de Sá e Benavides in seventeenth-century Brazil, it is his kinsmen and compadres; in nineteenth- and early twentieth-century rural Wisconsin it is populations of fellow immigrants from the same homeland, be it Norway or New England. In some cases relationships of trust and confidence are formalized and contractualized, as, for example, with the members of the Mexican and Nicaraguan investment groups, or the group of boarding-house buddies turned Board of Directors of the

Life Insurance Company of Georgia. In other cases the essentials of trust are built into the relationships from birth, as with the Chinese and Indians in Seychelles. In still other cases the relationships grow out of church or school affiliations, as with the planter-entrepreneurs of Natchez. At times the relationships are strong and far-reaching; at others they are tenuous and weak, easily shattered, and not to be depended upon over extended periods, such as among the Seychellois Creoles, or for the Peruvian entrepreneur in Professor Long's paper. The fact that these patterns are of importance in all the cases is due, we believe, less to the common orientation of the authors (which, in fact, does not exist) than to the fact that the subjects themselves perceived these units of trust and their characteristics as significant in the social settings in which they lived out their lives.

In the studies of entrepreneurship reviewed earlier in this essay the entrepreneur was looked at as an individual operating apart from existing social relationships. The cases presented here suggest that social relationships that engender confidence and trust are critical to the entrepreneurial process. The ability of an individual to mobilize such relationships might often be critical to the success or failure of his entrepreneurial venture. On the basis of this we might suggest that studying entrepreneurs isolated from their social contexts is like studying animals independent of their natural habitats, an activity not without some value, but one that misses the complex interactions upon which the selective process is dependent. On behalf of our colleagues, therefore, we urge that future studies of entrepreneurship treat their subjects and the decisions they make *in vivo*, which is to say that researchers should investigate the social relationships in which the individuals who carry out entrepreneurial activity are enmeshed, and on which their success or failure might depend.

NEW DIRECTIONS

While editing the papers Greenfield and Strickon concluded that most of the authors had analyzed their data in terms of an image and a set of assumptions that were not consistent with the evolutionary, developmental, and structural-functional perspectives that had informed the vast majority of previous studies of entrepreneurship. Instead, the papers in this volume are informed by decision-making and transactional perspectives that represent new directions in thought based on a different view of the world. In the final chapter of this volume Greenfield and Strickon present in abbreviated form what they call a populational framework for the analysis of social and cultural phenomena. It provides, we believe, an alternative way of approaching and understanding not only entrepreneurship, but other controversial issues in the social and cultural sciences.

PART 2

Entrepreneurs, Choices, and Decisions

2

Entrepreneurship and Dynasty Building in the Portuguese Empire in the Seventeenth Century: The Career of Salvador Correia de Sá e Benavides[1]

SIDNEY M. GREENFIELD

Department of Anthropology
University of Wisconsin-Milwaukee

The life-span of Salvador Correia de Sá e Benavides (1602–86) roughly coincided with the seventeenth century, and throughout it he played an important role on both sides of the Atlantic. He was actively, and at times decisively, concerned with such diverse matters as the exploration (and the exploitation) of the interior, the enslavement of the Amerindians, the struggle with the Dutch for the West African slave-market, and the revolution of Lisbon which resulted in the deposition of King Dom Affonso VI. No other historical figure symbolises so clearly the mutual depend-ence between Portugal, Brazil and Angola at the time, nor the nature of the connection between Portuguese and Spanish South America. . . . (Boxer 1952:viii–ix)

The following pages examine the career of Salvador Correia de Sá e Benavides as an entrepreneur, investor, builder of a financial and commercial empire, and founder of a dynasty. We shall focus on the decisions and choices that resulted in Salvador's success, with

21

due regard to the sociocultural system of his time—the system that was the context for Salvador's investment decisions and those of his contemporaries. We shall also take account of the social relationships that Salvador cultivated and used in attaining his goals and of the social networks that emerged in the process.

The literature on Salvador usually neglects his role as an entrepreneur and investor. His many biographers (Boxer 1952; Cardozo 1950; Carvalho 1941; Lamego 1913–25; Norton 1943; Pizarro e Araujo 1820–22; Ribeiro de Lessa 1940; and Varnhagen 1927–36) have viewed him primarily as a colonial administrator, servant of the crown, soldier, and seaman. While enacting these glamorous and often heroic roles, however, he also acted as an entrepreneur intent on building a family fortune—an activity in which he was so successful that his descendants were to be among the richest and most powerful families of Portugal.

Salvador was born into a family that could claim neither great wealth nor high nobility. He was the first son of Martim Correia de Sá and his Anglo-Spanish wife, D. María de Mendoza y Benavides (see fig. 2.1). The families on both sides were servants of the crown.[2] Salvador's maternal grandfather was to become governor of Cadiz, the city where Salvador was born and where he spent his youth. On the paternal side Salvador's family had a long and intimate association with Brazil. His grandfather, after whom he was named, had been the first governor of the city of São Sebastião de Rio de Janeiro (later shortened to Rio de Janeiro) on Guanabara Bay. The elder Salvador's uncle, Mem de Sá, the third governor general of Brazil, had appointed him to this post shortly after the territory had been taken from the French and the city had been founded by another member of the family, Estácio de Sá. Salvador's grandfather and father had both served as governor of the Royal Captaincy of Rio de Janeiro, in addition to holding other posts in the Brazilian colony.

Salvador's father and paternal grandfather had begun to accumulate the resources and properties he was to use in achieving his success. They had used their position as governor to obtain nearby cattle and sugar lands, and had promoted exploration for metals in the south of Brazil. Salvador's ultimate accomplishments, then, were partly a result of this foundation, upon which he skillfully built his financial empire. But to understand Salvador's entrepreneurial

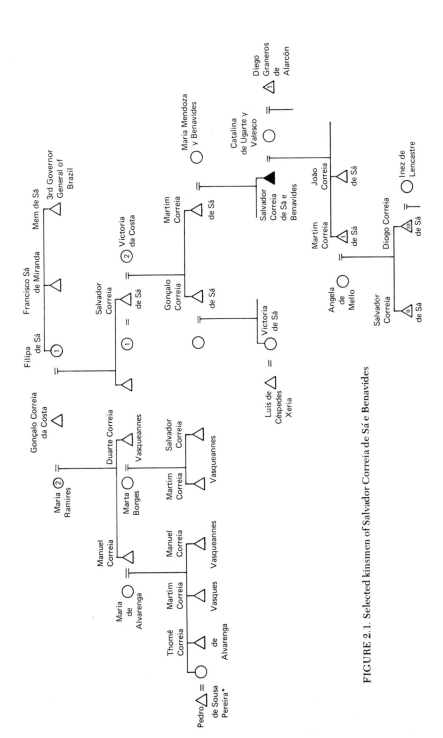

FIGURE 2.1. Selected kinsmen of Salvador Correia de Sá e Benavides

achievements, one must first have some basic knowledge of the system within which he had to operate: the seventeenth-century Portuguese economy and society.

From the beginnings of Portugal's expansion, civil servants and colonial administrators had been drawn primarily from the ranks of the lesser nobility and from among the second and third sons of the wealthy and prestigious upper nobility, who did not share in the estates of their families. By reason of his relatively modest origins, young Salvador was far removed from the station that symbolized success, leadership, and power in the hierarchically ordered society of his day.

Success and elite status in Luso-Hispanic society in the seventeenth century were based on two interdependent attributes: wealth and noble blood. "Blood and property" (o sangue e os bens), the eminent Francisco de Sá de Miranda (Salvador's collateral kinsman) had rightly asserted, "counted for more than anything else with his compatriots" (Boxer 1952:11).

We tend to think of noble status as something acquired by an individual at birth. In the Luso-Hispanic world of the seventeenth century, however, noble status could also be achieved. That is, the crown bestowed titles of nobility as rewards for service. To obtain a title an aspirant had to convince the monarch that his contribution to the crown and to the kingdom merited this reward. Once earned, noble status was then transmitted to succeeding generations in the male line according to the prevailing system of primogeniture.

In addition to performing a service, an upwardly mobile Iberian aspiring to elite status needed great wealth, both to "facilitate" his recognition by the crown (and its advisers), and as the patrimony for the noble house to be established with the title.

Salvador Correia de Sá e Benavides, the son of a modestly placed family, aspired to noble status and to the wealth, power, and influence such superior station symbolized. His life and career may be seen as an effort to achieve such an elevated position, an effort that was to meet with success when his eldest son, Martim, was made the first viscount of Asseca in 1666. To achieve his goal, Salvador knew, he needed both great wealth and the opportunity to demonstrate to the crown his personal worth and the value of his services. His first objective was to accumulate the wealth which his civil servant ancestors had lacked. It will become evident, however, that he managed to combine, in masterly fashion, service to his sovereign with the amassing of a personal fortune.

From the beginning of the great conquests and discoveries in the fifteenth century there had been three basic ways to acquire wealth in the Iberian world: international trade and commerce; the discovery of, or trade in, precious stones and metals; and the production and sale of plantation commodities, among which sugarcane and its by-products were paramount.

The Portuguese movement down the African coast in the fifteenth century and around Africa in the sixteenth to India and the Far East gave access to commodities for which there was a great demand in the markets of Western Europe. From the beginning, however, trade in such commodities had been preempted as a royal monopoly and was assigned to elites and favored foreigners in return for a percentage of profits paid to the royal treasury. By the seventeenth century there were few opportunities for the upwardly mobile in this international commerce. Contracts for the most lucrative trade already had been assigned. Furthermore, competition from Europeans also scrambling for the wealth of the world reduced the profits that could be earned once the skyrocketing costs of protecting the fleets from uncooperative natives and European rivals had been deducted. In any event, to people in Salvador's social position, trade and commerce in Asia and Africa did not offer much of an opportunity.

The spectacular Spanish discoveries of gold and silver in the highlands of South America and in the Valley of Mexico long kept alive in the humblest European colonist the hope of making a fortune in the overseas domains. Salvador was to devote a major share of his energies to the search for precious stones and metals, but without success.

There remained the third potential source of wealth, plantation crops, of which sugarcane and cane liquor were the most important. By the beginning of the seventeenth century, Brazil had become the major supplier of sugar and sugar products for the markets of Europe.

To produce sugar and to profit from it in the developing European world market required possession of (1) fertile, flat, well-watered, tropical or subtropical land; (2) plants and the technology for raising, harvesting, and processing the canes into sugar; (3) a source of energy both to run the mills and to transport the canes to the mill and the sugar and other products to a point of embarkation where they could be stored or shipped to market; (4) facilities for storing and shipping the sugar and sugar products to overseas markets; (5) a labor force to clear the land, plant and harvest the canes, work the milling and other machinery, and transport the sugars to storage facilities at the port of embarkation; (6) a supervisory-administrative staff to manage the mills, the labor force, and the other paraphernalia used in producing, transporting, and storing the sugar and sugar products; and (7) food and other supplies to maintain and care for the labor force and managerial staff. The model for the production of sugar in Brazil in the seventeenth century had been developed two centuries earlier in Madeira (Greenfield 1977) and was part of European colonial practice dating back to the First Crusade (Verlinden 1954, 1966, 1970).

The lowlands of Brazil's Atlantic coast from Rio Grande do Norte south to São Vicente satisfied the first requirement (see fig. 2.2B). When discovered and claimed by the Portuguese crown in the sixteenth century, these lowlands were distributed to individuals in *sesmarias* (land grants) through *donatários* (lord proprietors). Skilled technicians came from Madeira, and from São Tomé in the Gulf of Guinea, to which sugarcane production had spread at the end of the fifteenth century. Power to turn the mills and transport the cane from the fields to the mill was provided by horses and oxen brought from Europe and the Atlantic islands.

Labor was to be supplied by slaves, again following the precedent of Madeira. In Brazil the labor force was originally composed of Amerindians, but by the end of the sixteenth century they were replaced by African slaves. In time the Africans proved to be more reliable and effective workers, and they became the backbone of the plantation labor force from the seventeenth to the nineteenth centuries.

The selection of supervisory-administrative personnel was a special problem about which the literature has little to say. An entrepreneur aspiring to a title of nobility, like Salvador, had to be free from the daily routine tasks of industry and commerce if he were to perform the activities that might win the crown's attention and approval. He must amass wealth, but he could not afford to be tied to his planta-

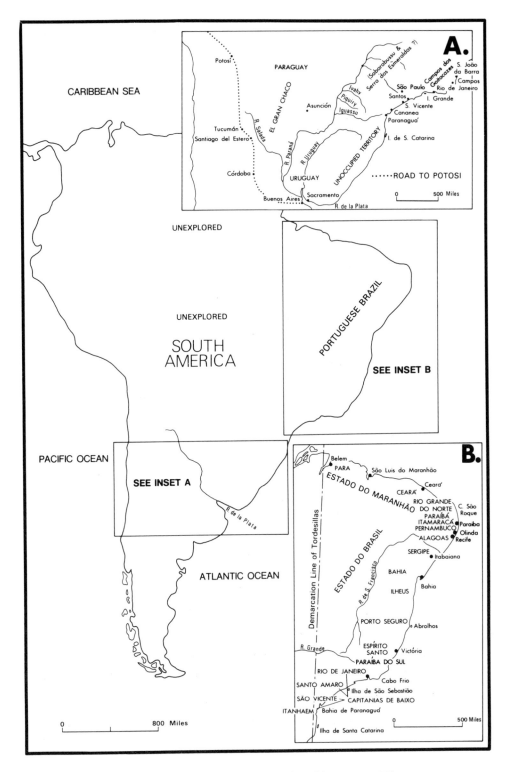

FIGURE 2.2. South America in the Seventeenth Century (adapted from Boxer 1952)
Insert A. Southern Brazil, Paraguay and Peru
Insert B. The Captaincies of Brazil in the Seventeenth Century

tions, mills, and warehouses. He must also be sure that the persons looking after his financial and other interests in the colonies would be loyal to him and would not use his assets to satisfy their own ambitions.

The Portuguese social structure of the period, and more specifically its kinship system, suggested a possible answer to this need for reliable overseers. That kinship system created strong ties of reciprocal rights and responsibilities between individuals. The Portuguese family was more than a nuclear unit. It was an extended family, including kinsmen of widely differing status, for kinship in the Iberian tradition cut across the rigid hierarchy of the system of social stratification. Kinsmen bound by reciprocal obligations often were members of different social categories or classes, and in the relations of mutual aid that bound them, the parties received differential benefits according to their respective positions in the status hierarchy.

Aspiring entrepreneurs could build on bonds of reciprocity, loyalty, and trust with kinsmen of statuses considerably lower than their own. Managerial tasks in branches of specific productive enterprises could be assigned these kinsmen. The bonds of trust and loyalty between the entrepreneur and his lower-status kinsmen enabled the former to leave his estates and other enterprises and serve his king and country in the hope of receiving recognition, from which his loyal kinsmen could expect to benefit.

In addition to kinsmen whose ties could be traced genealogically, Portuguese society also recognized relationships that have come to be referred to as fictive kinship. Such relationships included persons added to the family by means of adoption, plus godparents, godchildren, and *compadres*, or coparents derived from church rituals and their extensions. Any of these could be recruited as members of specific groups that performed activities necessary to the achievement of the career success of an entrepreneur. These strangers-made-kin (following the standard Portuguese opposition of outsiders to kinsmen), along with genealogical kinsmen, then formed a group that in one sense was interdependent with the entrepreneur in the attainment of his career goals and ambitions. Although subject to his authority and subordinate to him socially and legally, the members both contributed to his success and shared in his achievements. In the local setting they formed an interdependent group, based on

28

common material and other interests, that unified them against others in the geographical area.[3]

Supplies and provisions for the administrative staff and for the labor force were for the most part imported in the seventeenth century. This meant that the entrepreneur had to participate in world trade, not only to sell his sugar and purchase his slave labor force, but also to obtain the supplies needed to maintain his dependents. To do this he needed both storage facilities and access to ships.

The multiple requirements for the production and sale of sugar outlined above necessitated the mobilization of massive resources, i.e., capital investment. There were few if any individuals in Brazil in the seventeenth century, or in the Portuguese world, who had, or were willing to invest, capital that would enable them to integrate the production and trade of sugar. Instead, activities were generally separated and labor divided, with one group or sector growing the canes, another organizing and handling the milling, still another obtaining the slaves, a fourth raising the cattle, and yet another storing and shipping the sugar and engaging in the commerce that obtained supplies and provisions. Profits were earned at each step and from each of these activities.

The division of tasks resulted both in a division of profits and in a competition between sectors of the industry. As a result, the production of sugar and its related products was not always profitable to all the participants. Where what the modern economist would refer to as vertical integration was possible, however, truly great profits were to be earned. Therefore entrepreneurs strove to integrate as many of the several components of the industry as possible. But this was no simple matter, since each segment soon came to call for specialized skills and trained personnel. For example, the raising of cattle to transport the canes, run the mills, and supply food had to be separated physically from the growing of canes, lest the animals destroy the growing plants. This led to the development of cattle raising as an industry related to, but geographically separate from, sugar production.

The recruitment of slaves either from the native peoples or in Africa was another geographically separate activity vitally related to sugar production. For this recruiting and for warehousing and commerce special equipment and skills were developed, usually supplied by a distinct personnel.

Vertical integration was the ideal, but since few possessed both the necessary material resources and the loyal dependents with relevant skills, it was difficult for a single entrepreneur to amass truly great wealth from sugar. Salvador, as we shall see, came closer than most to integrating the industry vertically. Although sugar was but one of his economic ventures, it was to provide him with most of the vast fortune he was to accumulate as the patrimony for the House of Asseca.

Two significant sets of constraints affected the actions and decisions of an entrepreneur in the Portuguese world of the seventeenth century. First he was limited by the changeable interests of the crown, which determined what services it valued enough to reward the entrepreneur with the grant of a title of nobility. Second he needed to maintain good relationships with the supportive network of dependents who ran the enterprises.

To be aware of the crown's current interests, the entrepreneur had to gain access to influential elements in the royal bureaucracy and administration. The king often expressed his interests and concerns to close advisers, either informally or as members of formal groups. Such persons could be approached by aspiring entrepreneurs or their agents. In return for their patronage, highly placed advisers, generally members of the upper nobility, had to be rewarded directly or made parties to the enterprises. Since numerous entrepreneurs were striving for limited information and resources, the competition was intense. In order to succeed, an entrepreneur had to establish ties and exchanges with those close to the crown.

To be sure, at certain times and under very special conditions, an entrepreneur could make himself so indispensable that he was taken into the advisory circle of the king. Then, as an insider, he could both promote his own interests and act as a representative for other aspiring entrepreneurs while serving the monarch. (Accomplishing this unusual step is part of the reason for Salvador's later success.)

Sources close to the crown, however, were useless to an entrepreneur without a host of kinsmen, fictive kin, and other dependents who actually ran the enterprises that produced the wealth for the patrimony. As was true of the relationship between the entrepreneur and the advisers of the crown, however, relations with dependents and lower-status kinsmen had to be based on the mutual advantages received by both parties. On the one side, then, the entrepreneur was engaged in exchanges of mutual advantage with individuals above him in the social hierarchy, while on the other he was interacting reciprocally with persons below him.

In the process of making his career, then, the entrepreneur became a connection between local populations in scattered parts of the far-flung colonial kingdom and the interests of elites at court in the metropolitan capital. This, what might be thought of as a brokerage role, was a further constraint on the entrepreneur, who had to take into consideration the possible responses of parties on both sides in making his decisions. He had to protect and provide for those both above and below him socially and economically because they were interdependent with and interrelated to the attainment of his goals.

With this thumbnail sketch of the system within which Portuguese entrepreneurs in the seventeenth century operated, we now return to the life and career of Salvador Correia de Sá e Benavides.

Little is known about Salvador's boyhood. What formal education he received was from the Jesuits, with whom he was to be closely related for many years, and "whose Society," according to Boxer (1952:7), "he was at one time desirous of entering."

In 1614, at the age of 12 or 13, Salvador made his first trip to Brazil, accompanying his grandfather, who had been appointed governor of the recently created administrative unit for the *capitanias de baixo*, the lower, or southern captaincies (see fig. 2.2.B). These captaincies were but sparsely populated at the time and had as yet made but modest progress in comparison with the more prosperous settlements of Bahia and Olinda in the northeast.

The basis of the prosperity in the northeast was sugar. Little if any of the plantation crop, however, was being produced in the south, where the settlers had devoted themselves primarily to enslaving the Indians and to searching for precious stones and metals. The purpose of the administrative reorganization and the appointment of the elder Salvador as governor, it appeared, was "to encourage the development of gold- and silver-mining in the region of São Paulo, where a few golddiggings were already being worked and much larger mines were believed to exist" (Boxer 1952:37).

Young Salvador spent most of the next four years in the interior of southern Brazil, as did his father and grandfather. In their unsuccessful search for precious stones and metals they traveled extensively, and during this period the young man is known to have acquired both a knowledge of and a liking for the Tupi Indians of the region, whose language, which served as a lingua franca in the southern captaincies, he is reported to have learned to speak fluently (Boxer 1952:37).

Grandfather, father, and son are known to have been in Lisbon in 1618 when Martim de Sá was appointed garrison commander of Rio de Janeiro and its coastal district, a post which included supervising the neighboring Indian villages (Boxer 1952:38; Coaracy 1965:44). In that year young Salvador was knighted in the military order of Santiago (Saint James), having obtained a dispensation of the rule barring persons under twenty-one years of age (Boxer 1952:38).

Salvador then returned to Brazil with his father in the summer of 1618. When they stopped en route at Bahia, the colonial capital, the governor general asked them to help search for some mines in the interior of the captaincy of Sergipe (see fig. 2.2B). The venture met with the same lack of success as had the earlier efforts in the south. From Bahia they proceeded to Rio de Janeiro where in the following years Martim de Sá, in cooperation with his brother Gonçalo de Sá, who succeeded him as administrator of the mines of São Paulo, was to work intermittently on strengthening the coastal defenses of the captaincy. During that period of approximately five years Salvador probably spent much of his time in the backlands of São Vicente, either hunting for Indians, or prospecting, or both, in the company of the Paulistas (the settlers of the plateau) (Boxer 1952:38–39). (From 1620 to 1622 Martim also was governor of São Vicente.)

The effort to strengthen the defenses of the Rio settlement, and indeed those of the entire Brazilian colony and Portuguese territories in other parts of the globe, was in response to the expansionist thrust of newly independent Holland (Masselman 1963). The Netherlands had come into being as a nation in rebellion against King Philip of Spain, who was also to become king of Portugal. Not long after the Protestant provinces united and secured their independence, they began an overseas expansion comparable to that of Portugal and Spain a century earlier (Boxer 1969:109). However, when the Dutch began to expand overseas at the beginning of the seventeenth century, it had to be at the expense of the Iberian powers.

In 1494, papal authority had sanctioned the division of the globe into two spheres of control, ruled by Spain and Portugal respectively. This division of the world in favor of the Iberian nations left nothing for later arrivals on the colonial scene. The Dutch Protestants, however, were not bound by papal authority and hence did not recognize the provisions of the Treaty of Tordesillas, the instrument upon which Spanish and Portuguese claims overseas rested. Consequently, as they expanded they took land that in the eyes of European Catholics already belonged either to Portugal or to Spain. To retain the foreign lands they claimed, the Iberians had to defend themselves against the upstart Protestant nations.

From 1580 to 1640 both Spain and Portugal were ruled by the House of Hapsburg. In 1579 the throne of Portugal was left vacant by the death of King Sebastian of Portugal, and in 1580 Philip II of Spain successfully imposed himself as the new monarch, thus becoming also Philip I of Portugal (see fig. 2.3).[4] Philip's mother had been a Portuguese princess, and his claim to the throne, when backed by his financial and military power, enabled him now to rule both Spain and Portugal and their respective overseas domains (Oliveira Marques 1972:1:312–14).

As the seventeenth century dawned, the Dutch, through their East India Company, proceeded to attack Spanish and Portuguese holdings at their weakest points. After successful efforts in the Far East (Boxer 1969:106–12), the West India Company was incorporated in 1621. Preparations immediately were made for strikes in the New World. The first major effort was directed against northeast Brazil (Boxer 1952:41–44). Defending this region against the Dutch was to provide young Salvador Correia de Sá e Benavides with his first opportunity to serve the crown and to gain recognition for his efforts (Boxer 1952:57–59).

In 1624 the Dutch attacked the Brazilian colonial capital of Bahia, which fell to them in short order (see fig. 2.2.). In reaction to the loss, Portuguese and Spanish forces in Europe were mobilized for a counterattack, and the defenses of Pernambuco and Rio de Janeiro, the two most likely choices for the next Dutch attack, were reinforced and strengthened. Most of the reinforcements were sent to Pernambuco, with one ship, the *Nossa Senhora de Penha de França*, carrying eighty men and a small quantity of arms and ammunition, sailing for Rio. The commander of the forces heading for Rio was Salvador Correia de Sá e Benavides (Boxer 1952:57).

33

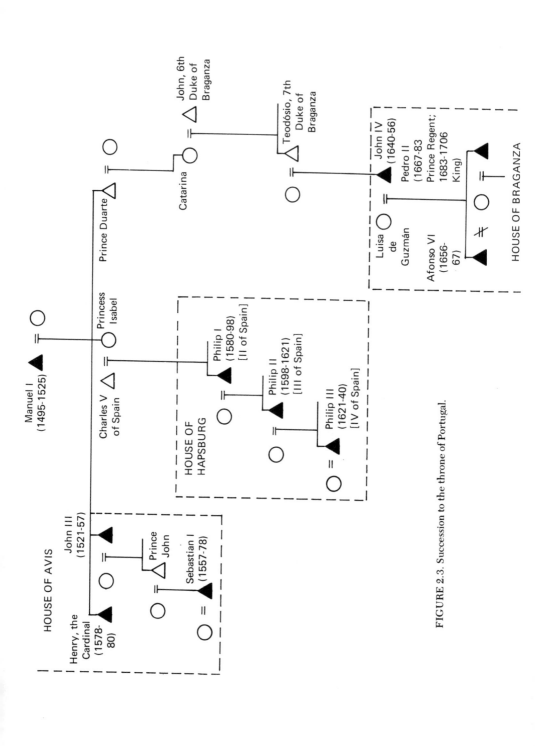

FIGURE 2.3. Succession to the throne of Portugal.

After an uneventful voyage Salvador was sent by his father, the governor, to São Vicente to raise men and supplies for the counteroffensive being mobilized against the Dutch in Bahia. He enlisted about one hundred Indians and eighty Europeans in São Vicente and Rio, leaving for Bahia early in 1625 in two caravels and six large war canoes (Boxer 1952:57). En route he stopped in the captaincy of Espírito Santo (see fig. 2.2), where he was surprised by four Dutch ships.

The Dutch vessels were commanded by Piet Heyn, who had left Holland the previous August to attack the Portuguese slave depot of Luanda in Angola on the West African coast (see fig. 2.4). Failing in his mission, Heyn had recrossed the Atlantic to attack Espírito Santo just as Salvador's party arrived. In cooperation with the Portuguese settlers, Salvador's group defeated the Dutch forces, which suffered heavy losses, most of them inflicted by the Indian archers Salvador had recruited (Boxer 1952:59). Following the victory, Salvador's party sailed on to Bahia, where they arrived in time to witness the final expulsion of the Dutch and the return of the colony to Portuguese control (Boxer 1952:62).

For his part in the campaign of 1624–25 Salvador was rewarded in 1628 by a royal commission appointing him *alcaide-mór* (military governor) of Rio de Janeiro "for all the days of his life" (Boxer 1952:66). The reward signaled his recognition as someone the crown could call upon when in need. In the decades to follow, the crown was to have increasing need of the military skills Salvador had demonstrated, since the Dutch, undaunted by their defeat in Bahia, seized the sugar-rich colony of Pernambuco, to the north, and managed to hold it from 1630 until 1654. They also were to take, and then to lose in part, Portuguese possessions on the African coast. Salvador was to serve the crown loyally and successfully during this period of danger and uncertainty; he also was to continue to build his financial empire.

As a result of the Dutch conquest of Pernambuco and the guerilla wars that were fought throughout the period of their occupation, the volume of sugar entering Europe from the Brazilian northeast declined. In response to the unsatisfied demand and to the profits to be made, sugarcane cultivation was introduced into the Recôncavo, the lowlands to the north of Rio de Janeiro. The Correias de Sá, as the dominant force in the administration of the Rio colony, were

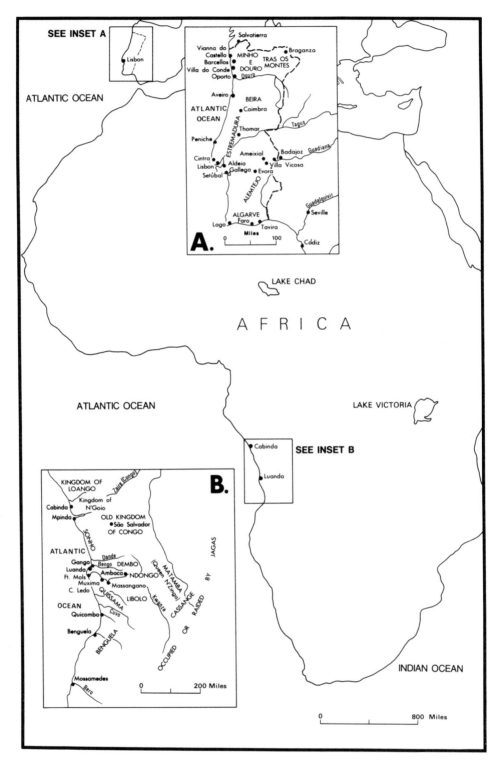

FIGURE 2.4. Portugal and Angola in the Seventeenth Century (adapted from Boxer 1952)
Insert A. Portugal
Insert B. Angola and the Congo

able to obtain for themselves and their supporters extensive land-holdings that soon were planted in sugar. Salvador would later expand production and add related aspects of the industry to his holdings. But before presenting these details, we first must take note of some developments in the 1630s that gave a dramatic twist to Salvador's career.

In 1630 Salvador left Rio on an overland journey to Asunción (see fig. 2.2A) to accompany his cousin, Victoria de Sá, who was to join her husband, Don Luis de Céspedes Xeria, the governor of Paraguay. In 1628 Céspedes had stayed with Martim de Sá, who was serving his second term as governor, in Rio while en route to take up his post in Asunción. On the eve of the influential but bankrupt hidalgo's departure, Martim and Salvador offered to him in marriage Victoria de Sá, daughter of Gonçalo Correia de Sá, Martim's brother and Salvador's uncle (see fig. 2.1). The bride brought a dowry of 40,000 ducats in cash plus sugar plantations and other properties. In return, the Correias de Sá expected to obtain from Céspedes support for slave raids into Paraguay (to capture Indians to labor on their sugar plantations); they also anticipated profits from the opening up of a new trade route to the famous silver-mining town of Potosí (see fig. 2.2A) in the highlands of the Andes. Their new in-law was in a position to make available to them important connections in Paraguay, the Río de la Plata, Tucumán, Potosí, and Spain (Boxer 1952:82–84).

Céspedes continued on to Asunción in 1628; two years later Salvador escorted the governor's bride to him. The party's arrival in the Paraguayan capital, however, coincided with an outbreak of Indian rebellions there and in the neighboring province of Tucumán. Céspedes offered the command of the punitive expedition to his young kinsman, who obtained at least a temporary victory.

On his return from battle to Asunción, Salvador met and in 1631 or early 1632 married Catalina de Urgate y Velasco, "a creole heiress of great wealth and prestige in Spanish colonial society" (Boxer 1952:96). Not only was Catalina descended from the conquistador aristocracy, she also was the wealthiest widow in the province of Tucumán. Her first husband, Captain Diego Graneros de Alarcón, had left her and their infant son, his sole heir, a fortune worth over 200,000 pesos, composed of three large cattle ranches, slaves, and jewels (Lizonado Borda 1936–38:3:174–80;

37

Boxer 1952:97). The estates, located in Tucumán, were in the region that supplied Potosí, whose market was certainly the most profitable in America at the time (Cobb 1949:45), if not in all the world (Boxer 1952:108).

By the time the news of his father's death in Rio in 1632 reached him, Salvador had acquired not only a bride, but also control over some of the richest properties in the Spanish New World, not to mention contacts with the most important and influential people in Spanish America. With his father's death, however, the governorship of Rio de Janeiro became his next objective. Therefore, after a brief visit to Rio, during which he was able to obtain a valuable contract from the municipal council (see below), he returned to Europe, where he obtained from King Philip IV (III of Portugal) a decree appointing him governor and captain-major of both the captaincy and its administrative center (Varnhagen 1927–36:1:112–13).

While Salvador was in Paraguay and Tucumán, the Dutch had captured Pernambuco. By the middle of the decade rumors were afoot that they were planning another attack on Bahia or Rio. Salvador therefore appealed to the crown for reinforcements for the Rio garrison; when they were granted, he left for the city he was to govern for the next six eventful years.

By this time, although scarcely thirty years old, Salvador already owned vast landed estates, including several sugar plantations in Rio and its environs. According to Boxer (1952:139), "He had about seven hundred slaves employed on his sugar plantations and cattle ranches and he was almost certainly the largest proprietor in the captaincy, possibly, indeed, the largest individual landowner in the whole of Brazil."

On his return to Europe from Paraguay and Tucumán, he had arranged with the municipal council of Rio to undertake a project that would add considerably to his wealth and involve him more deeply in the sugar-raising and -exporting activities of the captaincy. He had contracted to build a *trapiche*, or warehouse, at his own expense, on land rented from the city at a nominal fee. In return, he was granted sole right to weigh there all sugar exported from the captaincy. The producers were to pay him for this a fixed sum of forty *reis* for storage in the warehouse, whether the sugar was destined for export or for local consumption (Boxer 1952:114–15).

The merchants of Lisbon had been complaining for some time about receiving short weight in the sugar they imported from Rio. In response the municipal council had endeavored to construct such a warehouse and weigh station themselves as early as 1625, but their financial resources proved insufficient and the project was dropped (Boxer 1952:114). They had decided then to find a contractor who would undertake the project at his own expense.

Salvador signed the contract with them in 1636, but when he returned as governor in 1637 he enlisted the aid of his kinsmen and other council members to convert the original nineteen-year contract into a perpetual monopoly for himself and his descendants. "It need hardly be added," observes Boxer (1952:115),

> that this warehouse proved to be an immensely profitable investment for the Correia de Sá family, who clung to it for two centuries despite all efforts of the authorities to buy them out or otherwise abrogate this far-reaching concession. Not until 1850 did the imperial government succeed in buying out the family for an enormous sum.

In 1640, while Salvador was governor of Rio de Janeiro, Hapsburg control over Portugal come to an end. Following a successful revolt, John, the seventh Duke of Braganza, restored the Portuguese monarchy—and national independence—with the title of King John IV.

The dual monarchy had existed for sixty years, since 1580. When it came to an end, Hispano-Portuguese subjects like Salvador Correia de Sá e Benavides were faced with a difficult decision. Should they side with John and swear allegiance to the House of Braganza, or should they remain loyal to Philip of Hapsburg?

Salvador, it may be recalled, had been the child of a Portuguese father and an Anglo-Spanish mother. He then had married a creole aristocrat from New Spain. He had been born in Spain, but was equally at home in Portugal, in Brazil and, in Spanish America. Furthermore, he owned extensive properties and was engaged in enterprises both in the Portuguese and in the Spanish New World. Forced now to choose between the Braganzas and the Hapsburgs, between Portugal and Spain, the only thing that was certain was that he would be the loser. The question was, Through which choice would his losses be minimized?

If he went with Spain, he would lose not only the governorship of the Rio colony, but also his valuable and extensive sugar plantations, cattle estates, slaves, warehouse, and so forth. He also risked losing Philip's trust of a man with such family ties to the Portuguese New World; and that trust, it must be remembered, was essential if he was to obtain the title and status to which he aspired. To support John, however, meant that Salvador would forfeit the properties over which he had gained control through his wife, and the lucrative trade her connections made possible with Potosí. Furthermore, John also might have doubts of the loyalty of a servant with such strong Spanish ties.

The vulnerability of the new Portuguese monarch was to influence Salvador's choice. Having obtained the throne, King John was faced with the task of bringing the colonies, whose support and resources he desperately needed, under his control. At the time, it should be noted, Brazil was the richest and most important of Portugal's overseas domains.[5]

With Pernambuco in Dutch hands, the two key settlements in Brazil were Bahia in the north and Rio de Janeiro in the south. The viceroy at Bahia was D. Jorge de Mascarenhas, marquis of Montalvão, whose wife and two sons, according to Boxer (1952:145), "were rightly suspected of pro-Castilian sympathies." And the governor in Rio, of course, was the son of a Spanish mother married to a Spanish wife.

The royal dispatches from Lisbon, with the news of the restoration and the request for allegiance to the new regime, were sent to Brazil aboard a ship that landed first in Bahia. Montalvão reviewed the documents in consultation with the local leadership. With their consent, and probably under pressure from the Jesuits, who strongly supported Portuguese independence, he declared loyalty to John. He then dispatched the ship carrying the documents to Rio, adding letters of his own designed to win support for the new regime. These materials were placed in the hands of the Jesuit Provincial, Father Manuel Fernandes, who delivered them personally to Salvador when the ship landed in Rio. After consulting with the leading citizens, Salvador announced the decision he had reached. Following the examples of Lisbon and Bahia, the governor of Rio de Janeiro declared his loyalty to King John of Portugal. Then, in great haste, he sent his kinsman and secretary, João Antônio Correia, to Lisbon to secure from John confirmation of all the privileges and honors he had received from Madrid, including that of administrator of the gold and silver mines in São Paulo.

The confirmation was received in 1642, but shortly thereafter John held back on some of the promises he had made to Salvador. Questions had been raised in high places about his loyalty, and the king, as Salvador had feared, had developed reservations because of his Spanish connections.

In 1643, therefore, Salvador returned personally to Portugal, where, in a private audience, he convinced the monarch of his loyalty and usefulness (Cardozo 1950:149–50, 155). The king gave him a place on the prestigious and influential Overseas Council, which advised on colonial affairs. He also appointed him general of the escort fleet for Brazil, and promised him the title of Count, with an income of 4,000 cruzados, on condition that he return to the mines of São Paulo and extract from them 200,000 cruzados worth of precious metals (Boxer 1952:155). The king also sought Salvador's advice on the critical situation in Angola. Several years later he was to give him command of an expedition to recapture the portions of Angola taken by the Dutch.

Brazilian prosperity, so critical to the solvency of the royal treasury, was dependent at the time on Angolan slaves used in the production of sugar. The Dutch capture of Angola, combined with their conquest of Pernambuco, posed a serious threat to the prosperity of Brazil and, therefore, to the very existence of Portugal. As John IV himself so aptly if crudely characterized it, Brazil was his *vaca de leite*, or milch cow.

When Salvador accepted the command of the escort fleet for Brazil, the crown informed him that it could not provide him with the ships of war he would need. Instead, it expected that the Brazilians, through additional taxes, would pay for the protective convoy. When the already overtaxed Brazilians refused an additional levy, Salvador found himself with but two royal galleons in his command when he departed Portugal in 1644. His personal effort to enlist local support for the convoy system failed the following year when he was turned down by the municipal councils in both Bahia and Rio (Boxer 1952:189–90).

When he left with the sugar fleet in 1645 he had but a minimum protective escort. Then, to complicate matters, while en route to Bahia he was instructed to participate in a Portuguese attack on Pernambuco. After stopping in Bahia for orders, however, he chose to continue on with the sugar fleet to Lisbon (Boxer 1952:204–12). Needless to say, this action earned him nothing but enmity from the influential leaders of the Pernambuco affair.

On arriving in the Tagus with the twenty-five sugar ships of the Brazilian fleet intact, accompanied by a homeward-bound East India galleon, Salvador "lost no time in justifying himself to John, and asked for an official inquiry into his behaviour . . ." (Boxer 1952: 210-11). The inquiry most probably never was held. The king appears to have accepted Salvador's explanation of the events, since he lost none of his prestige and influence and was soon given additional responsibilities.

From his position on the important Overseas Council, to which he was reinstated, Salvador continued to advise the king on the major issues affecting the colonies. Although turned down in 1645 in his request for the governorship of Macao, Salvador did succeed in convincing the king of the benefits to be gained from establishing an independent administrative unit in the southern captaincies of Brazil, and gained for himself appointment as its governor and captain-general. But before he left to take up the post, news arrived of the death of Francisco de Soutomaior, who had been sent as governor of Angola to recapture the slave depot of Luanda, which the Dutch had taken in 1641.

Given the importance of Angola to Brazil, and of Brazil to Portugal, the king and his advisers decided that the best available man must be sent to replace Soutomaior. In 1647, therefore, Salvador Correia de Sá e Benavides was appointed as governor and captain-general of Angola, and provided "with as strong a force as could be assembled in the crown's penurious circumstances" (Boxer 1952:222). The king ordered that the new governor should be provided with two royal galleons, but "not of the best in the Armada, since they are needed here" (Boxer 1952:243), plus as many ships as could be chartered from private owners. Six hundred men, half to be recruited in Portugal and half in the Azores and Madeira, were to be assigned as reinforcements for the Angola garrison.

As Salvador prepared for the expedition, news arrived that the Dutch had landed a force at Bahia. The preparation of an armada to defend the Brazilian colonial capital against the imminent assault took precedence over providing supplies for Salvador's squadron. Only Salvador's stern personal refusal, which he presented directly to the king, prevented his forces from being incorporated into the fleet sent to defend Bahia. Short of both men and supplies, the new governor of Angola lacked the means to fulfill his mission. He therefore resolved to turn again to his long-time friends, associates, and kinsmen in southern Brazil for help.

Arriving in Rio with his skeleton forces at the beginning of 1648, he pleaded with the residents of Rio to provide a loan to pay for the Angola expedition. In response to his pleas, and aware of the importance of Angola to their well-being, the residents of Rio raised 60,000 cruzados to finance the project. As Boxer (1952:255) observes, this was "a truly remarkable cooperative effort, without which, as Salvador frankly acknowledged to the king, his armada could never have sailed." Salvador himself and the members of his family, it should be noted, were generous contributors to the loan.

While his armada was being prepared, Salvador was able to add to his own properties and business interests. In collaboration with the Jesuit Provincial, the Benedictine Abbot, and other close associates in Rio, Salvador used his influence to effect, by what his enemies later referred to as a combination of force and fraud (Boxer 1952:287), a redistribution of the *sesmarias* in the fertile, unsettled lands of the district of Campos dos Goitacazes (fig. 2.2A) to the north of Rio.

By the Composition of March 1648—the supposed official document providing for the redistribution of the *sesmarias*—the territory between Barra de Iguaçu and Lagoa Feia, extending inland in a northwesterly direction to the Paraíba River, was to be divided into twelve equal plots (*quinhões*) of approximately eighty square miles (Feydit 1900:35–39).[6] Three of the plots went to the Jesuits, four and one-half were left for the original recipients of the *sesmarias* and their heirs, half a plot went to the Benedictines, and one was awarded to Pedro de Sousa Pereira, Salvador's cousin and adopted son (see fig. 2.1), whom he had appointed *provedor* (purveyor) of Rio to control the finances of the captaincy and who had the authority to legalize the new composition. The remaining three plots went to Salvador himself (Leite 1938–50:6:84; Harrison n.d.:61–62).

The effort to gain control over the Campos dos Goitacazes clearly was aimed at converting the lush coastal lowlands into pastures. This in turn would enable Salvador to convert his cattle ranches near Rio into sugar plantations. By May, when Salvador left with his fleet for Angola, arrangements already had been completed to establish cattle ranches in the Campos dos Goitacazes.[7] When he returned from his miraculous victory in Angola four years later, the Jesuits are reported to have had nearly a thousand head of cattle grazing there (Harrison n.d.:66), while Salvador himself is reported to have owned seven thousand head (Boxer 1952:287), although we are not told where specifically they were located.

Salvador departed for Angola in 1648 with serious reservations about depleting the defensive forces of Rio when the Dutch might be preparing an attack there. By a combination of skill and luck (see Boxer 1952:263–70), however, within the next few months he was able to defeat the Dutch forces and to recapture the African colony.

After securing the victory, Salvador turned his attention to the slave trade. He not only revived regular shipments to Brazil but also, with King John's permission, made supplies available to Spanish America (Boxer 1952:282):

To help pay the debt still owed as late as 1650 for the forces raised for the recapture of the African colony in Rio, and to maintain the local garrison, Salvador convinced the municipal council of Luanda to impose a new tax of three milreis on each slave exported. Salvador himself had conflicting interests in this matter, being "one of the largest slave-dealers" to be affected by the tax and also one of the largest creditors to whom funds were owed on the loan (Boxer 1952:284).

While he was still in Africa, another of his projects, the Brazil convoy system, was to be expanded with the formation of the Brazil Company. The company, modeled after the East and West India companies chartered in Holland and England, was granted a monopoly on maritime trade with Brazil (Boxer 1952:290). Heated debate soon developed in high circles as to the desirability of the company, especially since it was to be financed largely with capital provided by Crypto Jews (Varnhagen 1927–36:3:171–74, 251–53; Boxer 1949:474–97).

Salvador, of course, was consulted on the matter. Not only was he the authority on the maritime defense of Portuguese interests in the South Atlantic, but he had been the driving force behind and the first commander of the convoy system. Before giving advice, however, he secured his personal interests "by obtaining a royal decree which enjoined all ships calling at Rio for cargo to reserve a tenth of their loading capacity for shipping the sugar produced by Salvador's own mills" (Boxer 1952:291). He then spoke out in support of the establishment of the company.

With his mission in Africa successfully completed, Salvador wrote to the king in 1650 asking to be relieved as governor of Angola. His request was not honored for two years, but by 1652 he was on his way to Rio to visit his family and see to his affairs in the colony, "taking with him a large number of Negro slaves" (Boxer 1952:286; see also Norton 1943:284–85).

44

> In the interval between his arrival at Rio early in June and his departure a few weeks later for Bahia and Lisbon, Salvador was very busy with the management of his vast estates in this captaincy. He stated next year that he owned five sugar plantations and forty cattle ranches in the *Reconcavo* of Rio de Janeiro, apart from his valuable urban property in the city of São Sebastião itself. . . . (Boxer 1952:286)

To these properties must be added his now extensive holdings in the Campos dos Goitacazes, where "he owned seven thousand head of cattle and one hundred and sixty Negro slaves. . . , as well as seventy saddle horses and much other property" (Boxer 1952:287).

Before leaving for Lisbon that year Salvador reportedly made an agreement with the Jesuits to combine the management of their six plots in the Planície (the plains in the Campos dos Goitacazes), with the profits to be divided equally between himself and the Jesuit college in Rio (Lamego 1913–25:1:117; Coaracy 1965:65–67, 125–26,136–37; Leite 1938–50:6:84–85). Before it could be implemented, however, the agreement is reported to have been voided, with Salvador then appointing a Benedictine as his *procurador* (legal representative) for the properties.[8] A cattle trail down the coast to the city of Rio de Janeiro then was opened to connect the cattle ranches in the new territory with the sugar plantations and other markets in the more established settlement. As Salvador sailed for Portugal in 1652, he was somewhat secure in the belief that the Campos dos Goitacazes were well on their way to being transformed into the cattle reserve he needed to enable him to convert his cattle ranches in the Recôncavo of Rio into sugar plantations, and thereby increase their value and his total income.

After arriving in Lisbon, he turned his attention to several other projects, of which the most important was the revival of his earlier proposal to the king to separate from Bahia the administration of the southern captaincies of Brazil, with Salvador himself as governor and captain-general. It will be remembered that the king had agreed to the idea, in part at least, and had given Salvador the appointment in 1646. Only the critical situation in Angola had delayed implementation of the project.

Salvador's primary reason for wanting control over an independent colony in the south was his desire to add mining properties to his already extensive holdings.

He estimated that the dazzling mountain of Sabarábussú was situated about three hundred miles from Rio de Janeiro, and about two hundred and forty from São Paulo. If so, it could not be very far away from the Serra das Esmeraldas, in the hinterland of Espirito Santo, so that it would be easy to combine the search for the two. . . . (Boxer 1952:302)

Shortly after his return, the Overseas Council, of which he still was a member, had suggested that Salvador be sent back to Rio, "to organize the mines of São Paulo and Paranaguá on a proper footing" (Boxer 1952:302). Salvador, of course, was willing, but tried to use the occasion to extract from the king the rewards and titles he believed due him for the services he had rendered the crown since 1614.

What Salvador was referring to, besides the creation of the autonomous southern captaincies, was the title and incomes John IV had promised him back in 1643 (Boxer 1952:155). At that time, the still somewhat insecure monarch had promised Salvador the title of Count, plus a substantial income, if he extracted a specified amount of gold from the alluvial mines in São Paulo. By 1652, however, the king, more secure on his throne, had changed his mind. For a combination of reasons, some real and others fabricated by Salvador's enemies who had the royal ear, he therefore informed Salvador bluntly that "if he did not wish to go without further bargaining, he would send someone else" (Boxer 1952:302).

Providence, however, was to assist Salvador unexpectedly. In November the monarch died, leaving his then-thirteen-year-old son, Afonso, to succeed him. For the remainder of the boy's minority the Spanish-born queen mother, Luisa de Guzmán, served as regent; and in 1658 she appointed Salvador governor and captain-general of the newly created, autonomous southern captaincies.

When Salvador returned to Brazil in 1658, he found himself, at the age of fifty-six, a man of great wealth, power, and influence. He had put together a personal fortune based on holdings that helped to supply the markets of Europe with the major commercial product of the period. He had become the principal individual landholder in the south of Brazil, and his cattle ranches and sugar plantations were equalled only by the properties of the religious orders. His plantations were adequately supplied with slaves by his own slaving interests in Angola, where he was one of the largest suppliers of chattel. His cattle ranches in the Recôncavo of Rio and in the Campos dos Goitacazes supplied his plantations with oxen to turn the cane presses and to transport the canes to the mills and the loaves of processed sugar to the coast for export. Furthermore, he had the monopoly for weighing and storing sugar in Rio and guaranteed maritime transportation from the Brazil Company. In addition, he had plans to build great ships of his own at Rio.

Missing from his holdings, however, was the other major source of great wealth at the time, mines of precious stones and metals. Also missing was the dramatic triumph of a title of nobility, thus far denied him by the crown in spite of his years of recognized service.

Salvador's personal interests, then, and the future of his family, would be best served if, on arrival in Rio, he devoted his energies to the mines. The discovery of gold and precious stones, now that he was administrator of the mines in the south, would not only round out his personal holdings but also, he believed, bring him the title he had so long coveted. The mineral wealth of Brazil was thought to be in the interior. Alluvial gold already had been discovered in São Paulo and in Paranaguá. The fabled Serra das Esmeraldas, or mountain range of emeralds, was believed to be located to the northwest of Rio and São Paulo, in the interior. After establishing himself in the government of the new colony, Salvador turned as quickly as possible to the real business at hand, the mines.

When the new governor and captain-general arrived in the capital of the newly autonomous southern colony, its affairs were in the trusted hands of his kinsmen and dependents. The governor of the royal captaincy of Rio de Janeiro, whom Salvador was to replace, was his cousin, Thomé Correia de Alvarenga (see fig. 2.1). The *provedor-mór*, or crown purveyor, was Pedro de Sousa Pereira, Salvador's adopted son, who was married to his cousin and was brother-in-law to Thomé Correia. Pedro was also acting administrator of the mines in São Paulo. Manuel Correia Vasqueannes, another cousin to the new governor, was president of the municipal council of the city, while still another cousin, Martim Correia Vasques, was commander of the Rio garrison (Boxer 1952:303–4).

With his kin caring for his interests in Rio, Salvador, after attending to the defenses of the city, was free to set out to search the southern captaincies for the mines that had eluded him through the years. He chose as a starting point for exploration the backlands of the captaincy of Espírito Santo.[9] But he was to have no success. When he returned to Rio, however, he left his son, João, to continue the unsuccessful search. On the latter's behalf Salvador had written to the Paulistas "asking them to send him a local jeweler and lapidary, together with 'thirty or forty white men, expert backwoodsmen,' promising rewards and promotion to those who would join his son's projected expedition" (Boxer 1952:306).

Once back in Rio, Salvador occupied himself with the construction of what is reported to have been one of the largest ships built in the seventeenth century, the *Padre Eterno*.

By October 1660, having pushed a stiff poll tax through the Rio municipal council to pay and secure the garrison, having commenced the building of the *Padre Eterno*, and having dispatched his son, João, on yet another expedition in search of the Serra das Esmeraldas, Salvador was ready to take charge personally of the mines in São Paulo and Paranaguá, where a new vein of alluvial gold was reported to have been discovered.

In São Paulo Salvador received the news that a group of settlers in the newly founded parish of São Gonçalo (established in 1647 across Guanabara Bay, where the city of Niteroi is now located) had refused to pay the taxes to support the Rio garrison. The rebels, led by his enemies, had presented a formal ultimatum to the acting governor, demanding an investigation of the government's accounts. When this request was refused, the rebels, joined by the soldiers to whom they had promised their back pay, sacked the houses of the absent governor and his local supporters (Boxer 1952:313). Then, after holding a meeting at which all Salvador's appointees were deposed and barred from holding office, his kinsmen and dependents were arrested and, with their families, were shipped off to Portugal, accompanied by a long list of charges against the Correia administration (Boxer 1952:314). Finally, the *ouvidor* (crown judge) was forced to organize an impromptu election to fill the positions vacated by the departure of Salvador's supporters.

Although Salvador's kinsmen and dependents had dominated the municipal council and the administrative offices in the captaincy of Rio, for some time there had been a small dissident faction in the local chamber strongly opposed to Salvador personally and to Correia domination in general. The ranks of this opposition had been increased by the heirs of the two landowners in the Campos dos Goitacazes who had lost their properties to Salvador in 1648. Still in possession of their plantations and *engenhos* in the Recôncavo of Rio, however, the two had succeeded in being elected to the municipal council of the city. With support from others also opposed to the Correias, they were able to rally additional citizens whose interests had been or were being prejudiced by the increased taxes just imposed on them and by the way the governor was using them, their city, and its resources in his effort to discover new mines in other captaincies. It was clear to them that Salvador was interested only in increasing his personal fortune and obtaining a title of nobility, with little consideration for the interests and well-being of the citizens of Rio—other than his dependents.

As long as the Correias controlled the colonial administration and the local municipal assembly, the laws would favor their interests to the detriment of their opponents. The only alternatives for the members of the opposition were to leave, giving up their homes and profitable plantations and mills, or to rebel. Their hope in choosing the latter course of action was that, given the precarious international situation and their influential friends at court, the home government might decide on expedience, and support whichever side was able to dominate the local scene by force. If they won, a new governor, without local ties and commitments, might be persuaded to reconcile his interests with their own.

With the support of the people of São Paulo, whom he had finally won over after years of opposition, Salvador issued a proclamation pardoning the people of Rio—with the exception of the ringleaders of the revolt—and abolishing the unpopular taxes that had precipitated the mutiny (Boxer 1952:319).

He turned down an offer from the Paulistas to accompany him to Rio. Instead, he chose to return on his own, anticipating the arrival of the Brazil fleet from Portugal led by two personal friends "on whose cooperation and support he felt he could rely" (Boxer 1952:321). Joined by his son, João, and the *bandeira* (band) that had been searching unsuccessfully for the Serra das Esmeraldas and the elusive Sabarábussú, Salvador moved to recapture the city, which he did with minimum effort on April 6, 1661.

His first act on regaining the city was to convene a summary court-martial at which the leader of the revolt, Jeronimo Barbalho, was tried, condemned, and executed, all on the same day. Following the execution, Barbalho's head was displayed on the pillory in the public square. This act, as Salvador admitted, was intended mainly "to terrorize the local populace and to discourage other attempts at rebellion, whether in Rio or in other Portuguese colonies" (Boxer 1952:322).

The victory was to be short-lived, however. When the Overseas Council received word of the news, it was presented with a dilemma. A marriage had been arranged between Catherine of Braganza and Charles II of England. Portugal, at the time, could not afford to have anything interfere with the wedding. War with Spain would be inopportune. If the rebels were not appeased they might seek an alliance with the Spanish forces in Buenos Aires, the result of which could have been war and the possible loss of the southern captaincies. The royal treasury, which was becoming ever more dependent on Brazil could not afford their loss. Hence, the councilors advised the queen-regent to appoint someone to replace Salvador as governor of the southern captaincies. From then on neither Salvador nor any of his relatives ever returned to Brazil as royal governor (Boxer 1952:327).

The complete results of the rebellion, however, were to remain in doubt for some time. Salvador and his supporters were recalled and even spent a short time in prison. The rebels, for the most part, also went to jail, where they remained until the case finally was resolved in 1668.[10] A new governor was sent to Rio, and Salvador returned shortly thereafter to Lisbon, where a new set of adventures and opportunities at court awaited him.[11]

Afonso, the young son of John IV and heir to the Portuguese throne, we learn from Sir Robert Southwell (Boxer 1952:341), "had suffered from paralytic seizure in his childhood, which had crippled him both mentally and physically. . . ." As he matured, he was given to overindulgence, drinking excessively and spending his days carousing and whoring. He appears to have had neither the interest nor the ability to govern. Recognizing this, the queen-regent favored her strong and vigorous younger son, the Infante D. Pedro, and, we are told, even "toyed with the idea of supplanting his older brother in his favour" (Boxer 1952:342).

The queen-regent had given Pedro his own household and apartments in 1662. In the same year, some of Afonso's more disreputable favorites were kidnapped and sent off to Brazil. The Count of Castel-Melhor, a young nobleman in the king's service, then insinuated to the king that the same fate might befall him if he did not take the government into his own hands. The impulsive Afonso, believing this a possibility, precipitated a palace revolution in June of 1662 which forced his mother into retirement and eventually into a convent, where she died. Afonso did not wish to be bothered with the affairs of state, however, so he left the decision making to Castel-Melhor, who soon became a virtual dictator.

Having secured his position, Castel-Melhor devoted his energies to an alliance with France, arranging a marriage for the incompetent king. The bride was Marie Françoise Isabelle of Savoy-Nemours, Mademoiselle d'Aumale. The wedding took place, after lengthy negotiation, in 1666. The new queen was ambitious, but she was to be frustrated in that ambition, first by her incompetent husband, and then by Castel-Melhor, with whom she broke openly within a year of the wedding.

Meanwhile, the *fidalgos* (noblemen) who had supported the queen-regent gathered around Pedro as the only alternative to Castel-Melhor. The young queen also turned to her brother-in-law as an ally, and the two, supported by the Duke of Cadavel and others, entered into a war of intrigue which they won, obtaining Castel-Melhor's dismissal and exile in 1667. The king, however, was not willing to hand over his throne without one last effort. He turned to those who had remained loyal to him, meeting in council on October 1, 1667. Among the half-dozen loyal intimates present was Salvador Correia de Sá e Benavides.

Salvador had supported Castel-Melhor's efforts to centralize the administration of the kingdom. Castel-Melhor, in turn, had rewarded Salvador by granting his eldest son the title of nobility Salvador himself had so long desired. In 1666, Martim Correia de Sá, who had served gallantly in the battle of Amiecial and had won distinction in the battle of Ormuz, was made Viscount of Asseca.

Now, in 1667, the plan devised by the king's advisers was for Salvador to lead four regiments of the Lisbon garrison in rounding up first the Infante D. Pedro, and then the other leaders of the opposition. The plot was leaked, however, and the enemy struck first, buying off the members of the garrison and then sending their own forces to deal with the organizers. Salvador, unlike some of the others, escaped, but eventually was jailed.

Pedro then took steps to take the government from his brother. Mademoiselle d'Aumale, the queen, meanwhile, retired to a convent, where she declared herself still to be a virgin, the wife neither of Afonso nor of any other man. The following year, she married Pedro, who took the title of prince-regent. Afonso then was exiled to the island of Terceira, in the Azores. He remained there until 1674, when he was brought back and imprisoned in the palace at Cintra, where he died in 1683.

Salvador was not to remain in prison for long, however. He had remained close to the Jesuits, whose wishes were important to the prince-regent. Not only was Salvador released, presumably through their influence, but soon he was back in royal favor. In 1669 we find him once again taking his seats on the Council of War and the Overseas Council, and also securing authorization for the collection of monies from Brazil owed him on account of the *Padre Eterno* (Boxer 1952:370). And this was not all.

With the throne secured, the prince-regent—at least until the death of his unfortunate brother in 1683—chose not to take personal control of the government. Instead, he left almost all decisions to the members of the various ministries and councils of state. Consequently, Salvador, now back on the important and prestigious Council of War and the Overseas Council, and the most experienced hand on colonial affairs, came to exert considerable influence on national policy, especially on matters pertaining to Brazil. It should be no surprise, therefore, that he added to his already extensive holdings in the colony.

The central government at the time was making every effort to populate Brazil and to develop its economic resources. Wars with Holland and England earlier in the century had cost the Portuguese most of their colonies in the Orient, and Brazil was the only hope left to replenish a depleted treasury. But since the royal coffers were low, Portugal went to the old expedient of granting captaincies to private citizens who were willing and able to defend and develop them at their own expense.

In 1674, then, on behalf of his two sons, Martim Correia de Sá, the Viscount of Asseca, and João Correia de Sá, Salvador reportedly requested and received twenty and ten leagues respectively along the coast of Brazil, extending from Cabo Frio in the south to the borders of Espírito Santo in the north (fig. 2.2.B). Consequently, the Campos dos Goitacazes were once again a private captaincy, now belonging to the Correia de Sá family and called Paraíba do Sul.[12]

Misfortune, however, was to prevent the two new lords proprietor from exploiting their domains. Within a month of the confirmation of the grant, Martim Correia de Sá died, his titles and properties passing to his infant son, named Salvador after his paternal grandfather. João, meanwhile, had gone to the Orient, first as general of the straits of Ormuz, and then to Goa, where he was to disgrace himself and the family first by assassinating his father-in-law and then by escaping to Spain—with his father's help—when sent home in chains to stand trial (Boxer 1952:375–77; Irvine 1907:3:159–60). By fleeing, João forfeited his share of Paraíba do Sul and an additional grant his father had been able to secure on his behalf in 1676.

In 1671, the aging Salvador had petitioned the crown for eighty leagues along the southern coast of Brazil extending to the La Plata River. He had promised to build fortifications in the no-man's-land and to protect it against aggression by the Spanish in Buenos Aires. The Overseas Council, as might be expected, looked favorably on the request, but insisted that the fortifications be constructed before it would grant the concession. Salvador had long before proposed the creation of the captaincy of Santa Catarina in this area. It was not until 1676 that a grant of seventy-five leagues was obtained in favor of João Correia de Sá and the young Salvador Correia, the Second Viscount of Asseca.

The provisions of the grant were somewhat confusing since they combined the new territories with the earlier grant of Paraíba do Sul. The intent was to give each of Salvador's heirs a total of fifty leagues of coast to govern. But since João was in hiding to avoid standing trial for murder, and had no legal heir, the entire one hundred leagues of coast (approximately four hundred miles), comprising several noncontiguous parcels, passed to the young viscount. The aging Salvador, of course, acted as the legal representative for his grandson.

The concession in the south gave the elder Salvador one more chance to add mining properties to the already large holdings that were entailed as the patrimony of the House of Asseca. He therefore appointed a loyal kinsman to govern Paraíba do Sul and turned his attention to the south, where he also was involved "in a scheme with the crown to establish a town on the La Plata which would serve as a base for the (illegal) silver trade with the Spanish mines at Potosí" (Harrison n.d.:105).

Salvador was never to discover the precious stones and metals for which he had been searching since 1614. Nevertheless, when he died, "at some unascertained date between 1681 and 1687" (Boxer 1952:391), he had come closer to achieving success as it was defined by the society of which he was a part than all but a few of his contemporaries. He was one of the richest men in the empire, if not in the world. In addition, on behalf of his eldest son, he had obtained a viscountship that was to make his descendants not only rich but also members of the Portuguese aristocracy. Furthermore, he had worked his way into the inner circle of advisers upon whom a series of kings and rulers of Portugal was dependent for the maintenance and at times even the survival of their thrones and kingdoms. He had wealth and power, which he was able to pass on to his descendants in a noble line.

His wealth, as we have seen, had come primarily from sugar, whose production and commerce he came very close to integrating vertically. From his father and a series of paternal kinsmen who had helped to found and to administer for the crown the Rio captaincy, he had acquired lands in the fertile Recôncavo. With the capture of Pernambuco and other parts of the northeast coast of Brazil by the Dutch, he had initiated the planting of sugarcane in the vicinity of the Rio settlement.

He then acquired lands in the Campos dos Goitacazes that later became his family's private captaincy, Paraíba do Sul. On these lands he established a cattle industry to supply food and animal power for his sugar estates in Rio and to help feed the inhabitants of the city. These ranches later replaced his cattle estates in Rio, which then could be converted into additional sugar plantations and mills.

Both in Paraguay and in Angola he had gained access to supplies of slaves to work his plantations. In Paraguay he was able to obtain native Amerindians, while in Angola he traded for black Africans.

In the captaincy of Rio de Janeiro he built sugar mills and storage facilities, in which his cattle and slaves were employed. In addition, as the result of a contract with the municipal council of Rio, he had a perpetual monopoly on the weighing and storing of all of the sugar produced in the captaincy. He also had guaranteed space for his sugars on the ships of the Brazil Company. In addition, he had built the *Padre Eterno*, one of the largest ships afloat at the time, in which sugar was carried to Europe and trade goods imported to Brazil.

His numerous properties and investments, when appropriate recognition is given to the differences between his era and our own, might be thought of as his investment portfolio. They included land, mills, cattle, horses, and slaves in the Rio captaincy, the warehouse in the city of Rio, lands, cattle, and slaves in Paraíba do Sul, lands, slaves, and other interests in Angola and Paraguay, an interest in the Brazil Company, the *Padre Eterno* and other ships, plus rights in lands and the territory between the captaincy of São Vicente and the Río de la Plata—which also was to become a private captaincy with his family as lord proprietor.

In the administration of these disparate areas and in the management of his personal affairs, Salvador judiciously placed loyal kinsmen and dependents able to protect his interests. In Rio, as we have seen, João Antônio Correia had served as his secretary and Thomé Correia de Alvarenga, landowner and sugar planter in his own right, acted for him as governor. Duarte Correia Vasqueannes, a half-uncle, held the governorship of Rio in the interim following the death of his father while also commanding one of the harbor forts. Duarte also had properties both in Rio and in Paraíba do Sul. Manuel Correia Vasqueannes, another cousin, was for a time president of the municipal council of Rio and a landowner both in Rio and in Paraíba. His brother, Martim Correia Vasques, also Salvador's cousin, was commander of the Rio garrison and the owner of lands and mills in Rio and cattle estates in Paraíba. Pedro de Sousa Pereira was married to Ana Correia de Sá, Salvador's cousin, and was brother-in-law to Thomé Correia de Alvarenga, Martim Correia Vasques, and Manuel Correia Vasqueannes. He also was Salvador's adopted son. Pedro served as *provedor-mór* (crown purveyor) at Rio de Janeiro and as deputy administrator of the mines in São Paulo. In his capacity as crown purveyor he had collaborated with Salvador in the redistribution of the *sesmarias* in the Campos dos Goitacazes, making possible Correia de Sá control of the area that later became their private captaincy.

In Paraguay Salvador had the support of Don Luis de Céspedes Xeria, the governor, who, at Salvador's initiative, had married Victoria de Sá, the daughter of Salvador's father's brother, Gonçalo Correia de Sá. Gonçalo, it must be remembered, also had served as administrator of the mines in São Paulo and had collaborated with Salvador and his father. Salvador also had important ties throughout the Spanish New World through his wife, who was exceptionally well placed.

We are not told who was left to protect the family's interests in Angola when Salvador was relieved as governor. We can surmise, however, that some trustworthy kinsman or dependent had been established to look after the slaving interests upon which the estates and mills in Brazil came to rely for labor as the Amerindian population became more difficult to obtain.

In each of these varied holdings that together have been likened to an investment portfolio, Salvador had trusted kinsmen and dependents whose interests were interdependent with his and whose future depended upon the success of his career. These kinsmen and dependents were almost all socially, politically, and economically inferior to Salvador, who was the leader upon whom all relied for guidance and direction.

For the success of his career and the well-being of his dependents, Salvador needed the support of the crown. The norm for the period was to obtain through negotiated exchange a patron in the inner circles of the palace. Salvador, however, by serving outstandingly in a period of uncertainty and flux, obtained positions on two of the councils that directly advised the crown. As a member of the War Council and the Overseas Council he gained direct access to the monarch, who came both to need and to respect him, and therefore to support him, at least in many of the requests he made for the promotion of his career.

Salvador might have preferred to receive a title of nobility from King John IV, whom he had supported after the restoration in 1640 and whom he had served until the monarch's death in 1656. But John never fully trusted Salvador, and he held back on the most important reward Salvador needed to achieve his life's ambition. Instead, he gave his loyal servant lesser benefits and made the coveted title of nobility contingent upon the discovery of gold.

Salvador was able to take advantage of the uncertainty and confusion surrounding the regency of the queen-mother, Luisa de Guzmán, and the intrigue and, later, open conflict between the incompetent King Afonso VI and his brother, Prince Pedro. From his positions on the Overseas and War councils, he was able to assist the Count of Castel-Melhor, an old collaborator, in his rise to the dictatorship of the kingdom. In return it was Castel-Melhor who named Salvador's eldest son, Martim, the First Viscount of Asseca.

Salvador's fortune at this point rose and fell depending on which side gained the upper hand in the struggle for the crown that lasted until the exile of the king in 1669. Then, just as he appeared to have lost everything by supporting the king, he was saved and restored to favor with the help of the Jesuits, with whom he had long-standing ties and whose interests had coincided with his for almost half a century. With Salvador restored to favor in the new regime, his holdings, now entailed in the House of Asseca, were increased by additional lands in Brazil and by the captaincy of Santa Catarina.

For reasons beyond his control, Salvador's achievements almost came to naught in his later years. By his personal determination and tenacity he had acquired wealth almost beyond belief and a title for his eldest son. That son, however, predeceased his father just after the title had been obtained. Then João, Salvador's second son and favorite, for whom a captaincy and other properties had been obtained, murdered his father-in-law while serving in Goa. The rest of his life he lived in disgrace in exile. Two other sons entered the church. One daughter survived and married.

The Viscountship of Asseca then passed to Salvador's grandson and namesake. In his old age, therefore, Salvador was still struggling to maintain his place and to manage the interests, properties, and dependents he had accumulated on behalf of his young grandson. He was still uncertain as to the future of all he had devoted his life to achieving. With his first son dead, the second in exile in disgrace, and two others in the church, Salvador had no sons left to carry on with what he had built. When he died, everything went to young Salvador, who himself died before reaching maturity. The estate then passed to the second grandson, Diogo Correia de Sá, who became the Third Viscount of Asseca. After several decades of uncertainty Diogo, aided by his sons Martim, who was to be the Fourth Viscount, and Luis, brought the Correias de Sá back to prominence in Portuguese aristocratic circles, where they were to remain into the twentieth century.

Salvador Correia de Sá e Benavides, however, had been the builder of the dynasty that linked the continents of the Portuguese Empire and articulated groups of kinsmen and dependents in a network that mobilized productive social groupings in Portugal, Brazil, and Africa. Through his life and career, one may gain some insight into investment decision making in the Portuguese Empire in the seventeenth century.

NOTES

1. A special debt of gratitude is expressed to Professor William F. Harrison of Northern Illinois University for his contribution to this paper. Not only did he make available to me his unpublished manuscript on the captaincy of Paraíba do Sul (Har-

rison n.d.), he also advised me on the literature of the period and served as a general consultant. In addition, he read and edited several versions of the manuscript. I alone, however, am responsible for the final form and content of the paper.

2. Although the crowns of both Portugal and Spain had been one since 1580 (see below), the two kingdoms had been administered separately and by distinct personnel.

3. We may think of them as a faction linked vertically to the entrepreneur by means of a set of exchanges. In this way we can refer to them as a dependency network that formed a faction vis-à-vis other groups linked similarly to other, often competing, entrepreneurs.

4. Since the monarchs of the Iberian nations are so well known in the English literature, and their names anglicized, we have used the English versions of their names throughout the paper.

5. Philip, meanwhile, also was making overtures to the Brazilian colonists while planning measures against supporters of the Braganzas. And the Dutch, who still controlled Pernambuco, continued to threaten the Brazilian colonists whose loyalty and support John so badly needed.

6. The two landowners coerced into agreeing to the new arrangements were less than pleased with its consequences. Both were sugar planters and substantial land-owners in Rio and of considerable importance in local affairs. Both, or their heirs, kinsmen, or dependents, now bitter enemies of the Correias de Sá, were to become members of the municipal council in Rio and to lead a dissident minority wishing to oust the Correias from control of the captaincy (see below; Coaracy 1965:133–34; Harrison n.d.:63).

7. The Composition of 1648 specified that each of the twelve plots was to have a *sítio* (ranch site) with eight corrals. Each corral was to have a grazing area of 500 *braças*—with 1 *braça* equal to 1.8 square meters. Additional corrals, however, could be constructed if the plot was large enough. Anyone found squatting on the lands, it stipulated, was to be expelled and his improvements destroyed (Feydit 1900:36; Harrison n.d.:62).

8. This act, followed by his granting of a large tract of land to the order on which to construct the *matriz*, or principal church of the captaincy, opened the door to an important presence of the Benedictines in the social, political, and economic life of the incipient colony (Harrison n.d.).

9. Salvador had insisted that the backward and sparsely populated captaincy be included in his new jurisdiction because he believed that the Serra das Esmeraldas was located in its hinterland (Boxer 1952:305).

10. Agostinho Barbalho, brother of the executed rebel, who also had been one of the leaders, was, however, speedily absolved of all blame for the rebellion. In addition, he was given various rewards as payment for previous services to the crown and, as Boxer (1952:348) supposes, "as some sort of solace for the execution of his brother."

One of the rewards was the island of Santa Catarina, the center of the captaincy between São Paulo and the Río de la Plata that Salvador had proposed be created for himself. Another was Salvador's former post as administrator of the mines of São Paulo and leader of the search for the Serra das Esmeraldas. Unfortunately for the Barbalho family, Agostinho died before he could benefit from these concessions.

Salvador also was ultimately absolved of any wrongdoing. His supporters were released and permitted to return to their families and properties in Rio. The other mutineers were given amnesty and the final decision was to forget the whole matter (Boxer 1952:348; Coaracy 1965:166–76; Varnhagen 1927–36:255–56).

11. Shortly after his arrival in the metropolis, however, as one contemporary source (Brazão 1940:144–45, 147–48) tells it, he was arrested and charged with accepting a bribe. He was alleged to have permitted four Dutch ships to have taken cargo in Rio when he was governor and proceed directly to Holland, thus defrauding the king of his dues and the Portuguese of their profits (Boxer 1952:347).

As usual, he responded to the charges with high claims. He boasted of his forty-nine years of service, while complaining of his age and health. He then protested against having his reputation questioned at a time when he had expected to receive great thanks and rewards. He concluded by asking to be allowed to take his place on the councils to which he belonged despite the judicial proceedings pending against him (Boxer 1952:347). The tactic seems to have worked since soon thereafter he is found participating on the councils and the bribery charges are dropped.

12. The provisions of the grant required each of the brothers to establish at his own expense a town with a church, houses for thirty married couples, and a building for the municipal government. If the condidions were not satisfied within six years, the grants would be forfeited (Harrison n.d.:102).

APPENDIX: Chronology of Major World Events and Personal Events Affecting the Life and Career of Salvador Correia de Sá e Benavides*

Date	Major World Events	Personal Events in Salvador's Life
1578	Defeat and death of the childless King Sebastian at the battle of Alcacer-Kebir.	
1580	After the short reign of the elderly Cardinal-King Henry, King Philip II of Spain occupies Portugal and assumes the crown as Philip I of Portugal.	
1581	Cortes of Tomar legalizes Philip's assumption of the Portuguese crown.	
1598	Death of Philip II (and I of Portugal) and accension of Philip III (and II of Portugal).	
1602		Birth of Salvador Correia de Sá e Benavides in Cádiz.
1614 or 15		First visit to Brazil with his father and grandfather in search of mines in the São Paulo area.
1618		Made knight of the Order of Santiago (St. James).
1621	Death of Philip III (and II of Portugal) and acession of Philip IV (and III of Portugal). Dutch West India Company founded.	
1624	Dutch forces capture Bahia.	Leaves Lisbon for Rio where he levies men and supplies in Rio and São Vicente to fight the Dutch.

Date	Major World Events	Personal Events in Salvador's Life
1625	Bahia recaptured in May.	Leads a skirmish against Piet Heyn in Espírito Santo in March.
1629		Luis Céspedes Xeria reaches Rio on his way to Paraguay and marries Victoria de Sá.
1630	Dutch capture Pernambuco, which they hold until 1654.	Escorts Victoria de Sá overland to Asunción in Paraguay. Between 1630 and 1635 serves as commander of forces to put down Indian rebellions in Paraguay and Tucumán. During that time he meets and marries D. Catalina de Urgate y Velasco, a wealthy widow, and visits Potosí.
1636		Signs contract with the municipal council of Rio to build a warehouse facility and weigh station.
1637	Dutch capture Mina on the West African coast.	Assumes governorship of Rio on the death of his father. Contract of the previous year with the municipal council of Rio converted into a perpetual monopoly for himself and his descendants.
1639		Birth of first son, Martim Correia de Sá.
1640	Dutch defeat Portuguese fleet. Riots in Rio, Santos, and São Paulo over the publication of Pope Urban VIII's brief on the liberty of the Amerindians. Jesuits expelled from São Paulo. Portugal revolts against Spain, with the Duke of Braganza proclaimed as King John IV.	
1641	Ten-year truce signed between Holland and Portugal in June, but Dutch seize Luanda in August and Sergipe and Maranhão in November.	As governor of Rio proclaims both his personal and the colony's loyalty to John IV.
1642	Jesuits reinstated in Santos. Loyalists rebel against Dutch in Maranhão.	Trouble with the Paulistas.
1643	Dutch attack other Portuguese possessions in Africa	Returns to Europe for a personal interview with King John.
1644	Dutch evacuate Maranhão.	Commissioned general of the Brazil fleets by the crown.
1645	Convoy system inaugurated at Bahia and Rio. Portuguese send expedition to Angola. Loyalists in Pernambuco revolt against Dutch.	Request for the governorship of Macao refused.

Date	Major World Events	Personal Events in Salvador's Life
1646	Jesuits again expelled from Santos.	
1647	Dutch defeat Portuguese forces in Angola.	Appointed governor of Angola and secretly commissioned to recover the colony from the Dutch. Departs Lisbon with his Rio-bound squadron.
1648	Spain recognizes Dutch independence. Brazil Company founded.	Recaptures Luanda, Benguela, and São Tomé with resources raised in Brazil. Effects the redistribution of lands in the Terras dos Goitacazes and establishes cattle ranches there. Also secures guaranteed space for his sugar on ships of the Brazil Company.
1649	First fleet of the Brazil Company departs under the Count of Castel-Melhor.	
1651	John IV seeks peace with Cromwell.	
1652	War breaks out between England and Holland.	Leaves Luanda for Rio. Founds Jesuit College at Santos.
1654	Recife and other Dutch strongholds in Brazil fall to the Portuguese.	Charged with the maritime defense of Lisbon.
1656	Death of John IV. Ascent of 13-year-old Afonso VI, and regency of queen-mother, Luisa de Guzmán.	
1657	Holland declares war on Portugal and blockades the Tagus.	
1658	Holland also goes to war against Sweden. Gold discovered at Paranguá, where previous finds had been made in 1629 and 1648.	
1659	Peace between France and Spain.	Returns to Rio as captain-general and governor of the southern captaincies and begins the construction of the galleon *Padre Eterno*. Abortive expedition made to the Serra das Esmeraldas.
1660		Second expedition to the Serra das Esmeraldas made under the command of João Correia de Sá, Salvador's second son. Leaves for the mines of Paranaguá. Revolt in Rio against the Correia de Sá family. Kinsmen Thomé Correia and Pedro de Sousa Pereira expelled by the rebels.
1661	Peace between Portugal and Holland. Anglo-Portuguese alliance renewed.	Recaptures Rio and executes rebel leader Jeronimo Barbalha.

Date	Major World Events	Personal Events in Salvador's Life
1662	Catherine of Braganza marries Charles II of England. Count of Castel-Melhor leads a palace coup against the queen-regent and forces her to hand over the government to the incompetent Afonso VI who turns it over to Castel-Melhor.	
1664		The *Padre Eterno* is launched.
1665	Second Anglo-Dutch war breaks out. Philip IV of Spain dies. Ascent of the sickly infant Charles II and regency of the queen-mother, Mariana of Austria.	
1666	Luisa de Guzmán dies. Afonso VI marries Marie Françoise Isabelle of Savoy-Nemours, Mademoiselle d'Aumale. Discontent with the Castel-Melhor dictatorship grows.	Martim Correia de Sá made first Viscount of Asseca by Castel-Melhor for his services to the crown and for the services of his father.
1667	Alliance signed between Portugal and Spain. Louis XIV of France invades Spanish Flanders. England and Holland sign the Treaty of Breda. After considerable intrigue Afonso VI is forced to dismiss Castel-Melhor and turn the government over to his brother Pedro, who takes the title of prince-regent. The queen seeks an annulment of her marriage.	Captured in a plot against the king's brother Pedro along with a few of the remaining supporters of the king.
1668	Peace between Portugal and Spain. Cortes meets. Queen's marriage to King Afonso VI annulled and she marries her brother-in-law, Pedro, the prince-regent.	Arrested and imprisoned. His sons sent into exile.
1669	Afonso exiled to Terceira in the Azores. The Infanta Isabel Luisa Josefa born to the queen.	Released and restored to favor, most probably through the intervention of the Jesuits.
1673	Plot discovered for the restoration of Afonso VI, with Spanish help.	
1674	Afonso brought back to Portugal and imprisoned at Cintra.	Martim and João Correia de Sá each receive extensive grants of land in Brazil.
1676	São Salvador de Campos and São João de Barra founded in Paraíba do Sul. Paulistas renew their raids in Paraguay and Uruguay. Bishopric of Rio de Janeiro created.	João Correia de Sá murders his father-in-law in Goa. Martim and João Correia de Sá granted additional territory in the region between São Vicente and the Río de la Plata.

Entrepreneurship in the Portuguese Empire

Date	Major World Events	Personal Events in Salvador's Life
1677	Unsuccessful expeditions for gold, silver, and emeralds in the interior of Brazil.	João Correia de Sá sent back under arrest from India via Bahia.
1678		Death of Martim Correia de Sá.
1679		João Correia de Sá breaks sanctuary and seeks refuge in Spain.
1681		Signs his last *consulta* in the Overseas Council.
1682		Presumed death of Salvador Correia de Sá e Benavides.
1683	Death of Afonso VI. Pedro becomes king in name as well as in fact. The queen dies.	

*Adapted with modifications from Boxer (1952:399–403).

The Changing Social Networks and Investment Behavior of a Slaveholding Elite in the Ante Bellum South: Some Natchez "Nabobs," 1800–1860[1]

MORTON ROTHSTEIN

Department of History
University of Wisconsin–Madison

For almost a generation, new modes of historical research and analysis, employing quantitative techniques and sophisticated behavioral concepts, along with uncovering abundant new or unutilized sources, have stimulated great interest in reexamining the record of plantation slavery in the ante bellum South. The storm of controversy in the popular press and scholarly journals that has greeted such recent books as those by Fogel and Engerman (1974), Genovese (1974), Gutman (1976), and David and his colleagues (1976) attests not only to their relevance for grappling with current social problems, but to the continuous effort dedicated to obtaining a better understanding of that history. The arguments over current research efforts and results (see *Reviews in American History* 1974) have generated much heat and shed important new light on many aspects of slavery in the United States, yet underlying much of the new literature, explicitly or implicitly, are assumptions and conclusions about the behavior of slaveholders as entrepreneurs. For the most part a consensus seems to be emerging that plantation owners were rational decision makers who responded to market opportunities and pressures in ways that, on the whole, made slavery profitable for them, whatever its costs to the region or the nation (see Parker 1970; Engerman 1975; Gallman and Anderson 1977).

There are some curious and important gaps in the work thus far advanced. The newer modes of analysis apparently work best on features for which highly aggregated data, in raw form or sophisticated samples, exist, yielding important insights into the total structure of the plantation economy. They are less usefully applied to those features that involve extensive periods of time or concentration on individuals, places, or other smaller units. In much of the new work, the planters, the slaves, and the plantation enterprise become disembodied entities, and presumably interchangeable "types," without regard to the specifics of time or place. The tendency to homogenize bits and pieces of evidence about particular persons or settings, to be sure, also marred many of the older, traditional studies of "plantation and frontier" in the United States (Phillips 1909, 1966; see Miller and Genovese 1974 and Mohr 1972 for some of the better recent work). Perhaps the deficiencies that arise from treating slave families or communities without allowing for real distinctions between the social contexts in which they functioned, or for differences over time, is an unavoidable cost of operating beyond the micro level, or local and individual firm level; the problem of assessing typicality always goes with such a study. It is undoubtedly one outcome of trying to reduce a complex, dynamic, and sprawling history to manageable form or size (Parker 1973; Rosenberg 1975; Boney 1974). Whatever the reasons, few recent works adequately explore such relationships as kinship networks or the importance of trust and confidence among members of entrepreneurial groups anywhere in the United States, much less the slaveholders of the Old South (see Hoselitz 1963 and Saveth 1966 for general theories; D. Smith 1970 and Ghent and Jaher 1976 for more recent efforts; and Davidson 1971 and Rogers 1971 for multidisciplinary approaches to the ante bellum South; see also Aronson 1970). It is an omission all the more puzzling in view of the new interest in family history and the persistent awareness of the importance of kinship ties at various levels of economic development in most areas of the world.

One obvious place for beginning such entrepreneurial studies of slaveholding is the Natchez district. There is considerable material, old and new, on the plantation owners who lived in or near that Mississippi River town. Located on the first great bluff of the Mississippi River's eastern bank as one moves north from New Orleans (see fig. 3.1), Natchez served as a focal point of settlement and development by overlapping and interrelated groups and families, including some of the ante bellum South's most prominent planter-entrepreneurs. Members of the elite slaveholding groups had established themselves early in the history of that district, acquiring property on both sides of the river from the beginnings of Anglo-American settlement. During the first six decades of the nineteenth century they shifted and extended their investments into a variety of enterprises. By intensively exploring the investment behavior of a segment of Natchez's elite, and the connections between business decisions and the complex network of the segment's familial and social ties, we can gain new insights into the importance of trust and business confidence in the development of a major plantation region. These intangibles were crucial in seizing chances to buy or sell land and slaves, and in undertaking sales and purchases of produce and supplies at the most advantageous time or place. They were also crucial in making transactions possible and reducing the risks, through loans that could be obtained from formal institutions (banks or merchants) and from informal sources, such as a cousin, uncle, or in-law, with appropriate guarantees always available in either case.

Many of the relationships upon which the network of trust and confidence among the leaders of the town's ante bellum society rested have been known and discussed in Natchez parlors over the years since the Civil War, as well as in considerable research by historians (James 1968; Scarborough 1973; Rothstein 1977). The written and oral traditions have reinforced a conviction that the district had been a unique center of ante bellum wealth in the United States. The feeling that Natchez had boasted more millionaires than almost any other city in the nation was strong as ever in the 1930s and 1940s, though by then a critical scholarly community could detect elements of mythmaking that would take on new dimensions with the introduction of the "Natchez Pilgrimage" (Cohn 1940; Hamburger 1963; Pilkington 1975). Some new research on the dis-

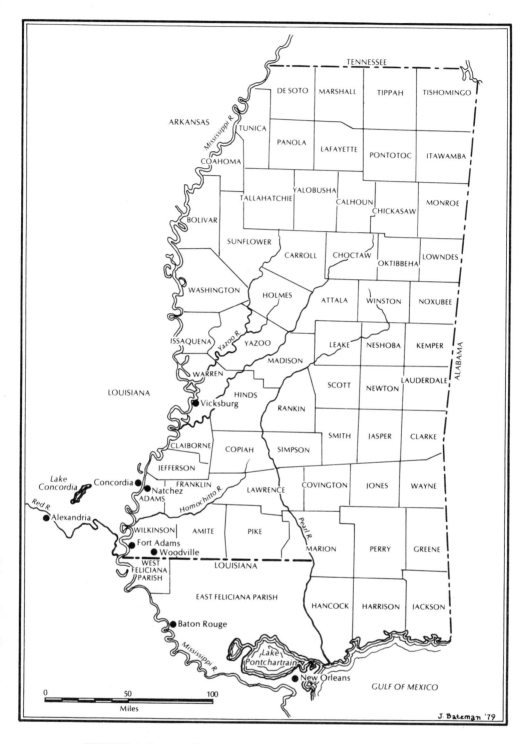

FIGURE 3.1. Counties of Mississippi, 1860.

tribution of wealth in the South and in the United States in the 1850s (Soltow 1975) shows that the region was a major pocket of affluence. According to the 1860 census, Adams County, Mississippi, had a higher proportion of adult white males whose estates exceeded $100,-000 in value than did either Newport County, Rhode Island, or the Eighteenth Ward of New York City, two comparable enclaves of wealth (see Foust 1967; Lee 1975; Degler 1974; Campbell 1974; and W. W. Smith 1968). In fact, the extent of holdings among the wealthiest 5 percent of the population of the Natchez district was probably much greater than this comparison indicates, since the counties that stretched along the Mississippi River on both sides, from Memphis to Baton Rouge, constituted one of the nation's greatest concentrations of wealth, and Natchez families owned considerable tracts, slaves, and other property within that set of counties and farther away. The census data, no matter how one examines them, do not easily yield information on multiple-unit ownership, or on the distribution of estates to children before the death of the first owner (who retains managerial control during his lifetime), or on the administration of large estates by family and friends who shared in the income from wealth listed in another name.[2]

Critics of the elite planter-entrepreneurs who held the largest share of wealth in the Natchez district referred to them as "aristocrats" or "cotton snobs" during the 1850s. More often, from the beginning of the nineteenth century, they were called—and called each other—nabobs. This term implies not only speedily acquired, ostentatious wealth, but also the use of that wealth by parvenu "outsiders" to acquire and hold political domination over the larger numbers of original settlers or inhabitants,[3] and to block equal access to opportunity for newcomers.

The prominence of a wealthy, virtually patrician class of landholders and merchants was characteristic of the Natchez area under both Spain and England. (Located on the Anglo-Spanish frontier, Natchez was ceded to Spain by the British in 1779.) Its small society was almost a Loyalist outpost during the American Revolution (Haynes 1976; Holmes 1965a, 1965b). The community's original "aristocracy," who came from various places in Europe and the North American mainland, were politically contentious and faction-ridden. But they were able to refrain from committing themselves too fully or freely to any group and clung to both lands and slaves when they came under the rule of the United States in 1798. Their economic prospects then were far from bright, since the crops on which they depended, indigo and tobacco, no longer had subsidies or protected markets. Their ranks began to split between supporters of their first territorial governor, the conservative New Englander Winthrop Sargent, and the next governor, William Claiborne, a Jeffersonian; the former group had a slight edge, at least in wealth and social standing (see Haynes 1965; Hamilton 1944, 1948). The beginnings of a cotton boom and the flow of migration came after the Louisiana Purchase (1803), and the more enterprising Natchez residents and absentee land claimants lost little time in snapping up choice tracts of land across the river in Concordia Parish (Calhoun 1932). The older leaders of the community and the new entrants into their midst had to contend with many uncertainties about titles to land, access to markets, and the effect of overseas wars and embargoes during the period from 1800 to 1816, but had little trouble in maintaining a dominance over the economic and political life of the community, so that it remained a stronghold of conservatives under the Federalist, Republican, and Whig leadership that emanated from national-level politics (Sydnor 1938).

By the 1820s, however, a second generation of planter-entrepreneurs—bulwarks of conservative, almost patrician, political traditions—was rising to positions of importance as businessmen and community leaders. They gained access to those positions of leadership through marriage or inheritance, but other factors aided them in obtaining opportunities, making good on them, and retaining leadership after the growth of the Natchez district and its hinterland reached new dimensions. They needed information that was reliable, short-term credit or loans, and connections in distant markets.

Perhaps the best way to identify the elements critical for the success of the Natchez elite in this period is to follow the careers and the complex family relationships among several representative planters who were reaching the top of the district's social order (see fig. 3.2). In spite of a plethora of genealogical, journalistic, and scholarly studies of various individuals and subgroups within the region's elite, no one has undertaken the kind of systematic, detailed examination of those relationships necessary to understand the cohesion and entrepreneurial behavior of this elite. It is now time to plunge into those details.

70

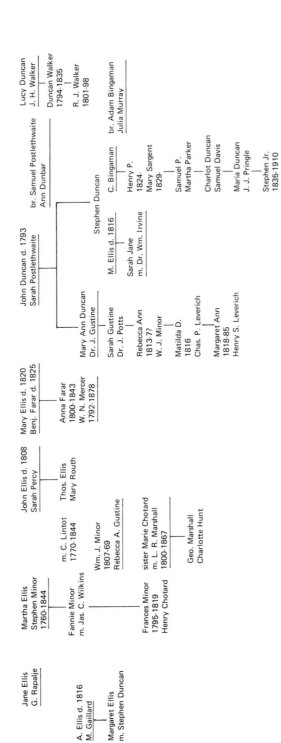

FIGURE 3.2. Genealogical table, Natchez planter group.

Sources: Butler 1948, 1954; Katherine D. Smith 1928; Weaver 1929; Sheppard 1871; Seebold 1941

One of the outstanding Natchez nabobs of this second generation was Stephen Duncan, who in 1860 was dividing an estate he
had built up to well over three million dollars by a conservative
estimate, making him one of several candidates for the title of the
richest planter in the South.[4] Duncan was born into a prominent
Carlisle, Pennsylvania, family in 1787, attended Dickinson College,
and went on to earn a medical degree under Benjamin Rush at
the University of Pennsylvania shortly before coming to Natchez
in 1808. His father was killed in a duel in 1793; his mother, the
former Sarah Postlethwaite, married again in 1797 and moved to
Philadelphia when her new husband, Ephraim Blaine, died in
1804. Mrs. Blaine lived with her daughters as the matriarch of the
Philadelphia household until 1850, when she died at the age of 80
(K. Smith 1928).[5]

It was probably through the interwoven family connections at
Carlisle, Philadelphia, and neighboring communities that Duncan
was induced to try his fortune at Natchez. The prominent Butler
family of Pennsylvania, to which he was related, had sent several
members to the Natchez district. Thomas Duncan, a judge in
Philadelphia and Stephen's most distinguished uncle, had strong
family connections to several leading settlers in the district by his
marriage to a Callender (see Seebold 1941; Dawes 1953). Most important, Stephen Duncan's uncle, Samuel Postlethwaite, had migrated to Natchez about 1800, traveling by river from Pittsburgh on
his own flatboats and setting up shop as a merchant. In 1805 he
married Ann Dunbar, daughter of one of the most prominent men
in the community, "Sir" William Dunbar, whose estate Postlethwaite administered for many years after Dunbar's death in 1810.
Administration of estates was often an important adjunct to business
activity; by controlling the Dunbar assets, Postlethwaite rapidly increased his personal fortune as a merchant and enhanced his role
among the cadre of founders of the Bank of Mississippi, which he
served as president from 1815 to his death in 1825, when his
nephew, Stephen Duncan, succeeded him (Weems 1953). This bank
was the leading financial institution in the state until the 1830s.

In a letter to the editor of the *Natchez Courier* (responding to the
paper's 1856 Unionist views), W. J. Minor claimed that Duncan had
arrived in Natchez with only one hundred dollars to his name, but
with great abilities and energy. "The first crop of Cotton he ever

grew, he ginned with his own hands," Minor claimed, and "the first crop of Sugar he ever made, worked as a hand every night at his own kettles."[6] Undoubtedly Duncan did have great managerial talents, but he was hardly a Horatio Alger hero. He would probably have found it more difficult to make opportunities, or respond to them, without the important connections he had in Natchez on arrival. Through his relationship with the prominent Butler family, he also joined the social circle of the Ellis and Farar clans. All three families were interrelated and held some of the largest and richest plantations in the district. In 1811, when he was a practicing physician, Duncan joined the local dancing club, where he met other socially prominent figures. At about this time he married Margaret Ellis, daughter of Abram Ellis, one of the first English settlers in the region. Duncan quickly learned about land purchases, plantation management, and financial affairs by helping with several family business matters. He acquired his own tracts on the nearby Homochitto River, where he built a plantation and gave it most of his attention, confining his doctoring to an occasional patient among his many new cousins and his many new slaves (Wainwright 1964; Butler 1948).

In 1817, after Duncan had spent five difficult years clearing land and facing uncertain wartime markets, his wife died. He sent his two children back to his family in Carlisle while he put his affairs in order and considered returning permanently North himself. Natchez, he felt, was an "unhealthy" region; the danger of cholera, yellow fever, and other afflictions made death more of a constant threat then it was in the North. An epidemic in 1820 wiped out several members of the Butler and Farar families, including Richard Butler, his wife, several of their children, and Mary Ellis Farar, all of them visiting Bay St. Louis, near New Orleans, that summer. The survivors were grateful for the attention during those illnesses of William Newton Mercer, a young surgeon in the United States Navy. He married Anna Farar, abandoned his naval career, and quickly entered the ranks of leading figures in West Feliciana–Natchez society as he took over the management of two large plantations that had devolved upon his wife. Mercer was from Cecil County, Maryland, near the Pennsylvania-Delaware border, and had studied medicine with Benjamin Rush (Butler 1948).[7] He became Stephen Duncan's closest friend, though he later spent more time on banking and land investments than on planting. By 1820, at any rate, Duncan was coming to his own critical decision about the future. He elected to remain in the Natchez area.[8]

Two wholly unrelated deaths of respected older friends, prominent in Natchez society's upper stratum, had a great impact on Duncan at this time, just when he was courting (and about to marry) a local belle, Catherine Bingaman. The first was the death of Winthrop Sargent, the first territorial governor of Mississippi, who had acquired considerable land through marriage into local wealth. He died in 1820 en route to New Orleans. Sargent's widow left Natchez and moved to Philadelphia almost immediately after her husband's death. She then negotiated the sale of much of her estate (acquired before and after her marriage to Sargent), while several of her cousins and her son stayed on to run their own plantations as profitable enterprises. Duncan was one of the planters who obtained choice town lots and tracts of land adjoining his own plantations from Mrs. Sargent between 1820 and 1825.[9] Lyman Harding (originally, like Sargent, from Massachusetts) also died in 1820. He was a leading member of the Mississippi bar, a steadfast Federalist leader in politics, and one of the founders of the Bank of Mississippi. Upon Harding's death, his house, "Auburn," then on the outskirts of Natchez, came on the market. Duncan opened negotiations for its purchase and obtained title a few years later. It would be his main residence, except for summers, until he left Natchez forever in 1863. It was much nearer town and his growing circle of friends and relatives than his previous house on the Homochitto plantation (see Van Court 1938; J. F. Smith 1941).

Duncan's new brother-in-law, Adam Lewis Bingaman, was a flamboyant character, heir to one of the Surget brothers' estates, a Harvard graduate, and husband of one of Winthrop Sargent's nieces from the Boston area (Kane 1947). By 1820, another of Bingaman's sisters was married to James C. Wilkins (who had earlier lost his first wife, a daughter of Stephen Minor), one of the leading merchants in Natchez district. Wilkins was about to enter a partnership with John Linton, a merchant-planter connected with the Surget and Bingaman families, who took charge of the firm's New Orleans office. Both Wilkins and Linton owned plantations, and bought and sold them over the years, but they spent much of their energies during the 1820s in mercantile and banking affairs.[10]

74

At the beginning of the 1820s, therefore, Stephen Duncan and William Mercer were just emerging into the ranks of the elite. Both M.D.'s, they were in their early and mid thirties at the beginning of the decade, and active in local affairs. They were superintendents of the Bank of Mississippi, founders of charitable institutions, promoters of educational efforts, and leaders in organizing both the Presbyterian church, in which some of their kinsmen were active, and the Episcopalian church, in which they served as vestrymen and the plans for whose building had been drawn up in Auburn shortly after Duncan moved into the house (Stratton 1869; Chisholm 1972; Steitenroth 1922). These activities sustained their social positions. During the rest of the decade, both men were as active in economic affairs as in religious and social spheres, and proved themselves extremely capable managers. Duncan assumed the presidency of the Bank of Mississippi, and Mercer helped found the Mississippi Agricultural Society. They were both very active supporters of John Quincy Adams in 1824, and again in 1828, helping to maintain the nucleus of old Federalist support that would reappear as the Whig party in the 1830s. Their connections with merchants and political leaders in New Orleans, and the information about new opportunities that they had access to, helped them ride out the cotton crisis of 1825. Information from these sources sent Duncan to the Attakapas region of the Louisiana sugar country, where he purchased land adjoining Alexander Porter's estate and began developing new plantations there by the late 1820s (Stephenson 1934).[11] Mercer was meanwhile becoming well known in New Orleans mercantile and banking circles. He invested in considerable real estate and warehouse properties in the city. Both men had also begun to make private loans to relatives and friends who wanted to expand investments.[12] The interests of both Duncan and Mercer were so complex, and their need to be close to the river and lines of communication (and away from their households' busy social life) so urgent, that they each bought buildings in town and maintained offices there in the 1830s, though in Duncan's case, at least, it was but a two- or three-mile ride from the bluffs of Natchez to Auburn, which is the site of the current city park. But he retained the office for conducting his business until the 1850s.[13]

Even during the 1820s, Stephen Duncan's success was already sufficient to attract relatives from the Carlisle area, as he had been

75

attracted by his uncle. Stephen's sister had married Dr. James Gustine, who had attended the same college and medical school as Duncan, and had spent some time in Natchez during the previous decade, but had returned home to help an ailing father (Weaver 1929). By the end of the decade the Gustines' second daughter was being courted by young William J. Minor, son of the famous "Don" Stephen Minor, who had been the most influential American in Natchez under the Spanish regime and had the landholdings to match that status (see Sitterson 1943; Wingfield 1950). Young Minor was at school in Philadelphia when he met Rebecca Ann Gustine, and their marriage took place after the Gustines settled in the Natchez district on a plantation that Stephen Duncan had arranged for them to acquire. Dr. Lemuel Gustine, James's brother, made the same trek shortly afterward, and with Duncan's help also found ways to combine a medical practice with large-scale cotton planting, land speculation, and banking. Meanwhile, two other of Duncan's numerous Carlisle cousins, lawyers rather than doctors, came to Mississippi in search of opportunity, and found it. Duncan Walker and his brother Robert J. Walker arrived there in the 1820s, rose quickly within the legal profession, and became active politically. But they were Jacksonians rather than steadfast Whigs, and although Duncan Walker died in an epidemic in the 1830s, Robert J. Walker built a long, distinguished career at the national level in politics after the Jacksonian revolution swept across Mississippi in the 1830s (see Shenton 1961 on Walker, and Sydnor 1938 for Duncan's reactions).

The 1830s were years of boom and bust, and of political struggles that would break the domination of the "Whig aristocracy" in Mississippi politics. The struggles were over banking facilities, and the opening of opportunities to speculate in and/or acquire new lands to the north of Vicksburg, which were being taken over by federal authorities from the Choctaw and Chickasaw tribes. Duncan was an unusually candid letter writer, and his correspondence shows that he was deeply troubled both by the extension of the plantation system and by the coming to power of groups that would remove all constraints on extension of credit to the rising parvenu planters. As president of the Bank of Mississippi, he had pursued a conservative policy. When the bank lost its charter as a result of Jacksonian political victories, banks that would replace his own institution were proliferating. He had been reluctant to accept even the opening of branches of the Bank of the United States at Natchez, much less the Commercial Bank of Natchez, which was in some ways the successor of that institution. But after 1837 he and Mercer were associated with the Planters Bank, and William J. Minor became president of the Agricultural Bank of Mississippi, both of which were also located in Natchez. They expected to retain financial power in spite of Jacksonian efforts to provide newer, if shaky, facilities to settlers in the more remote parts of the state (see Bentley 1973).[14]

For a brief period, the Natchez elite also hoped to use their control of the town's, if no longer the state's, banking facilities to help them bypass New Orleans and some of the traditional arrangements they had with merchants in that city or with houses abroad. They established a tugboat firm to bring ocean-sailing vessels up the Mississippi to Natchez, and tried to guarantee full cargoes for direct shipment to Europe—a rather audacious plan that actually got further in Natchez than similar efforts in older, and presumably richer, seaports such as Charleston and Savannah. In 1837, for example, just as the "panic" was about to set in, Frank Surget, W. J. Minor, and other members of the Agricultural Bank's board of directors pooled their cotton crops, some 20,000 bales, and consigned it to W. & J. Brown & Co., the Liverpool branch of the outstanding Baltimore banking and mercantile firm, with the proviso that Brown's New York branch would "make no charge for negotiating [exchange] for us."[15] It was clearly an arrangement designed to give the participants the same kind of advantage in dealing with foreign exchange that only a few of the more enterprising older planters, such as Duncan and Mercer, had begun to arrange for themselves previously. It is also further evidence of the way in which the loss of political power at the local level tended to divert the larger producers into more direct involvement in national and international economic and social circles.

Duncan and Mercer demonstrated this tendency earlier in their relationship with Washington Jackson, a merchant who began his career in Nashville, Tennessee. He had relatives in Philadelphia, two brothers in the leading Nashville mercantile circles (one was briefly his partner), and a partner named Riddle in the firm's office at Philadelphia, when he came to Natchez in 1811. He quickly entered the same social circle, including membership in the dancing club, that included the Ellises, Farars, and Duncan. By the 1820s, Washington Jackson and Company had a major house in New Orleans and was one of the first such houses to engage in shipping from the Attakapas region of Louisiana, where Duncan bought his sugar plantations. In the early 1830s, the Philadelphia branch was changed from Jackson, Riddle & Co. to Jackson, Todd & Co., and another branch was opened in Liverpool, where Thomas Todd ran the office and moved comfortably in British banking circles at least until the end of the 1830s.[16] Mercer, Duncan, and Frank Surget, along with the Minors, had hitherto sold cotton direct for export to George Green & Co., a Liverpool firm, which succeeded in the 1820s another Liverpool house whose partners had been visiting Natchez annually to negotiate contracts with large planters since the beginning of the century. But the friendship with Washington Jackson, who spent at least one month a year visiting friends and making deals in the Natchez district during the 1830s and 1840s, went deep. When Jackson, Todd & Co. of Philadelphia dissolved in 1841, and Todd, Jackson & Co., Liverpool, suffered enough losses of credit and capital to make their future uncertain, they were sustained largely by Jackson's "very good connexions" with planters "who are considerable shippers of cotton," such as "Dr. Mercer & Dr. Duncan" and Surget. These three men impressed a leading London banker, who personally investigated Washington Jackson's affairs in the winter of 1837–38 by visiting New Orleans and Natchez. He described the planters as "mighty men of the South, millionaires in Dollars," and, even more important, men who not only were not in debt but were "large lenders."[17] In the early 1840s, the same London banker recommended that Jackson be given further credit to ride through a financial squeeze, in large part because he was "respected & supported by so many of the best men in Mississippi—Duncan, Surget, Chotard, Marshall, and others," who came from the "distinct class of old French families with the settlers from other states possessed of fortune and education," as opposed to the "crowd of adventurers who brought with them into the State little either of capital or character."[18]

Meanwhile, some of the younger members of the nabob group were proving their mettle as businessmen in adjusting to the crisis of the 1830s. Mercer had avoided extending himself, or making many new loans, in part because his wife was undergoing a protracted illness which took him and the immediate family to Europe in a futile effort to restore her health. A new, important member of the inner circle, the chief nabob of the 1830s boom, according to a report Mercer received, was Levin R. Marshall, a handsome Virginian supposedly related to the famous chief justice, who had come to Woodville, Mississippi, as a youth in 1817 and within a few years was cashier of the town's bank, a branch of the Bank of Mississippi near the Mississippi-Louisiana border. Thus he was already known and trusted by leaders of the district's business group (Kane 1890, 1947).[19] In 1826 he married Maria Chotard, one of William Minor's cousins and daughter of another prominent Natchez planter. In 1831, Marshall moved to Natchez as the cashier (then a prestigious position) of the newly established branch of the Second Bank of the United States. His wife died soon after the move, and a few years later Marshall married Sarah Elliott Ross, daughter of one powerful planter-entrepreneur and widow of another, Isaac Ross, Jr., whose father had made the most publicized attempt at slave manumission in Mississippi's history. Along with his close friend, Dr. John Ker (son of one of the first territorial judges in Mississippi), Stephen Duncan was deeply involved in the family's struggle during the 1830s to make good on the manumission in the face of legal obstructions and legislative action. Ker, Duncan, and many of the other Natchez figures mentioned so far led the founding of the Mississippi Colonization Society, which tried to free blacks and move them to Liberia. This was in part a tribute to their support for Henry Clay, who was for a brief time a leader of the national movement, but in Duncan's case, at least, also represented an attempt to deal with fear of the possibility of a slave uprising (Sydnor 1966).[20] Most of all, Duncan and Ker were determined to carry out their friend's will after his death. The protracted suits brought both men closer to Marshall, whose wife they represented. At the time, ironically, Marshall was buying new plantations and slaves on a scale that eventually gave him large holdings in Mississippi, Louisiana, and Arkansas, and would make him one of the dozen leading producers of cotton in the nation by the eve of the Civil War (Menn 1964).[21] Marshall's position in banking at Natchez, which made him president of the Commercial Bank of that city after the demise of the Bank of the United States, and his connections with local and New Orleans merchants as partner in a leading house with branches in both places, undoubtedly helped in his acquisition of land and slaves. His abilities and business stature underwent some testing in the early 1840s, when Mississippi's repudiation of her own state bonds put an extra strain on her ability to obtain credit in Europe, but Marshall bought enough time and credit, in visiting the Liverpool and London markets and banks, to help his institution out of its difficulties and to enable him to continue extending his investments.[22]

One of the results of the Panic of 1837 was the completion of a shift that made New York rather than Philadelphia the national center of banking and other facilities for supporting foreign trade. By that time, Duncan's family was being enriched with a connection that would give them special links to the New York market, and through it to the international economy. The Gustines, whose daughter Rebecca Ann married William J. Minor in 1829, had two younger daughters, each of whom married one of the Leverich brothers in the 1830s and moved back into a northern social circle. Charles P. and Henry S. Leverich were the younger of four brothers from an old, respected Newtown, Long Island, family. They embarked on mercantile careers in New York during the 1820s under the sponsorship of a friend and neighbor whose family had also been in New York since the seventeenth century, George Rapalje, a prominent merchant-shipper associated with Peter Remsen. Many of the Rapaljes on Long Island had been Loyalists during the American Revolution, and one of them, presumably a fairly close relative, had married an aunt of Anna Farar, Mercer's wife (Rothstein 1968). It was an ill-fated match, and Rapalje later disappeared from the scene, but "Aunt Rapalje" was an important figure in the lives of Mercer and Duncan, since she left their children considerable legacies and appointed them to administer those legacies after her death in 1823 (Butler 1948). By that time James Harvey Leverich, the oldest of the four brothers, was in New Orleans, regularly visiting the Natchez area and doing business as a merchant with John Routh and other leading planters. By the mid 1830s, James and Edward Leverich were firmly entrenched in New Orleans, and had valuable friendships and business relationships, based on experience and trust, with James Colles, the Metcalfe family, Samuel J. Peters, and other leading merchant-banking figures with northern origins (De Forest 1926; Carey 1947).[23] They certainly could have obtained introductions to some of the Natchez planter families through any of those connections. James also entered the banking field in New Orleans and acquired several plantations in Mississippi and Louisiana. The two younger brothers, Charles and Henry, maintained a separate firm in New York which concentrated on the southern trade, for which they alternately made annual visits to the region. By the mid 1830s they were periodically at Natchez, courting Dr. James Gustine's two younger daughters. The success of their courtships made the Leverich brothers the husbands of Stephen Duncan's nieces and the brothers-in-law of William J. Minor.[24]

In addition to their new relationships, the brothers were well known in New York financial circles through their years of experience as successful merchants, and were knowledgeable about arranging coastal shipping charters, sugar and cotton sales, and the purchase of plantation supplies. They obviously could be trusted. From the late 1830s to the Civil War and after, the Leveriches performed many services for Duncan, Minor, Mercer, Marshall, and many other leading Natchez entrepreneurs. In 1848 they saved Frank Surget, who had remained independent in his New York business associations, from embarrassment at the hands of New York bankers. Surget switched from his previous agents, and the Leveriches had still another important loyal client. Through Duncan's recommendations, the Leverich brothers obtained consignments and orders from many leading sugar planters in the Bayou Teche region, most notably Mrs. Mary Porter, one of Duncan's neighbors, heiress and manager of the Alexander Porter estate, and William T. Palfrey, a prominent sugar planter of New England origins.[25]

For all of these clients, the Leverich brothers performed the wide range of extra services common among factors at that time. They made advances on consignments, ordered everything for the planters from short, light hoes for younger field workers to vintage wines and brandies, and looked after the sons and daughters who came north for schooling. They did even more for the Natchez nabobs. Almost every spring the Duncan and Minor families came north, visiting Philadelphia first to pay respects to close relatives there, then traveling to New York, Saratoga, and Newport. The Leveriches often entertained them at their Long Island farm (now part of Queens), then usually joined them during August at Newport, along with Mercer, Mrs. Porter, the Surgets, and the Marshalls, for a

81

month or more of cool breezes and associations with such people as the Winthrops and Belmonts, whose knowledge of investment opportunities was undoubtedly useful to the southerners. The Leveriches helped arrange many of the leases and purchases of living quarters at Newport, supplied the households with food and wine, and maintained the flow of information about markets and investments to the heads of the households.[26] Duncan also relied on the Leverich brothers to help with the affairs of his children, especially as he began, by the mid 1840s, to transfer more and more of his holdings to their possession, usually when they married. By then, the only surviving offspring of his first marriage were the two daughters of Dr. William Irvine; the five children of his second marriage were reaching majority. His oldest son married a Sargent (probably the granddaughter of Winthrop Sargent), the second a daughter of a prominent planter at Port Gibson, between Natchez and Vicksburg; the third child, Charlotte, married the son of Samuel Davis and moved to Philadelphia in the 1830s; and Maria Duncan married a prominent South Carolina planting-family scion. Stephen Duncan, Jr., who never married, began taking charge of the family's Attakapas sugar plantations, and corresponded regularly about supplies, boat charters, and purchases of machinery with the Leverich firm, which also passed on occasional imperious reprimands from the elder Stephen Duncan.[27]

Perhaps the most important category of service that the Leveriches provided was the funneling of reliable information about market conditions, crop prospects, credit ratings, and investment opportunities. Not only were they, in effect, members of the family, they had also demonstrated their business acumen and competence and the trustworthiness of the news and opinions they offered. After the mid 1830s, much of the elite's old network was changing rapidly, particularly with regard to connections with the national and international markets. The number of producers of both cotton and sugar had increased rapidly in the Lower Mississippi Valley after the removal of Indians from Mississippi, the opening of the Red River districts in northern Louisiana, and the development of new techniques for sugar growing and refining in southern Louisiana. Duncan tended to rely on his New York relations and on such old friends as Washington Jackson for a flow of information, constantly revising his estimates of cotton yields, sugar crops, and the impact of changes in either the weather or supplies of carryover from the previous season, as well as the rates of consumption in the North and in Europe. Mercer had recourse to the same network, in part, but his wife's death was followed in the early 1840s by his daughter's demise, and he lived more and more in New Orleans. He developed there a supplementary network of information that he shared with Duncan and other Natchez planters. The market in which these men operated may have been growing impersonal as it grew in size, but the access to constant flow of discussion about exchange rates, shipping charges, insurance availability, and above all the extent of demand was critical. In addition to reinforcing the local network by means of active church and social life, or serving each other's families during summer travels, the new social clubs for select leaders of a community also filled some gaps in testing the reliability of news and businessmen's reputations. In 1852, for example, William N. Mercer joined the Union Club of New York, which was the "Mother of Clubs" and represented the closest organization of a national elite among businessmen that could be found outside of certain exchange meeting rooms. The following year, Stephen Duncan, his three sons, and Levin Marshall joined. Most of them already had joined the Boston Club, in New Orleans, which would take over Mercer's house on Canal Street after the Civil War and is now one of the few buildings on that thoroughfare that was once a private residence (Landry 1938; Townsend 1936). All the club memberships enlarged the nabobs' circle of friendships and acquaintances among the nation's leading businessmen.

Not all of the inner group among the nabobs, whether close kin or not, could make their way as easily into such organizations, or benefit from membership. Adam L. Bingaman, for example, gradually dissipated much of his wealth and at the end of his life was a virtual outcast in New Orleans, though in the 1840s and early 1850s he was still active in public affairs, known for his lavish entertainments and ownership of racehorses. Stephen Duncan was concerned that William Minor would spend too much time, energy, and attention on his clubs and on horse races rather than tending to his administrative duties on plantations. In the 1840s, Minor was still having difficulties, and had borrowed heavily from Duncan and others in the Natchez area, but he moved from the old family homestead, "Concord," to one of his Louisiana plantations and emulated Duncan's example as a thorough, energetic manager of three plantations while paying off his debts and turning his landholdings into profit-making ventures. Few of the other planters of note on the fringe of this network—the Kers, the Nutt family, the Liddells, or the McGehees of the Woodville area (a third-generation branch of wealthy southerners whose paterfamilias in Mississippi was another claimant to the title of largest slaveholder)—carried their business connections farther than New Orleans. It was primarily Stephen Duncan, William Mercer, and Levin Marshall who attained the wealth, connections to the outside, and acquisitive instincts to give their entrepreneurial drive full scope. They were also among the few members of that small group who remained lenders rather than borrowers, and also investors in diversified portfolios. Duncan became particularly interested in railroad securities, accumulating about $500,000 worth in 1860. Mercer bought a tract of land that covered about half of Macoupin County in central Illinois. Marshall speculated in new cotton lands in Arkansas until the eve of the war. All three by then were advanced in years, though Duncan was busily accumulating new lands in the Yazoo Delta, buying slaves for them, and building levees when he was in his seventies. All three lived more and more of the time outside the Natchez region and had built homes in other cities. Mercer had his mansion in New Orleans, Duncan had a house at 12 Washington Square, New York, and Levin Marshall owned a mansion at Pelham Bay, on the outskirts of the Bronx, in New York.

None of them were very interested in politics any longer. They had been supporters and friends of Henry Clay until his death in the early 1850s; in fact, Mercer and Duncan are reputed to have saved the Kentucky senator from bankruptcy. But the Whig Party was in disarray after 1850, and a new generation of planters on the make was supporting a new generation of politicians who would lead them into secession. The nabobs' lack of interest in politics was largely due to impotence at the local level, and the growing natural rift over slavery had put enough pressure on the constituent families of the old, conservative network of the Natchez group, which was never wholly cohesive, to create deep political divisions. Many of the younger members came to support secession. Age, differences in success, and variable access to the currents of a wider world had transformed the network. The growing secession crisis fragmented it. The ties of mutual educational background, professional standing, family, and church could define membership in the large, loosely structured and overlapping networks of the district's upper class. The reinforcement of those ties by strong nationalistic feelings, self-consciousness of elite standing, and a premium on stability and ability as businessmen became less and less effective over time.

An isolated, ambivalent minority by the 1860s, they could not take a stand during the Civil War for one side or the other. Mercer remained in New Orleans, facing down the secessionists at first, and later tangling with General Butler, commander for a time of the Union occupation, over his refusal to swear loyalty to either side. Duncan tried to protect his holdings for his children, if not for the Confederacy, and shifted back and forth in his sentiments for three summers until 1863, when the war had become enough of a revolution in the South to compel him to leave and make his way first to Carlisle and then to his New York City mansion. He and Levin Marshall died in 1867 in New York, while Mercer, clearly a survivor, lived on in New Orleans as a major aide to Henry C. Warmoth—the "carpetbag" governor. He lived through the entire Reconstruction period. When he died in 1878 he left his favorite watch to his old friend Washington Jackson, who had retired in the 1850s to England, where his sons carried on a successful mercantile business well into the 1880s.[28] By then a new, completely different set of individuals was seizing whatever opportunities were available in postwar Mississippi, while the Natchez district itself fell into a long period of stagnation. The new planter elite had to create its own networks of trust and confidence, under greatly changed conditions.

NOTES

1. I wish to acknowledge the support of the American Philosophical Society, which funded travel necessary for the research that went into this essay, and of the National Endowment for the Humanities, for a Fellowship award at the Newberry Library, Chicago, in 1977.

2. The Soltow study is based on county data from the census and does not attempt to deal with multiple holdings and the like. Some effort to do that is available in Menn (1964), but it is based on census manuscript schedules and the units in them that reported fifty or more slaves for only four states—Louisiana, Mississippi, Alabama, and Georgia. The method is by no means satisfactory. The schedules contain misspellings of names, and they fail to identify multiple owners or clarify the inclination of older planters to list their children, who were often well into their majority, as owners and silent partners in many enterprises. Some of the difficulties are apparent even in Scarborough's (1973) careful use of manuscript census data to arrive at a list of planters at the top of the scale. Scarborough's list varies considerably from Menn's data and fails to indicate some of the connections between individuals that would reveal more concentration of wealth on a family basis. For Louisiana we are fortunate in having annual production figures of some reliability for sugar plantations, along with the recently published *The Civil War Tax in Louisiana: 1865; based*

on direct tax assessments of Louisianians (New Orleans: Polyanthos, 1975), with introduction by John Milton Price (Reprint of 1895 book published in Baton Rouge).

3. The earliest document using the term that I have discovered is a report from a member of the Claiborne family dated 1803 (signature unclear) in Miscellaneous Collections of the American Philosophical Society, Philadelphia. It is "A List of the Gentlemen Little Nabobs of the Mississippi Territory." It was clearly a term then in use, borrowed from English politics of the late eighteenth century, where it was a term of derision implying a sinister threat to the political system (see Holzman 1926). The term is used again in the 1830s in letters from Natchez to William N. Mercer (Tulane University Library) and by visitors to some of the large estates in the 1850s (see Leverich Family Papers, Columbia University). A settler in newly opened districts of central Mississippi referred to Natchez in 1840 as the "hot bed of Aristocratic Whiggery" (Duncan McLaurin Papers, Duke University, J. Stewart to D. McLaurin, July 30, 1840).

4. Gates (1960) suggests that Duncan may have been "the greatest planter and slaveowner in the United States in the 'fifties,'" but several others may have deserved the title, even beyond the list of top producers in Menn (1964). The estimate of wealth was Duncan's own, which he used to allocate legacies of over half a million dollars each to his six children (see Wainwright 1964).

5. For the founding of Dickinson College, and the role of the Duncan family in it, see Sellars (1973). The *Alumni Record* of the College (Reed 1905) yields a harvest of names that later appear in the Natchez area, such as James Gustine, Class of 1798 (p. 48); Thomas Butler, Class of 1799, who did not graduate; Jesse Duncan, Class of 1800 (p. 50), who was admitted to the bar in Carlisle, then "removed to Mississippi, where he died" in 1804; and Richard Gustine and Alexander Mahon, Class of 1805 with Stephen Duncan, as well as Duncan's younger brother, Samuel P., who was in the Class of 1808 and also "removed to Mississippi, where he became a planter and served as an M.D." before he died in Natchez in 1830. It is ironic that Duncan, William Newton Mercer, and several other planters who found entrepreneurship in planting more attractive than medicine, should have studied with Benjamin Rush, who became a leader in the abolitionist nucleus of the North after the Revolution (D'Elia 1967). Duncan is often confused in popular or journalistic accounts of the Natchez district with two of his cousins, both named Stephen, both of whom came to the New Orleans hinterland in the early years of the nineteenth century, not to speak of other Stephen Duncans who were spawned by the Kentucky and Ohio branches of the family. For his mother and her remarriage, as well as the preceding tragic duel, see Blaine (1920), which describes Mrs. Duncan's marriage and her long residence in Philadelphia. After Blaine's death she lived in one of the "elegant mansions on Walnut Street west of Twelfth."

6. William J. Minor to Editor, *Natchez Courier*, Oct. 1856, letterbook no. 2, Minor Family Papers, Department of Archives and Manuscripts, Louisiana State University Library, Baton Rouge.

7. See also James Smith to Dr. Rush, Oct. 31, 1810, Pennsylvania Historical Society microfilms of Library Co. manuscripts.

8. S. Duncan to Thos. Butler, May 30, 1818, Butler Papers, Louisiana State University Library, and several other notes between the men that year show Duncan worried about his children, who were staying with the Butlers in winter and going to the North and Duncan's mothers and sisters in summer. After his marriage to Catherine Bingaman, he was still uncertain about remaining permanently in the Natchez district because of health. In 1822 he wrote, "The time was, when there was no country I wd. prefer to this, but for the last 5 years we have had scarcely anything to speak of half of the year, but diseases and death. I do not think I shall ever spend another summer in it, and I am, at times, more than *half-resolved* to purchase a seat near Philad. and make it my *permanent*

residence" (S. Duncan to Thos. Butler, Sept. 29, 1822). This kind of concern undoubtedly had a powerful impact on the time horizons of the planter-entrepreneurs and affected their investment decisions accordingly.

9. L. M. Sargent, Philadelphia, to Geo. M. Lewis, Natchez, Nov. 21, 1824, and to Mrs. Mary Sargent, Philadelphia, Jan. 9, 1826, Winthrop Sargent Papers, letterpress copybook, reel 4, microfilm edition; see also Sheppard 1871.

10. There are scattered references to Wilkins and Linton in Claiborne (1880), and in the Linton letters to J. S. Johnston throughout the correspondence in the Johnston Papers of the Pennsylvania Historical Society. After Linton's death in the late 1830s, Mrs. Linton accompanied the Duncans on many of their annual treks north, and Stephen Duncan was administering her estate into the late 1850s, according to the Duncan letterpress books of plantation and financial records (Duncan Family Papers, Louisiana State University Library).

11. See also the Natchez *Ariel*, Feb. 2, 1828. One of the more important families already living in the Attakapas country was the William Palfrey family, originally from near Boston, Massachusetts. As early as 1811, they were writing Thomas Butler and other planters in Natchez about the problems of sugar growing. See also deGrummond (1948) on the Porter and Duncan holdings.

12. They kept careful account of these loans, and charged 8 percent on most of them, even when lending to each other when they had cash-flow problems or if they wanted to avoid transfer costs when traveling so that the loan was very short term. In other cases, according to the careful memoranda books, and lists of bills receivable in Mercer's papers, and account books of Duncan that remained after the early 1850s when the earlier ones were destroyed in a fire, they made the notes of friends or relatives part of the legacies they provided in wills and codicils. Duncan in particular had a reputation for extraordinary generosity in providing loans to people he considered reliable and helped several local businessmen and planters get started. See Moore (1967) for one example of a firm he helped start, and the John Knight Papers, Duke University, for examples of his aid to a storekeeper turned planter, who borrowed capital and ideas from Duncan about investments in cotton lands in Louisiana and Arkansas.

13. Mercer sold his Natchez town house while traveling in Europe with his ailing wife in the 1837–38 winter, and lived only at Laurel Hill, some twenty or more miles south of Natchez near Ellis Cliffs. Duncan's letters during the 1830 to 1860 period to the Leveriches often mentioned his working in the office in town (Leverich Papers, Jackson, Mississippi, State Archives Dept., and Leverich Papers, New York Historical Society).

14. Duncan could make his peace with the Bank of the United States easily enough, and was receiving friendly letters from Nicholas Biddle in 1830. Wilburn (1967) indicates something of way the "entrepreneurial revolution" that Jacksonian democracy is now seen to have brought was responding to wishes of people "on the make" rather than entrenched wealth and power. In Willard Hurst's famous phrase, it helped bring out the "release of energy" in the developmental process.

15. W. J. Minor to W. & J. Brown & Co., Nov. 2, 1837, Minor letterbook, 1834–38, Louisiana State University.

16. Jackson's early career in Nashville gave him several important contacts on his later mercantile operations. He began with his brother in 1806, became a partner of Kirkman and Erwin in 1814 (probably the latter was a relative of Joseph and Lavinia Erwin, who migrated to the Natchez district in the period from 1807 to 1836), and was well known as a Whig supporter in Tennessee and Louisiana. He was in the commission business with a Philadelphia partner as early as 1821. I am indebted to Dr. Anita S. Goodstein (1976 and personal communication) for this and other information about Jackson's early career.

17. Morrison, Cryder & Co., London from Thomas Todd, Liverpool, Jan. 4, 1837; Jan. 30, 1838; and Feb. 5, 1838 in Morrison, Cryder Papers, Guildhall Library, London.

18. From an extensive report on the "Houses of Todd Jackson & Co., and Wash. Jackson & Co." from C. Morrison, New Orleans, to Morrison, Cryder & Co., London, Jan. 10, 1843. The report on Washington Jackson & Co. in the Dun and Bradstreet books, Baker Library, Harvard Business School, indicated much the same thing, and in the 1840s assessed Jackson's means as "moderate," but his credit was good because he was the "particular" friend of Stephen Duncan. At one point in the 1850s not only did Dun and Bradstreet indicate that Duncan's credit was first rate and unquestioned, but they listed him as a man who could buy out two or three New Orleans banks (Dun & Bradstreet Repts., Mississippi vol. 2, Adams Co., p. 55).

19. Also see Marshall and Evans (1940) for material on his earlier career, and the James Sheppard Papers, Duke University, for material on his later holdings in Arkansas.

20. In the aftermath of Nat Turner's rebellion, Duncan wrote Senator Johnston about his fears that slaves would be sold rapidly in Virginia and Maryland and brought to Mississippi, where they were already numerous enough "to excite serious apprehensions for our safety. In this county (exclusive of the city) we have 4 blacks to one white; a disproportion sufficiently great to make every mother bring her infant more closely to her bosom.' . . . I am not myself, entirely free from apprehension. . ." (S. Duncan to J. S. Johnston, Oct. 11, 1831, Johnston Papers, Pennsylvania Historical Society).

21. See also Washington Jackson & Co., New Orleans, to James Morrison, M. P., London, April 16, 1841, Morrison, Cryder Papers, with enclosures, from the Browns, Levin Marshall, and other officers of the Commercial Bank.

22. Ibid.

23. See also Colles Papers, Long Island Historical Society, Brooklyn, New York.

24. Charles P. Leverich gained considerable distinction in banking circles after the Civil War and served as president of the Bank of New York, with which he had been associated since the 1840s, from 1873-76 (Domett 1884).

25. F. Surget to C. P. Leverich, April 26, 29, and July 22, 1848, Leverich Papers, Jackson, Mississippi. By the 1840s, the Leveriches were also handling business for such well-known figures in Louisiana as Mausel White, David Weeks, and Laurent Millauden.

26. For the association with Winthrop and Belmont, see A. Belmont to W. N. Mercer, Aug. 16, 1862, Mercer Papers, Louisiana State University.

27. In the mid 1850s, Duncan did employ a manager for the sugar plantations, A. McWilliams, who for a time also supervised the operation of Mrs. Porter's plantation and was given an opportunity to participate in the profits of Duncan's concerns, so young Stephen Duncan did not have the full brunt of responsibility. After the Civil War he did try for about fifteen years to pull together into profitable undertakings the enterprises his father had begun in Natchez, in Issaquena County, Mississippi, and in the Bayou Teche area.

28. When Mercer died in 1874, the New Orleans Item ran an obituary that dubbed him the "Judah Touro of our Protestant population," for his philanthropies, which included helping to establish the University of the South at Sewanee, contributions to hospitals and asylums in New Orleans, and the like. See Carter and Carter (1955); for his career in New Orleans during Reconstruction, see Warmoth (1930). The thesis that the secessionist movement was led by, and received its main support from, younger planters and politicians "on the make" is given considerable substance by Barney (1974).

4

Kinship and Friendship in the Emergence of a Family-Controlled Southern Enterprise: Life Insurance Company of Georgia, 1891–1950

JACK BLICKSILVER

Department of Economics
Georgia State University

Life Insurance Company of Georgia, a medium-sized, family-controlled stock company, selling life and health insurance throughout an eleven-state southeastern territory, underwent a series of significant changes during the mid 1970s. In 1975 the enterprise chalked up a record-breaking billion dollars in sales. This feat was made possible by an increased volume of high-face-amount Ordinary life insurance sold to upper-income southerners.[1] The company's leading individual producer was Alfred E. Thompson, Jr., grandson of one of the cofounders, I. M. Sheffield, Sr. Equally dramatic and more significant was the decision of the board of directors on May 20, 1975, to elect John M. Bragg, Canadian-born company actuary since 1956, president and chief executive officer. Although the positions of chairman of the board and chairman of the powerful executive committee were to continue in the hands of major stockholders, descendants of the founding families, for the first time in its eighty-four-year history the company's top management post was to be held by a person who was not a family member.

There were other signs that the close-knit, family-dominated character of the regional insurer (its $598.8 million in assets as of January 1, 1975, ranked it sixty-third in the nation) was gradually being replaced by a more broadly based group in both management and ownership. Two prominent members of the Atlanta business community were added to the board of directors in August 1975, making a total of six of the twenty voting members of the company's policy-setting body "outside" members. Seven of the remaining fourteen board members were nonfamily company employees. A comparison of the distribution of Life of Georgia stock holdings in 1971 and 1975 reveals that the number of shares held by officers, directors, and families declined from 78 percent in 1971 to 67 percent in 1975. During the four-year period, shares held by large shareholders other than officers and directors rose from 9 percent to 19 percent; shares held by employees in the profit-sharing plan, first instituted in 1966, grew from 3 percent of the total in 1971 to 6 percent in 1975.

The dramatic shifts of the 1970s were paralleled during the company's long history by other significant turning-point periods. Between 1944 and 1949, under the dynamic leadership of John Newton McEachern, Jr., son of the senior cofounder, the company enlarged its trade territory from six to eleven states, initiated the sale of Ordinary life insurance, and began the process of upgrading the field force to sell and service larger and more sophisticated products. This strategy, in turn, necessitated the employment of a spate of medical, actuarial, financial, and other specialists in the Atlanta home office to prepare, underwrite, process, and supervise the increasing flow of business and to channel the growing surplus and reserves into income-producing investments. Befitting the expanding scope of company operations, on May 27, 1947, the name Life Insurance Company of Georgia was adopted to replace Industrial Life and Health Insurance Company, the name under which the company had operated since June 26, 1903. Prior to that date the enterprise used the title Industrial Aid Association.

During the half-century prior to the late 1940s, the company's most significant change took place in 1918, when the initial mutual assessment society, the assets of which were legally owned by the policyholders, was converted into a stock company, tightly held by "the boys who built the business." During much of the quarter-century following this event, the company continued to stress the sale of limited coverage disability and death burial policies to lower-income southerners, collecting nickel and dime premiums on a weekly basis at the homes of the insured. Until 1931 virtually all policyholders were black, primarily working women and their children, a group with exceedingly high mortality rates, unable to afford the larger, infrequent premium payments of Ordinary insurance and largely ignored by the northern-based mass marketers of industrial (home service) insurance.

This chapter focuses on the emergence of the enterprise during its formative years, prior to the mid 1940s, and upon the interrelationships of the company's founders, their families, neighbors, and friends from the North Georgia counties in which they were reared, as well as the associates within the industry with whom they worked to solve common problems. The members of the founding families established the business in a high-risk industry, nurtured it through the nation's worst depression to that time (1893–98), set its direction, and formulated a series of basic policies that were to guide the fledgling enterprise through the intense competition and the socio-economic changes that reshaped in some measure the society within which the company functioned. Sporadic disagreements among the owner-managers intensified after 1928, with the death of the dominant cofounder, and paved the way for the more intense controversies, based on policy issues as well as personality clashes, that were to play a major role in propelling the enterprise during the favorable post–World War II environment into its present broad-gauged combination company status.

Life of Georgia was launched in the autumn of 1891 by a group of farm-bred white Georgians, native to a number of rural counties twenty-five to forty miles northwest of Atlanta. The dominant persons in initiating the enterprise and spearheading its growth during the formative years were thirty-eight-year-old John Newton McEachern and twenty-one-year-old Isham Mallie Sheffield. The two men had first met two years earlier, on a Sunday in the spring of 1889, on the porch of the Atlanta boardinghouse at which McEachern, still a bachelor, resided. Young Sheffield had recently arrived from Dallas, Georgia, in Paulding County, and was seeking living accommodations. The two men engaged in congenial conversation, agreed to share the facilities of the boardinghouse, and soon became firm friends.[2]

McEachern was employed as a solicitor for the Home Friendly Society, an assessment life and accident insurance company based in Baltimore, Maryland, one of the twenty-odd comparable enterprises conducting business in Georgia. The society's contract offered burial insurance and weekly indemnity payments for illness or accidents to persons aged two through sixty-five. Premiums, starting at five cents, were collected weekly at the homes of the insured. John McEachern had come to this occupation after a decade and a half of frustrating disappointments in attempting to run country stores, first in several towns in his native Cobb County and then, when these went bankrupt or burned down, in Beaumont, Texas, where an aunt resided. McEachern, born April 9, 1853, was the eighth of eleven children of David Newton McEachern, who at age twenty took his teen-age wife and trekked from the piedmont section of North Carolina to newly opened Cobb County, where he eventually became a large landowner and an influential citizen. John obtained limited schooling; when he was eleven years old, the Union Army reduced the McEachern home to ashes. From a pallet in a converted corn crib, John heard the cannon bombarding Atlanta. After the war, when John reached twenty-one, his father turned over to him a parcel of land, but he found farming unprofitable. Country storekeeping followed; when various mercantile pursuits failed, he doggedly tried, again and again. Lacking success in Texas, he returned to Atlanta in autumn 1888 and found the "phoenix city" of the "New South" expanding rapidly, with Atlanta *Constitution* editor Henry Grady its most articulate advocate. Hotels, hospitals, and factories were springing up in a city of close to 65,000 persons, about 40 percent of them black.

As solicitor for the Home Friendly, McEachern appeared finally to have found his preferred career. Highly disciplined, with a self-assured manner that inspired confidence, McEachern embodied the best qualities of a successful debit agent.[3] When he returned to Cobb County to visit family and old friends, the local weekly newspaper commented upon his "genial countenance" and happy frame of mind.

When I. M. Sheffield joined McEachern at the boardinghouse, the older man soon had his new friend soliciting business and paying claims for the Home Friendly. The ambitious young Sheffield, however, had his eye on higher goals. He was the first of five children born to William J. Sheffield, a second-generation Paulding Countian who had lost a leg in a battle near Petersburg, Virginia. Returning to his home community, the elder Sheffield taught for a time, was elected county tax receiver, and, after his marriage in 1869, made a success out of both farming and mercantile trade. Young Isham was able to enjoy some of the amenities of life that the war had denied John McEachern, and he obtained a better-than-average education, principally at the Acworth Normal School. The slender, blue-eyed youth, with his outgoing personality and ready laughter, was a popular clerk at his father's general store, but his ambition was to carve out a successful business career on his own. After a short time with the Home Friendly Society, he found a higher-paying job as salesman for a tobacco house headquartered in Winston-Salem, North Carolina.

On October 9, 1891, Isham Sheffield married Nellie Gray Owen of Dallas, Georgia; their families had been friends for many years. Nellie's brother D. F. "Felt" Owen had arrived in Atlanta in May 1891 and obtained employment as an agent for the Southern Industrial Aid Society, another small life and accident insurance company. After Isham's marriage to Nellie, he, Owen, and J. J. Carleton, a friend from Paulding County who worked for Felt's company, began to meet with the older and more experienced John McEachern to explore the possibility of pooling their capital and their combined knowledge and contacts to establish an insurance company in Atlanta.

After considerable conversation, an agreement was finally reached. Sheffield would contribute some $400, which he had saved during the preceding two years, and would join the two other men as full-time solicitors in the Atlanta area. McEachern would participate in an advisory capacity, retaining his position with the Home Friendly until the new enterprise was successfully launched. The three-man "field force" went to work, with their immediate aim the acquisition of sufficient insurance in force and assets to qualify for a charter under Georgia law. They made the basic decision to specialize in servicing the black market for burial and disability insurance. They had seen during the post–Civil War years blacks in growing numbers leaving the plantations where they had been held in bondage and relocating in southern towns and cities. Generally living in overcrowded, ramshackle housing, unskilled and insecure, they shared with the white poor a fear of illness and a dread of death. Their greatest dread was connected with the disposition of the body after death. Burial in nondescript cemeteries maintained by local governments was the fate of the uninsured poor. Even worse was the knowledge that the bodies of destitute blacks were sometimes consigned to medical schools, where they were dissected (Puckett 1926:87–93; *Southern Workman* 1897:18–19). Loss of income due to illness or accident was another pervasive fear of the poor, for people who had no money could not get medical attention.

Early progress in the business was encouraging, but the gradual process of accumulating assets soon was rudely interrupted. William A. Wright, insurance commissioner for the state of Georgia, learned of the operation and notified the four men by mail that they could not operate in this fashion without formal authority. The four obtained a personal interview with General Wright, assured him of their honorable intentions, and pleaded for permission to proceed. They were firmly refused. They then appealed directly to Governor William J. Northen. The governor was sympathetic to their plight and impressed by their sincerity, but his intercession with Wright failed to sway the commissioner. Finally, however, Wright did offer some hope. (Possibly he was swayed by their persistence or, in part, by the wartime experiences of Sheffield's father, since Wright had also lost a leg in the conflict.) Wright informed the quartet that if they crossed the border into Alabama, obtained a charter as a mutual aid association under that state's less restrictive statutes, and operated successfully there for a minimum of six months, he would then consider their application for a license to conduct business in Georgia. Led by the forceful McEachern, to whom abandonment of the enterprise after its promising start would have been an especially hard blow, the group decided to follow Commissioner Wright's advice.

Thus on May 9, 1892, five men stood before Notary Public John J. Moore, in Birmingham, Jefferson County, Alabama. Standing alongside McEachern, Sheffield, Owen, and Carleton was William L. Dodd, a former fellow agent in the Home Friendly Society. In 1890, Dodd had moved to Birmingham to organize the Southern Mutual Aid Association. An Alabamian and an established insurance executive, he was there to lend his presence and his name to assist his friends. The group obtained a charter under Chapter Three, Mutual Aid Association, of the Code of Alabama, for a corporation to be called The Industrial Aid Association. The general purpose of the corporation, as stipulated in the brief charter, would be "to comfort, aid and assist all persons who may become members . . . , morally, socially, and financially." Under the charter, bylaws were adopted providing that the board of directors should elect from their own number officers to operate the enterprise. The initial group of officers were John N. McEachern, president; D. F. Owen, vice-president; I. M. Sheffield, secretary; and J. J. Carleton, treasurer.

With the enterprise legally launched, McEachern returned to Atlanta to await the now foreseeable day when a permit to transact business in Georgia would be obtained. Sheffield, Owen, and Carleton went to nearby Anniston, an industrial town of about 10,000; 35 percent of the population was black. In a single room that served both as an office and as a bedroom for Owen and Carleton, the company's first headquarters was housed. Carleton soon resigned the office of treasurer and left the company. Owen remained with the company for the rest of his working life, most of it as manager of the Anniston office. Never a stockholder, he was often referred to in later company publications as the "first employee." At a retirement banquet in his honor on May 9, 1936, his brother-in-law I. M. Sheffield, then company secretary, and President John N. McEachern, Jr., traveled the eighty miles from Atlanta to Anniston and presented him with a loving cup, as a "token of our appreciation of your forty-four years of continuous loyal service."[4]

Sheffield remained in Anniston until the summer of 1894, when he returned to Georgia to launch operations in the middle and eastern sections of the state. He returned to Atlanta soon after the turn of the century to take up active duties as an executive officer. Company secretary from 1892 until 1943 and treasurer from 1897 until 1918, Sheffield remained a member of the board of directors until his death in 1953.[5]

During the company's formative era, while Sheffield pioneered in opening new debits and, as secretary, served as the link between the home office and the scattered field force, John Newton McEachern, on the basis of age, experience, and personality, emerged as the enterprise's dominant figure. During the six-month probation period, he marked time in Atlanta. Finally, on October 17, 1892, the company was duly licensed to conduct business in the state of its choice. Almost immediately, McEachern hauled a few pieces of used furniture to the old state capitol, which had been converted to an office building, and Room 40 became the first Atlanta home office of the enterprise. For a time he operated as a one-man home office staff, serving as combination general manager, bookkeeper, and superintendent of agents. He began to receive applications from the field and issued policies; reports accompanied by paid disability and death claims flowed in from the field offices. A close observer during the early years wrote in 1934: "Without special training Mr. McEachern had natural genius of a high order for system, accounts and statistics, and under his direction, the system of records, accounts and statistical information which has developed into a highly efficient system now in use in the home office . . . was inaugurated" (McElreath 1935:29). When business grew to sufficient proportions to warrant the services of a bookkeeper, John McEachern's nephew E. C. McEachern was employed. During the difficult times of the 1890s, John McEachern continued personally to cultivate the Atlanta market.

Despite the pressing need for small-premium life and health insurance protection throughout the southeastern United States, the industry remained unorganized and chaotic. Large northern-based companies, such as Prudential and Metropolitan Life, had not yet penetrated the South and, in any event, were reluctant to insure blacks because of their exceedingly high mortality rates (Hoffman 1900:137,209–11,302; James 1947:86,338–39). The industry in the South was dominated by financially weak if well-meaning church-affiliated fraternal and benevolent societies. Entry of commercially run companies into the industry was relatively easy; exits through mergers or bankruptcies were extensive. Unsuccessful enterprises were destroyed by a variety of factors: cutthroat competition, which kept rates inordinately low; too few reserves coupled with careless field underwriting; and, most often, incompetent management and weak organization structure. (In 1890, claims exceeded premium income for six of the twenty-five assessment life and accident insurance companies operating in Georgia. By the turn of the century, a majority of the twenty-five companies had failed.)

The founders of Life of Georgia hoped to avoid this fate by able management, a sound selection of risks, and rates which were perhaps somewhat above the average but which would be coupled with fair and ethical treatment of policyholders and especially with the prompt payment of fair claims.

Despite a commitment to sound business practices, company progress during the early 1890s was painfully slow. Gross premium income in 1896 was still under $25,000. Between 1893 and 1896, the number of policies issued by the company increased by 21 percent; claims paid almost quadrupled. (This was the first company experience with the typical insurance phenomenon of rising claims rates during periods of economic distress.) During the mid 1890s the nation experienced the worst depression it had ever suffered. Prices plummeted, businesses closed their doors, unemployment soared. Nowhere was the depression more serious than in the South.

Under these adverse circumstances, even insurance companies with highly favorable charters found survival difficult. This, indeed, was the experience of the Southern Industrial Aid Society, which had been chartered by special act of the Georgia legislature on October 3, 1891. The enterprise, which had briefly employed D. F. Owen in its early days, was virtually moribund by the summer of 1897. Its president, Atlanta physician Julian P. Thomas, had become disenchanted with the insurance business and was in immediate need of money. Dr. Thomas consulted with his attorney, Walter McElreath, regarding ways and means of raising ready cash. McElreath, nephew of John McEachern, had shared living accommodations with his uncle for some time after arriving in Atlanta in early 1895 with his law degree in hand. On many occasions he had heard McEachern voice a wistful hope of someday being able to conduct the insurance business under a strong charter, comparable to that held by the Southern Industrial Aid Society. Now, in 1897, McElreath proceeded promptly to act as intermediary in bringing the potential buyer and seller together. He suggested to Dr. Thomas that he knew of persons who would be interested in obtaining the charter of Southern Industrial Aid and who would most likely pay up to $100 for it. As McElreath later recalled, Dr. Thomas "eagerly accepted this offer."

On August 3, 1897, a meeting of the board of directors of Southern Industrial Aid Society was held and a new five-man board was elected. It consisted of John McEachern; his younger brother by two years, Samuel C., who joined the company in 1893 and was soon dispatched to Rome, Georgia, to expand field operations in the northern part of the state; I. M. Sheffield; his younger brother, Snowden; and Dr. J. D. Middlebrooks, a family friend of the McEacherns with a medical practice in Cobb County. The new board met immediately and elected officers: McEachern, president; Sheffield, secretary and treasurer; and McElreath, attorney. McElreath's first task was to take the necessary legal steps to secure an amendment to the charter of the society, changing its name to Industrial Aid Association. This was accomplished on September 4, 1897. On that day, the newly named enterprise assumed the assets and liabilities of the Alabama corporation, which then went out of existence.

The acquisition of a far more favorable charter—which for one thing permitted the enterprise officially to establish its home office in Atlanta—was soon followed by economic recovery. Between 1897 and 1902 company premium income increased fivefold. As prosperity returned, company officers hosted a banquet for agents, their families, and some invited friends in celebration of the company's sixth anniversary. On Friday evening, October 1, 1898, at the Kimball House, Atlanta's largest and most elegant hotel, almost a hundred guests—including W. L. Dodd, president, and B. M. Cross, vice-president of the Southern Mutual Aid Association—feasted on filet mignon, broiled spring chicken, and broiled trout and quaffed punch au Benedictine and coffee. The press reported that the guests were welcomed by McEachern "in a short and happy speech," and at the close of the banquet he was presented a "beautiful" cane by the company's agents in Atlanta.

Company expansion and profitability during the early years of the twentieth century led top management to decide, in 1903, to adopt a new corporate name, one that would more accurately reflect its purpose and more effectively enhance its prestige than Industrial Aid Association. The name the board of directors decided upon was Industrial Life and Health Insurance Company. On June 26, 1903, the amendment to the charter was approved. The new name was to grace company letterhead, policies, and advertising materials for forty-three years. Only when significant company developments in the mid 1940s made this name inappropriate was it replaced in 1947 by Life Insurance Company of Georgia. Soon after the name Industrial Life and Health Insurance Company was officially adopted, company officers and employees celebrated the occasion at John McEachern's rambling ten-room house in Atlanta's West End. The festive affair featured the new name—all thirty-nine letters—spelled out in bananas on the dining room table.

John McEachern had moved into his West End home almost seven years earlier, following his marriage at the age of forty-three to an attractive schoolteacher from Cherokee County, twenty-two-year-old Lula Cordelia Dobbs. In the years following her marriage, Lula, a woman of rare energy and intelligence, was to take an active and significant role in civic, religious, and educational affairs, particularly in sponsoring missionary work. She served several terms as president of the Woman's Missionary Society of the North Georgia Methodist Conference and was the first woman to hold the position of first vice-president of the International Council of Religious Education. After John's death in 1928, Lula assumed the post of chairman of the board and served in that capacity until 1948, except for a short hiatus in 1933. She was a company director from 1924 until her death in 1949 and second vice-president from 1926 until 1928.

Of more immediate and far-reaching importance to the expansion of the fledgling enterprise, the marriage of John McEachern and Lula Dobbs brought to the company the drive and talent of four of Lula's younger brothers as well as important contributions by numerous cousins and, subsequently, their children and grandchildren. By far the most common name in the chronicles of Life of Georgia after 1896 is Dobbs; the clan clearly dominated certain geographic sections of the company's expanding trade territory and occupied key posts supervising agency and financial affairs from the Atlanta home office.

The first of Lula's four brothers to join the enterprise was Rufus Howard. In 1896, after graduating from Powder Springs High School, Howard decided to follow the newlyweds to Atlanta. Three years later the next brother, A. Quinton, arrived, followed by Oliver Reid in 1903 and Henri Talmage in 1909. Howard's competence and contributions to the company made the others more eagerly welcomed and readily employed than they otherwise might have been. Conscientious and mature beyond his years, Howard was elected to the board in April 1900, just prior to his twenty-fourth birthday, and in August 1903 was named first vice-president, a position he was to retain, with the additional duties of treasurer added in 1918, for nearly thirty years. The sound and conservative investments he made during the 1920s served the company in good stead during the difficult early years of the Great Depression, from 1931 through 1935, when losses were suffered in field operations. In February

1933, Howard Dobbs was named chairman of the board and chief executive officer; in September 1933 he relinquished the former post and was named president and chief executive officer. In September 1933, he was also named president of the Industrial Insurers' Conference, a trade association of southern life and health insurers that John McEachern had helped found in 1910. R. Howard Dobbs, Sr., was at the peak of his intellectual powers and influence within the company and the industry when he suffered a sudden heart attack and died on December 10, 1933.

Howard Dobbs's only son, R. Howard Dobbs, Jr., was to follow in his father's footsteps as the company's major financial specialist. He later served as president and chief executive officer, from 1950 to 1969, and then as chairman of the board, from 1970 to 1975.

During his lifetime and beyond, the three brothers of Howard R. Dobbs, Sr., played important parts in company progress. A. Quinton went to work for the company as an agent in Atlanta in 1899 and became manager of the district six years later. He became a member of the board of directors in 1933 and a vice-president in 1938. He died in 1944. (A. Q. Dobbs was also active in various non-company activities. He was vice-president of the Dixie Realty Company and a director of the Pepsi Cola Company and the Tung Oil Company.) Oliver Reid Dobbs became an agent in Gainesville, Georgia, in 1903, later served in Macon and Athens, and rose to become the South Georgia division manager. During World War II he was brought to the home office as assistant treasurer and remained in that post from 1942 to 1948. He was elected a director in 1942 and a vice-president in 1944. He retired in 1954. H. Talmage Dobbs joined the company in 1909 as a bookkeeper after graduating from Young Harris College. He boarded with his brother Howard and sister-in-law Viola in their West End home for two years, and then moved his belongings down the street (from 251 Gordon Street to 272 Gordon Street) to the home of his sister Lula, where he boarded for two years. Talmage Dobbs remained in the home office for seventeen years, rising to assistant office manager (1919–22) and cosuperintendent of agencies (1922–26) along with John Newton McEachern, Jr. He went into the field to develop central Florida for two years, and then returned to the home office as superintendant of agencies (1928–33). In 1933 he was named first vice-president and was placed in charge of the agency force and field operations. In his

1935 history of the company, Walter McElreath termed Talmage Dobbs "the greatest dynamo of personal energy among the executive force of the company." (McElreath 1935:75). In 1942 Dobbs was designated executive vice-president and served in that capacity until February 1944. He also served as a member of the board of directors from 1924 to 1926 and then from 1928 to 1945. Talmage Dobbs's relations with other company officers, particularly John Newton McEachern, Jr., as described later in this essay, were to play, somewhat paradoxically, a major part in the dramatic turning-point period of the company's history, 1944 to 1950.

With completion of the first decade of operations, survival of the 1890s depression, and acquisition of a favorable charter, the stage was set for an accelerated rate of expansion. Early emphasis was placed upon financial solidity and upon the use of monetary incentives for both company officers and the field force in order to enlarge net earnings. Growth was to be a gradual, incremental process.

During the first half-century of its history, prior to the introduction of Ordinary life insurance in 1945, which made necessary the accumulation of sizable reserves, the financial objectives of the company were as modest as its scope was limited. In essence, the enterprise functioned as a money pump, drawing in a steady stream of premium income and pouring out large payments to policyholders in the form of disability claims and death benefits. The concept of an adequate surplus was embraced by the board of directors in its October 3, 1901, meeting, when it approved a resolution advanced by Second Vice-President Howard Dobbs to the effect that "the proper conduct of the business of Insurance requires that a certain surplus be kept to meet any unexpected demands and to insure the prompt payment of all disability or mortuary or other claims against the Association." The board also agreed that "such surplus be invested if possible so that it will yield some increment . . . and so that it can be quickly and readily converted at any time needed into cash without loss." The board then "authorized and directed" President McEachern to invest any surplus funds "which at any time he deem it advisable to invest" in United States or State of Georgia bonds "or any other safe and marketable securities."[6] Thus commenced the official building up of a surplus fund. By the end of the decade, the company held federal, state, and municipal bonds, with a total par value of $24,500 and first mortgages (on real estate) totaling $23,650.

With the protection of the policyholders accounted for, company profitability gained high priority. The decision was made to link the remuneration of home office officials directly to the flow of premium income flowing in from the field. Beginning in 1901, 20 percent of gross collections from the members of the association were to be set aside as compensation for company officers. At the same time, the board of directors resolved that "no extra assessment nor any funds arising from such extra assessments" should be considered in making the percentage allotment. At its December 5, 1904, meeting, the board fixed officers' salaries for the next three years on a weekly basis as follows: J. N. McEachern, president, $500; R. H. Dobbs, first vice-president, $100; S. C. McEachern, second vice-president, $100; I. M. Sheffield, secretary and treasurer, $100. As premium income grew, the percentage allotted to officers' salaries was reduced; in August 1906, it was dropped to 15 percent of collections. This method of compensation was later brought under attack by the Georgia Insurance Department, and attorney McElreath sought to defend the practice as "equitable, just and expedient. It sets a premium on executive ability, insures the utmost devotion to the interests of the company upon the part of the officers, and calls out every faculty for the economical administration of the company's affairs." An independent accountant, examining the company's books in 1912, concurred: "All of these officers," the report stated, "are actively engaged in and devote their entire time to the business. . . . The Company is an example of what can be done . . . when experience is combined with a constant supervision that is reflected in every detail of this organization."[7] The insurance department accepted the incentive compensation plan in principle; some policyholders viewed it in a different light and raised objections. Nonetheless, the allotment plan remained in effect, although as the business grew the percentage allotted was revised downward. Finally, the great increase in the number of home office officials after World War II made the percentage allotment system impracticable.

During the long period characterized by decentralized company operations, home office officials devised a variety of incentive plans for field managers. During 1902 a system of "remittances and increase" was devised for the managers of the company's three principal Georgia districts (Atlanta, Augusta, and Savannah), all of whom had been making the same salary. President McEachern, in announcing the arrangement, which would place each manager on his "own merits," emphasized its objective: "If one man is worth more in the business than the other, he should have it."⁸ A feature of the plan, often used in subsequent contests, was the requirement of a high persistency rate in premium collections. No salary would be raised and no prizes awarded with less than 93 percent collections of the current district debit.

An incentive arrangement of far-reaching significance was established in the summer of 1902, when the company entered into a contract with Julius Covington to develop the Savannah district. The contract called for Covington to pay all his claims, agents' salaries, and other expenses out of his premium income and to remit 15 percent of his gross collections to the home office. When collections exceeded $1,000 the remission rate dropped to 10 percent. The arrangement came close to being a franchise within the prescribed territory. At about the same time, comparable contracts were entered into with other managers to develop North Georgia and Alabama. Subsequently, and especially after the death of Covington in 1912, some of these contracts were surrendered to the company, and the managers placed on a weekly stipend. The company continued to regard the incentive arrangement with favor, and used it selectively. A characteristic contract, negotiated in 1924, was explained to the manager in the following terms: "It will be all right for you to take your salary each week and at the end of this quarter we will mail you a check for all above 20 percent you have remitted to us, and so on each quarter. Of course, if you should fall down and get in a hole one quarter it would be charged against you the next quarter. . . ."⁹ When remittances did fail to cover claims and field expenses, the home office sent a "to-balance" check to the manager. Managers whose remittances consistently fell behind their quotas could expect to feel the strong prod of home office disapproval. At the same time efforts were made to discover the source of the problem.

The system of incentive contracts plus the recruitment of managers from within agency ranks built a corps of aggressive, hardworking field leaders. There were some disadvantages and dangers in the system, both to the home office and to field management. Managers with so much autonomy could, if so inclined, detach debits and entire divisions from company control. And there were instances in which highly successful agents, when elevated to field leadership, proved mediocre as managers. On the whole, however, the recruitment of field managers from among the best agents served the company well.[10]

Company expansion during the formative years was accomplished by two major methods. One was geographic growth, the enlargement of the trade territory by opening new districts and entering new states. The other was the buying out of the business of other companies, primarily those in financial difficulty. Both methods were employed, although with characteristic caution.

North Georgia, as already briefly noted, was developed principally by Samuel C. McEachern, who joined the company in 1893, at age 38, with a diverse business background. His salient personality traits were assessed by a knowledgeable observer as follows: "Like his older brother [John], he was a man of indomitable will and untiring energy. He lacked the daring initiative of his brother, but he made up for the less brilliant quality by good, sound, conservative judgement" (McElreath 1935:70). Establishing his base of operations in Rome, Georgia, Sam McEachern remained there for a decade, supervising expanding company activities in Rome and surrounding areas. He became a leading citizen of the city, winning election as councilman in 1905. The following year he was appointed manager of field operations for all of Georgia, except Atlanta. Returning to the home office in Atlanta, he built a home in nearby Marietta, and in 1909 was elected councilman of the city's Third Ward. He continued to serve the company as second vice-president until his retirement at the age of sixty-nine, in 1924. In that year he sold his stock interest in the company (one of the few stockholders ever to do so), and for the remaining four years of his life devoted his still abundant energies to agricultural experimentation.

Whereas Sam McEachern was the dominant voice in guiding field operations throughout the northern half of Georgia, members of the Dobbs family (especially A. Quinton and O. Reid) played major roles in developing the eastern and southern parts of the state. When the decision was made, in 1904, to expand operations into the neighboring state of Florida, one of the key fieldmen who pioneered the peninsula was a member of the Dobbs clan through marriage: Arthur Landers Coffey, Sr. Born in Lula, Georgia, in 1885, A. L. (later nicknamed "Doc") Coffey arrived in Atlanta in 1902 and shared an apartment with his older sister Viola, who was employed by the Industrial Aid Association as a stenographer. Coffey soon joined the company; his task was filling in lapse sheets. He remained in the home office for eleven years. Viola, meanwhile, had fallen in love with R. Howard Dobbs, Sr., and she married him on July 20, 1904. In 1914, Doc Coffey left Atlanta to commence his career in the field. Accompanied by his wife, Grace, he served briefly in Valdosta, Georgia, and then crossed the border into Florida and began to build a large debit in the Little River and Coconut Grove communities of Dade County. He became a well-known figure, riding a bright yellow bicycle around the area in order to serve his widely scattered policyholders. In 1918, he was named manager of Miami, and ten years later was promoted to state manager. Coffey subsequently moved to Jacksonville, and from there guided Florida agency operations for a quarter of a century. During that time he served as a company vice-president (1948–54) and as a director (1945–58). Retiring in 1954, A. L. Coffey, Sr., left as legacy to the company (as did countless other veteran employees) his son. A. L. ("Art") Coffey, Jr., joined the company as an agent in Jacksonville in 1929, after graduating from the University of Florida. He served the company in Florida for thirty-seven years, rising to the position of Miami division manager in 1952, and retained that post until his retirement in 1968.

Company expansion throughout Alabama has been supervised and guided over the years by the Sheffields, first by cofounder I. M. Sheffield, Sr., and then during the 1930s and 1940s by his son, later chairman of the board, I. M. Sheffield, Jr. In 1909, when twenty-three-year-old Emmett Miller was selected to open offices for the company throughout southern Alabama, it was I. M. Sheffield, Sr., who described the company's basic precepts to him: "Explain the policy contract thoroughly and be careful about the risks you write." Also, concerned with the possibilities of heavy initial losses, Sheffield advised, "Endeavor to write small premiums."[11] The calm, conscientious Miller followed these instructions with great care. Arriving by train in Brewton, Alabama, a town of 2,000 situated just above the Florida border, Miller immediately acquired his license to sell insurance and began calling personally upon doctors, funeral directors, and storekeepers, passing out circulars and testimonials supplied by the home office. Having established a thriving office in

Brewton, Miller headed northward, and by the end of 1910 he had successfully launched operations in a number of Alabama towns—Evergreen, Tuskegee, Wetumpka, Clanton, Montevallo, Calero, Columbiana—ranging in population from 754 to 2,803.

The location of offices in such small communities, a phenomenon that characterized company expansion into other states as well, led eventually to a degree of sales imbalance.[12] The stress upon sales to rural southerners was justified, however, during the early twentieth century, when the bulk of the population, white and black, still lived on the land or in small communities. In 1910, only 20.2 percent of southerners resided in communities of 2,500 or more people, compared to 45.7 percent for the nation. As of December 1910, the number of company branch offices totaled seventy-five and included virtually all of the larger cities of the tristate trade territory. Since August 1906, when a number of offices were being operated in North Carolina, the total number of branch offices had increased by ten.

The company's experience in North Carolina illuminates some of the problems associated with combining decentralized field operations with a dogmatic and ruggedly individualistic group of owner-managers. In April 1901 the company applied for a license to conduct business in North Carolina, and by the early part of 1902 veteran field managers were establishing branch offices in the piedmont section of the state under the remittance-type contract. To defray the initial cost of operating the territory, S. M. Holland and E. N. Johnson borrowed $50 from John McEachern for a six-month period at 6 percent interest and signed a note promising as collateral "all debits built at Winston Salem, Concord and Salisbury. . . ."[13] Buoyed by a wave of economic expansion, company business in North Carolina burgeoned. In 1907, policies issued in the state accounted for 19.3 percent of all policies issued by the company. The state insurance commissioner began to question such matters as the form in which notices were given to policyholders regarding annual meetings and the arrangement by which company officials were being compensated. President McEachern responded to these questions in considerable detail, but apparently he did not completely satisfy North Carolina's Insurance Department. The company was asked to leave the state, and ceased operations on October 20, 1908.

The setback in North Carolina was especially serious, coming as it did during the course of a downturn in the economy. "On all sides we have been hearing nothing but complaint of hard times," McEachern reported to the board of directors on August 8, 1908. "Our sick claims have been much heavier as a result of so many people being out of work." Nevertheless, he viewed the future with characteristic confidence. "We have met all claims promptly and have maintained our reputation for honest dealings with policyholders and when other industries start up the business of the company will improve rapidly."

McEachern's optimism regarding longer-range prospects for company growth may have been occasioned in part by the acquisition of the business of a number of bankrupt life and health insurers. No entirely new markets resulted from these acquisitions, but existing debits were enlarged, considerably in some instances, and, moreover, at very little additional cost. Able fieldmen and potential managers were often obtained in this manner.

The first such company so acquired was the Georgia Aid Association, organized in 1896 by C. S. Drake, a distant relative of I. M. Sheffield who had been serving the company in the Macon office. Georgia Aid failed to flourish and, in 1897, its small debit was taken over by the company; Drake being named assistant superintendent of the Atlanta district office. In 1900, the United States Benevolent Association faced a crisis when its claims-to-premium income ratio reached 70 percent (compared to 27 percent for the company). The company agreed to buy its business for $1,000. This move doubled the size of the Montgomery debit and Sheffield arrived from Atlanta to help effect the transfer.

A wave of acquisitions followed the passage of the Georgia Insurance Act of 1905, which required all companies conducting an Industrial life insurance business in the state to post a $5,000 deposit and to keep on hand liquid assets fixed at $1.50 for each $100 of insurance in force. In the passage of this legislation, John McEachern, who was becoming recognized as an insurance authority, and attorney Walter McElreath played prominent parts (Knight 1930: 396, 399). The act amounted to a death sentence upon weak and insolvent beneficiary societies, although some companies found temporary respite in borrowing funds to meet the deposit requirement and subsequently issuing income certificates to meet operating expenses. The case of the Southern Life and Health Insurance

Company illustrates the process by which Industrial Life and Health took over several of these enterprises. Southern Life was obliged to borrow the required $5,000, using the proceeds to buy that amount of City of Atlanta water bonds. In 1906, John McEachern acquired title to the bonds, with Southern Life agreeing to pay him 10 percent of its gross receipts so long as he would keep the bonds deposited with the state treasurer as required by law. McEachern subsequently advanced to Southern Life an additional $4,000. By October 1908 the enterprise was insolvent, and Industrial Life and Health agreed to take over its business in exchange for payment of its total debt.

The next wave of acquisitions took place between 1911 and 1914. The Royal Mutual Insurance Association's $250 debit was reinsured in January 1911. In 1912, Industrial Life and Health paid $6,000 in cash and $7,000 in income certificates for the $425 debit of the American Assurance Association. In 1913, in a move that must have brought great satisfaction to the company cofounders, the management of the Home Friendly Society sought them out and suggested that they take over the society's Georgia business. The company agreed, paying $6,000 cash for the society's $680 debit. The company's final acquisition of the pre–World War I period took place in 1914 when the United States Health and Life Insurance Company transferred its Georgia debit and $15,000 in City of Atlanta bonds to Industrial Life and Health for $27,000.

Following the war, in 1919, the company acquired the $4,000 debit of the Continental Life and Health Insurance Company for $29,026. Among the agents retained by the company was Mamie Zachrey, a middle-aged woman. Assigned a debit in Savannah, she continued to work for the company for about six years. Zachrey enjoyed the twofold distinction of being the company's first female and first black agent.

With the reinsurance of the Continental's business, the era of acquisitions reached its peak. Times were changing, and expansion during subsequent decades was to take place primarily through territorial expansion and product development. One of the few acquisitions made after 1920 occurred in 1924 when the Carolina Life Insurance Company decided to withdraw from the sick benefit business. Carolina Life had been organized in March 1902 by A. B. Langley, who had gained his knowledge of industry practices as an agent for what was then the Industrial Aid Association, first under F. J. Walker, superintendent of the Savannah office, and then as a special agent in South Georgia.

Langley is one of a number of pioneer fieldmen who left the company to establish or manage other enterprises; some of them subsequently became highly successful. These men include T. T. Phillips, who founded Gulf Life Insurance Company in 1911 and served as its president until 1947, and C. S. Drake, previously mentioned, who was to play key roles in the launching of Kentucky Central Life and Accident Insurance Company in 1902 and Empire Life and Accident Insurance Company (of Indiana) in 1908. The founders of Kentucky Central included Frank J. Walker, veteran Industrial Aid field manager, and T. O. West, another long-time company agent. John N. McEachern, Sr., was named first president of Kentucky Central, although he served "in name only and did not come close to Kentucky." He was replaced in March 1903 by Walker, who remained president until 1936. Drake served as secretary-treasurer for about a year and then was replaced by West, who was secretary from 1903 until 1937. Drake remained with Kentucky Central as an agent until 1908, when he went to Indianapolis and started the Empire Health and Accident Insurance Company.

What seems clear is that, just as McEachern and Sheffield had profited from the training and experience they received from the Home Friendly Society, the company that they established proceeded to serve during the first decade of the twentieth century as a seedbed for a significant number of southern-based life and health insurance companies.

During the 1910s, McEachern joined with a dozen southern insurance leaders, some of them former coworkers, to organize a trade association which, since 1948, has been called the Life Insurers Conference. The concept of a trade association for southern life and health companies was advanced initially at a meeting of the top executives of twelve so-called casualty and surety companies in Mobile, Alabama, in September 1910; McEachern was among the dozen. The group reassembled in Atlanta in November, at which time the organization was completed. Its first conference was held in Atlanta, December 8–9, 1910. The *Insurance Herald* reported that McEachern "and his estimable wife assisted materially in the entertainment of the ladies of the visiting delegation. . . . The courtesies extended by Mr. and Mrs. McEachern added spice to the social features of the occasion and were much appreciated." John McEachern was selected as one of four members of the Law Committee. Prior to the second annual meeting, McEachern expressed his thoughts on the "Helpfulness of Association" in the September 28, 1911, issue of the *Life & Casualty Underwriter's Supplement:*

> I think that in the organization of the Southern Casualty & Surety Conference a great work has been started. . . . Of course, the members . . . well understand that merely being members . . . will not make our companies great, . . . but we can get information from each other at the meetings of the Conference that will be helpful to us in managing our business in a uniform manner. I like to meet the members of the Conference, as it is helpful to me to discuss business with them, and I believe it is helpful to others in the same way.

Therefore, McEachern averred, ever since his participation in the preliminary Mobile meeting of the conference, he had "felt disposed to render the organization every assistance within my power."

From its initiation in 1910, the conference has enjoyed the consistent and enthusiastic support of Life of Georgia's top management. Over the years, four company officers have served as president of the conference: R. Howard Dobbs, Sr. (1933); H. Talmage Dobbs, Sr. (1940–42); I. M. Sheffield, Jr. (1951–52); and R. Howard Dobbs, Jr. (1960–61). In addition, other company employees have served on a wide range of conference committees. After World War II, when Life of Georgia became a full-fledged combination company, it proceeded to join such industry-wide organizations as American Life Convention (1945), Life Insurance Association of America (1945), and Institute of Life Insurance (1946), and has played an active and significant role in most of them. It has continued to manifest, however, a major loyalty to the grouping of regional insurers which cofounder McEachern helped organize in 1910.

Despite the growing prosperity of the company during the early twentieth century and the enhanced prestige of its top management, the founders remained deeply apprehensive. Their main source of concern was that under the mutual assessment plan of organization there was always the possibility of being ousted from company control by an organized group of policyholders. This situation had occurred in the early days of the Prudential Insurance Company and the crisis of control thus created was resolved only when the New

Jersey legislature abrogated the voting rights of the policyholders. There is no doubt that Life of Georgia's tight-knit group of family-related officers, after a decade and a half of total involvement in the struggles and successes of the enterprise, had a deep desire to dominate its future direction. Indeed, a complaint was lodged by a number of policyholders to the effect that President McEachern "administers the property of the company as though it belonged to him personally."

With ultimate control the major consideration, company officers resolved to convert the mutual assessment enterprise into a stock company. The way had been prepared by the passage of the Act of 1905. On December 4, 1905, J. N. McEachern, I. M. Sheffield, R. Howard Dobbs, Samuel C. McEachern, and Julius Covington incorporated the Atlanta Industrial Life Insurance Company; its stated purpose was that of "carrying on the business of life insurance on the industrial plan." The objective of the incorporators was to have the new company assume the assets and reinsure the business of the Industrial Life and Health Insurance Company. They proposed to begin on January 1, 1906.

This was the plan, but it was never implemented. On behalf of three policyholders, a firm of attorneys in Atlanta promptly filed a suit seeking an injunction against the transfer of the company's assets. A temporary injunction was issued until a hearing set for later in the month. The company's board of directors expressed the belief that the suit could be defeated; but in view of the prevailing hostile state of public opinion—exacerbated by daily sensational disclosures in the press of the Armstrong investigation of insurance abuses in New York State—attorney Walter McElreath was instructed to settle the dispute out of court. Concurrently, the directors of the newly incorporated enterprise agreed not to transact any business during 1906. The proposed stock company remained moribund; it was never revived.

The founders of Life of Georgia continued to believe, however, that the stock form of organization was feasible and desirable. They awaited a more propitious time and searched for a better method to accomplish their purpose. Between 1909 and 1912, company general counsel Walter McElreath served in the Georgia General Assembly, where he was a member of the committee on insurance. In 1911 he was instrumental in the appointment of a commission to study and

111

revise the insurance laws of the state; he subsequently chaired that commission. The result of the commission's work was the General Insurance Act of 1912. Section 16 of the act enabled any mutual, life, health, or accident insurance company to become a stock company "by filing a certificate with the Secretary of State showing that three-fourths of its outstanding policyholders have voted in lawful meeting assembled to become a stock company, and the capital of such company is fixed at not less than $25,000. . . ."

Soon after the passage of this legislation, the company decided to take advantage of the new statute. In August 1913, company policyholders, through collected proxy votes, unanimously supported a resolution to instruct the board of directors to investigate the advisability of the stock form of organization. But some complications again arose, and World War I intervened. Finally, five years later, the time was ripe to accomplish the long deferred plan.

At their annual meeting on August 16, 1918, company policyholders resolved: (1) that the enterprise "become a stock company and that the capital stock . . . be fixed at the sum of Twenty-Six Thousand Dollars"; and (2) "that the assets belonging to the company at the time that it becomes a stock company shall never be used for the payment of dividends on any stock issued or upon any increase thereof." On October 29, 1918, an amendment to the charter was granted, changing the company structure from mutual and cooperative to a stock company, with capital of $26,000. At four o'clock that afternoon, the board of directors convened in special session, received subscriptions to the capital stock, and adopted new bylaws. The 260 shares, par value at $100, were subscribed for as follows: John N. McEachern, Sr., 100 shares; Isham Mallie Sheffield, Sr., 50 shares; Samuel C. McEachern, 50 shares; R. Howard Dobbs, Sr., 50 shares; Walter McElreath, 10 shares. The Company immediately invested the $26,000 in 4¼ percent United States bonds of the Fourth Liberty Loan.

George N. Spring, at the time a life insurance actuary in private practice and later a company employee, recalled that when he learned of the transfer from mutual to stock company he had "begged pitifully to be allowed to invest $1,000." President McEachern declined, remarking "There is not enough stock to go around for the boys who built up the business."[14]

There is another story, accepted by R. Howard Dobbs, Jr., that the original plan was to capitalize the company for $25,000, the legal minimum, and that McElreath was finally given 10 shares in payment for his legal work. In subsequent years, McElreath, an excellent historian, spearheaded the movement to establish the Atlanta Historical Society (1926) and was the prime mover in organizing the Atlanta Federal Savings and Loan Association (1930), which he served as president for two decades and saw develop into Georgia's largest savings and loan institution. When McElreath died in 1951, his will stipulated that the bulk of his estate (which in May 1947 contained 1,536 shares of Life of Georgia stock) be used, upon the death of his wife and sister, as an endowment fund "in promotion of the objects and purposes of [the Historical] Society." At the time of his death, McElreath's estate was estimated to be in excess of $1 million. His Life of Georgia stock alone, based upon the price of $1,200 a share for which it was being offered for sale after World War II, had a market value of close to $2 million.

With the successful conversion of the enterprise from mutual assessment to stock company status, the major work of the two cofounders had been accomplished. The changes that took place between 1918 and the dramatic turning-point era of 1944–49 were limited in number and moderate in impact. The company entered three additional states: South Carolina (1920), Mississippi (1931), and Tennessee (1931). October 1930 saw the completion of a six-story Home Office Building, costing $340,000, on the periphery of Atlanta's central business district, and the staff of thirty-four moved from the company's much smaller downtown office building (completed in 1916) to occupy two floors of the new facility. In 1931 a straight life-insurance policy for white clients was introduced, but agents found it difficult to cultivate a biracial market; the straight life policy for blacks, first issued in 1926, was a great success. The sound, conservative investment portfolio, accumulated principally by R. Howard Dobbs, Sr., prior to his death in 1933, was a major factor in company survival during the difficult years of the Great Depression. The 1936 assessment of the company by the prestigious *Best's Life Insurance Reports* disclosed that bonds represented 71 percent of the company's physical assets; very few were in default and more than one-seventh of them had "particularly high ratings from independent bond services." Overall, the bondholdings were rated "of very good quality."[15] Best also reported that none of the physical assets

113

were collateral loans or common stock, nor were any mortgages currently owned; "all companies holding mortgages," it noted, "have experienced trouble with them." The yield on assets as a whole was 4.6 percent in 1935, regarded by Best as "a very good rate of return." Although lapses were "above average," expenses had been kept "fairly low," and the claims ratios were favorable. Best concluded that the company had "moderate margins for contingencies," and that the results achieved were "above the average for the business."

Company operations were guided through the remaining years of the Great Depression and World War II by the rising second generation of the founders' families and by Lula McEachern's younger brother, H. Talmage Dobbs. I. M. Sheffield, Sr., continued as company secretary until 1943, but he devoted increasing time and attention to a secondary business interest—the purchase, sale, and rental of real estate through the Paulding Investment Company, which he organized and headed. Interested in improving the community's cultural level, Sheffield served as a member of the Atlanta Art Association and became active in the affairs of the High Museum of Art. He also was a charter member and one of the initial contributors to the Atlanta Historical Society. Beginning in the mid 1930s, when both his wife and his daughter Nellie died of cancer, Sheffield's major philanthropic interest became financing the treatment and eradication of that dread disease. He made many gifts to Georgia Baptist Hospital and in 1939 donated to the hospital land and sufficient funds to construct what was then called the Sheffield Clinic for the treatment of cancer patients.

Sheffield's long-time business associate, company cofounder John McEachern, was also interested in rural real estate. By the time of his death on December 6, 1928, he had acquired extensive real estate holdings, mostly undeveloped land, amounting to almost 1,000 acres in his native Cobb County and another 399 acres in Wayne County in southeast Georgia. A strong proponent of education, McEachern served as a member of Atlanta's board of education from 1916 to 1918. In 1907 he donated to the state of Georgia 80 acres of land for the establishment of the Seventh District Agricultural and Mechanical College and supplied funds for the construction of the main building. Throughout his life John McEachern remained active in civic and philanthropic affairs. He was a 32d degree Mason, a Shriner, a Scottish Rite Mason, and a member of the Knights Templar.[16]

McEachern's only son, John Newton McEachern, Jr. (called Newton or Newt by associates and friends), exhibited a great deal of his father's drive and initiative. Joining the company as an agent in 1918, at the age of nineteen, he was elected second vice-president in 1924 and two years later, when his ailing father assumed the position of chairman of the board, Newton McEachern, at age twenty-seven, was named company president. Handsome, strong-willed, his mood fluctuating in mercurial fashion, Newton McEachern strove as chief executive officer to centralize authority in the home office. He insisted upon approving all applications for field positions; he wanted receipts for all field management expenses. In attempting to alter the delicate balance of power between the home office and the field force, young McEachern ran into resistance from veteran managers. Moreover, with the death of J. N. McEachern, Sr., in 1928, the high degree of internal harmony among home office officials that had been imposed by the dominant personality of the senior co-founder gave way to considerable internal squabbling over the remuneration of various family-related employees and some jockeying for a larger voice in decision making.

A major home office claimant to greater influence in determining the pace and direction of company affairs was Newton McEachern's dynamic and ambitious uncle, H. Talmage Dobbs, Sr. Ten years Newton's senior, "Tal" Dobbs was widely admired for his drive and constancy of effort. A compact, wiry, 135 pounder, Dobbs would often "work all night; he never got tired," recalled a veteran field manager. Dobbs's aggressiveness as a supervisor of field operations was balanced by a happy marriage and harmonious home life. Newton McEachern, equally dynamic but less constant in his efforts, was beset with numerous personal problems. During the early 1930s, his marriage of a half-dozen years was dissolved. Soon thereafter he remarried, but the couple soon separated and divorce followed within a year. While Newton grappled with his personal difficulties he was sometimes away from the home office for extended periods. During one of these troubled times, in early 1933, also a period of economic crisis, R. Howard Dobbs, Sr., replaced McEachern as the company's chief executive officer. But when Dobbs died unexpectedly, on December 10, 1933, Newton McEachern was again named president and chief executive officer, and Talmage Dobbs was elevated to the post of first vice-president.

115

During the remainder of the 1930s, major home office attention was concentrated first upon company survival and then, with some degree of national economic recovery, upon improving company profitability. In the interest of achieving these goals, personal antagonisms and individual ambitions were subordinated. Lula McEachern, as board chairman, continued to exercise a moderating influence, as her son and younger brother played their respective roles in company affairs.

During the years of deepening depression, lapses mounted, sick claims soared, and premiums became increasingly difficult to collect. Much ingenuity was required to keep business on the books. More than one imaginative agent partially solved the problem by piling a pair of scales and a chicken coop into his car each morning and returning to the district office at the day's end with the auto bulging with hams, side meat, and squawking fowl. Policyholders' premium books would then be credited with money received from the sale of these farm items. Other agents, with urban debits, struggled to overcome resistance from some employers of policyholders. One agent later recalled having to "hide my book in my umbrella to keep the lady of the house from knowing for what I was collecting." This kind of opposition could be combatted successfully. One agent learned that once the community became aware of the company's ethical conduct, "these same ladies would call and tell me they had a new maid they wanted me to insure." Conscientious fieldmen could serve under various circumstances as the patron for policyholders, not only in providing sound financial advice and helping to keep insurance protection in force, but also in obtaining competent medical care in case of illness and as a character witness in the event of difficulties with the law. At the same time, fieldmen, whose performance continued during the 1920s and 1930s to be measured in terms of sick and accident claims as well as the percentage of collections on premiums due and the net increase in new business, were urged by field managers and the home office to uncover unethical physicians and eliminate undeserved claims payments.

To accomplish the overriding goals of increasing premium income and reducing claims, all home office officials during the 1930s made an increasing number of forays into the company's territory. Talmage Dobbs, offically in charge of field operations, was particularly effective in this capacity, conducting meetings where sales quotas

116

were established, contests were announced, and prizes awarded. A charismatic speaker, typically garbed in a tuxedo on these occasions, Dobbs invariably instilled a sparkle in sessions with managers and fieldmen. An impulsive, emotional gesture would sometimes stun his audience. At one meeting, after an agent's fine record was reviewed, Dobbs suddenly and publicly presented the man with a pair of champion hunting dogs.

By the late 1930s the worst of the depression was over. The year 1938 was proclaimed "the best" overall in the company's history. The extent of the company's financial progress from 1918 to 1938 was disclosed in the United States Congress's Temporary National Economic Committee investigation of economic concentration. On December 31, 1938, the company's capitalization stood at $500,000 (which included the original $26,000 invested in the enterprise plus stock dividends of $474,000). Cash dividends to stockholders since its organization in 1918 amounted to $1,083,391. Surplus funds, excluding possible contingency reserves, stood at $493,669. Information relating to stock ownership in the enterprise disclosed that 51 percent of the stock was held by four persons. John Newton McEachern, Jr., held 15.4 percent; his sister Christine McEachern Smith (mother of later chairman of the board Rankin M. Smith) held 11.5 percent; R. Howard Dobbs, Jr. (as trustee for the estate of his father), held 8.7 percent; and Lula McEachern and R. Howard Dobbs, Jr., in their own right, held 7.7 percent each.

Company progress markedly accelerated during the early 1940s as the war brought prosperity to the South. Although antagonisms among various home office officials occasionally burst through the surface calm, and threats to sell company stock to outside interests were voiced, key company officials continued to work together during the late 1930s and early 1940s in essential harmony, toward common goals. This harmony was manifest at the board of directors meeting on December 29, 1942, when the office of executive vice-president was created and President Newton McEachern nominated Talmage Dobbs, Sr., for the post; Dobbs was unanimously elected.

Relations between Talmage Dobbs and other top officials began to deteriorate, however, particularly during the early part of 1944. At the February 1, 1944, meeting of the board, Talmage Dobbs informed his fellow directors that he intended to sell his stock in the company to outside interests. During subsequent weeks, he continued to assert that his aim was to acquire control of the enterprise. Finally, on February 22, 1944 (Newton McEachern's forty-fifth birthday), Chairman of the Board Lula McEachern called a special meeting of the board. A resolution was offered to abolish the office of executive vice-president. The resolution passed by a vote of eight to three. Talmage Dobbs was immediately relieved of all duties and authority, except as company director.

It is important to keep in mind that the controversies between Talmage Dobbs and other company officers (particularly Newton McEachern) revolved around the vital question of the future direction of the enterprise as well as matters of individual ambitions and clashing personalities. As an insurance man, Talmage Dobbs was firmly committed to Industrial life insurance; he was irredeemably opposed to a broadening of the company's portfolio of contracts to include higher face value Ordinary insurance. Newton McEachern, on the other hand, caught the vision of a vigorous and dynamically expanding regional postwar economy which he hoped would be built on the bedrock of southern capital. The company goals he embraced by the early and mid 1940s included expanding the geographic scope of its operations throughout the Southeast (and eventually throughout the nation) and making available to potential policyholders life insurance that would cover every need "from convenient premiums for the small budgets of those in the lower income brackets, to policies required by those with great interests to protect." At the same time, McEachern hoped through the enlargement of the company's financial reserves to provide capital for investments in southern industry. He particularly wanted to assure reemployment and the possibility of advancement within his company to all returning veterans.

At first the expansion planned by McEachern seemed seriously threatened by the prospect of Talmage Dobbs organizing a rival enterprise and enticing away a host of veteran field managers. But this threat never materialized. And on Sunday, September 1, 1946, Talmage Dobbs drowned in the waters of a fishing lake on his Cobb County farm.[17]

The dramatic and rapid conversion of Life of Georgia, already launched with the expansion into Arkansas in 1944 and the introduction of Ordinary life insurance in 1945, was to continue undiminished through the remaining years of the decade.[18]

118

NOTES

1. There are many similarities between Ordinary and Industrial life insurance. The distinguishing features of Industrial life insurance, which Life of Georgia sold exclusively until Ordinary was introduced in 1945, were the frequency of premium payments (weekly or monthly) and the method of collection (by agents at the home of insured). In addition, Industrial insurers were much more likely to sell policies to all members of the family, and often without medical examination. The Ordinary system fixed a unit of insurance, say $1,000, and then according to age and plan, set a premium; the Industrial business first fixed the unit of premium, say 5 cents, and then, according to age and plan, set the amount of insurance that could be given for that unit of premium.

2. The information that follows is based principally upon the internal records of Life Insurance Company of Georgia, published materials in the employee magazine of the company, some correspondence in the possession of the author, and an extensive number of interviews conducted during the period from 1964 to 1975. The other major sources utilized were a short published history of the Company by Walter McElreath, a family-related employee since 1895, and his somewhat longer and, at some points different, unpublished version written in longhand; and a competent Ph.D. dissertation by George E. Manners, Sr., completed in 1959 at Emory University.

3. The term *debit* has a dual meaning. Originally it denoted the total amount of premium income collected weekly for which an agent was responsible. It also came to refer to the fixed geographic area assigned each agent for solicitation of new business and servicing of existing policies. The debit system made possible the efficient conduct of the life insurance business based on small, frequent premiums.

4. Owen's son Schuyler, then an agent for the company in Tennessee, wrote to President McEachern: "I appreciate all you have done for him. I hope some day to have a district that I can make a good showing on and make a name with the Company as my Dad has." In July 1945, Owen's younger son, W. Sheffield, at the time an Ordinary agent for the Sun Life Assurance Company of Canada, joined the company to spearhead the development of Ordinary operations. He was elected to the board of directors in 1959 and was named vice-president for business development in 1957, in which position he served until his death in 1965.

5. It is the contention of members of the Sheffield family that I. M. Sheffield, Sr., and J. N. McEachern, Sr., initially agreed to share the profits equally. When Sheffield's return to the home office in Atlanta was delayed due to serious illness, he allegedly agreed to turn over part of his share in the enterprise to other members of the family, presumably John's brother Samuel and his brother-in-law R. Howard Dobbs, Sr.

6. Minutes, Board of Directors Meeting, Industrial Aid Association, October 3, 1901. A complete set of minutes of the meetings of the stockholders and the board of directors of Life Insurance Company of Georgia, under its various corporate names, is housed in the historical archives of the company in its home office building, in Atlanta, Georgia.

7. George N. Spring to William A. Wright, Insurance Commissioner of Georgia, February 3, 1913. A copy of the report and cover letter is housed in the historical archives of Life Insurance Company of Georgia.

8. John N. McEachern to field managers R. H. Dobbs, G. E. Wester and J. T. Waldrop, February 28, 1902. Very little correspondence between McEachern and company agents remains. A copy of the letter cited is housed in the historical

119

archives of the company.

9. I. M. Sheffield, Sr. to S. W. Owen, January 11, 1924. See also letter of July 10, 1924. Cofounder I. M. Sheffield, serving as company secretary during an extended period, carried on an extensive correspondence with the managers in the field, particularly those based in Alabama. A considerable body of this correspondence remains, and is housed in the company's historical archives.

10. This generalization is true only for the period through the mid 1940s. As field operations became more complex and sophisticated, large numbers of veteran managers could not cope with the new demands. Consequently, home office officials selected and trained managers on the basis of qualifications far different from those of an earlier and simpler time.

11. I. M. Sheffield to Emmett L. Miller, April 29, 1909. A copy of the letter is located in historical archives of Life Insurance Company of Georgia.

12. An analysis of the locus of residence of the 208 agents who qualified in 1968 for the prestigious President's Club convention disclosed that 20 percent lived in towns with populations of less than 5,000 and another 26 percent lived in towns with populations of 5,000 to 25,000.

13. The note, signed by S. M. Holland and E. N. Johnson, is located in the historical archives of the company. A letter from John McEachern to A. H. Mowbray, insurance commissioner of North Carolina, September 12, 1908, also throws much light on the company's experience in conducting business in North Carolina from 1902 until 1908. A copy of the letter is located in the historical archives.

14. "Recollections of George N. Spring, former actuary of Company," undated (ca. 1956), in historical archives, Life Insurance Company of Georgia.

15. An insurance company's physical assets, as calculated by Best, included real estate, bonds, cash, interest and rents, and deferred and uncollected premiums. The difference between this figure and gross assets consisted of policy loans and premium notes. During the depression decade, Life of Georgia's physical assets and gross assets were the same.

16. An inventory of McEachern's estate disclosed some surprising facets of the Scotsman's personality. It contained extensive stock holdings in speculative enterprises: almost 6,000 shares in El Socorro Mining Company; 2,500 shares in the Georgia-Mexico Mining Company; 240 shares in Cuban-American Creosote Manufacturing Company; and 100 shares in Macoochee Gold Mining Company. The total cost of these shares of stock to McEachern was $46,000; they were appraised at the time of his death at zero value.

17. The inventory of H. Talmage Dobbs's estate revealed that he held 1,797 shares of Industrial Life and Health Insurance Company stock. He also held 1,000 shares of Eastern Airlines stock, 1,750 shares of Chicago and South Airlines stock, and 1,370 shares of Fulton National Bank (Atlanta) stock, as well as about $100,000 of common stock in a variety of other companies. He also held about 1,300 acres of land in Cobb County and other parcels of land in Atlanta and throughout the state of Georgia. On the day of Dobbs's funeral, the state capitol was closed and state flags were flown at half-staff. Governor Ellis Arnall, a close political associate whom Dobbs had served in several capacities, was a pallbearer.

18. A coda to the story of the relationship between H. Talmage Dobbs, Sr., and his kinsmen in the company may add to an understanding of the complex personal business motives of the participants. Dobbs's son, H. Talmage Dobbs, Jr., who had been employed in the home office as a clerk since 1933 and office manager since 1942, resigned on February 1, 1944 to join the U.S. Navy. His resignation was

accepted by the board of directors "with regret." When young Dobbs sought reinstatement with the company after his release from naval service in June 1945, he was informed that his position had been filled and that there were no openings. Dobbs persisted, and about a year later, following the death of his father, he did rejoin the company, in the Finance Department. Subsequently H. Talmage Dobbs, Jr., rose within the administrative ranks of Life of Georgia to become treasurer and chief investment officer. He was elected to the board of directors in 1948, and served as senior vice-president from November 1972 until May 1975. Subsequently, he served as vice-chairman and later as chairman of the board of directors.

5

Multiple Enterprise in the Central Highlands of Peru

NORMAN LONG

Department of Anthropology
University of Durham

An almost ubiquitous feature of underdeveloped economies is the phenomenon of multiple occupations or enterprise, the simultaneous participation of individuals or groups in more than one branch of economic activity. This pattern has been observed at different levels and in different sectors of the economic structure. It exists, at one extreme, among national and regional elites whose members invest in several sectors at once and who are thus able to move their capital between various enterprises as the market conditions require; and, at the other, among the poorest urban workers and peasants who combine independent employment with temporary wage-earning opportunities to eke out a precarious living. A similar pattern is found in the intermediate categories; for example, middle-class professionals often divide their time between two or more occupations or invest their savings in land or commerce. The same is true of small-scale entrepreneurs and traders, who frequently diversify their economic activities to cover both production and distribution functions.

This tendency toward economic diversification has been explained by reference to the structural conditions associated with underdeveloped types of economy, where resources are scarce, fragmented, and disproportionately distributed among sectors and social groups.

Studies have also suggested that multiple job holding is a feature of "transitional" societies experiencing incipient industrialization and a rapidly expanding opportunity structure, or that it reflects the essentially multistructural character of underdevelopment, where noncapitalist modes of production persist alongside—and are functionally related to—the dominant capitalist mode.

Other interpretations of multiple enterprise have focused more specifically on the particular life situations and interests of the social categories in question. Hence it has been contended that members of elite groups attempt to deploy their differential capital and resources so as to optimize their control over basic financial, commercial, and industrial institutions, whereas poorer people aim to spread their more limited assets over several fields in order to reduce risk or to supplement their inadequate incomes.

While such interpretations have the merit of placing the phenomenon of multiple occupations in some macro- or microstructural context, few studies have documented in detail how particular social categories or groups set about building the necessary networks of relationships for combining or switching among various economic activities or occupations. No individual—whether a poor urban worker or a peasant struggling to make ends meet or an entrepreneur wishing to expand his businesses—has a ready-made matrix of relationships and investments that remains constant over time. Even those who inherit businesses or occupations from their parents or other kin must, during the course of their economic careers, reconstitute and modify the sets of relationships involved. The aim of this chapter, then, is to develop an analysis of economic careers that combine different fields of activity and investment. The argument is elaborated by reference to data on rurally based entrepreneurs in the Central Highlands of Peru,[1] and focuses primarily on what Ansoff (1965) calls "strategic decisions," which lead to the emergence of new branches of production or business. The final part of the chapter examines the structural conditions associated with such careers.

SOCIAL NETWORKS AND ECONOMIC CAREERS

My main purpose is to analyze the ways in which particular networks of social relationships develop—networks that give a certain direction or trajectory to a man's economic career and enable him to combine or switch among branches of economic activity. I am especially interested in showing how particular social networks, once established, become a constraint as well as a positive influence on future decisions. New economic investments emerge out of a whole set of social investments in personal relations and themselves generate new or modified sets. A person's ability to combine different branches of economic activity and to develop certain types of entrepreneurial careers is, I maintain, crucially affected by the content of his existing personal network. This network of relationships is significant not only because it may provide access to essential resources like capital or labor, but also for the flow of information and for the support its participants can offer for various courses of action. Although certain aspects of a person's network may be preselected by family and community background, other aspects must be developed from scratch, like those based on friendship or on occupational criteria. The ways that a person, in a given sociocultural setting, attempts to evolve and maintain a dependable network of social ties which can be activated for specific purposes is, then, a matter of considerable analytic interest for the understanding of economic careers.

In previous papers (Long 1972, 1973a) I have discussed the management of interpersonal relations based on kinship, compadrazgo, and other kinds of ties in the running of small businesses in the Central Highlands of Peru. I have also explored the operational requirements and types of networks associated with running particular enterprises, showing how these networks have been established and sustained. A third theme has been the analysis of the mechanisms by which entrepreneurs attempt to increase the predictability of outcomes of specific relationships by injecting into them certain normative and symbolic content which they hope will create a higher degree of trust or specificity in the exchanges between them and the parties concerned. This chapter considers the broader problem of how networks influence both the setting up of new branches of economic activity and the types of economic careers pursued.

The work by Anthony Leeds (1964) on Brazilian social careers provides some valuable points on how one might develop this perspective. The main focus of Leeds's analysis is an identification of the mechanisms by which people advance their political and economic careers, giving particular attention to the higher status levels of Brazilian society. One of his conclusions is that patterns of informal organization based on personal ties are critical at every promotional level. These ties are loosely established in groups sharing a common interest. Usually, they represent a roster of all key socio-politico-economic positions. Such groups, *panelinha*, are operative at every level in the national hierarchy, so that the ambitious and successful leader must pass through a number in succession. He must, in addition, spread his tentacles 'out into differing fields of activity, thus keeping in touch with various types of social resources. Involvement in several niches or jobs at once is characteristically described in Brazil as *cabide de emprego* ("the employment hanger").

Leeds goes on to suggest that for each person there are specific "springboards" or "trampolines" that will project him into new branches of activity and into new levels of control and influence. These springboards consist of such ties as family, kinship, *compadresco*, politico-bureaucratic affiliations, commercial and industrial connections, and recreational and educational bonds. A major task for the ambitious person, therefore, is to establish the right network of contacts that will propel him into a more widespread and influential circle—something he can accomplish by cultivating and publicizing a particular image of himself and his capabilities. In the early and middle stages of a man's career, this normally entails investment in an ever-widening network of ties so that sources of support may be multiplied to cover a wide range of contingencies. He will also aim to build around himself a "tactical corps of supporters or aides, a kind of claque or coterie, called in Brazil a *rotary* or *igrejinha* ("little church")" (Leeds 1964:1336). If he is successful, he will later join a *panelinha*, which constitutes a body of individuals sharing roughly equivalent power and status, and hope then to move through a hierarchy of such informal networks at municipal, state, and federal levels (cf. Shirley 1971).

Leeds's discussion relates primarily to political careers at the regional and national level and describes a system that is probably far more structured and hierarchical than that in other Latin American situations. Nonetheless, his analysis raises considerations that might be applicable to the study of other types of social careers. The notion of springboards is particularly useful as it directs attention toward the

126

identification of major sets of relationships that become available to the individual at stages in his career and subsequently provide the means by which he can initiate new branches of activity. These relationships may be based on certain membership criteria (for example, kinship, friendship, or political and religious affiliation) and may be characterized by different types of transactions and social investments. An important focus for analysis, then, is the specification of how these various sets of connections are maintained, consolidated, or manipulated to achieve desired ends. It is also valuable to describe the conditions under which these relationships emerge and how, as springboards, they serve to promote career prospects or to send one off in a direction not fully anticipated.

Involvement in a specific network of relationships, however, may carry with it some negative consequences for career mobility since dependence on particular relationships will tend to impose boundaries or limits on the types of action or decision possible. Hence it may be necessary at times in a career to reduce or repudiate certain sectors of one's effective network. Also, subject to the prevailing circumstances, a man may fail to exploit the opportunities available and find himself immobile, encapsulated within a set of relationships. The processes by which people spin new webs of relationships and shake off old ones are still not adequately understood. This chapter aims to contribute an understanding of this problem through the analysis of economic career patterns. As suggested earlier, my main emphasis is on viewing changes in economic career as resulting from prior investment in certain networks of social relationships as opposed to interpreting decisions as the direct outcome of rational or purposive choice.

MULTIPLE ENTERPRISE IN MATAHUASI: THE CASE OF ROMERO

In the development of my argument, I shall examine the history of one large, multiple enterprise based in the village of Matahuasi, a settlement of some 4,000 inhabitants located in the Mantaro Valley of the Central Highlands of Peru. Besides agriculture, its major form of livelihood, Matahuasi has an important commercial and transport

127

sector. It has close connections with Lima, which is a five-hour drive by all-weather road, and with the mining towns of the Cerro de Pasco Copper Corporation.

The Mantaro Valley itself is one of the largest highland valleys and a primary source of foodstuffs for Lima-Callao. It is predominantly a *minifundia* (smallholder) zone specializing in the production of maize, grains, potatoes, vegetables, and livestock products. Attempts have been made in recent years to develop a high quality milk industry. In addition, certain villages are well known for both traditional and modern crafts which are sold either in the feria of Huancayo, the main city of the region, or directly to Lima-based export agencies. Huancayo acts as the administrative and service center of the area, and, situated at the south end of the valley, is the gateway to the highland cities of Huancavelica, Ayacucho, and Cuzco.

Matahuasi is in the middle of the valley on the main road and the railway line from Huancayo to La Oroya and the coast. Partly because of this location, the village boasts a fairly substantial commercial and transport capacity that serves not only its immediate environs but also spreads out to capture some of the business of the mine and coastal towns.

During the past sixty years, Matahuasi has become increasingly integrated into the regional and national economy. Its response to the new opportunities brought by the development of mines and the growth of Huancayo as an urban center has been positive. A great number of Matahuasi residents have migrated to various towns and cities, and in Lima they constitute one of the two largest populations of valley-born natives.

Family Background and Early Work History

Romero was born in 1909 of humble parentage.[2] His father was reputed to have been a bandit who operated in the southern part of the Mantaro Valley but who in later years devoted himself to small-scale trading of agricultural produce. His mother came from Matahuasi. During the last part of their lives, his parents settled in Matahuasi, making their living by purchasing small quantities of vegetables and transporting them by horse or donkey to the ferias (weekly markets) in the nearby towns of Jauja and Concepcion. The

128

father owned no land and the mother only a very small plot which she had inherited.

Both parents died when Romero was young, and he, together with his elder brother and sister, was then looked after by his mother's kin in Matahuasi. The Romero siblings never knew their kin on their father's side of the family. The small plot of land and the house left by the mother were inherited by the eldest of the three children, Isabel. The others were left to fend for themselves. Romero's brother, Eduardo, a young man at that time, migrated to Lima to find work; he has remained there ever since and now operates a small carpenter's workshop. At the age of ten, Romero was sent to live with his mother's brother, Maximo, a livestock trader who worked between the valley and the developing mining towns. At this time the mine company was installing a new copper smelter at La Oroya and had recruited a large labor force. Food was needed, and Maximo seized the opportunity to set himself up as a cattle trader. Later, through a series of critical investments, he rose to become a prominent commercial and political figure in La Oroya. Romero at first lived in Matahuasi working as Maximo's herdsboy, but he gradually grew to take part in the transportation and selling of cattle. With his uncle's help, Romero finished his primary education in Matahuasi and spent one year in a secondary school in Huancayo.

During these early years Romero learned the livestock and butchery business. Maximo rapidly cornered a large share of the meat market in La Oroya; he still operates a butcher shop and several stalls in the markets. As Romero gained in experience, he purchased, again with assistance from Maximo, a few head of cattle for himself and thus began his own small-scale transactions. He then— in the late 1920s—married a woman from Matahuasi with Maximo acting as *padrino* (sponsor) to the marriage.

Shortly after the wedding, Romero and his wife moved to Malpaso, a small mining town near La Oroya, where, through the uncle's business, Romero already had some contacts. His experience with livestock trading helped to establish him as a meat intermediary in Malpaso, while his wife opened a small canteen for mine workers. The latter strategy was particularly opportune, as there were few comparable facilities in Malpaso at the time and a growing mine population. The canteen, it seems, was initially financed by capital

129

from the livestock business; throughout these years, though, Romero was greatly assisted by his wife's parents, themselves business people who traded in meat and vegetables. Together, parents-in-law and uncle provided Romero the main contacts for the formation of a network of relationships with traders who came from different parts of the Central Highlands. Several of these early friendships and business partnerships assumed importance for him at later stages in his career.

The Move Toward Investment in Agriculture

A year or two after opening his businesses in Malpaso, Romero rented four hectares of land in Matahuasi which, with the help of his sister Isabel, he planted with maize and potatoes. The plot was looked after by Isabel, with Romero and his wife returning to Matahuasi during the planting and harvesting seasons. When necessary, they would also take on a few hired hands to assist with specific tasks.

Romero's interest in acquiring land was, it seems, in part related to the deteriorating employment situation in the mines, which were suffering through the Great Depression. Between 1929 and 1932 Cerro de Pasco Copper Corporation was forced to lay off a third of its labor force. Copper production, which had been steadily expanding throughout World War I and the 1920s, reached its peak in 1929, but in 1930 world copper prices slumped dramatically. This led to a major crisis in the copper industry. Malpaso and other small mines were completely closed down, and this was followed by a severe reduction in the La Oroya labor force and, early in 1931, by the closure of the mines at Casapalca. The drastic drop in mine labor had negative repercussions for the many traders and small businessmen who had thrived during the beginning phases of mine expansion; several businesses went bankrupt while the rest had to operate with much-reduced levels of income.

Romero's investment in agriculture, then, helped to compensate for the loss of both clientele and income and ensured that, despite fluctuations and uncertainties of urban income, subsistence needs could be met. The farm, in addition, gave support to his sister, who, barely making ends meet on her small plot of land, had had to work as an agricultural laborer for part of the year.

130

For the next five years, Romero and his wife combined commerce with small-scale farming and spent time regularly in Matahuasi. In 1937, Romero learned of the Church's intention to sell its land in the valley. The prospect of obtaining freehold rights over land appealed to Romero, especially since the plot he then rented was in fact Church property which he thought might be put up for sale. He immediately travelled to Huanuco to discuss with Church authorities the possibility of making the purchase. It was important for him to act quickly since several others were also interested. The Church finally agreed to sell the property, and Romero was faced with having to raise 3,200 *soles*[3] for approximately four and one-half hectares of unirrigated land.

Although he had some cash of his own, he was still short of the full amount. His first thought was to ask Maximo, his uncle, for a loan, but relations between them were strained at the time, as the separation of business interests which occurred after Romero's marriage had indirectly affected Maximo's own entrepreneurial plans. So Romero instead went to another maternal uncle, Enrique, with whom he had more distant, yet friendly ties. Enrique, also a trader operating between the valley and the mines, agreed to advance him some of the capital, though it is not known exactly how much. Romero was thus able to conclude the deal with the Church by paying 900 *soles* down and the rest over the next two years. The contract was signed and sealed on July 17,1937, in nearby Jauja.

Both Romero and his wife worked energetically at their various occupations to clear the debt. Their efforts were aided by the generally improving economic situation in the mine towns in the late 1930s as the international economy began to revive. They built a small house in Matahuasi with the intention of returning later to take up agriculture full-time. By 1940 they managed to pay off the outstanding debt and were ready to return.

The beginning of the 1940s marked a major shift in Romero's economic career when the family—he now had several children—decided to settle permanently in Matahuasi to devote itself to agriculture rather than trade. In retrospect, Romero gives as the main reasons for returning his wish to take full charge of managing his land, to attend to the education of his children (the educational facilities in the Mantaro Valley were generally superior to those in other places), and to live in a more agreeable climate, since the

mine towns were located at a higher altitude. The land he purchased was well sited—close to both the main Huancayo–La
Oroya–Lima road then under construction, and to the railway line.
It was also situated near a tributary of the Mantaro River from
which water could be easily tapped to irrigate the fields.

The late 1930s to early 1940s was a unique period in the history of
landholding in the Mantaro Valley, as this was the first time in a
hundred years that sizable plots of land were available for purchase.
Land Registry data in Huancayo since 1900 show very small turnover of any land for sale at all. The Church's decision to dispose of
its landholdings in different communities throughout the valley was,
thus, a once-in-a-lifetime opportunity, which Romero, and seventeen other Matahuasinos, seized upon. It is significant that all eighteen purchasers had experience as labor migrants—either in the
mines, coastal plantations, or metropolitan area of Lima-Callao—
and had accumulated sufficient savings to make the investment.
Several of them had little farming experience and worked at professional or other nonagricultural occupations.

During this second phase of Romero's economic career, it became
essential for him to build a network of dependable relationships in
his village of origin. This was important for two reasons. In the first
place, he needed a reliable set of ties which could be activated
whenever he required labor at harvest or other peak periods. Second, he wished to establish a reputation for himself which would
accord him some community esteem, thus making his task easier.

Investment in agriculture, however, brought with it a number of unintended and possibly unpredictable consequences. Romero's rapid
rise to landowner status was interpreted by many as the result of his
having found *tapado* (buried treasure of the colonial period); they were
unwilling to attribute his success to virtue or hard work. His was the
luck of a bandit's son, they said, and therefore illegitimate. This pre-
judice was later reinforced by the conflict that developed between
Romero and the community over the purchase of Church land. The
dispute centered on the complicated legal issue of ownership, since the
Church had over a long period of time accumulated its land through
bequests from people of the village. The land became associated with
various local saints and was administered by cofradias (religious
brotherhoods). Thus, although the title of ownership rested with the
Church, it was the community itself, through its cofradias, that
worked the land and used its products to finance religious fiestas and

maintain the saints' images. Consequently, the selling of these land-holdings to private individuals was argued to be illegitimate and against the interests and wishes of the community.

A long-standing legal battle ensued between the community and the purchasers of Church land. This struggle has persisted through the last thirty years and has recently acquired renewed vitality with the possibility of the community reclaiming such lands under the new agrarian reform law introduced in Peru by Velasco's military government. The prolonged successive litigation, nevertheless, has cost the community enormous sums of money for legal advice, with no positive result. Adjudication has always favored the Church. The main grounds for this were, first, that the Church was able to produce title deeds showing ownership and, second, that at the time of the sales the *comunidad indigena* (community), as a formally recognized legal entity, did not exist, having been registered only subsequently, in 1942 (for details see Winder 1974:81–91; also Long and Winder 1975).

This dispute has produced major social divisions within the village, polarizing the larger farmers, many of whom had acquired their holdings through the purchase of Church land, and poorer households. For Romero the situation has been particularly acute; at various times he has found himself in direct confrontation with his two maternal uncles. In the year preceding the commencement of litigation by the community, Romero was associated with Maximo and Enrique in an abortive attempt to establish in Matahuasi a consumer cooperative modelled on similar ventures undertaken by the nearby village of Muquiyauyo (Adams 1959). Later, however, his two uncles, who were concurrently mayor of the municipality and president of the newly founded community institution, became deeply involved in initiating litigation for reclamation of Church land—in direct opposition to the interests of their nephew and his fellow purchasers. Under these circumstances, it was inevitable that Romero's relationship with his uncles would become rather acrimonious.

Romero's investment in land, then, led to a lengthy struggle with the local politico-administrative authorities, to a souring of his relationships with his maternal kin, and to a gradual disaffection with community affairs. Romero has never held office in local government nor taken a major role in organizing or financing village fiestas. His only claim to public service is his continued interest in the parent-teacher association at the local school; for a number of years he has served as president of the association and has helped to raise funds for the construction of a new school building.

The difficulties that Romero had with the authorities and the people of the village were further compounded when he took over a small piece of land adjacent to his original plot and close to the main road. It was claimed that this land was the property of the municipality and that Romero had alienated it for his own purposes. As shall be seen, this action was part of Romero's plan for building a petrol station to serve the traffic on the main road.

An Expanding Agricultural Enterprise

Romero's economic career in Matahuasi is marked by a pattern of gradual diversification and shifts in various activities. He at first concentrated on agriculture, growing maize, potatoes, barley, carrots, and other vegetables. The work was mainly done by his wife and himself with occasional help from his sister and hired hands for sowing and harvesting. When his children were old enough, they too took part. Each year he exported his surplus to Lima, transporting it in hired lorries. The marketing of his produce was greatly assisted by the fact that his parents-in-law had expanded their small trading business into a large-scale agricultural intermediary business with all the necessary sales outlets in Lima. Some of Romero's earnings were later invested in the purchase of dairy cattle, and he began to move into milk production as well.

During this phase he was, it seems, a bold agricultural innovator. One story describes how a group of agricultural engineers visiting his farm were impressed that he had sown three species of pasture in the same field—alfalfa, trebol, and natural grass. When asked why he had done this, Romero replied that it produced a better quality food mix for the cattle and consequently much better milk yields. He also experimented with the intercropping of barley and carrots. These crops were grown exclusively for the Lima market and, with irrigation from the nearby river and careful tending, two harvests a year were produced, although the amount of labor involved in harvesting the carrots at times proved excessive. Eventually he rented an additional two hectares of farmland from a neighboring farmer who had also purchased Church land but was not fully utilizing it.

In addition to engaging in agriculture and livestock husbandry,

134

Romero built an artificial pond with running water channeled from the nearby tributary of the Mantaro River and stocked it with fish. In four years he had raised several thousand fish which he sold locally. This and other farming investments were supported by a loan he received from the Agricultural Development Bank which he was able to obtain with the guarantee of his four and one-half hectares of land and livestock and 9 percent interest. The loan totaled 50,000 *soles* and took him five years to repay.

Romero and his family spent fifteen years developing the farm and its various branches of production. Despite the frequent problems of labor recruitment—always a source of uncertainty—he was able to achieve high levels of productivity and a balanced system of production. In 1952 the government of Peru awarded him a gold medal and a prize of 20,000 *soles* for his work as the best farmer of the central region of the country. The award was presented at the Presidential Palace in Lima by President Odria himself. Romero used the prize money to establish yet another branch of enterprise—one that would eventually shift the balance of his interest away from farming back into commerce.

Restaurateur and Garage Owner

With his property close to the main road, Romero conceived the idea of opening a restaurant and bar. It took four years for the building to be constructed and everything readied for operation. His wife, with the experience of having run a similar but smaller business in Malpaso, managed the enterprise and organized the kitchen, while the elder daughter was made responsible for the general administration of the establishment. Romero, for his part, continued to supervise work on the farm, which had become increasingly concentrated on milk production. He was assisted by his three teen-age sons, who herded the cattle and cultivated the alfalfa. Requiring less labor input than crops, milk production was developed in response to the growing problems of labor supply, as few local peasant families would work for him if they could get employment elsewhere. His unpopularity was due to his isolation from the community on the land litigation issue and his reputation as an authoritarian who underpaid his workers.

While the bulk of the livestock and agricultural products produced on the farm was traded in Lima and the valley markets, the farm also provided food for the restaurant. A regular feature of the menu was trout from Romero's own fish farm. On weekends this attracted large numbers of visitors from Huancayo and Jauja. Romero recalls that one special customer—an airline pilot who flew between Lima and Jauja—never failed to come in for a meal when in the area. The restaurant quickly became a center for dining out for the middle classes of Huancayo and other towns of the valley. The establishment was strategically situated midway between Huancayo and Jauja, and during the late 1950s there were few rival establishments. A temporary setback occurred in 1960 when the trout experiment was suddenly and tragically brought to an end. One morning Romero discovered all his fish floating dead on the surface of the pond. Evidence suggested that they had been poisoned in the night by, as he put it, "his enemies in the pueblo." He never raised any more fish.

Rogelia, his elder daughter, turned out to be an exceptionally able administrator for the restaurant and became well known throughout the valley for the dinner dances she arranged. Indeed, the restaurant business prospered so much that it was necessary to take on additional help in the form of waiters and kitchen staff. For twelve years Rogelia worked for her father but eventually quit to attend to her young children and to start a small shop of her own. In retrospect, she complains that she had no real share in the restaurant business and was only given pocket money. The profits, she claims, together with the income from the farm were used primarily to educate Romero's sons, several of whom went on to complete their secondary schooling.

Rogelia was replaced by her mother, who tried to take over the administration of the restaurant and dealings with the customers. She struggled at the task for three years but gradually the quality of service suffered and the clientele diminished. The administrative problems involved were more than Romero's aging wife could handle, and as a solution Romero rented the restaurant for 900 *soles* a month to his son Andres. Andres was less educated than the other sons, had no specific occupation, and was married, with a rapidly expanding family. He and his wife took over the restaurant but, faced with the growing competition from new restaurants along the road, failed to attract customers.

136

It was at this juncture that Romero launched yet another branch of business. He opened a petrol station which he saw as a natural extension of having a restaurant. If a restaurant stood alongside a petrol pump, then lorry drivers would be encouraged to stop and have a meal after they filled their tanks. The idea of the petrol station originated in 1957 in conversation with a friend in Huancayo who knew the garage business well. This friend happened to be the prefect of Huancayo, a man with whom Romero had first become friends during the legal difficulties he experienced with the community over land and the use of community resources. It was not until 1961, however, that this new project got off the ground. A large loan was needed to finance the building of the pumps and tanks. The total loan, eventually obtained from the Industrial Bank, amounted to 1.5 million *soles* and was to cover the costs for both the construction of the petrol installations and the purchase of two petrol tankers. A loan application for a sum of this magnitude required the careful preparation of financial estimates and a presentation of the economic viability of the project. In this Romero was ably assisted by his friend the prefect—who had the necessary professional and political connections in government and banking circles in Huancayo—and by an old school friend in Matahuasi, a trained accountant who had worked at one time for a garage in the valley and knew firsthand the problems of running a petrol station.

Even with finance secured and installations completed, the opening of the station was delayed because of a conflict between Romero and the local municipality over the siting of the pumps. By placing the pumps alongside the road, Romero had illegally, the municipality claimed, taken over land that in fact was property of the local district. The dispute continued for two years, after which Romero was finally taken to court and ordered to pay a fine. During this time Romero applied to the provincial government for an operating license. With a change of municipal authorities and the election of a new mayor—a distant relative of Romero through his mother's family and a member of the same political party (APRA, Alianza Popular Revolucionaria Americana)—the problem was resolved. Romero was issued an operating license.

The large investment necessitated by the construction of the petrol station and the purchase of tankers meant that Romero was for some seven years weighed down by heavy loan payments. He claims

137

that this kept the garage from showing much net profit until about 1969. Since then he has achieved a fair degree of financial success. By 1972 he owned, in addition to the two tankers, a Volkswagen car and pickup truck. His son Andres was given charge of one of the tankers and made responsible for its operation and maintenance. His daughter Rogelia ran her own small shop and managed jointly with her father the petrol station, the farm, the restaurant, and other assets. The main emphasis of the enterprise, however, was shifted from the restaurant and farm to the development of the petrol business. Romero now had a set of regular contracts for the transportation of petrol, diesel, and paraffin from Lima to various garages and commercial establishments in Huancayo and other valley towns. At his Matahuasi garage he was beginning to put together a spare parts service. Figure 5.1 summarizes the present organization of Romero's enterprise, shows his kin and affines, and gives details on the occupations and places of residence of his children. From this it can be seen that Romero's kinship network contains within it a number of important entrepreneurial families.

THE INFLUENCE OF INTERPERSONAL NETWORKS ON INVESTMENT BEHAVIOR

At the beginning of this paper I drew attention to the value of considering the ways in which economic careers and strategic decisions, such as the setting up of new branches of economic activity, are influenced by the evolution of one's network of interpersonal ties. Social networks, I argued, are essential primarily for the flow of information and for the mobilization of resources necessary for shifts in economic investment. The case of Romero illustrates this point well, for at each stage in the development of his enterprise he became involved in a slightly different matrix of social relationships which in turn opened up new sources of information, assistance, and capital. Indeed, his whole career profile may be interpreted as the outcome of successive changes in the pattern of interpersonal ties based on kinship, affinity, friendship and locality.

In the initial phase of his career, Romero was closely involved as a dependent worker with a set of maternal kin who were emerging as important traders and businessmen in the nearby mine towns. In

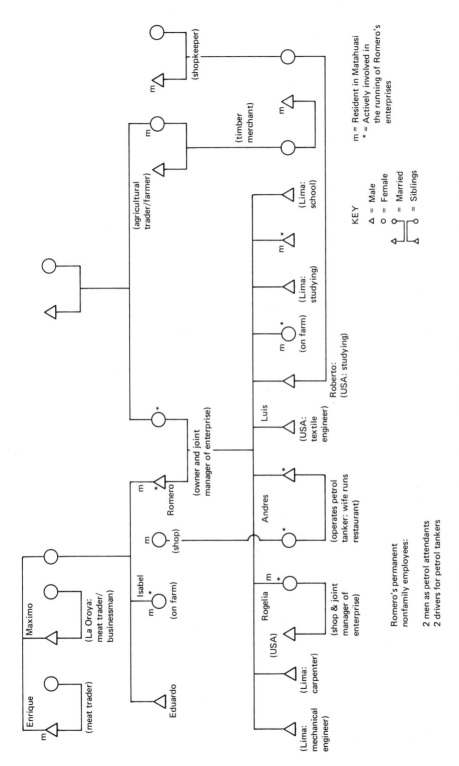

FIGURE 5.1. Genealogy of Romero's family, indicating participants in the multiple enterprise.

transactional terms, Romero's labor was offered in return for his keep and educational expenses. This period of dependence was significant for several reasons. For one, he acquired information and expertise which later proved beneficial when he sought to establish his own independent business. For another, it brought him into contact with his future wife and in-laws, since they were also trading in the towns of the region. After marriage he was able to consolidate this set of affinal ties and, together with his previous contacts, spin a wider web of commercial ties. At this time, his social network consisted predominantly of a combination of maternal and affinal relationships based primarily on commercial interests, and it was this network that determined the direction his investments took in the ensuing years.

The next stage in Romero's career was marked by his decision to rent land in the home community. Although his economic activities were located mainly in Malpaso, the buying of cattle and other products necessitated traveling regularly back to the Mantaro Valley and to nearby areas to build up clientele. In this way he was able to keep channels of information open at the village level, and when land became available for rent, he was quick to hear of it. Having acquired land, Romero and his wife then needed to return to harvest and plant and to supervise the temporary workers whom they employed. Enmeshed in a network of ties in the home community and increasingly involved with local people for the recruitment of labor, they learned early of the possibility of purchasing land from the Church. Romero's situation, in this regard, differed somewhat from that of his two uncles, who had concentrated on developing their businesses in La Oroya and the mine towns and were not therefore so closely involved with peasant production in the Mantaro Valley. Most of their contracts, in fact, were with the haciendas of the Cerro de Pasco Corporation, not with the smaller-scale peasant producer. It is also clear that the marrying of a local girl, whose family both traded and farmed, was crucial for orienting Romero toward land investment and eventual residence in Matahuasi.

Their return to Matahuasi to take up farming full-time could have led to the development of a dense network of local ties with various sectors of the population. Instead, however, whole areas of social relationships were closed off to them. The main reason for this, of course, was the hostility generated by the purchase of land attached

140

to the Catholic saints which the majority of residents regarded as inalienable community property—a hostility which became a political and emotionally charged issue isolating Romero and the other purchasers from the rest of the village. He further experienced difficulties with his fish farm, with the municipality over the expansion of his farming area onto land that was unused but officially under its jurisdiction, and with the site and operation of his petrol station. These particular problems were symptomatic of his generally poor and deteriorating social relations within the village. This situation threatened to affect seriously the running of his farm since he faced constant uncertainties over labor recruitment and over whether the community would win its legal case against him and confiscate his land. He had also acquired a reputation as a tough entrepreneur who exploited his employees. In addition, in 1972 a story circulated through the village that Romero had one day in a rage so severely beaten his young son, when he failed to carry out instructions, that the son died of injuries. According to the family, the boy apparently died of a lung infection.

These difficulties ramified to affect Romero's participation in community affairs. At no time did he hold office in local government or take a prominent part in organizing local fiestas. Even his consanguineal relations were attenuated and prone to conflict. He experienced major disputes with his two maternal uncles who frequently found themselves supporting the village against the larger landowners of the district. Maximo and his brother have always been interested in competing for political status and have held office in local government both in Matahuasi and La Oroya. Maximo, now too old to participate actively, has recently devoted time to furthering his son's political ambitions. During the early 1970s his son was successively mayor and *gobernador* (district governor) of La Oroya. While Romero has tried his best to maintain reasonable relations with Maximo and publicly manifests this once a year when he assists him at the fiesta of Candelaria for which Maximo has been responsible for the past thirty years, their relationship remains distinctly cool. Only during fiesta entertainments is there any attempt at reaffirming family solidarity, and this is very short-lived.

Over the years Romero has retained little contact with his brother in Lima. He occasionally visits him but there is no effort to develop close bonds. On the other hand, Romero maintains continued good

141

relations with his sister who helps on the farm; their relationship is marked, nonetheless, by a pattern of deference shown by her to Romero and to his daughter Rogelia. His links with his wife's kin constitute the most secure sector of his kinship network and it is with them that he interacts most frequently in business and recreational contexts. His most successful attempt to build new linkages in Matahuasi is through the marriage of his son Roberto to the daughter of the largest shopkeeper in the village. His son's father-in-law, a man from Arequipa, in southern Peru, is married to a Matahuasi woman and himself has an extensive set of ties with commercial and professional people both in the valley and elsewhere. Like Romero, he remains somewhat aloof from local affairs.

As a result of the deterioration of social relations in the village, Romero has been forced to develop new types of external ties. This first arose because of his need for legal advice and administrative support in his disputes with the community. Gradually he established a network of links with lawyers and members of APRA who held important positions at the regional level. During the late 1950s through 1960s, APRA dominated the politics of the Mantaro area and represented a broadly based rural bourgeoisie composed of farm6ers, businessmen, and middle-class professionals. It was in this context, then, that Romero sought to align himself with persons from outside Matahuasi who might recognize his entrepreneurial talents and give him support. Several of these newfound friends became godparents to his children and were thus tied to him through compadrazgo relationships. As I have argued elsewhere (Long 1973a), compadrazgo in Highland Peru takes two basic forms: it can be used to select out of an existing kin or affinal network relationships of special significance; or it can be used to create a set of strategically important non-kin ties that, for the most part, are located outside one's village of origin. Often the latter type of relationship is with a person of slightly higher social status or with a business partner or political ally. Table 5.1 shows that of five compadres of Romero, only one is a Matahuasino by origin, but even he has spent most of his life working outside the valley and is presently retired in Lima. Each of these compadres appears to have been chosen carefully for his access to important contacts outside. Two are large-scale middlemen who assumed significance in the marketing of Romero's agricultural and livestock products, one a senior official on

TABLE 5.1
ROMERO'S COMPADRES

	Place of Residence	Place of Origin	Occupation	How Contacted and When	Extent of Present Contact
1.	Tarma (Central Highlands)	Tarma (Central Highlands)	Agricultural Intermediary/Farmer	Through trading of farm products during 1940s.	Occasional visits.
2.	Miami (U.S.A.)	Cajamarca Valley (Northern Peru)	Businessman	Was trading partner for livestock during 1930s.	By letter only but helped sons in U.S.A.
3.	Huancayo	Huancayo	Lawyer/Administrator (now retired)	When he was Prefect of Huancayo in early 1950s.	Regular weekly visits.
4.	Lima	Matahuasi	Chief Telegrapher on Railways (now retired)	From 1930 onward when he transported livestock and meat products by train.	Occasional visits.
5.	Lima	Huancayo	Lawyer (now working in Supreme Court, Lima)	When he practiced law in Huancayo during 1940–50s. He was senator for the Department of Junin in the early 1960s.	Occasional visits but helped with road accident case.

the railway, and the other two, professionals with legal training and an extensive network of friends in regional government. The latter two were crucial in assisting Romero explore new types of investment. One of them—the prefect of Huancayo—originated the idea of a garage, as mentioned earlier, and put Romero in touch with his relatives who owned petrol stations. The prefect also helped in working out costs and presenting the loan application to the Industrial Bank. The other played his part by offering legal advice when Romero faced opposition from the municipality over the siting of the petrol pumps.

These stages in the development of Romero's enterprise were accompanied, then, by the evolution of a set of ties with persons of higher social status than himself who lived and worked in the major urban centers of the region. These were persons with whom he might not in the ordinary course of events have come into direct contact. Paradoxically it was because of the series of complicated legal cases involving him and the village that the occasion arose for him to develop these relationships. This is also brought out by the list of best friends he names: of six persons indicated, two are lawyers who worked for him during the land disputes and whom he has used more recently in connection with a road accident case. One lives in Concepción and the other in Jauja. The remaining four all currently live in Matahuasi but have urban experience and contacts (see table 5.2).

Unlike the petrol business, which was initiated by the development of an external network of friends and compadres, the restaurant and shop were primarily a response to the growth of Romero's nuclear family. As Benedict (1968) has observed, it is usual for family firms to begin new branches of production so that their adult children might be settled in their own businesses. A similar process occurred with Romero's enterprise, though the question of educational investment must also be considered.

Investment in the education of children provides an alternative to joining the firm, for it offers the possibility of entering professions or skilled occupations. As Figure 5.1 shows, several of Romero's sons were educated to the secondary or postsecondary level and practice occupations that, in the short run at least, seem unlikely to bring them back to Matahuasi to work with their father. Two of them live in the United States—one working as an engineer in a textile factory, the other studying fine arts and design—and four live in

144

TABLE 5.2
ROMERO'S FRIENDS

	Place of Residence	Place of Origin	Occupation	How Relationship Formed and When	Extent of Present Contact
1.	Matahuasi	Matahuasi	Accountant/Small farmer	Old school friends.	Regular visits; gives advice on accounts.
2.	Matahuasi	Matahuasi	Bar Owner/Electrician	Distant maternal kinsman.	Regular visits; gives electrical help.
3.	Matahuasi	Arequipa	Shopkeeper	Commercial relationship developed during 1950s.	Regular visits; daughter married to Romero's son.
4.	Matahuasi	Matahuasi	Carpenter (now retired)	Distant maternal kinsman; he was Mayor of Matahuasi during early 1960s; member of same political party.	Infrequent visits.
5.	Jauja	Jauja	Lawyer	Helped with disputes with community over Church land during 1940s and 1950s.	Regular weekly visits; helped with accident case.
6.	Concepción	Concepción	Lawyer	Same as above.	Regular weekly visits.

Lima—two working in skilled jobs, the other two finishing their secondary schooling. Of the remaining sons, one is young and still at school in Matahuasi; the other, Andres, works with his father in the petrol business. Romero's two daughters both received some education but left school before they had completed their secondary course. The elder, Rogelia, now plays a major part in the management of the enterprise, and her younger sister lends a hand on the farm and in the restaurant.

From this it appears that Romero has invested a fair percentage of his income in the education of his children, but this has resulted in several of them leaving home to seek fortunes elsewhere. Two of his sons and a son-in-law, the husband of Rogelia, eventually went to the United States, the others to Lima. After one of these sons, Luis, had unsuccessfully tried to enter the Engineering University in Lima, he was sent to complete his education at a U.S. college in Miami, Florida, where Romero's compadre from Cerro de Pasco had himself settled. With assistance from the compadre, Luis finished his training and is now for all intents and purposes permanently settled in the United States; one index of this is that he was drafted into military service and sent to Vietnam for a year. After his return to Miami, he married a Cuban woman and was later joined in Miami by his brother and brother-in-law. They likewise seem committed to making careers for themselves in the United States. It is, of course, possible that when Romero dies they will return to Peru to try to secure a share of the family property, but for the time being they remain abroad and uninvolved in the family business. The recent marriage of the other son, Roberto, into a prominent commerical family in Matahuasi—a marriage Romero seemed instrumental in arranging—can be interpreted as a way of encouraging his closer involvement with the family network in Matahuasi. After the marriage, however, the young couple traveled to the United States to live.

The establishment of the restaurant, which followed the difficulties Romero faced in expanding his farm, was aimed at giving his wife and the elder daughter an area of special responsibility within the enterprise. The daughter assumed an increasingly larger role in the restaurant business and later graduated to share joint management of the petrol station as well as other economic concerns.

146

Rogelia also manages her own shop, which she operates independently of the family firm. One son, Andres, also tried the restaurant business but on a formal contract basis; that is, he was expected to rent the facilities from his father at a fixed monthly rate. Andres and his wife, however, took over the restaurant at a time when competition was fiercer, and they had no flair for the task. Romero eventually offered Andres financial backing for the purchase of a new petrol tanker which Andres would operate himself within the already established petrol business. By handing out financial incentives of this kind, Romero, it seems, was maneuvering to keep these two children closely tied to the family business. This was essential for survival of the family firm, for his commitment to educating his sons had worked against him and he was unable to utilize their labor and skills in further expansion of the business. The first signs of his family slipping away occurred early on when he found difficulty in securing enough labor for agricultural production. At this time several of his children were teen-agers who could have helped regularly but for the fact that they were away at school. This was one of the factors affecting his decision to shift to livestock production and to open a restaurant which would make better use of the female labor available. After this decision, his strategy has been to diversify more, moving away from agriculture toward providing services for road transport, and to employ more labor permanently from outside the village rather than depending upon temporary workers recruited locally. Indeed, in 1972 only one of his four permanent employees was from Matahuasi.

The later period in Romero's career, then, has been a joint product of increasing external ties which have integrated him more effectively into the regional commercial structure, and of pressures existing within the village and within his own nuclear family as a result of earlier decisions made about his children's education. He is a true cosmopolitan in orientation: his main sets of relationships extend well beyond the village to the towns and cities of the region, to Lima, the metropolitan capital, and to the United States. The only viable set of local relationships he maintains is with the small number of families in the area who have relatively high economic status as traders and farmers and who, for the most part, form the central links in his network of kin and affines.

SPRINGBOARDS AND CONSTRAINTS

Although I have not been able to document fully the specific transactions and social investments made by Romero, the entrepreneur, during the development of his economic career, I have attempted to show, following the work of Leeds (1964), the importance of identifying the emergence of social networks that served as springboards to new forms of economic activity. I have also suggested that the notion of springboards deals with only one side of the matter since continual use of particular social ties tends to impose boundaries or constraints on actions and decisions. In order to explore this latter aspect adequately, it would be necessary to provide a detailed account of the norms and expectations associated with each type of relationship, as well as an evaluation of the costs and benefits involved. A closer analysis of Romero's relationship with his uncle Maximo, for example, showing how the pattern of transactions and normative expectations were modified over time, would have been useful. A similar analysis might be made of the various compadrazgo relationships which Romero established during his career.

The kinds of springboards associated with Romero's enterprise are, I believe, of more general significance for understanding economic careers in the Central Highlands of Peru. In the first place, there exists a closely knit kin network which—depending on the skills, contacts, and resources of the particular people concerned—initially determines the direction of a person's early career. This is especially the case when entering the urban labor market for the first time since the neophyte will likely gravitate toward fellow kinsmen and paisanos (persons of the same rural origin) who in turn are likely to help him to find work in the same economic sector as their own (Long 1973a; Alderson-Smith 1975; Laite 1975).

A second springboard is the set of affinal relationships which a man derives through marriage and which may open up new fields of participation, making available new types of material and nonmaterial resources. In a previous paper (Long 1973a) I illustrated the kinds of social transactions that occur between brothers-in-law and showed their significance for the exchange of labor and information. Affinal relationships between members of the same generation do not, it appears, exhibit the same degree of tension and competition

148

or conflict that characterizes bonds between siblings. A main reason for this is that the parties involved do not directly vie with one another for control over inheritable wealth.[4]

Another important set of ties is that which a man develops through membership in a political party or regional association.[5] Ties of this type frequently crosscut rural and urban areas and thus become important in orienting the individual to a wide range of rural and urban contexts. Membership in such organizations seems particularly significant for entrepreneurs specializing in transport or in the marketing of agricultural produce. These fields are highly competitive, and associational affiliations provide protection against competing groups (Long 1972, 1973b).

Another springboard, which in Romero's case was critical, is the set of links with professional persons such as lawyers, doctors, and administrators. This network is valuable for the flow of general information and specialist advice, and for the provision of additional contacts with government personnel and institutions. Like Romero, most aspiring entrepreneurs will attempt to cultivate professional friends who may help them lobby the government or who will introduce them to persons of political or economic status.

Certain types of entrepreneurial careers require, in addition, a springboard into the system of social relationships at the local level. This is particularly the case if a person is originally an outsider and operates in a field of economic activity—for example, an agricultural middleman—that requires close connections with the peasant population in order to know when and where produce is ready for purchase. The maintenance of such a network calls for considerable skill and tenacity on the part of the entrepreneur who may be expected to participate actively in village fiestas or other voluntary activities.

While emphasizing the positive aspects of these springboards it is equally important to note the kinds of restrictions which they may effect. The continued use of the same set of ties will tend to give rise to a highly dense and involuted network which can impose considerable constraints on the person (Bott 1957; Long 1973a). Sometimes the very restrictions and pressures that develop lead to new ventures and new phases in a career, even if this requires the repudiation of relationships where there is a high degree of affective and normative content. One aspect of this process is illustrated in

149

the case of Romero when the entrepreneur breaks close ties with his maternal kin in order to consolidate an affinal network. The difficulties with his maternal kin are further exacerbated in the conflict with the community over Church land. These same problems, however, lead in the longer term to his establishing various external relationships which generate new and different forms of economic investment.

Hence an analysis of economic careers must allow for a dialectical process whereby a person builds up a set of springboards but later finds that in order to advance he must reject these and proceed in a different way. These changes and shifts in career pattern, I suggest, are best seen as contingent upon the person having developed certain relationships or having made certain investments which themselves produce unintended or unforeseen consequences. Moreover, it is characteristic of the situation in which Romero finds himself that careers are discontinuous in that they are not clearly predetermined from the outset by skills, assets, and occupational niche. In the Mantaro region, as in other Third World contexts, there are but few instances of bureaucratic careers where the steps in the ladder have been clearly placed according to a fixed pattern.

ECONOMIC CAREERS AND THE FLOW OF INFORMATION

Implicit in the foregoing discussion is the significance of information as a factor in the development of careers. Several scholars have suggested that in analyzing the flow of information one must distinguish between two zones or sectors in a social network:[6] that which is a tightly organized set of ties, often focusing upon particular institutional contexts or social groupings, for example, family and kinship groups or religious and political associations; and that which comprises a more extended, loosely knit network of dyadic relationships. The latter, it is argued, functions as the means by which information is fed from one institutional context or social grouping into another. Accordingly, the study of entrepreneurial careers requires close attention to the form and structure of social networks and to the ways that information of various types flows within them. Viewing this process diachronically, one can see that during an entrepreneur's lifetime the significance and composition of these two sectors of the network will vary. Romero's career, for example, consisted of a combination of a tightly organized core of ties and a more dispersed, loosely organized set. The types of relationships constituting the central core changed over time: he was first enmeshed in a set of maternal kin, then in an affinal grouping, and lastly in a friendship and compadrazgo network which extended well beyond the bounds of village. The passage of time also saw certain ties in his nuclear family assume importance. Other entrepreneurs exhibit a slightly different pattern. For example, transporters in Matahuasi develop close bonds of friendship with one another and with intermediaries through their joint membership and control of a fiesta club. This provides a flexible institutional framework where social and economic exchanges take place and acquire symbolic meaning (Long 1972).

The two sectors of an entrepreneur's network become further significant for the flow of information brought to bear on different types of decisions. Information pertaining to strategic decisions—that is, concerning changes in the branch of economic activity pursued or relating to new forms of investment—generally flows through a series of weak ties which form part of the extended network, and not through relationships where there is a high degree of interaction and normative consensus. On the other hand, information concerning the availability of basic resources or inputs necessary for the everyday operation of an enterprise will tend to flow between persons whose ties are strong and consolidated. This latter point is illustrated by the way traders and transporters maintain close bonds among themselves and with their business partners in order that information about contracts and available produce can be passed on easily. A similar pattern operates for commercial farmers who regularly organize exchanges for labor and information with their neighbors and kinsmen.

The significance of weak ties in social networks has recently been emphasized by Granovetter (1973) who suggests their importance not only for the manipulation of networks but also for their function as channels through which ideas, influences, and information socially distant from ego may reach him.[7] Granovetter develops this idea in relation to information on job mobility and to general literature on the diffusion of innovation. Information, he contends, travels more quickly if it travels through weak ties that link together clusters of relatively dense sets of relationships. Moreover, the more weak ties a person has, the more information he is likely to receive, and conversely the better placed he is to distribute it, directly or indirectly, to a wider range of people. In job seeking, for instance, a loosely knit network of weak ties will provide access to more varied sources of information from a greater variety of people than a more dense personal network which lacks extensions beyond the common circle. On the other hand, once information is received concerning the availability of a job or the possibility for a new type of economic investment, it is obviously better to activate strong ties where trust and support are important if one wishes to make the fullest use of the information. Weak ties may help with the provision of vital information but they will not necessarily bring the best results.

The success of an entrepreneur, therefore, lies in his ability to integrate both these elements in his network. He must spin a widespread network of weak ties and keep their channels open while he develops a set of closely knit, dependable relationships to assist him in utilizing his resources effectively. The structure of his network will alter over time—some strong ties will become weak and some weak ties strong. There will be shifts in the emphasis placed on particular types of relationships and their contents. Depending on the sociocultural context, the viability of some relationships, like kinship, will change considerably. And there will be differences in the ways relationships within a common frame are activated and consolidated. The social costs involved in keeping open weak ties will, I believe, vary according to the type of relationship. Some, like consanguineal bonds or ties of compadrazgo, require little effort beyond the basic requirement of occasional interaction, for they form part of a persisting cultural framework with generalized norms and values. Other relationships that are more instrumental or transitory in character, like buyer-seller relationships or political alliances, will cease to exist once specific types of exchanges are terminated. The latter, therefore, need constantly to be renewed through the joint participation of the parties concerned.

Some weak ties function to link two or more relatively dense sectors in a network or between networks. Granovetter (1973) calls these relationships "local bridges"; others (Boissevain 1974; Allen and Cohen 1969) have suggested the terms "broker" or "gatekeeper" for the person occupying such a position. Brokers are important in the

152

flow of information as they command access to socially distant relationships and resources, and hence often play a significant role in opening up new sources of economic activity and investment. In the case of Romero there are several examples of brokers. First, Maximo, with whom he now maintains a rather distant relationship, has connections with businessmen and political figures in La Oroya and the mining towns in the event Romero needs to use them, as he did as a trader in Malpaso. Second, his compadre in Huancayo, at one time the prefect, provides links with influential persons in commerce and politics at the regional level. Third, his other compadre, who lives in the United States, offers indirect contacts with various persons and institutions which have proved helpful for Romero's sons. Finally, the Matahuasi businessman whose daughter recently married Romero's son, Roberto, is integrated into a network of links with local Matahuasino farmers and shopkeepers which could be useful should Romero decide to align himself more firmly with the local economic elite. This last relationship could become strategically important in the near future as the group has recently assumed control over the municipal government (Long and Winder 1975).

These comments on the significance of interpersonal networks in the flow of information must suffice. The direction of the argument here is toward recognition of the need to analyze the effects of interpersonal ties on the development of economic careers.

THE STRUCTURAL CONCOMITANTS OF MULTIPLE ENTERPRISE

In concluding this paper I wish to return briefly to the phenomenon of multiple enterprise posed at the outset. My aim is to identify the structural conditions associated with the development of economically diversified careers like that of Romero. I concentrate on the broad features of the regional socioeconomic structure.[8]

The main features of the regional system in the Mantaro area may be characterized as follows. The system is highly diversified in terms of the economic functions it encompasses. There are important mining centers near the valley, and the majority of the labor force for these mines is supplied by villages in the valley. This same

153

population has also worked on the coastal cotton plantations and was a major contributor to the growth of the labor force of Lima. The surrounding highlands are the location of Peru's largest and most modernized cattle haciendas, which have recently been affected by the government's land reform program. The primary city of the area, Huancayo, which in 1972 had a population of 116,000, is one of Peru's fastest growing cities, is a major commercial and administrative center, and once possessed a textile industry employing some three thousand workers. The rural-agricultural scene exhibits great diversity of interrelated forms of production and land tenure. There also exists a system of markets and marketing ranging from traditional barter exchange through rotating village markets, *ferias*, catering to local consumption needs, to large distribution markets that buy the local surplus for Lima-Callao. Alongside these markets, and in many ways more important than they, are the individual traders and middlemen of the villages who are responsible for the movement of most of the 25 percent of Lima's food needs that this area supplies. Some villages engage in small-scale craft production which is aimed mainly at a tourist market. As a whole, the region comprises a complex mix of agricultural, commercial, craft, industrial, and service activities. It also possesses a considerable variety of organizational forms. Hence there exist both household- and firm-based enterprises, a large number of production, distribution, and service cooperatives, various types of recreational and welfare associations, and an abundance of government development agencies.

A second major feature of the socioeconomic structure is the relatively low degree of economic integration and centralization in the region. For example, the bulk of agricultural produce is marketed directly from the villages to the principal centers of the coast; it does not pass through Huancayo or through the hands of Huancayo-based entrepreneurs. Though there is a major wholesale market in Huancayo, it derives most of its business from trade with the more remote provinces outside the area, and the volume of business it handles is much less than that of valley traders. Moreover, although Huancayo is a distribution center for dry goods and manufactured items originating from the coast, its function in this regard is diminished by the fact that the major villages make purchases directly from firms in Lima. This practice has been facilitated by the development of excellent road communications with the coast since the 1940s. Even in the field of administrative services, there is a general tendency to negotiate directly with the government in Lima, often using Lima-based associations representing village and provincial interests in the capital, rather than with the regional government based in Huancayo. The same tendency to use Lima as a center of activity is reflected in the higher proportion of the area's university and secondary school students in Lima than in Huancayo, which also has a university and good secondary schools. Labor migration data, furthermore, indicate no consistent stage migration such as has been documented in other Latin American contexts. That is to say, large villages like Matahuasi, only ten miles from Huancayo, have greater out-migration directly to Lima than to Huancayo or the mines.

Another feature of the area is that economic resources are highly dispersed. In the field of agriculture it is common for a household to have its land (average size of landholding in the valley is about one and one-half hectares) divided into a number of small plots located in different parts of the village or adjoining settlements. Some families also hold land in the distant tropical lowlands or in other places outside the valley. The different systems of land tenure, which range from private freehold to various sharecropping and renting arrangements, have the consequence that some plots are held by persons living temporarily or permanently outside the village. On the other hand, villagers may themselves own, and from time to time use, houses in Huancayo, Jauja, La Oroya, and Lima. This dispersal of property holding is often associated with the operation of trading and small industrial enterprises. There is, for example, a group of traders who live in Matahuasi but control property and businesses in La Oroya; another group resides in the nearby village of Sicaya but runs a small garment industry with workshops located in Huancayo. The operation of transport, timber processing, or agricultural intermediary businesses likewise necessitates networks of relationships in different localities. For example, timber, purchased in small lots from farmers in the valley and the tropical lowlands, is sold in the mining and urban centers of the region.

This dispersal of economic resources is, in part, an outcome of the valley's critical variations in microecology and climate. Another factor is the long history of labor and household mobility which has

155

enabled villagers of the valley not only to colonize labor centers but also to acquire land in the tropical lowlands and the highland pastoral zone. These different places constitute valuable resources for the people of the Mantaro Valley, in the same way that the valley provides for those who reside outside it and wish, for whatever reason, to retain active involvement in village affairs.

The counterpart to the dispersal of economic resources is the small-scale nature of economic activity. In Huancayo and in the small towns and villages there are no large-scale stable enterprises. This is evident in agriculture, where the tendency has been for holdings to fragment and where, in the absence of large permanent out-migration from the countryside, no significant consolidation of land has taken place. The same is true for the organization of transport which is made up of independent operators who maintain close informal ties but have not developed any corporate form. Thus, although there are some several hundred trucks operating in the valley, there is not one trucking company. A transport cooperative does exist, but its members own their trucks individually and profits are based upon individual effort. The primary function of the cooperative is the dissemination of information on loads and contracts. Eighty-one bus companies are registered in Huancayo, but most are made up of single bus owners who combine in order to secure a route, coordinate timetables, and share the expenses of running an office. Similar patterns are found in trading and industrial ventures. Apart from some of the Lima-owned and foreign trading companies in Huancayo, large-scale, formally constituted, trading or industrial firms are nonexistent. Indeed, the tendency has been for the large firm to be replaced by small ones. Huancayo's large-scale textile industry, which at its height employed three thousand workers in four factories, has now been replaced by four hundred textile workshops, each with an average of seven employees, and by a newly formed textile cooperative of two hundred and fifty members. None of the larger trading, industrial, or agricultural ventures in the rural sector employs more than seven permanent workers. So apparent is the prevalence of small-scale business that one is led to compare this to the Indonesian bazaar-type economy described by Geertz (1963).

The persistence of small-scale enterprise is, I believe, largely explained by the diversified, dispersed nature of resources, the generally low-level capitalization of the economy, which continually

156

suffers a drain of resources to the coastal metropolis, and by the high degree of uncertainty that exists in the regional and national markets. Despite these unfavorable conditions, many cases of successful entrepreneurship by persons of peasant origin can be documented. Such persons succeed in expanding their businesses by investing capital in new, though often complementary, enterprises. Economic expansion through increasing specialization of function seems unlikely; heavy losses might ensue should the market suddenly contract.

These multiple enterprises, like that of Romero, are often organized in terms of a division of labor between the members of a household or extended family and operate on a profit-sharing basis. This pattern of organization reduces labor costs and provides junior members with some leeway in the pursuit of their own economic strategies—though it can at the same time lead to conflicts of authority and status. Much depends, it seems, on the management skills of the senior partners who, in order to generate profit and maintain a stable set of internal ties, must establish recognized conventions and operating standards. They must also negotiate with the parties concerned to define more precisely the nature of the rights and obligations and, if necessary, attempt to differentiate them from the more diffuse kinship norms and expectations. An analysis of these internal organizational problems is, as I have argued elsewhere (Long 1973a), fundamental for assessing the viability of enterprises and for appreciating the specific sociocultural forms that characterize the entrepreneur in the Mantaro Valley.

An additional dimension is the entrepreneur's external network of social relationships. The network provides him with information and other resources relevant to the running of his business. The form and structure of this network is, as I have shown, a major determinant of the career his pursues. The foregoing case study has developed this idea and explored how setting up new branches of economic activity was to a large degree a consequence of already existing interpersonal ties. The kinds of opportunities and relationships that emerged, however, were conditioned also by the nature of the regional socioeconomic structure and its transformations over time. The last part of this chapter has attempted to characterize in broad outline the main features of this macrostructure. Hence, while Romero's career is unique in that it can be viewed as a prod-

157

uct of the evolution of particular patterns of interpersonal relationships, it is, I maintain, also typical of certain forms and styles of entrepreneurship which have emerged in the Mantaro Valley. How similar are the patterns and processes which occur in other Third World contexts remains to be seen.

NOTES

1. The field material on which this paper is based was collected in 1971–72 and formed part of a larger project, "Regional Structure and Entrepreneurship in a Peruvian Valley." This project was jointly directed by Dr. Bryan Roberts (University of Manchester) and myself, and was funded by grants from the Ford Foundation and from the Social Science Research Council of the United Kingdom. Mr. Teófilo Altamirano of the Catholic University, Lima, assisted with the collection of field material for this paper.

2. In order to retain the anonymity of all persons, pseudonyms have been used.

3. At the time 4 Peruvian *soles* were roughly equivalent to one U.S. dollar. The Church sold about 140 hectares in Matahuasi. There was no valuation of land, no public auction, and the land was sold below the market value. The price per hectare varied considerably: early purchasers like Romero paid about 500 *soles*, whereas three years later the price had risen to 1,500 *soles* or more.

4. The inheritance system is bilateral with equal division of property among children of both sexes; how far the rules are followed, though, depends on the family circumstances and whether or not the property is formally registered.

5. Regional associations are organizations whose main function is to bring together migrants from the same village or region. They vary considerably in their activities, some catering primarily to the recreational needs of their members and others combining this with fund raising and lobbying activities in order to promote the development of home communities. Associations of this type are common in the mine towns and in Lima-Callao. For details, see Mangin (1959), Doughty (1970), and Long (1973b).

6. See Aubey, Kyle, and Strickon (1974), who distinguish between formal groups and informal, extended networks; Epstein (1963), who differentiates between "effective" and "extended" networks among miners on the Zambian Copperbelt; and Leeds (1964), who draws attention to what he calls dispersed networks and organized cliques among members of the Brazilian elite.

7. Granovetter (1973) does not explicitly define what he means by "weak ties," but from his definition of "strong ties" (1973:1361) we can conclude that the term refers to relationships where no pronounced mutal investment occurs but where there is some mutual acknowledgment of the relationship beyond merely being acquainted. Weak ties, then, are more than nodding relationships.

8. For a fuller treatment, see Long and Roberts (1975).

6
Ethnicity and Entrepreneurship in Rural Wisconsin

ARNOLD STRICKON

Department of Anthropology
University of Wisconsin–Madison

The analysis of elite social structure and investment behavior in Latin America by Robert Aubey, John Kyle, and myself (1974) was based upon the investigation of large, powerful, nationally significant, kinship-focused social aggregates in Latin America. We realized at the time that this model, which examined the social and economic variables that produced both investment decisions and social structural arrangements, was probably not limited in its applicability to wealthy Latin Americans. Not only was there a question of the degree to which this model was "culture specific," but also there was a question of how far this model was applicable as the scale and complexity of resources was reduced. A research project planned several years ago on ethnic differences among European immigrants in a rural community in Wisconsin presented the unanticipated opportunity to address these questions.[1]

The original Aubey, Kyle, and Strickon (1974) model was in contrast to standard portfolio investment models that assumed equal access to information by all participants in the market at no cost. Our model assumed instead unequal accessibility of information at a cost. It demonstrated the reduced risk an informational edge affords,

159

but it also showed that the cost of the reduced risk is a smaller return (that is, the gross return less the cost of information gathering).

At this point, however, several anthropological and sociological concepts were plugged into the revised portfolio model. Information, it was suggested, becomes part of a series of social exchanges and transactions—prestations in ongoing social relationships—and, as such, may be without a direct financial cost. Under these conditions, the marginal financial cost of information is "zero," and the possessor of that information has an equally high return as well as a reduced risk vis-à-vis "outsiders." This flow of information, imbedded in multiplex transactions and prestations, will reinforce existing social relationships and help to create new ones.

In the case of the Latin American examples with which the 1974 paper dealt, the core of the social groupings was large, extended family networks with individual members scattered widely and ensconced in a variety of significant positions in the society. Around the kinship core were other persons, sometimes linking several families through marriage, tied by a complex series of social and economic transactions.

Even the most cursory examination of small agricultural service centers in the midlands of the United States would reveal no kinship-structured investment groups comparable in extent, resources, influence, or power to the "great families" analyzed in the 1974 paper. Yet the analysis was not of kin-focused investment groups but rather of the processes which led to the generation, emergence, and persistence of these structures. The question, then, is to what degree this model of process can also, with appropriate alterations in inputs of variables and changes in the relevant parameters, "explain" or order investment practices and associated structural arrangements in a small agricultural community in the American Midwest.

The rest of this paper will concentrate upon three men who were active entrepreneurs in the same Wisconsin county. The first of these men, Albert Field, was an early pioneer. The other two, Martin Bekkedahl and Jens Vigdahl, were Norwegian immigrants whose careers spanned the last decades of the nineteenth century through the early 1970s.

THE SETTING[2]

In 1851, three years after Wisconsin had achieved statehood, the state legislature in Madison raised the township of Bad Axe, in Crawford County, to the status of a county in its own right. Eleven years later, the legislature changed the name of Bad Axe County to Vernon County according to the wishes of its residents. Since that time, little of historic note has occurred there. A recent history of Wisconsin (Nesbit 1973) does not even mention the county by name, except in tables, in over five hundred pages of text. Rather, the ups and downs of Vernon County's economy, the waves of its immigrants, the building of its railroads and highways, and the peaks and valleys of its political changes are dealt with within the sweep of state and regional movements.

Today Vernon County covers 814 square miles of southwestern Wisconsin and is home to some 25,000 people. Extending about forty-four miles from its western boundary on the Mississippi River to its eastern edge near the city of Hillsboro, the county lies athwart the unglaciated, driftless zone of southwestern Wisconsin. Angular in shape, the county looks on a map like an abstract drawing of a hand with its index and middle fingers pointing east, with its wrist at the Mississippi River. The county seat, Viroqua, is located in the center of the county—less than one hundred miles from the state capital in Madison and about thirty-five miles from La Crosse, the major urban center of western Wisconsin. The county is equidistant from metropolitan Milwaukee and the urban complex at Minneapolis–St. Paul, the latter tending to draw more local people than the former.

As it has always been, the county today is predominantly rural. About one-fourth of the population of 25,000 lives in the three cities of Viroqua, Westby, and Hillsboro, with over 3,000 in Viroqua. Another 16 percent of the population resides in nine incorporated villages which have an average population of 426, ranging from 215 to 750. The other 59 percent of the population of the county lives on farms scattered through the open countryside, with a few in unincorporated "places."

The driftless zone in which Vernon County is located is an area of great natural beauty, a fact appreciated by its residents. A large

161

rolling prairie bisects the county in a north-south direction while to both the east and west of this prairie the land is carved by deep, steep, heavily wooded valleys generally known as coulees in the western part of the county and as hollows ("hollers") in the eastern part. This rough landscape runs into the valley of the Kickapoo River, which cuts the county from north to south at a point fourteen miles west of the county's eastern boundary. Geologically the county rests upon sandstone, limestone, and quartzite strata which are covered by a variety of loams (Hole et al., 1968; Martin 1974). The natural cover of the area is hardwood forest although this has been almost completely cleared on the large central prairie and at the bottoms of the coulees.

This is a county of family farms; it has one of the highest incidences of family-owned and operated farms in the state. At present, Vernon County is devoted largely to dairy farming and is one of the top dairy producers in the state. Another major crop is tobacco, and again Vernon County is one of the state's major producers. The tobacco farms are located in the central prairie and adjacent valleys—generally the same areas which are centers of Norwegian settlement. Although tobacco is found elsewhere in the county, the concentration is less than it is in the central prairie.

The contemporary distribution of crops has altered since earlier periods of the county's history. The region was initially devoted to wheat, while hops and other industrial crops were raised widely. Plant blights as well as changing market conditions have led to the shift in crop patterns.

The population of Vernon County derives from a multiplicity of backgrounds. The first European settlers in what is now Vernon County were from New England and northern New York State. These "Yankees" established themselves in the central prairie and founded the town of Viroqua, arriving in the mid 1840s, a few years before Wisconsin statehood in 1848, when the area was still a township of Crawford County. By 1850, however, the Yankees lost their monopoly of the county, as numerous European immigrants moved into the region. A small Italian population settled on the banks of the Mississippi River. This group, northern Italians and Italian Swiss, had apparently come north from the lead mines around Galena, Illinois. They set up businesses to serve river traffic, fished, and later moved to farm the adjacent ridges and coulees. Around them settled a Catholic German population, as Lutheran Germans put down roots in the northwestern corner of the county.

Immigration also came to the central prairie. English, Scottish, and Irish immigrants fitted easily with the early Yankee settlers living in the southern part of the prairie. In the 1850s, large numbers of Norwegians began to move into the area. People from Sognefjord in western Norway now settled where only Yankee and English-Irish populations had lived a few years earlier. A few miles to the north of this area, other Norwegians, mostly from Gudbrandsdal in eastern Norway, moved into a previously unsettled region.

Farther to the east, in the Kickapoo River Valley, the Yankee population was added to by settlers from border states and the southern mountains. This area was known throughout the 1850s as a nest of Copperheads, as the group's southern sympathies remained untemporized until the actual outbreak of the Civil War.

The eastern part of the county, centering on Hillsboro, was settled somewhat later than the rest of the county, in 1852. Unlike the other areas of the county, where Yankees were clearly the first settlers, many of the earliest immigrants to the region were Germans. They, and some Irish as well, had come to Wisconsin after earlier settlement in other midwestern states of the East Coast. These waves of immigrants also reached Hillsboro. Since 1880 and continuing through the present, there has been a continual movement of Bohemians (or, as they now prefer to call themselves, Czechs) into the area.

The distribution of these various European immigrant groups over the county remains essentially the same to this day.

A YANKEE PIONEER-ENTREPRENEUR

The Yankees were the pioneers, or so they pictured themselves. They were the first to settle what is now Hillsboro, and they were the first to settle in the county. In American folklore these pioneers are generally portrayed as farmers. At best, this view is an oversimplification. Although it is true that they farmed in the early years, for many of them farming was a means of survival until more significant opportunities came to fruition. Whatever else they might have been, farmer, businessman, or doctor, they were ready to take advantage of business opportunities. In the case of Hillsboro, business speculation was more the attraction than the availability of inexpensive government land to farm.

The Hills brothers, founders of Hillsboro, were the first to lay claim to land in eastern Vernon County and the first to plat what was to become the village of Hillsboro. They displayed another Yankee characteristic—the desire, at times the drive, to move on, to go west, to seek a new frontier. Within a few years they did exactly that, leaving no descendants and making no further mark on the community.

Actually Albert Field, a New Englander, was the effective founder of Hillsboro. Born in Maine in 1821, he arrived in Vernon County in 1852. In 1854 he made the first settlement on the site of the village.

For Field and his fellow settlers, Hillsboro offered few amenities. Since the village was cut off from the rest of the county, wheat had to be carried to Baraboo, a distance of thirty-five air miles, to be ground into flour and then either traded for other items or returned for home use—a two-or-three-day round trip. Yet, Field imagined, a branch of the Baraboo River could provide the power for a water-driven mill in Hillsboro itself. The mill could produce flour not only for Hillsboro but also for the areas north and east of the new settlement. The water power potential offered other opportunities as well, the most obvious and crucial of which was a sawmill. The area was growing, towns and farms were springing up, and the landscape lay deep in a hardwood forest. It was this potential which had in fact attracted Field to the area in the first place.

The potential of the area also struck the fancy of one Edward Klopfleisch, a German-born resident of New York City. Klopfleisch had traveled through the West, seeking an appropriate location to develop a lumber mill. Hillsboro was to be the site. With Albert Field's financial assistance, Klopfleisch and his partner, another German immigrant named Otto Hammer, became the owners of the village plat in the autumn of 1854. Almost immediately, Klopfleisch, now working with his brother-in-law, a Mr. Schlolmilch, began the erection of a sawmill. The following year, Hammer moved his family from Jefferson County, adjacent to the growing city of Milwaukee, north to Hillsboro, committing himself to the new community.

164

Simultaneous with the construction of the lumber mill, Field began work on the flour mill he had envisioned, aiming to attract the business that had previously gone to Baraboo. Then Field and Klopfleisch and their associates began construction of the dam which would be utilized by the two mills. Joining in on the sawmill enterprise was another Yankee by the name of B. I. Bailey. As far as I can determine, none of these men was primarily a farmer. Like many of the German immigrants they were artisans and relatively well educated by the standards of the time.

Field seems to have become involved in these businesses only on the financial end. His activities instead were concentrated upon the acquisition of more land. By 1884 he owned some two thousand acres, much of it in and around the village of Hillsboro and some in the eastern end of the county. He also retained control of the flow of water that supplied the lumber and flour mills with energy. The control of this flowage remained with the Field family long after Field and the last of his descendants had left the area. It was only in the summer of 1974 that, with great ceremony and fanfare, one of Field's descendants, a professor at an Ivy League university, presented the city of Hillsboro with these water rights.

What did Field do with all his land? He neither worked it nor turned it into some kind of Yankee hacienda. What he did with it was to speculate and sell to his neighbors, to raise some cattle, and to cut the timber. The timber, of course, was fed into the sawmill in which he had a financial interest.

Field wore still another hat that was particularly valuable to a man in his position. In the early years of Hillsboro, he was the town "banker." This was not in any formal sense of the term since Hillsboro was to wait many years before it had its own bank. In fact, chartered banks were illegal in Wisconsin from 1848 to 1853 (Nesbit 1973:186–87). Field's bank was in his hat, so to speak. He would lend money to farmers and settlers who wanted to buy land—most likely his land. More often than not, mortgages were provided not with any signature or collateral, but on the basis of his knowledge of the people he was dealing with.

There were other ways that Field situated himself strategically in the social structure of the new community. When people moved into the area, he would put them up in his own home until they found a place to live. At least once a year, he would give a huge party for the people of the village and the surrounding area. He was a deacon of the church, and before a church was erected, services were held in his home. He knew, personally, just about everyone in the area.

Needless to say, Field had access to capital. Although details are lacking, it appears that he financed his operations through kinship connections from the East—something he was not alone in doing. About a generation after Field's activities in Hillsboro, Fred W. Ekhart, who will come up again later, was founder of the State Bank of Viroqua, builder of grain elevators, buyer of livestock, grains, and tobacco, as well as a community leader. His Viroqua empire was built at least partially with funding provided by his family in Chicago.

In the first twenty years of Hillsboro's development, Albert Field played a central role as community financier, leader, and entrepreneur. He was, however, by no means the only financier in the area. Land speculation and personal loans to new settlers building their own farms were common. The lender frequently increased his holdings by foreclosure in bad times. Although I have seen no reports indicating whether Field did this, the activities of other private lenders in the county were notorious. One private source of mortgage funds in Viroqua in the late nineteenth century, an illiterate man, was said to have owned at one point seventeen farms from foreclosures.

In these early years, land speculators and financiers were always Yankees. This was especially the case in Hillsboro, where, as we have seen, the "industrialists" tended to be German. Yankees were known as well to venture into retail trade even when they had other professions to follow. The first doctors in town, at least through the turn of the century, ran pharmacies, stables, farms, and other businesses. An English-born, Scottish-trained physician settling in Hillsboro at the end of the nineteenth century found the involvement of the "professional class in trade" shocking. "He would have none of that," his daughter, now in her eighties, told me, "he would have none of that. That's why I am on welfare today."

The pattern of Yankee financing and shopkeeping continued as Germans, still prone to industry, began to open a few shops. Later a brewery was built, run by a Mr. Ludwig, a German newcomer with financing from local Yankees, among them Albert Field. Also involved in the brewery business were Otto Hammer and his relative Ambrose Armbruster. Like Hammer, Armbruster was German born, had settled in the East, and had moved his family to Hillsboro after first looking the situation over. By 1861 Armbruster was settled in the community, and by the next year he owned interest in Hammer's lumber mill, having bought out Hammer's brother-in-law, Schlolmilch. Schlolmilch, in turn, used the money to leave Hillsboro and go on to other things. Deeply involved in business and land speculation, Yankees were less inclined to begin "institution building." This is more evident elsewhere in the county than in Hillsboro, where the large German population was instrumental in building the first churches at a time when Albert Field was holding services in his home. In 1860 the *Western Times*, Viroqua's newspaper, pointed out that the Norwegian settlement seven miles north of Viroqua boasted a school and a church; Viroqua, on the other hand, after fifteen years and with a population of three hundred, lacked both, though the town was dynamic in other ways. The situation was much the same in the larger area near Genoa on the Mississippi River. Even in the early 1880s, a contrast could be drawn between the Catholics, who had raised a church and had an active congregation, mostly of Italians with some Germans, and Yankee Protestants, who were still holding services in the homes of the congregation members.

Nonetheless, although slow in building a church and in establishing a formal school system, the Yankees did not avoid the responsibilities and benefits of government. The first village officers of Hillsboro numbered eleven men. Of these, eight—including, of course, Albert Field—were Yankees. The three German village officers, Hammer, Ludwig, and a Mr. Manhart, all had been involved in businesses in which Field had financial interest. This pattern was to continue—Yankees dominating local government and Germans slowly adding their numbers to the governing board, with those achieving such positions having previously been involved with the central Yankee group in business undertakings.

When later in the century Bohemians began to move into the area, the pattern was repeated. The first Bohemian business was a brewery started by the Bezoucha family apparently with the help of local financing. It was, however, not until forty years later that Bohemian names appeared with any regularity on lists of local officers.

167

Around 1900 Yankees, seeking new frontiers, began to move out of the area in large numbers. One "survivor" of this Yankee exodus described the situation in terms well known to every school child and moviegoer—the lure of the frontier, the need for elbow room, the need for new challenges and new worlds. At the time, new worlds translated into the Oklahoma Territory, then opening up, and, to a lesser degree, Alaska, where people rushed for gold. This Yankee migration was made up of the sons of the original Yankee settlers and entrepreneurs, who had by now retired or, like Albert Field, returned to the East, or died. Still, the flame of adventure burned in their descendants. The Yankee migration took with it the remaining descendants of Field and a number of other Yankee business, financial, and government leaders of the early years, almost all of whom had been involved with Field in one undertaking or another.

This "flight of the Yankees" was not confined to Hillsboro. Similar flights took place in and around Viroqua. Those who left likewise counted among themselves many of the early pioneering families. As a result, few families in Viroqua today can trace their ancestry back to the town's founders.

They who left were not only pioneers, but, more important, entrepreneurs. These were men who had taken the almost free land with its many opportunities and built up towns and villages, farms and hamlets, stores and roads. Opportunities had become fewer by the turn of the century, or at least less obvious, and returns on investment smaller than in the early days. So they moved and sought new frontiers.

In Hillsboro those who remained were businessmen of German background. Unlike the departed Yankee entrepreneurs, they saw a future for their businesses and the town itself. In time they became the town's major businessmen, entrepreneurs, and leaders.

HILLSBORO: THE POSTPIONEER ENTREPRENEURS

In 1902 these men, under the leadership of Edward Hammer, son of Otto Hammer, founded the Hillsboro and Northeastern Railroad. All 4.8 miles of the railroad—reputed to be the smallest working commercial railroad in the world—was financed and built with local funds. Among the investors in the railroad was the village of Hillsboro itself which purchased several thousands of dollars in bonds at the vote of the village board. It goes without saying that there was considerable crossover between the board members of the railroad and the village. Eventually the bonds were retired and the taxpayers of the village of Hillsboro were not stuck with a bad investment.

The intention of the railroad's founders was to link the town's businesses with the outside world. In doing so, they hoped to attract outside businesses into town. The Hillsboro and Northeastern joined with the Chicago and Northwestern in Union Center and indeed provided an outlet for the Hillsboro breweries and creameries. Many of these small local businesses remained locally owned and managed until the 1920s when they were sold to outside interests and incorporated into large regional or national concerns.

The establishment of the first local banks, ultimately combined into the present Farmers' State Bank, shows the same group of people involved. The first officers of the Hillsboro Bank, for example, were Otto Wernik, Robert Hammer, and Peter Hammer. Edward Hammer, founder of the Hillsboro and Northeastern Railroad, later became president of the bank. In addition, he was manager of the gristmill (no longer in existence) and co-owner of the Hammer Brothers Lumber Company. He held interest in the Hillsboro Brewing Company, served as chairman of the Hillsboro township board, and was president of the village of Hillsboro. His career was not an unusual one for the area, though clearly it was a successful one.

It is interesting to compare Hammer with Albert Field. Field's small empire in and around Hillsboro was based primarily on land and business interests. The land, however, was for speculation and his business interests were largely financial. The more successful he was, the more land he sold; the more successful his financial undertakings, the less he was tied to Hillsboro as a community. The ease with which the Yankee entrepreneurial families disengaged themselves from Hillsboro is one indication of this. Hammer, on the other hand, and others like him, became more strongly tied to the community.

By the early 1900s, the Bohemians were becoming a significant element of the population of Hillsboro. Unlike the pioneers who obtained land from the government or from speculators, the Bohe-

169

mians purchased farms already settled. This land had been previously farmed by the Yankees and Irish, both of whom are today almost completely gone from the farms in the Hillsboro area.

Although at this time there were banks in the community, the earliest Bohemian settlers turned to fellow countrymen for financial assistance. This was true well into the twentieth century. Like the loans made by Field to those he knew, so these loans by Bohemian to Bohemian were based upon trust and often involved no exchange of documents. Frequently the lender was a farmer who used the return on the loan to further his own farming capabilities or to move into other activities.

A case in point is a Czech farmer, now in his late eighties, who loaned money to other Czechs to purchase farms. From this base he went into the livestock purchasing business. That all the livestock purchasers were "Americans" (that is, non-Czechs), he contends, had nothing to do with his decision to enter the business. He does allow, however, that the vast majority of his customers, who came to him from the other dealers, were Bohemians. His success he attributes to the fact that he spoke Czech (though he was born in this country), that he came from a respected Bohemian family in the area and would "help out" his customers with loans and advances, and that his prices were at least as high, if not higher, than those of his competitors.

This same man, at various times of his life, was also a local politician, an insurance agent, and the first president of his community's bank. The community, by the way, was not Hillsboro but a satellite of it with a population to this day almost exclusively Bohemian.

Although some Bohemians were active and successful in their communities, they were at the bottom of the economic and status scale of Hillsboro at least through the 1930s. As one older informant put it, "The bosses were Yankees and Germans. The workers and poor folk were Bohemians." The situation has since changed, and today the Bohemian farmers of the area are doing very well indeed. Nevertheless, they remain predominantly farmers and, given their large numbers in the population of the area, extremely underrepresented in business and the professions. Yet they play an important role in local and county politics.

For the Bohemians as for the Yankees before them, investment patterns in their broadest sense operated in the earlier years primarily within a network bounded by ethnic or subethnic lines. As with the Germans, the first Bohemians to break into the town's central group were a few people with skills—in this case the Bezouchas with their knowledge of brewing—which could be utilized by the entrepreneurs of the larger community.

THE NORWEGIANS

Norwegian immigrant settlement in the prairies and coulees of central Vernon County began shortly after the first Yankees came to the area in the late 1840s and early 1850s. Yankee settlement had been by individuals, nuclear families, and occasionally small groups of siblings and their families. Norwegian settlement, on the other hand, was of a more organized pattern. The first Norwegian settlements in the southern Wisconsin and northern Illinois region near Lake Koshkonong were veritable colonies. Even after Norwegians began to spread into a wider area, the Lake Koshkonong location continued to be a prime staging area for initial settlement before moving on to other less developed regions.

New frontier areas as well, though not formally colonized, developed into settlements whose populations were drawn from specific regions and towns in Norway.[3] In Vernon County the pattern of local and regional ties is revealed in the two concentrations of Norwegian subpopulations. On the prairies around the county seat of Viroqua in central Vernon County, the Norwegian population was overwhelmingly from the Sognefjord in western Norway. In the coulees and prairies starting eight miles north of Viroqua, a population primarily from the Gudbrandsdal Valley in eastern Norway settled in the areas surrounding the modern towns of Westby and Coon Valley. Sandwiched between these two regional concentrations was a narrow band of people from the Flekkefjord in southern Norway. Each of these populations spoke a different Norwegian dialect. This tended to turn social relations inward toward those of the same dialect—a pattern of social relations which continued even after English became used first as a lingua franca and then, after several generations, as the prime language (Munch 1949).

The two areas differed in more than dialect. The Viroqua settlement had been developed previously by Yankees, and the Norwe-

171

gian farmer immigrants had to settle in the interstices of the Yankee farms, spaces that had been left after the sale of land by local Yankee speculators. Short on cash, long on family size, and willing to work hard, the Norwegian immigrants labored as hired hands and servants for the Yankees in addition to farming their own land. Through the second half of the nineteenth century the Norwegians were the lower class, the Yankees the upper; the Norwegians, the farmers, the Yankees, in growing number, the townsmen.

The situation which the Gudbrandsdalers faced around Westby, Coon Valley, and the adjacent prairies was different. The area had not been significantly settled by Yankees before the arrival of the Norwegians. Here the immigrants did not have to fit into marginal slots in a Yankee-dominated social order. The links to the larger political and economic systems, however, were still held by non-Norwegians. In the terminology of the Norwegian immigrants these people were called "Americans," regardless of their actual ethnic background.

Despite these differences—their places of origin in Norway and their situations in Vernon County—the Viroqua and Westby Norwegian populations shared numerous similar features. Both populations were drawn from lower rural strata, who were landless, land-deprived, second sons in a society marked by powerful rules of primogeniture. It was society, furthermore, where land, family, and personal identity were deeply interwoven. Though within Norway there did exist an aristocracy, largely of Danish background, and a native bourgeoisie, none of these emigrated to Vernon County. Accordingly, among the Norwegian immigrants who came to Wisconsin—landless, or with barely enough land to survive on—the values and etiquette of a fierce egalitarianism thrived.

The Norwegian pattern of open country neighborhoods, with family farms scattered over the countryside, fitted well into North American practice. In Norway as well as among their neighbors, the neighborhood was the next basic social unit above the family farm itself. The center of the Norwegian rural neighborhood was the small Lutheran church, standing in the open country alongside its small cemetery. Until as recently as World War II, services in these churches were held in Norwegian. School, too, was taught at least partially in Norwegian until 1889 when the Bennet law required instruction in English. They were usually one-room affairs and often associated with the church or built on donated land. Though legislation which set down homesteading practices required that a section of land be established in each township to support a school, such was not everywhere the case. As noted earlier, Norwegians in Coon Valley had schools and churches both, while Viroqua had neither.

The complex of farm, family, and church—the hallmark of Norwegian settlement as it had been in the homeland—continued in Vernon County and other areas of agricultural Norwegian settlement. Like other farmers in the area, the Norwegians originally grew wheat. By the latter part of the nineteenth century, though, wheat blight, the burgeoning markets at Chicago and Milwaukee, and the rapidly expanding railroad network all contributed to a shift from wheat to dairy farming. To this day, dairy farming remains the major economic activity. Tobacco, a secondary cash crop brought by the Norwegians from the Koshkonong settlement, spread to other farming populations in the area. Later, however, it diminished again, so that today it is a heavily "Norwegian" crop.

Even with the change in crops, there was no significant change in the marketing patterns. The commodity dealers for both dairy and tobacco were still Yankee. The sources of formal commercial credit, the political positions, the positions of power and prestige at the community level were still dominated by non-Norwegians. Only at the lowest-level political offices in Westby and Coon Valley could one find Norwegians.

THE GRAND OLD MAN OF TOBACCO[4]

Born in the Gudbrandsdal Valley, Norway, in 1862, Martin Bekkedahl came to the United States at the age of twenty-five. His cousin, who was clearing a farm in southwestern Wisconsin, was his sponsor, and, as was common in such arrangements, Martin was expected to repay the passage money. This he did within eight months, both by working his cousin's land and by cutting ties for a railroad line then under construction. As a hired hand on farms and as a worker in lumber mills, he in time earned enough money to send for his brother John from Norway.

By now proficient in English, Martin settled in Westby with his brother. Martin worked as a clerk and bookkeeper—a crucial position since non-Norwegian storekeepers required Norwegian-speaking employees to attract Norwegian customers. In an area such as Westby, however, the need was likely the other way around; someone who could manage transactions with salesmen and wholesalers in English would be most handy. For the next several years Martin used his position in the store to begin small speculations in lumber, livestock, and horses. He purchased these from Norwegian farmers in the surrounding area and shipped them to the buyers or processors outside the community. The first step in a wildly successful career was taken. Martin Bekkedahl had positioned himself between the community and the outside, between Yankee and Norwegian. The rest of his career was a masterful cadenza on this theme.

While clerking in Westby, Martin made many contacts among the traveling salesmen operating out of Milwaukee and nearby La Crosse. One salesman, on the verge of retirement, talked Bekkedahl into taking over his territory, which consisted of Vernon, Jackson, and Trempeleau counties, all areas of heavy Norwegian settlement. After a short while at the task, Bekkedahl decided that the job required more time and energy than its returns warranted. He had realized, perhaps, that greater opportunities lay at the boundaries of the Norwegian community rather than in only one aspect of what had already proved a successful equation.

In his year as a "traveling man," Martin spent his slack times on productive activities. His wife, whom he had married in 1892, was the daughter of the owner of the Westby Hotel. There he met several tobacco salesmen and took them to the farms of the local tobacco growers, translating for them. By 1893 he had gone into the tobacco business himself in a small way. He would buy low quality leaf and stems that the regular tobacco buyers would not touch. Within a short time he was clearing $8,000 a year on this low quality tobacco.

As Bekkedahl displayed business acumen by capitalizing on tobacco that professional buyers rejected, the possibilities for expanded operations were recognized by others as well. Two German-American bankers and a Norwegian doctor from Viroqua advised him to invest in a business of his own. They suggested that he purchase a building and hire labor to clean and prepare the tobacco for market, and they themselves invested money in the undertaking. Bekkedahl was now prepared to compete with the regular tobacco buyers. He, however, had at least one outstanding advantage over them.

In the late 1800s the most lucrative aspect of the tobacco business, not surprisingly, lay in buying and speculating rather than in growing. The tobacco buyers in western Wisconsin were Yankees or, in any event, non-Norwegians. They would travel from farm to farm and bargain with each farmer individually. Since the area was predominantly Norwegian-speaking, the buyers had to operate through translators—a role that introduced Martin Bekkedahl to the business.

Not well acquainted with the condition of the commodity market, the tobacco farmers felt themselves at the mercy of the buyers. Buyers had contacts and information which they lacked. Buyers were conspiring to keep tobacco prices low—or so the farmers imagined.

Bekkedahl, on the other hand, was different in the eyes of the local farmer. Not only was he Norwegian speaking, but also he was from the area. His knowledge of the farmers was not limited merely to an annual business contact. He knew them from the store, he knew them from the hotel, his wife's family was known to them. When Bekkedahl came to their door, it is safe to guess that conversation was not restricted to the business of tobacco buying.

Likely there was more to it than that. Since Bekkedahl was himself a member of the community, he would in all probability be responsive to community sanctions. Word about a dubious deal or word about airs of superiority over his neighbors would travel quickly and widely (as a Viroqua Yankee who had business dealings in Westby once remarked to me, "If you step on a Norwegian toe in Westby, the whole town says, 'Ouch.' "). Aware of community feelings, of the same background, language, and society as his clients, Martin Bekkedahl very likely played the game by the same rules his farmer-clients did.

"We always sold to Bekkedahl and even turned down other buyers," a local informant told Westby researcher Robert Ibarra (1976). And well they should have. When Bekkedahl bought tobacco before harvest, he kept to the agreed-upon price even if damage occurred later in the fields or during harvesting; other buyers would lower the price. "He dealt hard but took it the way he bought it," one of Bekkedahl's sons remarked to Ibarra. "We bought more cigar tobacco than all the others put together."

As the nineteenth century ended, Bekkedahl expanded his operations beyond Westby into the tobacco belt of southwestern Wisconsin. By 1910 he had established links with eastern tobacco firms and was producing record sales and packing record crops. He had become the richest man Westby had ever produced.

Bekkedahl's strategy of positioning himself between community and ambient system, between Westby and the world, between Yankee and Norwegian, had paid off well indeed. He brought his sons into the business. Seeking to gain vertical control over the materials needed to pack his tobacco, he expanded into lumbering in northern Wisconsin, against his sons' advice. It was this move, according to one son, which would trigger his downfall when the financial world collapsed in 1929.

But that was yet a long way off, and there were still potentials to be developed in the world he knew well. He moved into banking, once again with the advice and support of his early allies from Viroqua, the bankers Linderman and Ekhart.

In the early 1920s Linderman and Ekhart wished to expand their banking interests into the Westby area, but a number of problems stood in their way. First, Wisconsin banking law forbade the establishment of branch banks. Second, entering Westby meant entering the Norwegian community—a community which differed in dialect and in relative isolation in their social networks, even from other Norwegian communities in the area. Once more the bankers turned to Martin Bekkedahl.

They assured Martin that he would be granted the charter of a small local bank which had recently closed in Westby and which was then held in receivership by the state. Together, the three men went to the state capitol in Madison. The charter was assigned to Bekkedahl who, with the financial assistance of his two friends, opened the bank in 1922. It financed real estate expansion in the Westby area, both in the town and in the surrounding agricultural areas.

Though he ran a tight business, in banking as well as tobacco, the common touch had not escaped Bekkedahl. Ibarra relates the story of how Bekkedahl, sitting in his bank office, overheard a local farmer turned down for a loan by one of the bank's officers. Running out the back door, Martin intercepted the farmer on the street and made him a personal loan; the farmer could pay off the loan from his tobacco crop, he said. Such personal loans, even after the establishment of the bank, were not uncommon. According to Bekkedahl's family, he never lost money on any of them. He knew and accepted the fact that repayment would not always be immediate, that it might not always be in cash, but he trusted that it would come.

Personal loans were not the only means through which Bekkedahl maintained his ties to the community. Though not an active member of any of the area's Lutheran churches, he actively supported church-building programs, often without being asked. Also, working with three of his brothers who had remained in Norway, he arranged for the immigration of Norwegians who came to work in the homes and farms of the area. These arrangements were informal in nature, but all loans were paid back. Most of these people remained in the Westby region after their obligations were fulfilled. As a result, Bekkedahl's links to the people of the community were even wider and deeper.

In the crash of 1929 Bekkedahl lost everything. As indicated earlier, the collapse of his lumbering enterprise in northern Wisconsin was thought to have led to the collapse of the entire Bekkedahl empire. While to explain his business failure by a single error in judgment may seem unwarranted, that this venture should be singled out is of interest. The issue will be discussed more effectively in a comparative and theoretical context later in the chapter.

The crash of 1929 brought down not only Bekkedahl but also a number of people involved with him—farmers whose mortgages he held, workers in his tobacco enterprises. Apparently, there was no hostility directed at him or his family. The financial investments had been lost, the social ones had not. Bekkedahl had followed the rules; he had not raised himself, in his behavior and his dealings, above his fellows. Perhaps the best measure of this good feeling is the fact that Bekkedahl's descendants today still reside in Westby, comfortably to be sure, but no longer positioned at the economic peaks which the grand old man of tobacco had achieved.

ETHNIC ENTREPRENEURSHIP: IT'S NOT ALL FOR MONEY

The early part of the career of Jens Vigdahl shows a remarkable parallel with that of Martin Bekkedahl. One major difference from that of Bekkedahl, and from that of Yankee pioneer Albert Field as well, was that Jens Vigdahl did not become rich. This is not to say that he failed. Though he began with the same resources as Bekkedahl did, the social as well as economic opportunity structure was profoundly different. For one thing, Vigdahl lived and worked in the Yankee-dominated town of Viroqua, not the Norwegian world that was Westby. For another, Vigdahl appeared on the scene a generation later than did Bekkedahl.

At the end of the nineteenth century and during the first decades of the twentieth, the economic and political power, prestige, and influence of Viroqua lay in the hands of Yankees, some businessmen of German background, and others whom the Norwegians of the area identified as "Americans" to distinguish them from themselves and the Bohemians (Czechs), Italians, and Germans whose ethnic communities were scattered throughout Vernon County. The Norwegians from Sognefjord who had settled around Viroqua had had to fit themselves around Yankees and other earlier-arriving English-speaking peoples. As in Hillsboro, the "Americans" quickly came to dominate the political and economic life of Viroqua. They became the politicians, commodity dealers, teachers, bankers, and owners of the large retail establishments. And they lived in the large Victorian mansions that clustered on the eastern side of town.

The egalitarian frontier had been transformed into a class-structured society in which the social classes roughly paralleled the ethnic structure—the "Americans" at the top, the Norwegians at the bottom. Though a few Norwegians had broken the pattern and realized financial and social success, they had done this largely by separating themselves from the Norwegian population. Unlike Martin Bekkedahl of Westby, they played the game by "American" rules.

The growing prosperity of the area's Norwegian farmers had already sown the seeds which, along with accompanying conditions, were to change the pattern of ethnic stratification. The career of Jens Vigdahl took place amid this period of transformation; it was a transformation which he himself played a part in effecting.

The fifth child of a retired Norwegian army officer, Jens Vigdahl was born in 1890 in Fortun, Norway, in the Sogn district. Having completed middle school, he was offered the opportunity to follow in his father's footsteps by attending military school. Vigdahl refused, and instead, in 1908, joined an uncle visiting Fortun from

178

Vernon County and immigrated to the United States. He spent a year on his uncle's farm before moving to Viroqua. Here he began a career which would bring him honors from the nation he had left physically, but not spiritually.

His first job was as a clerk in a Norwegian-owned grocery store in Viroqua. Its customers, like those of the store Bekkedahl had begun a generation earlier, were Norwegian-speaking. Vigdahl remained at the Ostrem and Davidson store until 1914 when he returned to Norway on a tour with a Norwegian-American choral group. It was the first of many trips back "home," and it revealed to him his love for Norway and its culture, a love that was to remain his touchstone for the rest of his life.

Vigdahl returned to work for the Ostrem and Davidson store until 1916 when, with another Norwegian, he bought out a Norwegian-owned grocery. This partnership lasted until 1921, when he took over the business. In 1938, he was advised, because of his bad heart, to give up the grocery business and go into another line of work that was less physically demanding. He chose insurance, a business whose basic resource, contact with people, he had mastered by spending almost thirty years in retail trade.

The people with whom he had dealt in his grocery and in the Ostrem and Davidson store were largely Norwegian and Norwegian-speaking. According to his widow, "All the people who had traded in the store came to him for insurance." Perhaps it would be more accurate to say that he went to them. The insurance business began as a small-scale affair, dependent upon the numbers of clients rather than upon the size of the policies. Premiums—nickel and dime amounts—were collected monthly, as Vigdahl drove through the countryside, stopping at the farms or homes of his clients. As often as not, the collection was a minor part of the visit. News of Norway and local affairs would be exchanged, a will would be written for a client, a letter in Norwegian written or translated.

This same sort of rural network, in this case among the Sognings (the people of Sogn) of Viroqua, had brought Bekkedahl success in his career. Yet the niche and the opportunities that Bekkedahl had exploited so well were not available to Vigdahl. "American" commodity dealers had the area sewn up tight and, after the crash of 1929, cooperatives took over their function. The economic potential for the social networks Jens Vigdahl had developed in the course of

179

his career as tradesman and insurance salesman were limited. Insurance remained his business base until his retirement in the 1960s. Jens Vigdahl's entrepreneurial skills, then, were not activated to economic ends but to social ones. When he died in early 1974, he was economically comfortable but not, by any definition of the term in an American context, rich.

One clear direction that his wide knowledge of people in the community could lead to was a political career. He was appointed justice of the peace and was reelected to that position, which he held for ten years running. But that was as far as his political career went.

His interests and energies were turned to Norway and things Norwegian. In this he shone. It was an "avocational career," the payoff for which was only secondarily monetary, if at all. Instead, the rewards were in terms of his standing in the community. Significantly also it was avocational entrepreneurship which paid off for the Norwegians of the area, symbolizing the changing economic, political, and social position of the Norwegian community in Vernon County.

From the time that he arrived in the area, Vigdahl was active in both formal and informal Norwegian groups. He was a member of Viroqua's major Lutheran church, and as mentioned earlier, sang with a Norwegian choral group which returned to Norway for a season of performances. He also remained deeply involved with the Sons of Norway, a national Norwegian-American insurance and social group, until his death in 1974. It was in the *bygdelag* (regional or district lodge) movement, however, that his efforts were expended most and had the greatest impact on the local community.

Professor Odd S. Lovoll (1975), who wrote the definitive history of the *bygdelags*, maintains that the movement grew out of the immigrant's attachment to kin and neighbors in their old home districts in Norway. These district lodges were less special interest groups than social groups (Lovoll 1975:1).

According to Professor Lovoll, the word *bygd* refers to a "topographically and socially defined community of farmsteads. . . . To a Norwegian, the word connotes a sense of sharing, of living together; it represents a unified area of customs and traditions" (1975:2). When the *bygdelag* movement began in the United States in the late nineteenth century, it suffered the opposition of Norwegian-

American and immigrant intellectuals who feared a reawakening of old *bygd* enmities. They were concerned that the movement would undercut their own support for an emerging, sophisticated, national culture of a Norway which was only then breaking its last links to the government and crown of Sweden (Lovoll 1975:21).

The rank and file membership of the *bygdelags* was rural in both Norwegian origin and American location. They had relatively little education and were heavily influenced by a pietistic Lutheran clergy. Eighty percent foreign born (though the actual figure is probably less since only family heads were counted), many had come before World War I from their home *bygde* in Norway directly to new farm neighborhoods in the Midwest (Lovoll 1975:18).

The *bygdelag* existed primarily for its *stevne*, the gathering of its members (Lovoll 1975:15). These gatherings might occur as often as monthly, or semiannually, depending on the density of settlement. The major *stevne* of any particular *bygdelag*, however, was its annual meeting toward which all the efforts of the officers were directed anyway.

The *bygdelag* movement consisted of different *lags* (lodges), each deriving from a specific region or community in Norway. *Lag* memberships ranged from a particular kin group who admitted others from their home area in Norway (Lovoll 1975:15), to people from a large area such as Hardanger, Gudbrandsdal, or Trondheim. Jens Vigdahl belonged to the *lag* of Sogn, Sognelag.

Founded in 1908 in Albert Lea, Minnesota, the Sognelag grew to be one of the largest *bygdelags* in the United States. It was the organized center of what historian Hjalmar Rued considered "the largest cohesive folk group in America" (Lovoll 1975:61).

The beginnings of the Sognelag coincided with the arrival of Jens Vigdahl in the United States. Wishing to see his friends, who were scattered over the Midwest, Vigdahl soon joined the Sognelag. In 1923 he became one of the directors of the organization, serving until his retirement from the national organization in 1959. For nineteen of those thirty-six years he was president, and when not the president, he was usually the secretary (*Vernon County Broadcast Censor* June 10, 1965, p. 1). Many of the *bygdelags* were directed by Lutheran ministers; the Sognelag remained in the hands of secular officers.

According to Lovoll (1975:20),

181

The work required to plan and execute the annual *stevner* and other *lag* projects excluded from leadership those who were not willing or able to contribute time and effort without prospect of reward. . . . As the *lag* gained support within the Norwegian immigrant community, a certain amount of prestige attached to the functionary positions. That this fact might have been reward enough for many individuals to serve as officers is evidenced by the numbers of willing candidates and by the politicking engaged in by some.

Although Lovoll's investigation of the *bygdelags* has revealed no major reward for its officers and no significant function other than social, one wonders at the heavy politicking for the functionary positions. I would suggest that the rewards for participation in the *lag* were reaped in the home community of the *lag*'s leaders. Perhaps unconsciously, they aspired to these rewards.

The people of the *lags* were rural and small-town folk, and it was to rural towns and small cities that they went for their annual *stevner*. Up to the time of the Sognelag's fiftieth anniversary in 1958, there had been forty-two annual conventions (some were missed during the depression and the two world wars). Of these, twenty-five were held in the founding state of Minnesota. Seven were in the Dakotas and Iowa. The other ten were held in Wisconsin—one in the state capitol of Madison, four in small towns, one near the Minnesota border, and four in Viroqua. A fifth Sognestevne was held in Viroqua in 1965 when Mrs. Kristin Vigdahl was president of the *lag* and Jens Vigdahl secretary.

It is the Viroqua *stevner* which are of interest here. These were held in 1923, 1934, 1952, 1958, and 1965, all years when Jens Vigdahl was an active participant in the organization. Except for the *stevne* of 1934, a depression year, when attendance dropped to six hundred, the usual flow of people into Viroqua for the three or four days of the meeting was one thousand to two thousand people, a number not to pass unnoticed in a town of fewer than four thousand. It should be further noted that Vernon County, and the Viroqua region in particular, is one of the larger regions of Sogning settlement in the United States.

In addition to the convention itself, the *stevner* were occasions for parades and street and store displays. Advertisements in the local newspaper, some in Norwegian, greeted the delegates, and there was other public recognition of the event as well.

As great a spectacle as they were for this small town, these conventions probably did not add a great deal to the coffers of local businessmen. Even today Viroqua has only three small hotels and half a dozen restaurants of varying size and quality. Many of the delegates stayed and ate with friends and relatives. Others, for the most part, were housed in private homes arranged through the Lutheran churches of the town. Similarly the banquet and public dining affairs which were a part of the *stevne* were organized by the women of the local Lutheran churches. They prepared and served the meals as a kind of huge church supper.

What these conventions did do, however, was to attract public attention to the community. Newspaper articles appeared in Madison and Milwaukee reporting the events in considerable detail. Members of the Norwegian parliament came specifically to participate as did members of the Wisconsin state government, including the governor. In addition, the convention was addressed by the Norwegian diplomatic mission. The local elite, bankers, federal circuit court judges, and the like, Norwegian or not, took part in the proceedings. And Jens Vigdahl was at the center of it all.

Building on his reputation as an organizer for the Sognelag, Jens Vigdahl moved into the group of men who represented the leadership of the community. These men were called upon frequently to plan activities in their capacity as, for example, president of the Lion's Club, chairman of the drive for a new hospital wing, or justice of the peace. In his efforts to promote a relief program for Finns during the Russo-Finnish War of 1939–40, Vigdahl drew upon his contacts both locally and from the network of *bygdelags*. Similar energies for the Bundles for Norway program during World War II were so noteworthy that, in recognition of his service, the king of Norway presented Vigdahl with a citation after the war.

All this was exciting for a small town, especially for the Norwegian community who remembered well being at the bottom of the Viroqua social hierarchy, when, as one Norwegian put it, "We were Viroqua's 'niggers.' "

Vigdahl had tapped the Norwegian community, as had Bekkedahl before him, but similar financial opportunities did not seem to exist for him in spite of his community involvement. There were, however, other benefits, both for Vigdahl himself, in prestige and self-satisfaction, and, perhaps more important, for his community.

When Jens Vigdahl arrived in Vernon County early in the twentieth century, the Norwegian population of the area, and especially of Viroqua and its hinterlands, was just beginning to struggle out of their lower-class position in society. Even with wealth, land, and prestige more widely distributed among the different ethnic populations, rather than concentrated in Yankee hands, Norwegians generally remained at the bottom of the social hierarchy. The status hierarchy and the ethnic structure of the community essentially paralleled each other.

By the end of World War II the situation had changed. The ethnic structure could be seen, conceptually, to have been rotated ninety degrees so that it now intersected the status hierarchy vertically. Norwegians were now one of several socially coequal ethnic populations within the area. Not all of this, of course, was due solely to the efforts of Jens Vigdahl. These were times of transition, and political and economic power of Norwegians and other immigrant populations had grown. In addition, the depression had ruined or driven out much of the older, remaining Yankee elite. These vacated Yankee positions were taken over by people with different backgrounds. Particularly significant as well was the fact that economically powerful commodity dealers were almost completely replaced by producers' and consumers' cooperatives, organized and managed by people drawn from "ethnic" populations.

What Jens Vigdahl and the Sogn *bygdelag* accomplished was to place the symbolic imprimatur on the changing, and changed, status of the Norwegian population. At the moment that the old elite passed from the scene, diplomats and foreign dignitaries, university presidents and scholars, governors and high government officials, and business leaders of the country were journeying to Viroqua to pay homage to the Norwegian immigrants. They did this in the midst of parades and flags and oceans of bunting. News of these events was carried on the press and radio throughout the state. This represented public recognition of a changed social structure, a changed status of the Norwegian population that was based not on their assimilation but rather on a renewed, public affirmation of their Norwegian origins.

ETHNICITY AND THE BOUNDARIES OF TRUST

Two themes run through the careers of Albert Field, Martin Bekkedahl, and Jens Vigdahl. First, the three men were grounded firmly in a distinct culture and history. Their ethnicity was distinguishable from other ethnic populations among whom they lived. Second, relations with their own people were based upon "trust," a concept which they themselves articulated and which remains within the contemporary community as an understanding necessary for business activity.

What does trust mean and what is the connection between trust and ethnic affiliation? Crucial to this concept of trust is the related concept of honoring one's word, of meeting one's obligations and responsibilities, without need to force compliance. This is not to say that no sanctions are involved. Rather, failure to fulfill one's obligation is met first with informal sanctions, the rupture of social relations, and the loss of reputation in the wider community which will sharply strain relations in the future. To go beyond informal sanctions and to appeal to impersonal agencies represents a total breakdown in a relationship based upon trust. This is as true for the person who makes the appeal to the formal agency as it is for the person who has failed in his obligation. If in the eyes of the community the appeal for formal support is made too soon, the implication is that the person appealing for institutional support himself trusts neither the person against whom the action is taken nor, more important, the effectiveness of the community to ensure that obligations are satisfied. In other words, the appeal to formal sanctions can be as threatening to the plaintiff as to the defendant.

As seen earlier, Albert Field made business deals and personal loans on the basis of a handshake. This practice exists not only in the past. An informant in Viroqua told of a personal loan he made to a friend beginning a new business. The business failed, bankruptcy was not declared, and the informant was out five thousand dollars—or so it seemed—along with the other backers. "You've written off the five grand?" I asked. "Good Lord, no!" my informant replied. "X is a good old boy. He'll try again in another business and when he makes it he'll pay us back."

A man in Hillsboro, similarly well known as a source of private loans to farmers, sealed his loans with a handshake. One local Yankee informant reported that he knew personally of a $4,500 loan that had been made without exchange of signatures or documents and even without witness. "Of course," the informant continued, "Wopat would do this kind of thing only with other Bohemians."

Indeed, "this kind of thing" was not uncommon, and occurred

frequently with people of the same background. Cultural boundaries were crossed only with hesitation, as trust did not cross ethnic lines easily.

It would be easy to attribute this lack of trust to simple xenophobia, but there is more to the issue than that. In reality one could not be sure what the standards of other ethnic groups were. One did not attend their churches or know who their heroes were, or why. One did not know whether the standards of honesty and trust, clearly applicable in dealings among themselves, would be honored with outsiders.

The fact that a person was of one's own ethnic background was, of course, no guarantee that he was trustworthy. For example, Verna King Gruhlke, in her account of growing up in the 1900s in a small Wisconsin town not far from Vernon County, tells of the time her Irish father was brought to court for allegedly defaulting on a loan.

> Dad hung his head. "I haven't got any receipts. *I trusted him. He's a Catholic and an Irishman and I trusted him.* I relied on my own figuring just as I've always done—I never needed another man's receipt before this." (1971:98; emphasis added)

Trust ultimately rested upon personal knowledge of the person being dealt with. Nonetheless, one assumed that people of the same background would be trustworthy. A common ethnicity seemed to increase the probability that the person would honor obligations of trust.

The lack of trust between different groups was not an impermeable barrier. It could be crossed by personal knowledge of the person and the sense that he would indeed honor his obligations. In the cases discussed here, the motivation to breach the boundary— the Yankee Albert Field seeking links with the German craftsmen, artisans, and specialists, and the "American" bankers of Viroqua advising and financing Martin Bekkedahl—arose from the fact that those with less wealth and status commanded resources which could be utilized for mutual benefit. Among these resources was the trust which people of similar ancestry would grant to their own kind but withheld from an outsider. That is, when Martin Bekkedahl replaced the "American" tobacco buyers in Westby, the Norwegian tobacco farmers did not suddenly become sophisticated in the complexities of the commodity market. More likely, it was that Bekkedahl could be trusted not to cheat them, whereas previous tobacco buyers, who were neither Norwegian nor of the community, could not.

186

The boundaries of trust are verbalized in terms of, first, personal knowledge, then knowledge of individuals, knowledge of families, knowledge of the ethnic group, and knowledge of the people of the community, in order of increasing uncertainty. Beyond the community, dealings are the more constrained by a formal system of sanctions. Unless these dealings, too, can have the trust generated by personal knowledge, they become suspect. Hence, in spite of the fact that Martin Bekkedahl lost everything in the depression, there remains the lingering—and symbolic—belief that if he had not expanded his business interests beyond the Norwegian community he would have died the Tobacco King still.

The limitations of trust are borne out similarly in a Hillsboro morality story. According to this legend, a local man invented the roller bearing. Local business leaders saw its potential and invested money to produce pilot models by a local machinist and to build a factory to manufacture it. They soon realized, however, that they lacked sufficient resources for the large project and took it to a Chicago concern for testing and analysis. The model failed the test but company engineers suggested that the fault lay with the materials rather than the concept. Thus, they would attempt to reconstruct the model from materials unavailable in Hillsboro. The Hillsboro investors agreed to this and returned home, whereupon they were informed that the reconstructed model had also failed to live up to expectations. After the group closed up shop and cut their losses, the Chicago company, so the story goes, publicly announced *their* development of a radical new type of bearing, the roller bearing.

Whether the story is true or not, the moral is the same as that to be drawn from Bekkedahl's career. Trust rests upon knowledge, and business relations should rest upon trust. Go beyond that knowledge, beyond that trust, and the probabilities of betrayal increase. Institutional controls and sanctions, standing alone, cannot be depended upon.

CONCLUSION

At the beginning of this chapter, the question was raised of the applicability of a model designed to analyze the processes of elite social structure formation in Latin America to those in a rural and small town setting in the midwestern United States. My emphasis here has been upon the social arrangements within which business and financial activities operated.

In the Latin American case, these social arrangements centered upon a series of kin-based groups linked together by social networks. These kin groups and networks provided the paths for the flow of information, including information about the reliability of information and consequently the reliability of those kin groups and associated social networks who had provided the information. The ideology of kinship assured that members of kinship groups—and participants in their networks—would fulfill the obligations without the need to appeal to formal sanctions. Furthermore, while betrayal of the kin group could certainly provide handsome profits, these would be one-shot returns. The betrayer would thereafter be isolated from these groups which themselves were among the most significant resources in the society (Aubey, Kyle, Strickon 1974).

In the small midwestern communities here discussed, the processes involved in generating social structures seem to be very similar to those of Latin America although the resulting structures appear quite different. Rather than the homogeneous population within which the Latin American elite families operate, in the Midwest the population is culturally heterogeneous. Instead of a few families controlling the vast majority of the society's basic resources, these are relatively widely distributed and become, with the passing of time, increasingly so (Soltow 1971:123, 127).

In both cases, however, the basic processes seem to focus upon the same assumption by the actors. That is, the formal systems of control and sanctions of the society are to be avoided if at all possible. This is best accomplished if people live up to their obligations because of the rewards for doing so, because of the informal controls that might be applied if they do not, and, finally, because within their respective worlds they have been reared to do so.

In Latin America the core of these relationships of trust was the kin group. In the towns and farm neighborhoods of Wisconsin, the core of these units of trust was the people of common historical and cultural background who settled the area, or whose ancestors had.

Conceptually, then, the social core of the model rests upon those institutions, beliefs, and values which define the parameters of interpersonal trust in a particular society. The crucial social networks in Vernon County were those which linked together these ethnic cores and channeled the flow of resources and information, and of trust, between them. If the opportunity structure permitted, these network-linked ethnic cores could provide the social base for widespread and highly lucrative returns. Even when the opportunity structure, or the motivations of the actors, did not afford massive economic payoffs, these social arrangements made for significant and lasting effects on the communities.

The historical, economic, and political parameters of the elite families of Latin America were profoundly different from those that worked to constrain Albert Field, Martin Bekkedahl, and Jens Vigdahl. Even under these circumstances, these three men helped to mold and to develop their communities. The processes of creating and utilizing social relationships, of making crucial decisions, and of tapping critical resources, however, permit us to analyze the phenomena in terms of a single model, once the different situations in which they operated are made explicit.

NOTES

1. The research in rural Wisconsin was supported by HEW Grant MH 24587. I would also like to express my thanks to the Research Committee of the University of Wisconsin–Madison for providing support for the pilot project which preceded the full-scale research. The fieldwork phase of the research took place between July 1974 and December 1975.

2. As this paper was written only a few months after the end of the fieldwork, detailed documentation for the data presented in the rest of this paper must await later publications. Many of the data derive, except where otherwise noted, from interviews.

3. Even today I have authenticated data on families which have lived on neighboring farms since the period of settlement whose ancestors, in turn, had lived on neighboring farms in Norway for hundreds of years.

4. The biographical data on Martin Bekkedahl were obtained from Dr. Robert Ibarra, who, as my assistant on the Vernon County research, did a study of the community of Westby. Further material on Bekkedahl will be found in his dissertation, "Ethnicity: Genuine and Spurious," Department of Anthropology, University of Wisconsin–Madison, 1976.

7

Entrepreneurship in the State Sector: CONASUPO of Mexico

WILLIAM P. GLADE

Department of Economics
and
Institute of Latin American Studies
University of Texas at Austin

For several reasons, Mexico affords a particularly suitable arena for examining entrepreneurial decision making in the public sector. For one thing, a great deal has been written about the workings of the Mexican political system. Although important questions remain obscure, this literature nevertheless provides considerable general insight into the decisional territory in which public policy is made. Further, since the 1920s, the Mexican state has been increasingly involved in a variety of entrepreneurial operations—a fact which, in turn, has generated numerous observations of the phenomenon (Glade and Anderson 1963). In few cases have bureaucratic entrepreneurs been moved to write of their own work. One exception was Antonio J. Bermúdez (1963), the man who from 1947 to 1958 held the reins of Petróleos Mexicanos or Pemex, the national oil company, in a clearly critical period of that enterprise. Many of the public sector entrepreneurs are still alive and supposedly available for interviews, as are a multitude of observers, friendly and otherwise.

The case of the Compañía Nacional de Subsistencias Populares, S.A., or CONASUPO, provides an example of the lines such an inquiry might take. Through this agency and a whole set of parastatal financial institutions—today known as the Banco Nacional de Crédito Agrícola, the Banco Nacional de Crédito Ejidal, the Banco Nacional Agropecuario, the Fondo de Garantía y Fomento para la Agricultura, and several others—the government intervenes in both marketing and credit systems, two of the chief organizational systems which mediate the contact of the farmer with the outside world. Thanks to an evolutionary course spanning almost four decades, CONASUPO's functions have come to embrace far more complex operations than those with which it started out, ramifying into warehousing, rural education, urban merchandising, and even manufacturing. From a relatively minor appendage of other, more consequential public enterprises, it has emerged as one of the largest of the many decentralized or semiautonomous government-owned companies in terms of operating budget. Knowledgeable observers place the company at or near the top of the lengthy list of organizations that play influential roles in national agricultural policy. Controversial in some respects and with a seemingly great potential for attracting criticism on grounds of corruption and inefficiency, CONASUPO has succeeded in building what is a remarkably positive reputation among nearly all segments of Mexican society (Hilger 1976). Public respect, if not adulation, has come its way at home, and its possibilities as a prototype have been studied by groups from Guatemala, Ecuador, and Peru, to mention a few of the official state visitors.

Clearly, bureaucratic entrepreneurship has, in this instance, had very real payoffs: for the enterprise itself (as reflected in its growing assets and scale of operations), for the government stockholder (in terms of goodwill and the management of discontent), and for the politico-technocratic bureaucrats who, as entrepreneurs, have managed the organization's fortunes along the way.

THE ORGANIZATIONAL GENEALOGY OF CONASUPO: CEIMSA FROM 1937 TO 1961

The institutional ancestry of CONASUPO dates back to 1937, an era in which, to borrow more recent language, there was a rash of institution building in the Mexican public sector, especially in relation to rural society and economy. Land redistribution had been accelerated with the beginning of the Cárdenas administration (1934–40), the Banco Nacional de Crédito Ejidal in 1935 had spun off from the older Banco Nacional de Crédito Agrícola y Ganadero as a more specialized lending agency, and the Almacenes Nacionales de Depósito (ANDSA) was set up a year later as a government-run warehousing and storage company. Agricultural schools were organized, the Comisión Federal de Electricidad, begun in 1937, launched, among other things, rural electrification programs, and ejidatarios were brought into a new official interest group organization, the Confederación Nacional Campesina, which was created in 1938.

Shortly after the Banco Nacional de Comercio Exterior was formed in 1937 to promote Mexican foreign trade, it—in collaboration with Nacional Financiera, the two government agricultural banks, and the central bank—found it convenient to organize a subsidiary commercial company to carry out certain trading operations which were directly proscribed for banking institutions. This company, known as the Compañía Exportadora e Importadora Mexicana, S.A., or CEIMSA was, in effect, a department of the Foreign Trade Bank. About the same time the government also formed, separately from the foregoing, the Committee to Regulate the Wheat Market, which was soon superseded by a Committee to Regulate the Market for Staples. Regulation was done through a combination of price supports, imports, and exports, with the fluctuating prices of farm products—owing to bad harvests and speculation—a primary concern. Within the Ministry of National Economy, a Dirección General de Precios was set up to administer price controls at the retail level, and two other governmental entities, the Consultative Committee on Articles of Necessary Consumption and the Vigilance Committee for Commerce, operated temporarily also in this general area. A secondary concern was to prop up the incomes of small farmers who suffered from both shortfalls in harvests and the effects of crop speculators. Not long after, however, war-induced scarcities and internally generated inflationary pressures shifted the emphasis to more or less continuous price regulation to contain the rising prices of staples in urban areas, for example, corn, beans, and wheat. CEIMSA was accorded a virtual monopoly in staple imports in an effort to augment domestic supplies and restrain price increases. The Committee was reorganized in 1941 and became known as the Nacional Distribuidora y Reguladora, S.A., an agency with approximately the same functions as the predecessor committees. At the time, CEIMSA also shared these functions, both appearing to have been financed by the Foreign Trade Bank. A certain amount of organizational tacking and hauling was evident as the Avila Camacho administration (1940-46)—with limited money, manpower, and information—attempted to cope with the many dislocations produced by the war, the aftermath of the depression, and the massive push for agrarian reform. Unclear theoretical guidelines for policy, divergent political tendencies, and simple administrative inexperience combined made it difficult for CEIMSA and associated agencies to define and accomplish its institutional mission unequivocally.

By 1949, however, the earlier food shortages had abated, although some problems lingered on, and a further reorganization ensued. The Nacional Distribuidora y Reguladora was liquidated and its responsibilities were transferred to CEIMSA. From that point on, CEIMSA was the centerpiece of the government's program to regulate supplies and prices of beans, wheat, corn, as well as any other articles determined to be of prime necessity by the Ministers of Economics and Finance. Rice, for example, was once regulated, and so was lard, when shortages of cooking oil developed. In the mid 1950s intervention was applied temporarily to eggs, meat, and milk. On occasion, exports of staples, especially rice, were prohibited in order to retain larger supplies for consumption on the home market; meat exports were sometimes restricted for the same reason. Much more frequent were the cases when CEIMSA procured additional supplies from abroad, selling these imports at a loss to subsidize national consumers. For the farmers, the purpose of CEIMSA was said to be to support prices; for the consumers, it was to keep them from rising too high. For both, ostensibly, prices were to be stabilized, with crop storage and importation utilized to even out seasonal variations. To carry out its complex, even contradictory tasks, CEIMSA had at times to rely on interagency support. For example, credit sanctions from the official banks, fines, and other measures were sometimes used to coerce producers into selling their harvests to CEIMSA. Such compulsory sales were particularly common in the corn and bean markets before the late 1950s. As the situation suggests, what were proclaimed as price guarantees or price supports were, in fact, often converted into price ceilings. When the predictable disincentive effects appeared, the rationing of credit and irrigation water was employed to induce a greater production of staples.

It should be remembered that the entire period in question—the administrations of Alemán (1946–52) and Ruiz Cortines (1952–58)—was one of rapid structural transformation in the Mexican economy, and direct state intervention was evolving dynamically. A variety of state enterprises came into being, particularly in the industrial field, and some of the new regional development commissions made their first appearance on the scene. The conventional presumption of bureaucratic immobilism—of bureaucracy as a rule-bound, rule-keeping, conservative force in society—did not seem an apt description of the Mexican case. On the contrary, innovation abounded, and functionaries of the public sector were anything but passive in their sundry roles. Cumbersome the government's bureaucracy may have been; static it was not. Throughout, the government's administrative elite struck out on its own to introduce new policies and to work through new policy instrumentalities to upset the older order and generate new relationships. It is hard to escape the impression that this elite enjoyed a fair amount of autonomy in its tutelary role of charting the course of economic change, but overall policy consistency was not a necessary concomitant of such circumstances.

Within this general context of state-led modernization, CEIMSA gained importance and ventured into a variety of new activities. While presently one may tend to view functional innovation and organizational expansion as recent CONASUPO achievements, the older CEIMSA, for all its problems, was not devoid of a certain amount of mission refinement and improvement. The policies followed through the 1940s, for instance, had been aimed at influencing general supply and demand conditions and at regulating wholesale margins thought to be too high. It became evident, however, that retailers and food-processing industries were among the major beneficiaries of these policies, along with consumers from more privileged segments of the income structure. Subsequently, in the 1950s, CEIMSA endeavored to develop new policy instruments to convey its subsidies more directly, and exclusively, to the target populations. Price control agreements were instituted to restrict the markup of staples in small retail shops catering to the urban poor (for example, nixtamal millers and bakers), and in a growing number of cases CEIMSA opened its own retail outlets in the poorer neighborhoods of the federal district. Among the products sold in these shops, besides those mentioned earlier, were sugar, coffee, bread, assorted fruits and vegetables, dried fish and shrimp, and crackers. By 1958, the agency began to employ social workers to counsel and educate low-income housewives to take better advantage of the dietary improvement opportunities afforded by the CEIMSA retailing network. As part of the attempt to become more selective in its subsidization of urban consumers, CEIMSA even operated mobile vending units in order to reach poor families living at greater distances from the organization's retail shops.

Although at one point CEIMSA's rural buying stations were abolished and replaced by buying offices of the government's agricultural banks, they were later reopened and increased in number. Storage capacity was similarly enlarged. During the 1952–58 period, CEIMSA opened the first of its food-processing facilities—coffee-roasting plants, bakeries, and nixtamal mills—constituting a still more vertically integrated distribution channel for staple goods and food products.

For several reasons, CEIMSA attracted considerable criticism, and many seem to agree that its record was not a particularly distinguished one. Part of the problem was the ambiguous policy guidelines by which the agency apparently ordered its affairs. Evaluating the agency, two respected scholars wrote,

> The most salient characteristic of the work of CEIMSA, until recently, has been its lack of orientation. There has been no doctrine to guide its activities. Not only has such a doctrine not been [explicitly] defined, but the facts have also demonstrated that none was [implicitly] followed and that the agency was inspired by the greatest confusion of ideas. (Fernández y Fernández and Acosta 1961:201)

The "confusion of ideas" and "lack of orientation," however, are diminished if one disregards one of the formal objectives of the organization: that of safeguarding the economic interests of farmers producing staple crops. In practice, CEIMSA and other related agencies were geared to the consumer interest rather than the producer interest. While the operations of CEIMSA purported to supply all regions of the country with the output of the regions producing staples, it was the urban consumer who actually benefited most from the ministrations of the organization, at least in the short run. More specifically, the lion's share of attention was devoted to people living in the Federal District. They enjoyed, for at least part of the time, preferentially low prices in relation to consumers in less favored (and essentially poorer) sections of the republic. Consumers coming from outside to shop in the Federal District at its subsidized prices were at one time even considered to be engaged in contraband traffic!

Granted that the practical objective of CEIMSA was more narrowly construed than its formal institutional mission, a number of its policies could still be faulted for their shortsightedness and antieconomic consequences as well as their adverse welfare effects. They attracted, in addition, the animosity of those allied with the interests of both producer and private sector marketing intermediaries. Negative comment was further directed against the huge federal subsidies required to finance CEIMSA operations, subsidies which ran from 180 million pesos to 352 million pesos annually between 1954 and 1958.

EXPANSIVE MANAGEMENT AND ORGANIZATIONAL GROWTH

Criticism and substantial operating deficits, together with changed agricultural conditions (that is, larger national production), led eventually to a reexamination of CEIMSA's activities. In the early days of the López Mateos administration (1958–64), it was announced that CEIMSA would undergo a total reorganization. Although the overall pattern of operations did not actually change much at first, there were some significant adjustments. For example, agreements were negotiated during the reassessment phase for CEIMSA to supply private retail merchants and other businessmen with large quantities of the basic foodstuffs in which it dealt. This included substantial sales of corn to millers and various corn-product firms in several states and the thirty-four most important cities of the country. Peace was made with CONCANACO, the National Confederation of Chambers of Commerce. More realistic support price policies were announced and general consumer subsidies were on their way to being scaled down and phased out. Storage functions were shifted to

ANDSA, which thereupon multiplied its capacity from 394 bodegas in June 1959, to 1,112 bodegas a year later. By this time, the number of CEIMSA buying stations had grown to 168, so that fewer farmers complained of problems of inaccessibility. Compulsory transactions were infrequent. Meanwhile, wheat was sold to millers through their trade associations and eggs were purchased through associations of poultry raisers. In both instances the channels of transactions were institutionalized so as to mollify organized interest groups which might otherwise have mobilized opposition to the agency.

In 1961, the proposed reorganization was finally put into effect and CEIMSA was transformed into CONASUPO. Broader powers were bestowed on it—along with presidential attention—and a long and sustained period of expansion began. More food products were added to the line carried in CONASUPO's retail outlets, the number of outlets was increased, and clothing and shoes were introduced on a broader scale into the retail operations. In 1965, the enterprise structure was modified again, this time in the direction of administrative decentralization. Regional offices were established in each of the states of Mexico to provide more effective oversight of the assorted CONASUPO operations: small supermarkets, small grocery stores not handling fresh meat, market stalls in the public markets, stores located on the collective farms, and private shops and factory commissaries licensed to sell CONASUPO-brand products. The number of mobile vending units—functioning as grocery stores in some instances, as dry-goods shops in others—was also increased, as well as the number of buying centers. In due course, the mobile vending units included not only trucks but also a few specially designed railway cars and boats to serve communities not reached by highways.

By various means, exercising the subtle and not so subtle techniques which have been polished to a fine art, the Mexican government induced private manufacturers of such items as packaged foods and wearing apparel to supply the CONASUPO outlets at preferential prices. CONASUPO thus operated a transfer payment scheme by subsidizing the low-income stores and by selling at higher prices to marketing outlets in middle- and upper-income areas. The frequency and intensity of official inspections, the ease of securing permits to employ specialized foreign technicians, the level of duty applied to imported supplies all were leverages used by the government to obtain advantageous prices for the CONASUPO distribution network. Additional types of consumer items were eventually added to CONASUPO retail shops, these also on a preferred price basis. Brand selection, new products, improved packaging (including smaller package options for those with meager cash incomes), sanitary and attractive displays, and other aspects of modern merchandising were not least among the innovations brought by CONASUPO to the urban poor. In passing, one might note that a sizable portion of the manufactured goods carried by CONASUPO has come from the Mexican subsidiaries of large multinational corporations. These corporations, by participating in CONASUPO operations, have in effect become agents of the state in taxing the more affluent segments of the market.

Broadly speaking, the expansionary thrust which began during the López Mateos administration continued, at an even more stepped-up pace, under the administrations of Díaz Ordaz (1964–70) and Echeverría (1970–76). So large and complex has the operation become that it would not be feasible either to provide a detailed profile of CONASUPO's present activities or to recount how they have evolved over the past fifteen years. It will have to suffice to summarize some of the highlights of the record to indicate major qualitative characteristics and quantitative dimensions.[1]

As an organizational apparatus, it may be noted that CONASUPO proper, headquartered since 1971 in a conspicuous downtown site in the national capital, operates essentially as a state-owned holding company. The number of affiliated companies is reported to have grown from five to seventeen between 1970 and 1975, with the administrative decentralization begun in 1973 resulting in the construction of twenty-one *delegaciones estatales*, regional administrative headquarters and large central warehousing facilities in state capitals. Also regionalized in this period were the retail sales operations, most of which are now grouped into the six regional subsidiary sales companies of Distribuidora CONASUPO, S.A. de C.V. (DICONSA). The respective number of outlets and monthly sales volumes of these regional sales networks in June 1975 are shown in table 7.1.

According to one calculation, the total number of retail outlets grew from twelve hundred in 1971 to over six thousand in 1975. The

TABLE 7.1
CONASUPO REGIONAL SUBSIDIARIES, JUNE 1975

	Number of Outlets	Monthly Sales Volume (in millions of pesos)
Diconsa del Norte	523	53.2
Diconsa del Centro	646	35.6
Diconsa del Noroeste	308	32.9
Diconsa del Sur	497	49.1
Diconsa del Sureste	436	37.1
Diconsa Metropolitana	494	138.4
	2,904	346.3 million pesos

latter figure, however, evidently includes many outlets other than those of the DICONSA networks, incorporating some three thousand special small retail centers on ejidos, which sell a limited range of products (mainly five basic staples), small *tiendas concesionadas* leased to private operators, and *tiendas institucionales* or shops set up in conjunction with other government agencies. Included in these figures were the aforementioned *ferrotiendas* (begun in 1971 in collaboration with the Ferrocarriles Nacionales de México), the *barcotiendas* (coordinated with local government authorities), the *lecherías*, the market stalls, and such cooperative ventures as the *tiendas rurales* of the ejidos and the *tiendas sindicales* operated in association with trade-union organizations. Clearly, then, the range of CONASUPO retail outlets encompasses variations far more than ordinary grocery stores, supermarkets (self-service CONASUPER stores opened in 1971), and stores selling dry goods and household items. In recent years, consumer durables have been added to the line of goods carried in the more important retail outlets and farm tools are now sold in *tiendas rurales*. In 1974 the company invested in the building of CONASUPO shopping centers in the more heavily populated areas. Another development of note in the retail distribution field is the introduction of some two dozen CONASUPO-brand products (for example, cleaning products, corn meal, wheat flour, crackers, evaporated and powdered milk, powdered chocolate, instant coffee, honey, and cooking oil), some of which are also sold in private stores with resale price agreements. Some of these products are produced by CONASUPO manufacturing subsidiaries, while others are produced under contract by private manufacturers according to CONASUPO specifications. In several instances, CONASUPO-brand products have gained favor among consumers of the more privileged segments of the income structure. Combined with the retail operations in recent years has been a CONASUPO program of consumer credit for rural customers. The program was designed to provide farm families with relief from usurious rates of private moneylenders and to enable farmers to avoid having to pledge crops at disadvantageous price terms to marketing intermediaries in return for consumer credit extended before the harvest season. CONASUPO outlets accordingly allowed farm families to charge their preharvest consumption purchases and then to redeem their accounts by proceeds either from open-market sales or from sales to CONASUPO at a guaranteed price, whichever is higher. One CONASUPO estimate figures that in 1975 the rural retail systems of CONASUPO served, through both credit and cash sales in the *tiendas rurales* and *tiendas institucionales* (and the special small-scale sales units mentioned previously), rural communities totaling thirteen million people.

The national retail network of CONASUPO has been used, in turn, to develop two backward linkages, although limitedly thus far. On the one hand, the avowed intention is that the regional sales organizations should endeavor to develop to the extent possible new supply sources of products within their respective regions. It is not known to what degree this strategy has been successful as a means of promoting regional development. On the other hand, CONASUPO sales have also been used to further vertical integration through operating the system's own manufacturing plants—for example, subsidiary companies as LICONSA (milk processing and packaging), MINSA (corn processing), and TRICONSA (wheat products). Although present priorities seem to emphasize consolidation and improvements in existing system management, it would not be surprising were the future to bring an expansion of the variety and scale of the CONASUPO manufacturing affiliates. For the time being, however, top management has placed in the forefront commercial and regulatory functions and such technical matters as improved warehousing, inventory management, and promotion of rural production from the ejidos and smaller farm units. Manufacturing development is only a secondary consideration, notwithstanding the potential of the CONASUPO complex—which also serves institutional customers—to provide mass markets for national public and private concerns. What is sought, in most instances, is simply a large enough share of the market to exercise an influence, not expansion for its own sake.

Another aspect of CONASUPO's growth, that of warehousing, has had even more spin-offs. The urban-centered part of the CONASUPO warehousing-storage operations is now largely consolidated into ANDSA, a state company which has worked with CEIMSA and then CONASUPO for years. The shares of ANDSA were recently acquired by CONASUPO, converting it thereby into one of the subsidiary undertakings of this growing holding company. In 1975 ANDSA operated 644 urban bodegas. The last few years have seen, additionally, CONASUPO acting in collaboration with the Banco del Pequeño Comercio to erect more urban storage facilities to serve small-scale vendors; associations of small businessmen have worked out agreements with these two public enterprises to supply them with goods from the special bodegas of this system.

Rural storage facilities have figured in the CONASUPO operations since the days of CEIMSA. Both number and storage capacity of rural "reception centers" have grown. Beginning in 1966, however, a special campaign was undertaken to build "people's silos," with campesino labor and loans financed by CONASUPO. By the end of 1969, some 2,400 conical silos, resembling Indian teepees, and rectangular storage facilities had been built on the rural landscape. Technical and managerial problems at first often created operational difficulties. CONASUPO managers experienced conflicts with campesino customers over buying prices, storage costs, and other policies. Allegations of irregularities in the procedures for accepting crops for storage were also made at this time (Johnson 1971:106). Another problem was that storage was but one of several services needed by the campesinos at this stage of the production process. Private, and allegedly exploitative, marketing intermediaries known as caciques continued to supply sacks, transport, husking, as well as certain producer goods, thereby diminishing the intended welfare effect of CONASUPO intervention. The same cacique group was said to have lent money for consumer credit in further exploitation of the farmers.

Studies were made of this situation, and under the next CONASUPO directorship, new policies were installed to cope with such problems. It was ascertained that campesino confidence—and employment and income—would be improved if the rural storage

202

facilities were locally managed by the campesinos themselves within the framework of CONASUPO system management. To accomplish this was no small task. It involved administering, from 1972 on, an extensive rural training program to enable the ejidatarios to play a more active role in the marketing process. In collaboration with both the Secretaría de la Reforma Agraria and the Confederación Nacional Campesina, twenty residential training centers and a widespread extension education system were set up to "capacitate" ejidatarios in grading, weighing, and storing techniques, along with the necessary bookkeeping and managerial operations. By the end of 1974, sixty thousand campesinos had completed some form of training and begun to assume major responsibilities at the reception centers. To deal with middleman "exploitation," CONASUPO introduced new policies of lending, free of charge, sacks to the farmers, hiring transport services for CONASUPO rural operations, and providing facilities for husking—all this together with the previously mentioned consumer credit policies begun in 1974. Whereas consumer credit was handled by DICONSA affiliates, the storage and other ancillary services were organized under another CONASUPO subsidiary which had been established in 1971, the Bodegas Rurales CONASUPO, S.A. de C.V., or BORUCONSA.

The diversification of BORUCONSA services—representing scale economies derived from the basic organizational framework—did not stop with the foregoing. Associated with the rural bodegas of the BORUCONSA system were complementary functions such as the sale of fertilizers manufactured by Guanos y Fertilizantes de México, S.A., or GUANOMEX, and improved seeds developed by Productora Nacional de Semillas, or PRONASE, both public enterprises. Farm implements and CONASUPO-produced livestock feed and construction materials also entered into the distributional apparatus. With cooperation from the Secretaría de Agricultura y Ganadería, technical assistance programs were launched to aid farmers in the regions served by the bodegas of the rural reception centers. The number of these centers grew from 1,109 in 1971 to 1,250 in 1975. Larger facilities then under construction reportedly increased storage capacity from one to one and one-half million tons. Agricultural machinery stations were also available at some of these facilities, reflecting the prevailing view at CONASUPO of rural reception centers as "micropoles" of development.

Consistent with the new importance of social welfare functions in the 1970s, the BORUCONSA network of reception centers became sites for medical clinics or consultation offices as well. These clinics were administered by the Instituto Mexicano de Seguro Social in collaboration with CONASUPO. About a hundred such facilities were opened in 1974, and about two hundred and fifty were in operation by the close of the following year.

The 1970s also saw the Social Improvement Commission, another arm of CONASUPO, initiate a range of programs to upgrade rural life: assistance in planting more productive family gardens and orchards, organization of credit unions, publication of a newspaper, production of a special soap opera for broadcast over three hundred radio stations—written so as to convey useful information on CONASUPO marketing services, crop prices, and the like. Cultural and sports activities were encouraged as part of the CONASUPO community development efforts. It was claimed that by the end of 1975 a new CONASUPO-sponsored "peasant theater" group had played before two million farmers.

To round out this somewhat panoramic picture of CONASUPO activities, it should be noted that one or another division of the company has, in the past few years, promoted the development of milksheds; organized and financed the production of fruits, vegetables, cheese, jams and jellies, as well as construction materials; organized relief efforts and provided for victims of natural disasters; and bought, stored, and sold crops such as corn, beans, wheat, sorghum, rice, soybeans, copra, sesame, barley, safflower, and sunflower. In connection with these commercial operations, continuing efforts have been made to strengthen the incentive aspects of CONASUPO pricing by adjusting frequently the price quotations for crops (now sold only on a voluntary basis to CONASUPO) to allow for changes in the cost of production, projected demand, and harvest forecasts. The purchase of crops, both domestic and imported, amounted to 2.7 million tons in 1970 and reached 7 million tons in 1975. Unfortunately for the country's balance of payments, these figures included substantial imports in 1973, 1974, and 1975.

The CONASUPO patrimony grew from 1,700 million pesos in 1971 to 6,000 million pesos in 1975. Assets rose from nearly 2,500 million pesos to 11,500 million pesos in the same period. The total operating budget increased from 4.8 billion pesos in 1971 to 32 billion pesos in

1975. It is a source of pride to the enterprise management that administrative costs, at least as figured by the company, represent no more than 2.8 percent of the operating expenses and that the upper- and middle-level cadres bring to the organization a high level of technical proficiency.

A further source of pride is the fact that the level of integrity in CONASUPO operations is generally recognized to be high. A few people outside CONASUPO have charged that abuses at, say, the level of shop cashiers, are attributable to lax management and that payoffs may occasionally be involved between CONASUPO buyers and external suppliers. Yet these allegations seem on the whole to be fairly petty in light of the level and volume of possible impropriety. Rather, one is struck by the relative infrequency of such criticism for so widely observed an organization.

The higher echelons of CONASUPO—and so far as could be determined, the lower ranks too—see the agency as exceptionally flexible and receptive to innovation. Not without good reason, one might add. A large part of CONASUPO's effectiveness in the difficult milieu of small ejidal farmers and other campesinos is attributed, again not without justification, to the comprehensiveness of its services and functions, at least in comparison with other institutions working in agriculture. Commercial farmers are affected by the actions of CONASUPO, but the explicit attention given the smaller agriculturists is seen as the real challenge and hallmark of success. CONASUPO officials speak of their function as redistributing income and welfare and as correcting injustices—the usual language of the revolution. Particularly on the rural side of their operations, this was, more often than not, seen as a concomitant of productionist measures. For instance, the pricing policy for crops was almost always described in terms of incentive effects, the stimulation of production, increased savings out of higher farm incomes, and so on, with farm welfare a by-product. Outright social welfare programs are not denigrated. On the contrary, CONASUPO sponsorship of these is held to be unquestionably justified, but they do not seem to consume much of the CONASUPO budget. Even in the case of the urban retail outlets, the social welfare function is often linked explicitly with the contribution of the system to national marketing efficiency. At the same time, with a refreshing candor, many of the interviewees told of the local-level political benefits reaped by various projects. Local and regional political factions are often deliberately brought into the consultative processes in order to avert, or at least mute, hostile criticism of CONASUPO operations. This important role of constituency building was acknowledged without euphemism or apology.[2]

THE RELEVANCE OF ENTREPRENEURIAL ANALYSIS

The history of CONASUPO operations has been recounted at some length, although in summary form. Like many private corporations, CONASUPO has sought new functions for its institutional charter, diversified its undertakings, changed its organizational structure, served new clientele groups in new ways, and all the while managed to secure requisite resources (funds, skilled personnel, inter-organizational cooperation). Particularly notable has been its growth since the mid 1960s. That it is not a profit-maximizing or even profit-making entity in no way negates the fact that expansive management and growth in organizational resources have been characteristic of its activity in recent times. Thus, it is here posited that the concept of entrepreneurship can be readily applied to CONASUPO's performance and that, with modification, the social structural correlates of entrepreneurship in the private sector may also be useful in understanding the entrepreneurial phenomenon in the parastatal sector. In other words, somewhat different but essentially similar types of social structures appear here to play the role which family networks and investor coalitions or business groups have been described as playing in the literature on private entrepreneurship (Benedict 1968; Aubey 1970).[3]

It is the central contention of this chapter that the social links or nonformalized ties of interaction which grow out of what Leeds (1964) and others have described as multiple jobholding, *panelinhas*, and *igrejinhas*[4] provide—along with the *clientela*[5] relationships which La Palombara (1964) has examined—the elements of a model for analyzing the phenomenon of entrepreneurship in the parastatal sector. The concept of parentela[6] networks, moreover, supplements the *panelinha* notion. Taken together, these elements permit one to refine and specify with greater clarity the decisional analysis of organizational process and bureaucratic politics models (Allison 1969).

206

The operations of this complex of structures reveal themselves to be, in several respects, functional equivalents of the relationships depicted by Aubey, Kyle, and Strickon (1974). While from one point of view, such personalistic interlocking networks may be considered a "contamination" of the impersonal, instrumental relations ascribed by Weber, Parsons, and others to "modern" bureaucratic processes,[7] they are, it is here argued, important to understanding how entrepreneurial behavior can be manifested in public investment decisions in the prevailing Latin American context. In a sense, these are facilitating mechanisms, just as business groups and investor coalitions in underdeveloped private economic sectors are partial surrogates for the market mechanism which is as yet only imperfectly and incompletely constituted (Aubey 1970).

It must be admitted that the evidential basis for the model being proposed is fragmentary and, in large measure, inferential in character. In the first place, few studies of public-sector entrepreneurs have been made. Votaw's insightful treatment of Enrico Mattei and the development of the Ente Nazionale Idrocarburi is an outstanding record dealing with a sociocultural setting not wholly unlike the Latin American case. While the analytical segments of the work (Votaw 1964: 94–141) tend to confirm the general importance of alliances of a parentela nature and to hint at the presence of *igrejinha* and *clientela* relationships and multiple jobholding, none of these is fully developed as a subject of inquiry. Unfortunately, no investigation similar to Votaw's has been made, or at least published, for Latin America, leaving a great void in the available data base. Yet, as Allison (1969:716) has pointed out, organizational process and bureaucratic politics models of decisional analysis, the models of which the present is a variation, require large amounts of information to be applied effectively.

Second, most studies of entrepreneurship in Latin America are like that undertaken by Derossi (1971) in Mexico or by Lipman (1969) in Colombia. The nurturing role of the government vis-à-vis private entrepreneurship is discussed at length in Derossi and mentioned in Lipman, the direct entrepreneurial function of the state is clearly recognized in Derossi, and a perceived restrictive impact of public intervention on private sector leadership is acknowledged in both. What is not explicitly analyzed, however, is the entrepreneur who operates within the public sector.

A third problem is that many of the excellent studies made of aspects of the public sector deal with policy formation and decision making in areas which are, in varying degree, remote from the exercise of parastatal economic entrepreneurship (Cleaves 1974; Ugalde 1973; Wynia 1972). The studies do provide information essential to understanding the general decisional context we are discussing, however. Much closer is the account written by Antonio J. Bermúdez (1963) of his work as a bureaucratic entrepreneur in Petróleos Mexicanos, but this, too, slides quickly past data of present concern.[8] Even the Posadas' provocative work on the Cauca Valley Corporation (1966), which perhaps comes closest to yielding the necessary types of data, does not really focus enough on the entrepreneurial facets of the topic. Interbureaucratic decision making, in many instances what parastatal entrepreneurship involves, is a particularly neglected field.

The interbureaucratic aspects of parastatal entrepreneurship have been addressed in several Brazilian cases. For purposes of comparison they are discussed briefly. The role of General Edmundo de Macedo Soares e Silva and the Brazilian officer corps in establishing the National Steel Company, for example, has been described in a way to suggest relationships here hypothesized (Rady 1973:117–197; Wirth 1970:71–129). To some extent, the same may be said for the role of General Julio Caeteno Horta Barbosa and his backers, military and nonmilitary, and of the civilian bureaucrat, Rômulo de Almeida, and his group, in the tangled functional disputes which eventually gave birth to Petrobrás (Wirth 1970:133–216). Less informative but nevertheless illustrative is the account Hirschman provides of the formation of SUDENE, with passing mention of the inception of two other state enterprises, the São Francisco Hydroelectric Company and the Bank of the Northeast of Brazil (1963:13–91).

In consequence of these evidentiary limitations, support to establish a minimal presumptive basis for the network model will have to be drawn from a wide variety of admittedly suboptimal sources. In no sense is a claim being made that the model is anything more than a very preliminary, still crudely stated hypothesis. As such, it is at this stage less the basis for forming specific, testable propositions for building theories than a general frame of reference for collecting and organizing data.

208

ENTREPRENEURIAL FACTORS IN CONASUPO EXPANSION

During 1974 and 1975, extensive reading of various news sources together with numerous semistructured interviews with persons related and unrelated to CONASUPO were done to determine whether (a) the general network notions could be deemed plausible descriptions of the modus operandi of Mexican parastatal entrepreneurs in general and of CONASUPO in particular and (b) any putative networks could be described for the entrepreneurs in question. The almost universal consensus was that the social network approach did serve to describe the nature of the entrepreneurial reality. On the second research objective any clues proved remarkably elusive.[9]

For all the publicity accorded the public activities of the Mexican political elite, the more private and personal dimensions of their lives often remain a matter for conjecture and gossip. Everyone acknowledges the practical importance of the family, including the extended family of uncles, aunts, and cousins. Virtually all informants agree that this kind of family closeness can mean a whole constituency of support and encouragement. Instances of the use of kinship ties as means of mobilizing resource support can definitely be found in the Mexican public sector. For example, under the administration of Luís Echeverría, a particularly favored regional development project was the Comisión de Desarrollo del Sur de Jalisco, in which the Vocal Ejecutivo was Sr. José Guadalupe Zuno Arce, the president's brother-in-law. Also active in the agency's operations was the president's son, Lic. Alvaro Echeverría Zuno, until he moved into the regional development section of the Secretaría de la Presidencia. One might speculate, too, that the Mexican Federal Electricity Commission's expansion during the 1960s was not harmed by the fact that the president and chairman of the National Executive Committee of the PRI, Mexico's dominant political party, was Alfonso Martínez Domínguez, brother of Guillermo Martínez Domínguez, director general of the Federal Electricity Commission. Other examples of nepotism and kinship networks abound, but colorful though they may be they do not seem to figure significantly as components for public-sector decisional analysis. Mexican family

209

networks are large but nevertheless dwarfed by the size and complexity of the labyrinthine governing apparatus. Family networks also tend to be fragile, given the rapid turnover of positions in the administrative and political hierarchy. Although there is broad agreement that friendship and other nonfamilial networks function similarly and on a much more widespread basis, these probably shifting coalitions turn out, upon inquiry, to be far less visible and in composition much less certain.

In the case of CONASUPO, after its reorganization out of CEIMSA in mid 1961, a promising young politico, having just completed a term as federal deputy, was placed in charge of the newly important sales division from 1961 to 1964. Carlos Hank González, a native of the state of Mexico, was born in 1927, graduated from the Escuela Normal Superior de México at Toluca, and worked for four years as a mathematics teacher before becoming a government functionary.[10] His political career began with his participation, as a teacher, in the National Teachers Union and the PRI. The rapidity of his political rise in the 1950s would appear to be prima facie evidence of his exceptionally well-placed political connections. The launching pad for this career seems to have been Hank's membership in the informal group or camarilla surrounding Isidro Fabela, an influential *cardenista* governor of the state of Mexico.

In 1952 Hank left teaching to take the post of director of secondary education and professional schools for the Department of Education of the state of Mexico. In 1954, he served as treasurer of the city of Toluca and was mayor in 1955–57. From 1958 to 1961, before his appointment as sales manager of CONASUPO—at the time, much more active in its retail operations in the Federal District and the adjacent state of Mexico than in other parts of the republic—Hank served as a federal deputy from the state of Mexico in the Chamber of Deputies. In 1964, after his tenure as sales manager, he was promoted to the post of director general of CONASUPO, a position he held until 1969. Under his direction, CONASUPO grew considerably. He hired many young *técnicos* to raise the effectiveness of the organization, and his reputation as a hardworking, exceedingly capable, and politically astute administrator was consolidated. From 1969 to 1975, he built further on his reputation as governor of the state of Mexico, then well into a dynamic phase of economic expansion.[11] With patronage, he was able to strengthen his already solid base of support in the state while securing the backing of the important industrialists. Known to have a wide political following, Hank is generally thought to have been particularly close in his political associations to such key figures as Gustavo Baz, twice governor of the state of Mexico, Luis Enrique Bracamontes, a minister of public works, Alfredo de Mazo, Hugo Cervantes del Río, Emilio Sánchez Piedras, Gonzalo Martínez Córdoba, José Ortiz Avila, Juventino Castro Sánchez, Rafael Moreno Valle, Rómulo O'Farrill, Sr., Leopoldo Sánchez Celis, Mario Moya Palencia, and possibly Adolfo López Mateos, among others. With an assortment of business investments in his portfolio—trucking fleets, a truck factory, and other companies held in common with his father-in-law—Hank has accumulated considerable wealth, adding thereby an economic base to his political one. His earlier alliance with a *cardenista*-oriented group came in time to be replaced by the role of a conservative modernizer, somewhat after the fashion of Alemán.

Hank's eventual successor as director general of CONASUPO was Lic. Jorge de la Vega Domínguez, who served in that capacity from 1970 to 1976, when he resigned to run for the governorship of Chiapas. Under his direction, CONASUPO experienced even more innovation and expansion than it had under Hank. Born in Comitán, Chiapas, in 1931, de la Vega had spent most of his adult life in the Federal District where he took his degree in economics at the National University in 1958.[12] In 1958–61, de la Vega was subdirector of Diesel Nacional, a government-owned firm, and in 1960–64 he taught public finance at the National Polytechnic Institute, where he was director of the Advanced School of Economics in 1963–65. For an overlapping period, 1964–67, he served as federal deputy from Chiapas. His term in the Congress, where he sat on committees for natural resources, money and credit institutions, and budgets and accounts, provided a broad familiarization with the national economic scene. Further career benefits were conferred when he headed, for a brief period, the Department of Public Expenditure in the Office of the Presidency. During the early 1960s he also served as a subdirector of the Banco de Pequeño Comercio. In 1965 de la Vega was one of the talented young technocrats that Hank González had brought into CONASUPO, where de la Vega worked as sales manager until mid 1968. De la Vega was also, it should be noted, a founder of the Colegio de Economistas, of which he was president for a time in the sixties.

In short, the early public career of de la Vega reveals a pattern of rapid professional mobility and prominence. His career drew on opportunities which added new ones, resulting in mutually productive associations in strategic places. In addition, it provided a decidedly superior access to political and economic information, a most advantageous access, given the singularly imperfect information market which operates—particularly outside the institution—as regards the decision-making processes in the inner councils of the Mexican government.

De la Vega's rapid rise in party/government circles from his days as leader of the economics students' association at UNAM owes much, undoubtedly, to his ability and intelligence. But he was not without added advantages. He was the nephew of Belisario Domínguez, a distinguished senator from the earlier days of the revolution. From the time he arrived in the Federal District to attend the prestigious National Preparatory School, de la Vega seems, according to all accounts, to have gravitated easily into a select circle of friends and acquaintances. Reportedly, this continued during his studies in the National School of Economics. De la Vega is also mentioned as having been close in the 1960s to both Gustavo Díaz Ordaz and Luis Echeverría, whose regard for him rose even further after his constructive role as one of two presidentially appointed negotiators during the student disturbances of 1968. He was sales director of CONASUPO when he was selected to serve from 1968 to 1970 as head of the Instituto de Estudios Políticos, Económicos, y Sociales of the PRI. A key organization, IEPES flourishes as the party's organ for studying and defining issues and proposing solutions every six years before the elections. In this role, de la Vega traveled widely and frequently around the republic, organizing a series of seminars with the local political leadership (Alisky 1973:55–56). Thus, as in many other spheres, de la Vega's assets took on a cumulative aspect. The directorship of IEPES both reflected political accomplishment and provided the means for further political advancement.

As in the case of Hank González, the politically useful associations of de la Vega Domínguez remain a matter of conjecture. In addition to Hank González, and the two presidents mentioned above, the names sometimes associated with de la Vega's career trajectory include, outside CONASUPO, Moya Palencia, Eliseo Mendoza Berrueto (an undersecretary in the Secretaría de Industria y Comercio), Rodolfo Becerril Straffon (of the same ministry), José López Portillo (Finance Ministry), and, at one time, Horacio Flores de la Peña when he headed the Secretaría del Patrimonio Nacional. Occasionally mentioned was Lic. Carlos Torres Manzo, a CONASUPO official who went on to become the Minister of Commerce and Industry. Still other persons were suggested as having played supportive roles, but much was made of the key friendships with Díaz Ordaz, Echeverría, and López Portillo. While confirmatory evidence was not readily available from the interviews or other sources, the question of network differentiation was nevertheless raised by some of the responses. In other words, there may be two levels or types of networks operative. One is a broader, more diffuse, and more fluid set of associations, an extensive network which serves to monitor the environment and gather and transmit information. The other, smaller, more intensive, and more stable, serves to mobilize influence and other resources to act on the "investment opportunities" spotted by the first network level.

Within CONASUPO, the members of the de la Vega team are said to have included such high-level administrators as Fernando Solana, Gustavo Esteva, Enrique Díaz Ballesteros, and Jorge Aguilera Noriega. Further, it might be worth noting that among the other able technicians and administrators serving with de la Vega were Diego López Rosado, a professional economist, and Rubén Zuno Arce, an in-law of the president. The two exemplify well the range of affiliations involved in staffing the upper echelons of an agency like CONASUPO. The proposition that, by and large, CONASUPO functionaries had at least adequate technical qualifications (and often much more than that) found general acceptance throughout the interviews. For example, respondents indicated that a large percentage of the managerial cadres in CONASUPO were professionally trained in economics, administration, accounting, agronomy, or engineering. All of these educational backgrounds were assumed to be relevant to the work of the enterprise. However, most knowledgeable observers, especially outside the enterprise, saw a further attribute present *and relevant to the work setting:* direct friendship with higher level enterprise management or personal recommendations from external friendship connections of the CON-ASUPO leadership. How far this actually pervades the personnel structure of the enterprise could not be ascertained, but it seems, for a number of fairly obvious reasons, to be entirely functional and efficacy-enhancing from the standpoint of the organization itself.

What one deals with, in these presumptive groups, is not a single network but rather constellations of interlocking networks, which are moreover characterized by a fluidity through time. The association of the name of de la Vega with the Moya Palencia camp and that of Hank with the Cervantes del Río *alianza* in the prenomination phase of the 1976 election provide another illustration of this point. It does not necessarily imply any breach between Hank and either de la Vega or Moya, with whom Hank has also been grouped. Given these apparent characteristics of the informal associations, the term clique, which is sometimes used, seems inappropriate. These intersecting sets of people, admittedly based on assumed relationships rather than fully delineated ones, seem to indicate another characteristic of a provisional nature—namely, a certain pragmatism: that is to say, doctrinally derived political factions do not necessarily constitute the basis for these *alianzas*.

THE SOCIAL STRUCTURES OF PARASTATAL ENTREPRENEURSHIP: A PRELIMINARY MODEL

Following an earlier effort (Glade 1967) to develop an analytical framework for the study of entrepreneurship, I should like, in conclusion, to examine the demand and supply conditions for parastatal entrepreneurial behavior in terms of a bilevel situational analysis that takes account of factors operating at both macroenvironmental and microenvironmental levels. One component of a situational analysis of this kind involves the consideration of variables in economic structure that shape the demand for entrepreneurial abilities. Put differently, these variables affect the design of the opportunity structure. In the case of private entrepreneurial behavior, the relevant macroenvironmental variables include factors such as changes in the level and composition of aggregate demand, the structural characteristics of the production of the different goods and services demanded, and so on.

214

In the case of parastatal entrepreneurship, demand analysis begins with the foregoing considerations, but there are two further analytical steps to be made. The first is a consideration of those product features which channel the demand for particular goods and services to the public sector rather than the private sector. Deferred profitability aspects, the target rate of growth, externalities which create net social gains in excess of net private gains, a negative preference for foreign ownership and management, considerations of scale when a profitable project exceeds the capital mobilization capabilities of the domestic private sector—such factors must be explicitly taken into account, along with any priority for public control determined by the social preference function. This is not, of course, intended to be either an exhaustive or a systematic listing of the special factors in demand analysis which Eckstein (1958), Mark (1959), Johnson (1967:1–16), and others have discussed. To the listing, however, one may wish to add country-specific considerations. In Mexico, for example, a "six-year scramble" regularly produces a large turnover of top posts in government as a result of the "no reelection" principle that prevents elected officials from serving successive terms. As top elected officials come and go, so, too, do their appointees. With each shuffle among elective offices, cabinet posts, parastatal management positions, and other federal appointments, new faces enter the arena while others leave. An occasional Bermúdez or Hernández may stay on for a long time at Pemex or Nacional Financiera, but the general effect of the turnover is to multiply the opportunities for well-placed individuals to gain access to entrepreneurial positions, at least for a while.

The second special modification of the demand analysis derives from the fact that public enterprises, as extensions of the public sector, meet the demand for their output in two distinctly structured "markets." They, like other firms, deal in part with a social preference function (SPF_I)—a composite of the individual utility functions of households and firms, weighted by disposable income. Economic bargaining constitutes the mode of interaction in this market. Public enterprises must also cater to a demand pattern (SPF_{II}) which is generated by the political processes of the system: the preferences of the citizenry as filtered through political parties and movements, interest groups, political leaders in the legislative and executive-administrative branches of government. Political bargaining consti-

215

tutes the mode of interaction in this second market. CONASUPO, for example, deals in some conventional commodity markets where factors such as income, tastes, and knowledge determine the level of demand for its services. Just as clearly, it has also had increased opportunity, since the days of López Mateos, to expand its operations in response to the growing demand in the political market for redistributive policies.[13] Moreover, in view of the structural and demographic characteristics of the Mexican economy and the political climate of the times, one can, with a fair degree of reliability, forecast a continuously rising demand for both the goods and the redistributive services supplied by CONASUPO. This would hold true in rural no less than urban markets of each type. Just as the pecuniary sale of "economic" outputs provides the public or parastatal enterprise with financial resources, the nonpecuniary sale of political benefits yields a return in constituency building, power, and influence. The two "currencies" enjoy at least limited or partial convertibility so that, for example, earnings from the political market may sometimes be transformed into financial resources. These resources might include increased appropriations on behalf of the enterprise from the central government's treasury, a greater volume of loans from the central bank, and special concessions and subsidies. By the same token, greater financial resources may obviously be converted into higher political earnings. Both the monetary (Y_I) and non-monetary (Y_{II}) streams of "income" serve to provide the enterprise with command over real resources. Thus construed, the maximizing or satisficing behavior of the firm, whichever one believes to be applicable, involves increasing the value of Y_I, or Y_{II}, or both.

Two further observations on the nature of the demand function of parastatal entrepreneurship may be in order here. One is that in the markets of the public as well as of the private sector, there are opportunities to adapt to changing market conditions. The record of CONASUPO indicates this well. Although CONASUPO sought at first to offset the influence of private marketing intermediaries by providing storage for small farmers, it eventually discovered that the private middlemen retained their grip on the rural population through the multiple functions (transport, provisioning with staples, bagging, consumer credit) they had customarily provided. In the early days when simple storage was supplied, it was often the private

216

middlemen who brought the corn and beans in for CONASUPO storage. Competition for the small farmer's business, then, resulted in CONASUPO's functional diversification so as to supply more adequately the complete range of services required by the clientele.

Second, where state enterprises enjoy a degree of autonomy from supervisory scrutiny and control from both executive and legislative authorities or where the state itself enjoys a certain latitude for "independent" action, the laxity of external constraints on bureaucratic choice gives rise to a self-induced demand element. In other words, one may also have to consider a regime preference function or planners' preference function (SPF_{III}) emanating from either the administrative apparatus or the parastatal entity itself.[14] Votaw's study of Mattei and ENI indicates perhaps the maximum extent to which a public enterprise can derive its resource allocation pattern from its own utility function.

SPF_{II}, for instance, will normally involve extramarket considerations of a system-maintaining nature. These would include, for example, the subsidized provision of credit or electricity to rural groups in order to secure political loyalties for the incumbent regime. SPF_{III} may go further and involve system-formation criteria for allocation—for example, the establishment of state-operated basic industry to create a new clientele, domestic industrialists and urban workers, on which the parastatal enterprise or even the government in general can count for support. It is by now a familiar observation that the service and regulatory bureaucracies tend to develop their own powerful constituencies, both inside the legislative and executive branches and out, so that it becomes difficult to curb their powers or to diminish their size. As noted previously, the dynamics of a system such as Mexico's also leads to a self-induced organizational expansion as a derivative of the demand for patronage. Patronage here is based on the value of building larger camarillas which entrepreneurs like Hank González or de la Vega Domínguez can subsequently count on for support.

On the supply or entrepreneurial response side of the situational analysis, a macroenvironmental examination of the conditions of opportunity appropriation reveals "a structure of differential advantage in the capacity of the system's participants to perceive and act upon such opportunities" (Glade 1967:251). In this, a decisive consideration is control of or ability to obtain key relevant resources.

Access to capital, to influence over complementary investment or other economic policy decisions, to information networks, to transactional security arrangements, and so on may all constitute resources. Each is an element which may contribute to the success of the enterprise in realizing its usually multiple purposes. The far-flung activities of CONASUPO, for instance, reveal a pressing and continuing need for interagency cooperation, especially in the crowded field of Mexican agricultural policy. Given Mexican history, it is doubtful that formal bureaucratic mechanisms such as the interagency Comisión Coordinadora del Sector Agropecuario (CO-COSA), on which CONASUPO is represented, would yield the kind of resource provision which CONASUPO had evidently secured from other bureaucracies in the halcyon years of de la Vega Domínguez.

At this point, the relevance of the earlier hypothesized social structures becomes apparent. It is through their multiple jobholdings that would-be bureaucratic entrepreneurs gain access to assorted formal and informal networks. This affords them an accumulated information base with which to evaluate opportunities in terms of the subjective probability distribution of returns (both Y_I and Y_{II}). To some extent, reductions in the cost of gathering information are a function of the variety of the positions held. At the same time, movement through the bureaucratic-political structure, while providing career mobility, also enables potential entrepreneurs to build up associations of the parentela and *panelinha* types.

These social networks, in turn, serve three functions. First, as extensive monitoring systems they reduce uncertainty in the estimate of expected returns on alternative "assets" or opportunities. In the process, they reduce estimates of the standard deviation of the distribution of means in the Bayesian-modified Tobin-Markowitz decision theory suggested by Aubey, Kyle, and Strickon. Both aspects work to place the persons involved in comparatively favored positions for making entrepreneurial decisions. Second, parentela-*panelinha* associations (that is, the intensive transactional systems) constitute a source of influence over lending policies, budgetary appropriation policies, tariff policies, legislative policies, national planning and labor policies, all of which are involved in resource mobilization activities[15] and in reshaping the transactional environment of the entrepreneur. Consequently, the ability both to attract external resources and to accumulate resources internally in the organization may be bound up with such linkages, as the Votaw study of Mattei also makes plain. The series of prestations and counter-prestations that, in time, make up the fabric of such groupings themselves acquire increasing asset value for their participants. While from one point of view, the lateral transactional streams are the essence of bureaucratic politics (Downs 1967; Blau and Meyer 1971; Rourke 1969), in the political economy framework of this chapter they may be taken as the functional equivalent of trading in accounts receivable, or dynamic debt management.

The third function of these networks of communication and influence is, for the administrative elite, to provide part of the asset base on which vertical patron-client groupings, the *igrejinhas* or camarillas, may be built. Thus, the goodwill assets accumulated in the lateral or horizontal transactional streams of parentela and *panelinha* may be further capitalized into vertical flows of prestations and counter-prestations. These, in turn, expand the asset base of the public sector entrepreneur. On the basis of interviews with aspiring young *técnicos*, one may venture that potential members of a camarilla ordinarily examine closely these capitalization possibilities before casting their lot with a particular band. In this nuanced view of networks, a form of leveraging one's social capital is involved with the aim of enlarging sources of influence or bureaucratic "funds." In principle, the *igrejinha* networks include supporters and aides of subordinate status—both inside and outside the formal entity managed by the bureaucratic entrepreneur—who perform functions that Leeds has described. That such hierarchic subgroupings gather around the "careerist" to whom they are attached reflects, according to Adams (1970), the relative impermeability of the boundaries between the status positions occupied by the elite and those held by their followers. This is especially the case in societies where the career mobility systems available are still limited, even when the elite, as is increasingly common, are themselves upwardly mobile. As power brokers mediating between different levels of the social opportunity structure, the bureaucratic entrepreneurs may be double beneficiaries of the scarce career mobility systems—directly in terms of the more valued statuses they themselves come to occupy and indirectly in terms of the brokerage charges they exact from those who depend on them for access to higher circles of power, influence, or prestige.

In short, the bureaucratic entrepreneur's success in Mexico depends

219

on his ability to orchestrate these several social structures. Accordingly, he must organize his enterprise by supplying to its two markets the economic and noneconomic benefits from which earnings in the form of pecuniary and nonpecuniary command over resources derive—essentially the organizational function which Harbison (1956) sees as the heart of the entrepreneurial role. The affirmative purpose of the organization (Galbraith 1973:40, 100–109) is essentially the growth of the firm with all its implications for expanded promotional opportunities, managerial perquisites, and "the enhanced prestige and return of the technostructure"—including, of course, the prestige of the empresario. A protective purpose is served, too, for "as organization develops and becomes more elaborate, the greater will be its freedom from external interference." As Allison and Halperin (1972:49, 53, 54) have stated, "Organizations are often dominated by the desire to maintain the autonomy of the organization in pursuing what its members view as the essence of the organization's activity. . . . Decisions are rarely tailored to facilitate monitoring. . . . Where a [policy] decision leaves leeway for the organization that is implementing it, that organization will act so as to maximize its organizational interest within constraints." In very obvious ways, the interest of the organization is in this respect coincident with that of the bureaucratic entrepreneur.

CONASUPO provides an unequivocal example of an entrepreneurially directed parastatal firm that has been successful in developing a clientele and in operating in two kinds of markets, supplying two distinctive kinds of outputs. Its notable success in meeting the two types of demands is understandable in view of its innovative product mix and organizational changes—and reflected in the increasing volume of resources at its disposition. Evidence, albeit of a circumstantial sort, is strong as well that the two bureaucratic entrepreneurs associated most with this growth were able to bring to, and perhaps expand in, their jobs the useful networks which count for so much in the Mexican political system. Without these networks, advancement, almost automatically, does not come.[16]

NOTES

1. All data came from CONASUPO sources. The complexity of the operation, however, results in a variety of figures reported for certain activities, depending on how interpretations are made (in CONASUPO) on what to include in a particular statistical presentation. For our purposes, discrepancies may be disregarded.

2. This political element in the organization's objective function seems generally recognized in Mexico as legitimate in the behavior of a government corporation; political gains can be converted into resource gains for pursuing the organization's stated mission. It was, interestingly, never interpreted as either dishonesty or corruption, even by the interviewees who were not enthusiasts of CONASUPO. Thus, the willingness to work with various local factions—including most non-PRI groups except PAN—in developing projects does not contradict the earlier statement that the probability of large-scale corruption is not too likely, as the agency is watched closely by those who would like to use it as a target for criticizing the government. Criticism, when directed at more than picayune matters, appears mostly based on divergent ideological positions. It is the perceived irreconcilability of revolutionary ideology and PAN ideology that has led the CONASUPO management to eschew "political bargaining" with the activists of that party.

3. The existence and importance of these networks, as assets, has long been recognized in practice, if not in social science theory, as in old-fashioned observations on the advantages of having "connections."

4. Called, in Spanish, a camarilla, a group of *seguidores* or followers but popularly known, in Mexico, as *compinches* (a gang of henchmen).

5. The term *clientela* relationship is used to indicate the alliances which develop between bureaucracies of public agencies and interest groups which relate to them as clients. For present purposes, it is sufficient to speak of an interpenetration of interest groups and bureaucracies rather than to differentiate along a scale of relative degrees of subordinate-superordinate relationships.

6. Literally the members of the large extended family (blood ties and marriage ties) in the loose, modern sense (rather than in the more close-knit earlier sense), but used here to include groupings of close political affinity. La Palombara uses the term with Italian Christian Democratic party members as the chief referent, but it captures quite well what Brandenburg (1964b) means by the revolutionary family of Mexico and what other writers have in mind when they speak of the political factions which are smaller and more closely knit than a political party normally is.

7. Clearly, bureaucracy is used in this chapter to refer to a structure of organizational roles. It does not necessarily designate a form of "rational decision making" in a strict Weberian sense and does not, as in popular usage, associate particular structures with rigidity and conformism. With respect to the latter, it is obvious that private corporate bureaucracies have not stultified innovation; neither have public ones. The strict Weberian usage suggests a clear-cut division of labor and specialization of function (and role purity) which does not characterize the bureaucracies of Mexico—or of many other countries, one suspects.

8. It is clear, however, from Bermúdez's account of his tenure of office that he enjoyed substantial support from other parts of the Mexican government, during the presidencies of Miguel Alemán and Adolfo Ruíz Cortines, in dealing with such particularly thorny issues as labor relations and corporate finance. The latter problems originated with the politically set low prices charged and the special social subsidies conferred on assorted groups through Petróleos Mexicanos operations.

9. Simple ignorance of the details of others' lives undoubtedly accounted for part of this problem, but impression management on the side of some interviewees presented additional research difficulties. Moreover, the members of various groups and *alianzas* shift through time and may in some instances lose their value through disclosures. Full disclosure is the antithesis of the conventional operating style of the Mexican political system.

10. Born in Santiago de Tianquistengo in the state of Mexico of a Mexican mother

and a German father who had come to Mexico after World War I, Hank would be precluded by Mexican law from the presidency—a position which he might otherwise have been considered for, according to some observers.

11. Hank's tenure as governor of Mexico saw a notable growth in the state's financial base, progressive tax reforms in the state's fiscal system, and significant improvements in state government administration. There were organizational and procedural reforms, the employment of qualified young technocrats, and the institution of training programs for existing officials. Huge amounts of federal funds were secured for the state to assist in such programs as housing, school construction, teacher training. The industrialization of the state, with its affiliation with multi-nationals and the foregoing developments, provided many opportunities to make patronage appointments, just as the expansion of CONASUPO had also provided opportunities for rewarding protégés and building a camarilla.

12. During his student days, de la Vega worked in the economic studies section of the Secretaría de Industria y Comercio and, for a while, was manager of the Tampico branch of the government-owned Banco de Pequeño Comercio.

13. The profit-sharing legislation which López Mateos pushed through was another conspicuous policy response to this demand.

14. The looseness of market constraints on firms in the parastatal sector may be the result of several sources: relatively open access to both the lender of last resort (the central bank) and the investor of last resort (the national treasury) and enjoying substantial discretionary power as regards the pricing of output (and, possibly, the purchase of various inputs). Weak legislatures and deficiencies in the administrative organs of monitoring and control make for weak governmental constraints as well.

15. Since parastatal firms do not customarily go to the security exchanges and other loci of investors for their sources of venture capital, interagency contacts become vital for capital supply.

16. Generalizing, one may postulate that, on account of the mobility and varied career paths traced by Smith for the circulating Mexican political elite, the Mexican public sector is heavily interlaced by the vertical and horizontal networks depicted. Such social systems would tend both to support the kind of entrepreneurial behavior which seems characteristic of the parastatal sector and to facilitate the interagency (and extra-governmental) communication which must underlie the informal national planning system described by Shafer.

PART 3

Results and Outcomes:
Social Patterns and Groups

8

Capital Mobilization and the Patterns of Business Ownership and Control in Latin America: The Case of Mexico

ROBERT T. AUBEY

Graduate School of Business
University of Wisconsin–Madison

This study is concerned, primarily, with the capital mobilization process and how changes in this process influence the ownership and control pattern of business enterprise in the private sector. The study will examine specifically how economic units in the private sector adapt to changes in their environment during the industrialization process by modifying the capital mobilizing mechanism. Second, the influence of this adaptive technique the structure of business ownership and control will be examined. Finally, the current ownership and control patterns in Mexico will be analyzed to illustrate some of the implications of these patterns.

Although capital mobilization is a generalized term implying a set of functions beginning with savings and ending with investment in real assets, this study concentrates on the linkage between savings and investment rather than on either function. The linkage connecting these two functions, the capital market, will be referred to as the capital mobilization process. It should be noted at this point that while recognizing the increasing importance of the state in eco-

225

nomic affairs in Latin America, the focus of this study is on the capital mobilization process in the private sector.[1]

The first aspect of the capital mobilization process in Latin America that must be understood is that it is different from that found in more developed countries. In the United States, for example, the savings function and the investment function are separate and performed by different segments of the population. On the one hand, the investment function is highly institutionalized and is focused in the operation of large business firms. The savings function, on the other, is carried on by a large number of rather small savers. The small number of investors and large number of savers are brought together by a complex system of financial institutions which constitute the capital market. The capital markets, centering particularly on the security exchanges, provide the mechanism by which capital mobilization takes place.

The highly organized and institutionalized capital markets found in developed countries do not exist in the countries of Latin America. Financial institutions exist, to be sure, but they do not act as independent links between two otherwise unrelated groups. Three major aspects illustrate the difference of capital market systems in developed and developing countries. First, in Latin American countries, there is no large group of small savers interested in relatively long-term investments. The vast majority of savers in the developing countries are what may be termed "consumption savers." In general these savers are not seeking an interest return; they are, instead, short-term savers who focus on the purchase of a washing machine, a television, or similar consumer-related items. Second, financial institutions based on contractual savings plans—for example, life insurance companies, private pension funds, savings and loan associations, and public retirement funds, which have played major roles in the American system—have not made any significant contribution toward capital mobilization in most Latin American countries. The major exception to this has been the *financiera* system of Mexico, which we will examine in detail. There are, of course, commercial banks in every Latin American country, but their operations are generally limited geographically as well as in terms of the segments of the population served. Third, organized security exchanges, which exist in most developing countries, do not provide any impersonal evaluation or linking function in Latin America. For the most part, the coverage of business firms by organized security exchanges in Latin American countries is extremely limited, and the volume of transactions which take place through them is small compared with the total volume of security transactions in the economy. Even for Mexico, where the exchanges have experienced considerable growth over the past decade, this is still true (Basch 1968).

Although the process by which capital is mobilized in developed countries does not exist in Latin American economies, there can be little doubt that the private sector continues to channel significant amounts of capital into industrial ventures. Accordingly, any understanding of industrialization requires a knowledge of the process by which capital is directed toward industrial investment.

CAPITAL MOBILIZATION IN A CHANGING ENVIRONMENT

The capital mobilization process in Latin America, and indeed in most developing countries, appears to respond to changes in the development process by adopting new, more productive mechanisms for their changed environment. In the early stages of development the family acts as the mechanism by which capital is directed toward private business investments. As the capital resources of the family or extended family become inadequate for newly emerging investment opportunities, the mobilization process must be modified to provide a supplementary mechanism which can function as a channel for external funds. It is at this point that "investment groups" develop to perform the function of capital mobilization. The major characteristic of each of these adaptations will be analyzed in the following section.

The Family Firm

In the early phases of industrialization, the family and, by extension, the family firm, appear ideally suited to play a leading role in the process of economic development. In general, economic activity is dominated by a few wealthy families who have come by their position through landholdings, agricultural production, or commercial establishments stocked with imported consumer goods. Alongside

227

this highly concentrated power structure is a financial system which was originally developed to serve the agricultural economy.

The financial system in operation exhibits few of the characteristics needed to provide capital for risky industrial ventures. There is often no organized security exchange, and if one exists, government securities are dealt with almost exclusively. The few financial institutions which do exist and the commercial banking system both are greatly restricted in their activity. The wealthy families that control the production and commercial activity in the community also dominate commercial banking. It goes without saying that they have considerable political influence as well.

The importance of the family during the early stage of industrial development is directly related to three major factors:

1. *Access to capital.* Perhaps the most important single factor is the control over economic resources in general, and financial resources in particular. The family controls the former through its agricultural and commercial holdings and the latter through the commercial banking system.

The family's position provides it with an opportunity structure that also is invaluable. Accordingly, the established family is afforded access not only to capital but also to information about market developments, new production techniques, and government incentive programs.[2]

2. *Levels of technology.* Industrial ventures which are feasible during early industrialization can be adequately financed and managed by family members. These early industries are frequently those that produce consumer goods with the use of a relatively simple technology, requiring a small capital investment per worker. At this stage, items most commonly produced are matches, sugar, soap, cloth, apparel, flour, and beer (Hagen 1968).

3. *Culture.* Besides the obvious advantages the family may gain from the economic structure, it can also derive benefit from the cultural environment. In less developed areas, such as Latin America, where financial systems are in their beginning stages, legal and contractual arrangements difficult to enforce, and loyalties stronger to family than to nonfamily business associates, outside sources of capital are difficult, if not impossible, to arrange. Under these conditions, the family may be the only reliable source of funds for new business ventures.[3] Rather than impeding industrial development, strong family units may become an extremely important

228

facilitating mechanism.[4] Everett Hagen, in his book *The Economics of Development*, expresed a similar view.

> Where one can neither trust a stranger nor an acquaintance as a business associate, nor persuade him to lend one money, then the extended family may be a necessary source of capital and a necessary bond between business associates. Its abolition would not modernize the society; in the circumstances it would merely paralyze large-scale relationships (1968).

While these conditions prevail in many parts of the world, among Latin American countries the dominance of the family and the family firm is most evident in Central America. The case of El Salvador is a prime example. In the past, presidents of El Salvador had such family names as Dueñas, Regalado, Escalón, and Quiñónez.[5] All of these families today have substantial agricultural, commercial, and industrial holdings. The commercial banking system, as well, is dominated by old Salvadorian families with names such as Dueñas, Escalante Arce, and Guirola.

The Investment Group

The process of industrialization is basically one of increasing technology and complexity in production methods. As technical advances are made and interrelationships become more complex, additional capital investments are required. The increased capital requirements in turn require more sophisticated managerial skills which, at some point, surpass the capacity of many families to provide. When this happens, the capital mobilization process responds by adopting a supplementary mechananism appropriate for the prevailing environment, an adaptation characterized by the emergence of the investment group. The transition from family to investment group as the dominant mobilizing mechanism is a slow process, more evolutionary than revolutionary. The shift is one of emphasis and is most evident in institutional arrangements.

By *investment group* is meant a cluster of industrial, commercial, and financial institutions related by ownership and control. This definition highlights the major distinction between the family and the investment group—the incorporation of financial intermediaries into the business structure. Within the investment group, financial institutions act as the mechanism through which capital is channeled to the various industrial and commercial activities. The existence of such business groups has been noted by several studies of ownership structure in Latin America. Richard Lagos reported that in pre-Allende Chile eleven groups controlled 70.6 percent of business capital investment (1962) and Tomás Fillol found similar groups in Argentina (1961). Howard S. Ellis observed groups that closely resembled these in Greece (1964).

MEXICAN INVESTMENT GROUPS

In the preceding section it was suggested that the process of capital mobilization is directly related to industrial development. The hypothesis contended that as methods of production become more technical and complex (capital-intensive), capital mobilizing methods adapt to fit needs for capital as they emerge. It should not be assumed, however, that the dominant capital mobilization can be defined in terms of a particular technology or a particular industrial structure. The dominance of a particular mechanism, and indeed, the structure of a given mechanism itself, result from the interaction of a number of elements. For example, the transition from family domination to a group structure depends on such factors as the absolute wealth of the family as well as its managerial capacity and willingness to assume risk. This transition is influenced not only by the characteristics of the family but also by the structure of the political, social, and economic environment. The investment group is, therefore, a response to a change in environmental conditions and can only be understood in relation to those conditions.

Structure and Formation

The structure of the investment group has been described as a cluster of individual, commercial, and financial organizations. Its formation has been related to increased capital demands resulting from industrial development. This does not explain, however, how the groups developed or why they assumed their new structure. Since environmental factors are critical in this process, the investment group phenomena in Mexico will be examined as a basis for analyzing the more general capital mobilization process. The following analysis of the Mexican situation will focus on the structure, formation, and evaluation of the investment groups.

230

Although it is logical to assume that the structure of individual investment groups will vary considerably, in Mexico they also exhibit a number of common elements. The most important Mexican investment groups are structured around a primary core—a commercial bank and a *financiera*. Attached to this primary core are less important financial institutions consisting of a number of commercial banks and *financieras*, a mortgage bank, and an insurance company. Orbiting around this core are industrial and commercial enterprises. Some of these enterprises will have other types of operations, such as real estate or mutual funds, but on the whole this is not common (Brandenburg 1962).

An examination of the structure of the investment groups currently operating in Mexico clearly indicates that the family and concentrated family control have been important for several of the larger groups. At the same time, there are groups where ownership and control appear to be in the hands of a semi-stable group of investors consisting of both family members and outsiders or solely of independent investors with no family connections. An example of the latter would be the so-called Bruno Pagliai group centered around the *financiera* Continental. There seem to be no family connections among the major backers of this group.

Research has shown that the investment group itself evolves through several phases as different persons dominate the decision-making process. The various phases can be related to the needs of the group at a particular point. Although we will do no more than to suggest this as a line of future research, it can be hypothesized that the investment group in its formative period will be dominated by entrepreneurs or industrialists. Later, during its growth period, the need for organizational control will call for leadership by people with administrative abilities. At other stages the needs for funds may bring the banker to the forefront. These stages, of course, would not have to follow any particular sequence or pattern.

In contrast to the non-family-related groups, the more important Mexican groups can be traced to individuals and families. Probably the best known of the Mexican family groups is the Monterrey group, which is directly related to and dominated by the Garza Sada family. Although the Garza Sada or Monterrey group certainly dominates Monterrey and the surrounding area as regards the republic of Mexico, it is overshadowed by two Mexico City–based

231

groups, the Bancomer group (Banco de Comercio) and the Bana-mex group (Banco Nacional de México). Both of these groups had their genesis in old, established families. The Bancomer group was started by the Jenkins and Espinosa Yglesias family and is still controlled by Manuel Espinosa Yglesias. The Banamex group under the Legoreta family became important after the revolution; Augustín F. Legoreta is still the managing director.

Although the underlying control of these groups has been common knowledge for years, the use of the term *group* is of relatively recent orgin. Officially, the group headed by the Banco Nacional de México became known as the Banamex Group in February 1969, when it changed the name of several related financial institutions to include the word Banamex. In this way, its major *financiera* changed its name from Credíto Brusatil, S.A. to Financiera Banamex, S.A. Before the name change, it was not uncommon to hear these institutions called the Banco Nacional de México group, but neither the bank nor its related financial institutions ever publically referred to themselves as a group. Similarly, the Bancomer group was frequently called the Espinosa Yglesias group.

Referring to investment groups in this way was not restricted to larger groups. Before the late 1960s, only rarely were smaller groups referred to except by the name of the dominant individual or family. For example, it was always the Carlos Trouyet group (Banco Comercial Mexicano, S.A.) or the Raúl Balleres group (Crédito Minero y Mercantil, S.A.). It is now usual for group members to refer to themselves as a group. Thus, besides Bancomer and Bancomex, we have the Serfin group (Garza Sada) and the Cremi group (Raúl Balleres). Now, even the government refers to the group in which it has a dominant part as the Somex group. Others continue to be called by the name of their dominant financial institution. The Banco del Atlantico group, a recently formed group dominated by prominent but unrelated businessmen, is one example. Some of the more important groups and their affiliated financial institutions, the core of the groups, are given in the Appendix to this chapter.

Evolution from Family to Investment Group

Of all the groups currently of importance in Mexico, the Garza Sada group, Serfin, provides the best framework for understanding structure and operation. Because Serfin evolved initially from a family firm, it also can serve to illustrate how such groups operate and function.

Monterrey has a highly complex economic structure with activity concentrated in a few dominating industries. The giants of each industrial category are served by a few large firms together with a number of smaller enterprises. In addition, a set of financial institutions attends specifically to the industrial and commercial activity. Although a significant part of the activity of Monterrey is controlled by the Garza Sada family, the majority is not, and there are several other important family and nonfamily groups. Some of these are independent of the Garza Sada group, but several maintain strong connections with it.

The economic structure and groups of Monterrey differ according to the angle from which they are viewed. One study of Monterrey identifies nine local groups, while another uses an industrial breakdown and separates the Garza Sada group into three separate parts. For the purpose of this study, Monterrey will be considered from the perspective of the Garza Sada family and examined for its economic interests in three major industrial groups: the brewery group, the glass group, and the HYLSA steel group. The steel group is particularly interesting in that recently it was reorganized and expanded; it now formally goes by the name Grupo Industrial Alfa. The following discussion concentrates on those features relevant to the characteristics of the organization and the pattern of relationships among the owners.

The Brewery Group

The brewery group of companies began with the brewery Cervecería Cuauhtémoc, S.A., founded in 1890 by José A. Muguerza; his brother-in-law and attorney Lic. Francisco Sada; their nephew José Calderón Muguerza; Sada's son Francisco G. Sada Muguerza; Sada's son-in-law Isaac Garza Garza; and a technician, José M. Schneider. The following companies were incorporated into the brewery group: Fábricas Monterrey, S.A., begun in 1903 to produce metal bottle caps; Empaques de Cartón Titan, S.A., incorporated in 1926 to produce cardboard boxes; and Celulosa de Chihuahua, S.A., a "sister firm" of Titan from which Titan gets its pulp.

233

In 1936, the brewery's transition from a single company to an industrial group came about when a major reorganization was undertaken. The bottle cap and cardboard box plants were spun off as separate corporations, as were Malta, S.A., which makes animal feed, and Técnica Industrial, S.A., the administrative and technical services department. These firms, as well as the brewery itself, were placed under the control of a holding company, Valores Industriales, S.A.

With the glass and textile groups, the brewery group started the Banco Industrial de Monterrey, S.A., and sold it in 1952 to the Banco de Londres y México, S.A. The same groups also purchased a controlling interest in a commercial bank, the Banco de Nuevo León, S.A., established a mortgage bank, the Banco Capitalizador e Inmobiliario de Monterrey, S.A., and a life insurance firm, Monterrey, Cía de Seguros, S.A. In 1936, the brewery group alone founded the Cía General de Aceptaciones, S.A., a development bank and private lending institution. In 1942, the brewery group purchased a steel mill to remelt tin for bottle caps. Hojalata y Lámina, the firm operating the mill, has since developed into the HYLSA steel group.

Also part of the brewery group are Almacenes y Silos, S.A., Avícola Comercial Azteca, S.A., Cervecería de Sonora, S.A., Cía Operadora del Pacífico, S.A., Fomento Comercial, S.A., and Inmobiliaria Industrial y Comercial, S.A.

The Glass Group

The glass group began in 1909 when Francisco G. Sada, José A. Muguerza, José Calderón, and Isaac Garza—founders of the brewery group—and a number of other businessmen from the Brittingham, Zambrano, Rivero, Hernández, Cantu, and Garza Guerra families, started the Vidriera Monterrey, S.A., a glass bottle plant made to supply bottles to the brewery and other local users. Other firms established by the Vidriera Monterrey are Troqueles y Esmaltes, S.A., Gas Industrial de Monterrey, S.A., Planta Eléctrica Grupo Industrial, S.A., Distribuidora Monterrey, S.A., Comisionistas Monterrey, S.A., Consorcio Manufacturero, S.A., and Talleres Industriales, S.A.

As mentioned earlier, the Vidriera Monterrey joined with the brewery and textile group companies to establish the Banco Industrial de Monterrey; S.A., which was absorbed by the Banco de Londres y México, S.A.

In 1936, the glass group, as *did the brewery group, underwent reorganization. A holding company, Fomento de Industria y Comercio, S.A., was set up to control companies in the group, and the various sections of the Vidriera Monterrey were spun off as separate corporations. These are Vidriera Monterrey, S.A., Vidrio Plano, S.A., Cristalería, S.A., Representaciones Generales, S.A., Distribuidora Nacional, S.A., Proveedora de Hogar, S.A., Comercio Occidental, S.A., and Vidriera, México, S.A.

As noted earlier, along with its partners in the Banco Industrial, S.A., the glass group acquired in 1939 and 1940, the Banco de Nuevo León, S.A., founded the Banco Capitalizador e Inmobiliario de Monterrey, S.A., and established the life insurance company Monterrey Cía de Seguros, S.A.

Other firms and banks established by the glass group are Cristales Mexicanos, S.A., Fabricación de Máquinas, S.A., Vidriera de los Reyes, S.A., Industria de Alcalí, S.A., Financiera del Norte, S.A., CYDSA Chemical Group, Vidrio Plano de México, S.A., Peerless Tisa, S.A., Cía Vidriera de Guadalajara, S.A., Materias Primas, S.A., Silicatos y Derivados, S.A., Almacenadora del Norte, S.A., Máprimex, S.A., and Vitro-Fibras, S.A.

HYLSA Steel Group (Grupo Industrial Alfa)

The HYLSA steel group, fully owned by the brewery group, was started in 1942 to produce tinplate for bottle caps. By 1970, HYLSA had grown to become a major steel producer, with major links with such firms as Hojalata y Lámina, S.A., Las Encinas, S.A., Fierro Esponja, S.A., Aceros Alfa Monterrey, S.A., Aceros de México, S.A., Talleres Universales, S.A., and HYLSA de México, S.A.,

Since that time the steel group was reorganized as the Grupo Industrial Alfa and expanded to include some firms not related to the steel industry. Some of the non-steel firms are Empaques de Cartón Titan, S.A., Empaques de Cartón Corrugado, S.A., Industrial de Mexico, S.A., Servi-Empaques, S.A., Television Independiente de Mexico, S.A., Television del Norte, S.A., Television del Golfo, S.A., and Television del Puebla, S.A.

Functions of the Investment Group

The process of industrial growth and development impose new requirements and demands on business operation. The investment groups are well structured to answer at least three major demands—the requirement of increased capital, the necessity to bring nonfamily members into the business, and the heightened need for information. We have already discussed how industrialization influences the demand for capital and how in the early stages family-owned-and-operated firms are adequate to meet these demands. We have also noted that the continuously increasing capital demand will, at some point, outgrow the capacity of the family to provide. The increased demand for capital comes from several levels. To be sure, capital is needed for plant equipment. As firms expand, they become involved with more suppliers and more customers and this calls for an increase in operating capital. In other words, the process of growth itself increases the capital required for operation.

In developed countries, these demands are met through the issuance of stock or debt instruments and the increased use of commercial banking facilities. In the developing countries, however, these alternative sources of funds are seldom available. Few active security exchanges will issue stocks or bonds for the funds required. For some of the older firms, funds can be obtained from the commercial banks, but these are restricted mainly to short-term funds.[6] New firms, lacking connections, typically will find it difficult to obtain adequate funds from the commercial banks. It is only logical, under these conditions, that businessmen should develop a means for providing themselves with what are in effect captive sources of capital. An analysis of the operations of these groups leaves little doubt of this fact, which appears to be a major part of their purpose.[7]

The investment group structure has not only served as a direct source of capital but it is also well suited for another aspect of financing business operations. As existing business expands and new ventures become feasible, businessmen often find it desirable to use leverage—that is, the financing of business activity by using increasing amounts of debt, or borrowed capital, relative to equity capital. This is desirable because it both reduces the risk exposure of the owners in any one organization and can be used to increase the rate of return on the equity investment. The investment group structure facilitates the use of leverage by providing a mechanism through which debt instruments can be issued. These debt issues go first to financial institutions within the group and through these institutions to outside investors.

The investment group, by incorporating nonfamily members into the group, is capable of dealing with expansion-generated problems and the need for expertise and specialization.[8] Family members simply are not able to fill all the roles required. Yet the prevailing environment during this transition period resembles that of the time when the family firm was the predominant form of business organization. That is to say, positions of responsibilty are clearly positions of trust. Of course, some positions are filled by people with whom a personal trust relationship has had to be built. This possibility would appear to be limited, however, and certainly such a relationship would not be as strong as among family members.[9]

The investment group—with ownership and control of all units concentrated in a few hands—can get around this problem by having outsiders perform some functions of responsibility while family members or trusted persons continue to perform those functions demanding the greatest degree of trust. This will naturally be easier during the earlier part of the transition and become more difficult as the number of positions to be filled increases.

In terms of growth, this may well be a limiting factor. No doubt, in some cases this barrier has kept groups small. In cases, for instance, where groups which have expanded their operations, the barrier is probably broken through and the result is a relatively impersonal organization. The degree to which impersonal relationships are developed will of course vary from group to group. For the present at least, ownership and thus final control of even the larger group remain in the hands of a few trusted persons—a situation which is in most countries facilitated by the geographical concentration of industry. In light of this it is interesting to imagine that, although the investment group structure has its negative aspects, it may also serve to introduce more impersonal or nonfamilial relationships into the society, assuming that impersonal relationships have some beneficial attributes.

A third way in which the structure of the investment group appears to serve a function is in the area of information flows. As an economy expands, the relationships among business units and segments of the economy become more complex. There is a need for more information on sources of supplies, markets, technical advancements, government, and on many other factors. The investment group suits this purpose in at least two ways. First, all units of the group have some access to the technically trained people employed by the group; and second, since each unit within the group has its own outside connections through which information can be gathered, the group, on the whole, can have multiple sources of information. In addition, the connection with financial institutions would be, for any operating firm, an invaluable source of information. Given the environment of developing countries, such information could not be easily obtained by other means.

Although the investment group has facilitated the introduction of increasingly large economic units in the private business sector, negative aspects can also be noted. In the first place, the ownership and control patterns that have been described as characteristic of the investment group have also resulted in a heavy concentration of financial resources. In 1966, six investment groups controlled 71 percent of the private banking system resources in Mexico. The level of concentration can also be measured by the number of institutions controlled by the group, and the same six groups dominated a total of sixty-nine financial institutions. In 1971, the level of concentration had grown even higher, with the six major groups controlling 85 percent of banking system resources.

In addition to the high level of financial resource concentration resulting from the operation of investment groups, the possibility of two other adverse consequences should be noted. First, with the high concentration of resources in the hands of few, the potential effect of their activities on the investment patterns of the principal sectors is obvious. Indeed, it has been suggested that the extremely rapid drop in investment in 1971 and the resulting slowdown in economic activity can be directly traced to the actions of the investment groups. Second, evidence points to times when certain aspects of official monetary policy has been offset by the ability of these groups to move funds from one financial institution to another. Clearly, the potential for abuse by the investment group exists, but the extent to which it has been used to benefit the few is difficult to document.

APPENDIX: *Investment Groups in Mexico*

TABLE 8.1
BANCO DE COMERCIO

	Resources*	Activity
Banco de Comercio, S.A.	6,996	Com.
Financiera Bancomer, S.A.	22,357	Fin.
Hipotecaria Bancomer	5,280	Mortgage
Banco de Comercio de Chihuahua, S.A.	536	Com.
Banco de Comercio de Sonora, S.A.	579	Com.
Banco de Comercio de Yucatán, S.A.	163	Com.
Banco de Comercio de San Luis Potosí, S.A.	179	Com.
Banco de Comercio de Puebla, S.A.	579	Com.
Banco de Comercio de Michoacán, S.A.	541	Com.
Banco de Comercio de Tamaulipas, S.A.	443	Com.
Banco de Comercio de Durango, S.A.	192	Com.
Banco de Comercio de Guadalajara, S.A.	847	Com.
Banco de Comercio de Coahuila, S.A.	392	Com.
Banco de Comercio de Guanajuato, S.A.	693	Com.
Banco de Comercio de Sinaloa, S.A.	429	Com.
Banco de Comercio de Veracruz, S.A.	465	Com.
Banco de Comercio de al Laguna, S.A.	220	Com.
Banco de Comercio de Aguascalientes, S.A.	268	Com.
Banco de Comercio de Campeche, S.A.	79	Com.
Banco de Comercio de Hidalgo, S.A.	326	Com.
Banco de Comercio de Baja Calif., S.A.	1,086	Com.

*Millions of pesos (December 1971)

TABLE 8.2
BANCO NACIONAL DE MEXICO

	Resources*	Activity
Banco Nacional de México, S.A.	15,850	Com.
Financiera Banamex, S.A.	18,118	Fin.
Financiadora de Ventas Banamex, S.A.	3,807	Fin.
Affiliated Banks		
Banco del Centro, S.A.	246	Com.
Banco Ganadero, S.A.	114	Com.
Banco Regional del Pacífico, S.A.	78	Com.
Asoc. Hipotecaria Mexicana, S.A. de C.V.	1,944	Mortgage
Banco Agricola Industrial de Linares, S.A.	19	Com.
Banco de Oriente, S.A.	179	Com.
Banco de Tuxpán, S.A.	n.a.	Com.

*Millions of pesos (December 1971)

239

TABLE 8.3
GRUPO SERFIN

	Resources*	Activity
Banco de Londres y México, S.A.	4,619	Com.
Financiera Aceptaciones, S.A.	10,359	Fin.
Banco de Jalisco, S.A.	178	Com.
Banco Veracruzano, S.A.	257	Com.
Banco de Jarez, S.A.	267	Com.
Banco Azteca, S.A.	344	Com.
Banco Hipotecario Azteca, S.A.	522	Mortgage
Financiera Azteca, S.A.	234	Fin.
Fomento de Tampico, S.A.	168	Fin.

*Millions of pesos (December 1971)

TABLE 8.4
BANCO COMERCIAL MEXICANO

	Resources*	Activity
Banco Comercial Mexicano, S.A.	3,496	Com.
Financiera Comermex, S.A.	6,532	Fin.
Financiera de Industria y Comercio, S.A.	141	Fin.
Hipotecaria Comermex, S.A.	278	Mortgage
Banco Mercantil de Chihuahua, S.A.	184	Com.
Banco Comercial Mexicano de Monterrey, S.A.	159	Com.

*Millions of pesos (December 1971)

TABLE 8.5
GRUPO "SOMEX"

	Resources*	Activity
Sociedad Mexicana de Crédito Industrial, S.A.	7,225	Fin.
Financiera Comercial Mexicana, S.A.	439	Fin.
Banco Mexicano de Occidente, S.A.	228	Com.
Banco Mexicano, S.A.	1,537	Com.

*Millions of pesos (December 1971)

TABLE 8.6
BANCO INTERNACIONAL

	Resources*	Activity
Banco Internacional, S.A.	1,621	Com.
Banco Industrial de Jalisco, S.A.	778	Com.
Banco Internacional de Fomento Urbano, S.A.	589	Mortgage
Banco de Crédito Inmobiliario, S.A.	497	Mortgage
Banco Internacional del Norte, S.A.	283	Com.
Banco de Campeche, S.A.	66	Com.
Banco Internacional del Centro, S.A.	123	Com.
Financiera Internacional, S.A.	1,900	Fin.
Banco Internacional del Noroeste, S.A.	n.a.	Com.

*Millions of pesos (December 1971)

In 1972 the Mexican government obtained majority control of the Banco Internacional.

240

TABLE 8.7
BANCO DEL ATLANTICO

	Resources*	Activity
Banco del Atlántico, S.A.	1,288	Com.
Banco Inmobiliario del Atlántico, S.A.	1,101	Mortgage
Banco Internacional Inmobiliaria, S.A.	53	Mortgage
Banco de Yucatán, S.A.	62	Com.
Financiera del Atlántico, S.A.	2,657	Fin.

*Millions of pesos (December 1971)

TABLE 8.8
GRUPO "CREMI"

	Resources*	Activity
Crédito Minero y Mercantil, S.A.	1,678	Fin.
Crédito Hipotecario del Sur, S.A.		Mortgage
Banco Industrial de Jalisco, S.A.	811	Com.
Crédito Hipotecario, S.A.	3,441	Mortgage
Banco Minero y Mercantil, S.A.	282	Com.
Banco del Sureste, S.A.	163	Com.
Banco del Sur, S.A.	184	Com.
Financiera del Sureste, S.A.	169	Fin.

*Millions of pesos (December 1971)

NOTES

1. From the perspective of the United States, the level of state intervention in Latin American economies appears to be rather high, but it should be remembered that in most cases the private sector is still dominant. For example, in Mexico when the government has not hesitated to intervene in economic affairs, the Inter-American Development Bank reported that the share of banking system resources controlled by public institutions actually declined from 39.6 percent in 1969 to 37.7 percent in 1972. Another study indicated that the public sector's share of investment declined from 45 percent in 1964 to 38 percent in 1970.

2. For a discussion of the sociological aspects of the family firm and its relationship to economic development, see Benedict (1968).

3. Benedict, in his study of family firms in East Africa, gives several illustrations of how family relationships can be used as means of obtaining funds (1968:11–12).

4. It has often been argued that strong family ties are detrimental to development and that in those economies where the family firm is the predominant type of enterprise, industrialization is hindered. The validity of this is certainly open to question. For one example of the argument that the family orientation of the Latin American culture works to slow down economic development, see Cochran (1960). For the opposite view of the effect of family-dominated enterprise, see Khalap and Shwayri (1966) and Benedict (1968).

5. For a more complete discussion of the structure of family ownership of business firms in El Salvador, see Aubey (1969).

6. Latin American banking laws generally restrict, in varying degrees, commercial bank lending to the short-term field. There are, of course, ways that banks can and have used to get around this restriction, such as continuous renewal of short-term loans, which by its very nature is available to only the best customers. For comments about the short-term nature of commercial banking and the general reluctance of the banking system to provide funds for new ventures in Mexico, see Meyers (1954).

7. Brandenburg in his study of Mexican entrepreneurial groups comments on group financing as follows: "Each of the nine [groups that he has identified] which together control financial institutions possessing a majority of the nation's private bank capital, by and large finances its own industrial and commercial promotions. Inasmuch as the big nine utilize their banking capital to become owners of new promotions, other entrepreneurs can acquire credit from them only at relatively high interest rates" (1962:22).

8. For a discussion of how some family firms have tried to meet the challenge and the effects of the introduction of nonfamily members, see Benedict 1968:13–16.

9. Benedict has argued that the extremely close relationship which is established among members of the family firm is one of its strong points and that this relationship is formed over a relatively long period of time through what he calls "transactions." There is no reason, of course, why transactional relationships could not be formed with nonfamily employees as well. However, it is also obvious that in those societies which are still family-oriented, relationships with outsiders would never be as strong as those with family members.

9

Nicaragua's Grupos Económicos: Scope and Operations

HARRY W. STRACHAN

Instituto Centroamericano de
Administración de Empresas
Managua, Nicaragua

Nicaragua, like most of its sister republics in Central and South America, has several business groups, both large and small, which dominate the commercial landscape. Locally, the larger groups are called *grupos económicos*, *familias*, and on occasion *argoyas*. The smaller groups are referred to as *grupitos*, or subgroups, or protogroups.

These groups can best be described as long-term associations of many firms and the men who own and manage them. While there are many traits common to business groups—for example, family ties, geographical ties, interlocking directorates—three key characteristics can distinguish a full-fledged business group from other types.

1. Diversity of enterprise. A business group has a great variety of enterprises in different sectors of the economy.

2. Pluralistic composition. A business group is a coalition of several wealthy businessmen and families. While a group may have a leader and may carry his name, the business group is more than a one-man business empire, more than a single corporation with its vertically integrated subsidiaries, and more than the diversified holdings of a single wealthy family.

3. *Fiduciary atmosphere*. The relations which bind group members together are characterized by a loyalty and trust similar to that normally associated with family or kinship groups. A group member's relation to other group members usually employs a higher standard of fair dealings and disclosure than that which generally is found in arm's length commerce.

The objective of this chapter is to describe the composition of the Nicaraguan business group and its style of operation. The initial pages describe the principal groups and their relations to each other in the period 1970–1975. Succeeding sections deal with the boundaries of the groups, that is, who belongs to the group and who does not; the magnitude of the groups as compared with the rest of the economy; the formation of groups; the ways in which they grow to dominance; roles and decision making within the groups; and finally, some of the principal obligations of group membership. The information presented here was gathered in field interviews in Nicaragua in conjunction with research for a doctoral dissertation from the Harvard Business School (Strachan 1972) published in 1976 in the Praeger Special Studies Series entitled *Family and Other Business Groups in Economic Development*.

The chapter is organized as a straightforward description of groups rather than as a rigorous testing of hypotheses about them. Nevertheless, a number of questions concerning these groups might be kept in mind.

1. Why are groups formed? What functions do they perform for their members? My basic hypothesis is that the principal function provided by these groups is financial intermediation in which the group facilitates both the making of investments for members with excess savings and the securing of credit for members with net capital needs. Secondary but significant benefits include intragroup business and protection from discrimination by outsiders, especially the government. Other potential benefits, like market control, social status, preferential treatment by nonmembers, and mutual administrative and technical support, are not, in my opinion, major factors in explaining the existence of groups.

2. Are groups an "adaptive" or "efficient" organizational form? If so, in what environments and how? My hypothesis, based on my

244

research in Central America and limited evidence in the literature, is that business groups appear when a country embarks on the process of industrialization and when financial institutions are established. In this environment—normally characterized by new economic opportunities, underdeveloped capital markets, ambiguous governmental policies and practices—business groups are an adaptive organizational form and they thrive. Later, in an environment of more sophisticated financial institutions, more reliable markets and infrastructures, and more stable political structures, these groups lose their relative prominence.

I suspect that they are adaptive because they combine many of the characteristics of families and the modern corporation. They make use of the existing social and cultural relationships to gather information and to create the climate of trust necessary for successful financial intermediation and entrepreneurial activity. At the same time, they have greater freedom to incorporate new members on the basis of competence, wealth, or internal design.

IDENTIFICATION OF NICARAGUA'S GROUPS

In 1975 businessmen, economists, and persons both inside and outside business groups identified the major business groups of the country. Of the two unmistakable groups, one was clustered around the Banco de América (not to be confused with the California-based Bank of America), and the other around the Banco Nicaraguense. A "special" third group, which consists of enterprises belonging to the ruling family in Nicaragua, is the Somoza Group. An emerging fourth group is the firms related to AISA/La Nacional/INFISA. In addition there are numerous smaller groups.

Figure 9.1 is a visual summary of these major groups and their relations to each other. Examples of the smaller groups are included to show that the *grupitos* may be components of a larger group, as is SOVIPE in the Banco de América Group; or have ties with both major groups, as does the Manuel I. Lacayo Group; or be largely independent, as is the Terán Group. AISA is an example of a protogroup which in 1970 was considered a part of the Banco Nicaraguense Group, but has since moved out of this group to establish closer ties with the Somoza Group and other subgroups.

245

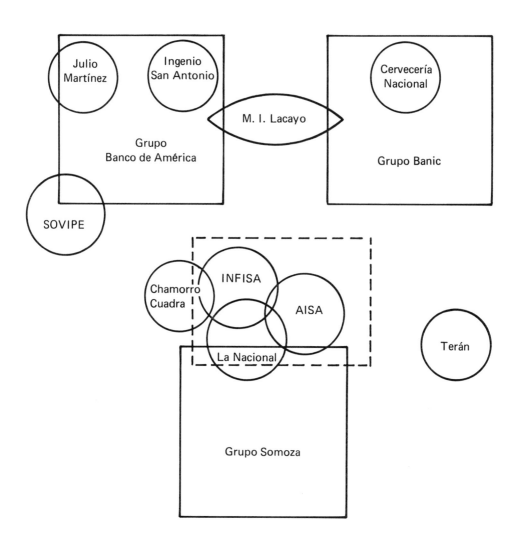

Julio
Martínez

Ingenio
San Antonio

M. I. Lacayo

Cervecería
Nacional

Grupo
Banco de América

Grupo Banic

SOVIPE

Chamorro
Cuadra

INFISA

AISA

La Nacional

Terán

Grupo Somoza

☐ = Major Group

◯ = Subgroup, Protogroup, *Grupito*

⌐ ̅ ⌐ = Emerging Major Group

FIGURE 9.1. Nicaragua's major business groups, 1971-75, and a sample of smaller groups.

Nicaragua's Grupos Económicos

Banco de América Group

Five distinguishable kinds of businesses were identified with the Banco de América Group. One is an agricultural complex, consisting primarily of the Nicaragua Sugar Estates, a large sugarcane plantation established in 1890. The sugar operations have been diversified and today the Ingenio San Antonio, as it is known, is one of Nicaragua's largest rum distillers and distributors as well as cattle raisers. The Pellas family is the dominant shareholder in Nicaragua Sugar Estates, although since its inception, the plantation has been a joint venture of several Nicaraguan families. There are a number of other agricultural concerns, such as coffee farms, which belong to group members, but these enterprises are generally not regarded as group firms.

Most of the founding members of the Ingenio San Antonio were merchants. Many of their commercial houses and import-export firms, which continue to be important today, form the nucleus of a second type of group businesses, commercial establishments. In addition to these old commercial houses, some of the most successful new retailers, such as Julio Martínez, an automobile dealer, and Felipe Mántica, an owner of a modern department store and chain of supermarkets, are also members of the group.

A third kind of business in the Banco de América Group focuses on construction and land development. SOVIPE, a complex of firms in the construction industry, is the major subgroup here. SOVIPE, begun about twenty years ago, engages in the production of electrical appliances and construction materials in addition to its more traditional building and land development activities. Since the 1972 earthquake, younger members of the Banco de América Group have formed their own holding company, Santa Monica. This has also become involved in the development of commercial centers, recreational activities, among others.

A fourth component of this group is the industrial firms. These include a number of factories which process coffee, produce vegetable oils, or make shoes. Some of the firms of the Manuel I. Lacayo Group work in this area.

These agricultural, commercial, construction, and industrial elements are linked together by a set of financial institutions, the fifth component of this group. The Banco de América was established in

1952 by a circle of businessmen led by Don Silvio F. Pellas, uncle of the current leader of the Banco de América Group, Don Alfredo Pellas. Over the years, the bank has grown until today it is the largest private bank in Nicaragua. In 1966, the Wells Fargo Bank bought a minority interest in the bank and founded the Corporación de Inversiones, S.A. (CID), with members of the Pellas, Lacayo, and SOVIPE subgroups. This holding company has interests in several *financieras*, a savings and loan association, an insurance company, and several construction material businesses. In 1973 a credit card company, CRED-O-MATIC, now linked with the Master Charge chain, was established.

Any description of the Banco de America Group would be incomplete without noting that its roots are in Granada, an ancient city of Nicaragua, and that it is generally identified with the Conservative Party.

The Banco Nicaraguense Group

The Banco Nicaraguense Group had its roots in León, another ancient city of Nicaragua, and is identified with the Liberal Party. Although certain members can trace their relationships with one another back to the nineteenth century, this group is more clearly a product of the last twenty years.

The distinguishable components of the Banco de America Group have their counterparts in the Banco Nicaraguense Group. A number of members are active in coffee and cotton farming, and several group firms work closely with the agricultural sector, for example, a cotton brokerage firm and a processor of vegetable oils.

Numbered among the Banco Nicaraguense Group are some of Nicaragua's most prominent merchants and commercial establishments. The group is also active in the industrial sector. INDESA, the group *financiera*, has equity interests in a variety of firms including lumber and fish processing. Firms established by Dr. Guerrero Montalbán, a founder of this group and an active industrialist, work closely with the group. One of these, La Cervecería Nacional, the largest brewery in the country, is the cornerstone of the group; its role parallels that of the Ingenio San Antonio in the Banco de America Group.

248

The group also has interests in land development and construction, but probably on a smaller scale than either the SOVIPE or AISA complexes.

As in the Banco de América Group, the key firms here, those which link other elements together, are the financial institutions. There are five of these which advertise jointly as Grupo BANIC: The Banco Nicaraguense, founded in 1952; Financiera de la Vivienda, a savings and loan association; INDESA, a *financiera* and investment company; La Protectora, a large insurance company; and ALMACENTRO, a bonded warehouse established at the end of 1973.

The Somoza Group

In 1971, 65 percent of the interviewees identified a Somoza business group, although 15 percent of these indicated that it was a special type of group, not as clearly delineated in the economic realm as in the political. By 1975 there was unmistakable evidence that this group was taking on many of the characteristics of the other major business groups and emerging as a major economic entity. Subgroups were forming within it, considerable diversification was taking place, and the firms were beginning to organize themselves more definitely around financial institutions. "Special" differences, however, most notably in the access to and use of political power, continue to differentiate this group from the other two in the opinion of most members of the business community.

The Somoza group consists principally of the extensive economic activities of the Somoza family. The family, first in the person of General Anastasio Somoza G., and later in that of his sons, Luis and Anastasio Somoza Debayle, has controlled Nicaraguan politics since 1933. During these forty-five years, the family has been an active investor in almost all sectors of the Nicaraguan economy. Today it owns cattle, cotton, sugar, and rice farms. It has equity investments in an airline, shipping and fishing fleets, a cement plant, and a slaughterhouse. Its real estate holdings are extensive.

Since the 1972 earthquake, the group has moved aggressively into construction and land development, into commerce, and into the financial sector with the establishment of the private Banco Centroamericano and Interfinanciera. The sons of Doña Lillian Somoza de Sevilla have founded their own financiera. Many of the credit functions for the Somoza enterprises, however, continue to be performed by the Banco Nacional, the nation's agricultural development bank. Until 1952, this bank was the principal financial institution in the country and is today still larger than any private commercial banks.

AISA/INFISA/La Nacional

In 1971 approximately 70 percent of the interviewees identified AISA as a major business group and about half that percentage also listed INFISA and La Nacional as a group.

AISA, founded in 1958, is a vertically integrated set of firms in construction and related activities. It has grown rapidly by applying modern techniques to the construction field and by diversifying into areas related to building. In 1963 it established a commercial outlet for furniture and electrical appliances and later joined with General Electric to assemble these appliances. In 1964 through 1966 it established a rock and gravel processor, a factory to make such wood products as cabinets, windows, and doors, and a firm to make concrete products. Diversification began in 1965 when AISA acquired minority interests in a hotel. In 1970 it expanded into several neighboring Central American countries as a partner in large development and mass housing projects.

Since 1973, on the crest of the postearthquake construction boom, AISA has continued to expand. Cutting off its special relationship with the Banco Nicaraguense group, it helped to establish the new Banco Centroamericano with the Somoza Group.

In the early 1970s, INFISA, a *financiera* with interest in land development firms, and La Nacional, the country's largest insurance company, owned in part by the government, interchanged stock to form what observers call a protogroup. Since that time, AISA and INFISA and La Nacional have interchanged stock and participated in a number of new joint ventures.

What is perhaps more significant is that executives within these institutions consciously seek ways to strengthen these ties and, by doing so, to establish a fourth major group. In 1975 several interviewees stated that AISA/INFISA/La Nacional was the largest protogroup in the country and was emerging as a major business group.

Other Groups

Numerous subgroups or protogroups work independently or are linked to the major groups. Only a sampling of these smaller groups have been included in figure 9.1. One, the Manuel I. Lacayo Group, is of particular interest. It is the case of a businessman who, although economically able to form his own group, chose instead to become a member of both Banco Nicaraguense and Banco de América Groups.

Manuel Ignacio Lacayo, a Nicaraguan engineer and constructor, became a multimillionaire in Venezuela during the decade following World War II. When he returned to Central America, he settled in Costa Rica but invested his money in a variety of Central American firms. In Nicaragua, a sample of his firms includes a hotel, a bottling company, a shoe factory, and a car dealership. When the two Nicaraguan banks were established in the early 1950s, he joined both. He was the largest single shareholder in the Banco Nicaraguense, where his brother, Róger Lacayo, served until his death in 1975 as vice-president of the board of directors. (The Lacayo firms directed by Róger work closely with the Banco Nicaraguense and are considered part of that group.)

Because Manuel Lacayo was also a large shareholder in the Banco de América, some of his firms, which were fierce competitors of important companies in the Banco Nicaraguense Group established a close working relation with the Banco de América. Lacayo was at one time a director of the Banco de América; he is now represented on the board of directors by his son-in-law, who is active in those Lacayo firms associated with the Banco de América.

GROUP BOUNDARIES

Identifying groups in Nicaragua proved easier than defining their borders. However clear the existence of a business group and the identity of its major members, there are always those people and organizations whose status in the group is vague. Hazari, for example, in describing groups in India notes,

> The group is not always a closed circle. Rather, it may be compared to a series of concentric circles. The innermost circle may be said to consist of the decision-making authority (whether it

can be detected straight away or not) which exercises control and influence in varying degrees . . . over the series of outer circles . . . .(1966)

The image of the group as a series of concentric circles is an apt one. In Nicaragua, interviewees felt that a nomenclature in which men and firms were classified as key, regular, or marginal members reflected the picture accurately. At the center of the group are those men who are the key leaders of the group and those firms of key importance. Next come the regular constituents, businesses controlled by group members which work with other group firms and the influential, trusted men of the group. Firms controlled by group members but closely integrated into group activities and with little influence or limited ties to the group are marginal. Occasionally there is a special case, like that of Manuel Lacayo—a man too important to be regarded as marginal yet too aberrant to qualify as a regular or key member.

As table 9.1 indicates, the area of vagueness in the types of firms in the business group is not great. There is near unanimity that the financial institutions and the nonfinancial firms controlled by these institutions are group firms. Personal businesses are regarded by a majority of respondents as groups firms, especially when the enterprise is owned by an important member of the group or works closely with other group firms. There is also great agreement that simple clients of group firms, such as suppliers or borrowers from the bank, should not be classed as group firms.

A cross-check of these opinions, obtained by asking interviewees to categorize specific Nicaraguan firms, show that 90 percent classified as group businesses examples of personal businesses of important group members that work closely with other group firms, even though only 60 percent had defined such firms as within the group.

It is more difficult to draw a precise line between people inside and outside a group than it is between firms inside and outside the association. Nevertheless, there is still considerable agreement about who is a group member, as table 9.2 demonstrates. Major shareholders, directors in group firms, and chief executives of important group enterprises are regarded by everyone as members of the group. Most of the respondents also classify hired executives and major shareholders without a voice on the board of directors as group members. Minor shareholders and employees are not considered members. The son of an important group member or a trusted consultant is generally included as a group member, but an intimate friend of a leader is not.

TABLE 9.1
TYPES OF FIRMS DEFINED AS PART OF GROUP

	Interview Responses		
	Yes	No	Other
1. The commercial bank	100%		
2. The financial institutions controlled* by the bank	100%		
3. The nonfinancial institutions controlled* by the bank and its related financial institutions	93.9%	6.1%	
4. The personal business of one or several of the directors of the bank or its related financial institutions	63.7%	30.3%	6.1%
5. The firms with loans from the bank or its financial institutions	3.0%	94.0%	3.0%
6. The suppliers to or distributors for firms controlled* by the bank	2.9%	91.2%	5.9%

*Control was defined as the power to designate, directly or indirectly, the majority of the board of directors or the top management positions in the firms.
Source: 33 interviews by author in Nicaragua in 1971.

TABLE 9.2
TYPES OF PERSONS IDENTIFIED AS GROUP MEMBERS

	Interview Responses		
	Yes	No	Other
1. Minor shareholders	11.8%	88.2%	
2. Major shareholders	52.9%	47.1%	
3. Major shareholder/director	100%		
4. Principal executive with profit sharing	97.1%	2.9%	
5. Executive without equity or profit sharing	76.5%	20.6%	2.9%
6. Employee	17.7%	73.5%	8.8%
7. Son of major shareholder/director	64.7%	29.4%	5.9%
8. Intimate friend of major shareholder/director	29.4%	58.8%	11.8%
9. Regular consultant	58.8%	38.3%	2.9%

Source: 33 interviews by author in Nicaragua in 1971.

The comments accompanying the answers in table 9.2 and the manner in which specific individuals were identified reveals the repondents' criteria of classification. Major shareholders without administrative roles and second echelon executives, if they are loyal to the group, are also classified as group members by about 85 percent of the interviewees. Their status within the group, which averages between marginal and regular, depends largely on their influence in group affairs and on how trusted they are by the other group members. Sons of key group members who are economically active in the family businesses are regarded as regular group members, more because of the future influence they are expected to wield than as a measure of their current importance. A consultant working exclusively with a group is identified within that group, his status purely a function of his influence. One consultant of long standing was rated a key member by a majority of the interviewees even though most of the other consultants on the list of names were generally classed as marginal.

If control and working with other group firms are the major criteria for determining whether a firm is a part of the group or not, then influence is undoubtedly the major criterion for determining whether or not a person is a member of the group. This influence can stem from the ownership of a major block of shares, the ability to turn this ownership into positions on the board of directors of various group enterprises, personal competence, or a position of executive responsibility. In exceptional cases, it can stem from influence over a key member of the group, for example, a relative or trusted consultant.

The nature of the criteria of group membership, as revealed in Nicaragua, makes it clear that there will always be uncertainty concerning the precise point at which a group ends. If, for example, being controlled and working with other group firms are the measures for determining whether or not a firm is placed within the association, one can expect that there will always be reasonable doubt as to whether a given firm is sufficiently controlled or is sufficiently integrated with other group firms. Rather than sharp divisions, concepts like control and influence reflect continua. Nevertheless, the Nicaraguan experience also demonstrates that vagueness of definition is limited to a small number of cases and is much more the result of difficulties in measurement or application of criteria than of an innate vagueness in the concept itself. For most Nicaraguans, the idea of business groups is clear even if it is not always known whether a particular firm or businessman meets certain requirements.

RELATIVE SIZE

Interviewees in 1971 were asked to calculate the size of the major groups relative to the rest of the economy. Where possible, these estimates were checked against statistical data. The average estimate for these is summarized in table 9.3. If accurate, it suggests that these groups account for 20 percent of the gross national product and exert potential influence on close to 40 percent of it.

TABLE 9.3
ESTIMATES OF GROUP ACTIVITY IN NICARAGUA 1971

| | | Sectors of the Economy | | | |
	Finance	Construc-tion	Industry	Agri-culture	Commerce
Group firms (including firms of groups members)	68%	71%	25%	22%	35%
Influenceable group firms[a]	13%	17%	39%	58%	31%
Estimated activity of group firms in relation to GNP[b]—20%					
Estimated influenceable activity in relation to GNP[c]—40%					

a. Influenceable firms were described as firms which could potentially be influenced by the groups because of family, credit, or client relationships.
b. The estimates of group activity by sector multiplied by the portion of GNP represented by that sector. The sectors of industry, agriculture, and commerce are all much larger than those of construction and finance.
c. The estimates of group activity plus influenceable activity by sector multiplied by the portion of GNP represented by each sector.

Sources: Estimates of group activity from interviews. GNP by Sector from, *Informe Anual 1971*, Central Bank of Nicaragua

Even more interesting than the overall figures, which have a large margin of error, is the fact that groups so completely dominate the financial and construction sectors. In the much larger sectors of agriculture, industry, and commerce, their impact is smaller.

FORMATION OF GROUPS

The birth of the Banco Nicaraguense Group according to its leader, Dr. Eduardo Montealegre, occurred as follows:

The development of the group was not a conscious activity planned from the start but something which gradually developed . . . .

255

In 1952, approximately, I returned to Nicaragua with some experience in banking in Guatemala and in Washington with the IMF. I had the idea at that time of developing a bank which might also provide other intermediary services like those of a savings and loan bank. At the time I had ideas and experience but not capital.

My initial concern was to find supporters with capital, business connections, governmental influence, and sufficient position in the community to create the good will and confidence necessary to ensure the bank's success.

The first person I approached was a friend of my family, a lawyer who was quite an entrepreneur, Dr. Salvador Guerrero Montalbán. He agreed that the idea was a good one. Together we contacted a select group of people to join us in the venture. All were men of business but we also selected several men in the government . . . and people not only from Leon but also from Managua, Diriamba, and other parts of Nicaragua. These men were all approached individually but the final planning session was held with everyone together in one of the hotels. In that meeting we put forth the plan which called for the raising of some $2,000,000 in capital. Half of the capital was to be sold to the assembled group members and the other half was to be sold in small blocs to businessmen who we hoped would become customers of the bank. No one person was to buy more than 10 percent of the outstanding stock.

A major hurdle was getting government permission to open a bank, a project accomplished by convincing General Somoza (the father of the president) that the time had come for this sort of institution in Nicaragua's development. Somoza also subscribed to a group members' bloc of stock in the bank. The final group of owners included people who had been in the business of lending money before and also several foreign residents in the country who had some appreciation of sophisticated finance.

I resigned my position in the United States to become general manager of the bank in January. By March or April the Bank was opened. By the end of the year we had made a profit and paid shareholders a 10 percent dividend. The bank expanded rapidly . . . .

Within two years, the savings and loan operation was begun as a separate institution for legal reasons. First, we found a dynamic young manager to head the operation. Then in preparing the capital subscription we eliminated several of the bank's original subscribers and added several other people, especially those with construction business contacts. Shortly therafter the savings and loan bank founded a construction company, although later the stock of the construction company was issued as a stock dividend to shareholders of the savings and loan association.

Later the bank and several of its shareholders purchased 30 percent of the stock of La Protectora, an insurance company, but we did not take over management until five years ago when earnings were down to only 16,000 córdobas. At that time, the directorate was changed, the manager replaced, and the firm reorganized. Earnings grew to a level of 2,000,000 córdobas this past year.

The group's next move was into an investment banking operation called INDESA, which was established in 1966. About this time the group began to think of itself more as a group and we began to take steps to organize ourselves as such. The bank took out the ownership interest in the *financiera*. We wanted the bank to own over 50 percent of the stock but were only allowed to own 25 percent and so had to ensure by clauses in the stock a right of veto power over board of director decisions and other personnel decisions . . . .

Dr. Montealegre's remarks illustrate several aspects of group development mentioned by others and supported by subsequent findings. First, the process of group formation is generally not "a conscious activity but something which gradually develops." Another interviewee meant much the same thing when he said that groups had developed in *una manera suave* (in a soft manner), that is, gradually, without sharp beginnings and endings. Another added, "The groups did not begin as groups; they were born naturally. Only in the last few years has the concept of groups become well known by many people." Remarked another, "At the beginning we got together to form a bank, not a group. Only later as we expanded and started other businesses did we begin to think of ourselves as a group."

As these comments imply, the group is something more than the bank and more than the complex of businesses which later developed. Each specific project has its own clearly defined group of owners and managers, but each project also reinforces a set of relationships among the joint venture partners which cannot be found in a legal document.

What kind of business project is likely to lead to the formation of a group? Again, Dr. Montealegre's remarks contain a clue. "I had ideas and experiences but no capital," he indicates. "My initial concern was to find supporters with capital, business connections, gov-

257

ernmental influence . . . ." Indeed, a characteristic of all major groups in Nicaragua, some of the protogroups, and the major industrial concerns which fathered the groups, is that they began as business ideas, requiring for success technical expertise including professional management, considerable amounts of capital, possibly governmental influence, and goodwill from the business community. This was true of both banks, the two construction companies, the brewery which is an important supporting industry of one group, and the sugar plantation and refinery which is the parent company of the other group.

One member of a protogroup who aspires to the creation of a new group stated in an interview:

> It is not easy to integrate or form a group. It is very difficult. Before you can have a group, the following must be accomplished:
> (1) learning to work together as a team and forgetting personalism, feeling a cohesion of interest and philosophy;
> (2) developing a balanced leadership;
> (3) developing absolute confidence among the members, a confidence which is practically blind;
> (4) having individual capacity among the members; and
> (5) having enormous financial, social, and political backing.

When groups form to work on projects that require a variety of contributions from different types, the diversity of contributions tends also to result in a diffusion of ownership and membership. The prominence of group leaders and the presence of some people clearly more influential than others make it easy to confuse a group of the type we are describing with a one-man or one-family business empire. Although there is some evidence that the Nicaraguan groups could be described as family concerns—and several of the interviewees felt this to be the case—one of the key distinguishing characteristics of the major groups is that they represent an association of men powerful and independent in their own right. The distribution of both power and ownership within these groups is greater than in the traditional one-man or one-family empire.

In the Banco Nicaraguense, as Dr. Montealegre mentioned, it was agreed that no man would subscribe to more than 10 percent of the outstanding stock. This, as one wealthy interviewee reported, was a new idea at the time. He, for example, had until then made it his policy not to invest in a project unless he controlled it or someone he trusted controlled it. Another example of the power distribution within the groups was the participation given to professional management when the groups formed. This was also a groundbreaking innovation in Nicaragua.

In the two ways mentioned above, the Banco Nicaraguense may be regarded as atypical. Nevertheless, even in the Banco de América group, the group most like a family empire, no one person or family—with the exception of the Wells Fargo Bank—owns more than 15 percent of the stock. As the following quotation from one respondent reveals, even those who see the Banco de América group as a series of family links will often admit the multi-family base of the group.

> In the Banco de América, the members are more linked by family ties than in the Banco Nicaraguense, because that group [Banco Nicaraguense] began when various men joined together in an economic cell which later became a group . . . the Banco de América is a mixed case. Actually, contrary to popular belief, the Pellas family did not originate the Banco de América Group. In the Nicaraguan Sugar Estate [Ingenio San Antonio], the Pellases are perhaps the largest shareholders, but there are also other strong shareholders. Already at the time the Nicaragua Sugar Estate was founded, it was more than a family. The Nicaragua Sugar Estate was a case of several Granadino businessmen working together, for example, Palazio, Benard, Chamorro, Vivas [who later sold out] and Pellas. They were all Granadinos and in a sense they have by now almost become one family.

A fourth item of interest in the development of the groups is the gradual formalization of group relations. Dr. Montealegre pointed out that by the time of INDESA's establishment in 1966, almost fifteen years after the beginning of the Banco Nicaraguense Group, there was a conscious desire on the part of the members to "organize ourselves more as a group." Earlier in the group's history, each new venture was made by a new stock subscription. The tendency was to distribute the stock of subsidiaries. For example, the savings and loan association, which established the land developing company FINANSA, later issued the shares of its subsidiary as a stock dividend. Since 1966, however, the tendency has been to consolidate group holdings. As new ventures are formed, the core institutions try to take out a majority of the stock and subsidiaries are now known even to purchase shares of the parent. Virtually all of the groups have also formed holding companies within the last few years.

A tendency has also developed toward more formal relationships among the group members. One member of a smaller group noted, "Before, when we were smaller, the organization was much more informal. Now with a larger number in the group, a council representing different institutions must get together to make decisions." Several other respondents spoke of more formal relations as one of the changes between 1970 and 1975.

Obviously a reason for the tendency toward formalization of the group relationships is size. Two other pressures encourage more formal relations: the fragility of personal ties and the problem of succession. One of the interviewees mentioned both when he said, "In its cohesiveness, the group tends to oscillate. Even during the last two years, I would say, we have gone through two cycles of tension and cohesion. Also, if a person dies, that can be a great blow to the group. New people come in . . . ." When an organization is based primarily on intangible relationships, there are numerous events that can break up these relationships. The leaders of these organizations, aware of the fragility of these bonds, try to buttress the personal relationships with clear institutional patterns. At the same time as the institution progresses and its leaders grow older, they become concerned with the problem of succession and take steps to cope with the vacuum and disequilibrium which their deaths could create. "We are currently in the process of trying to set up institutional arrangements so that on the death of a leader, the whole group does not come apart," one of the group executives mentioned. "We have thought about holding companies, and other arrangements but have not yet decided what to do."

THE PROCESS OF GROWTH

Each of the groups appears to have grown rapidly in the last twenty-six years. Most of the group's financial and construction enterprises did not exist twenty-five years ago. Yet today they perform 80 percent of all business activity in these two sectors. In the commercial sector, a roster of the successful businessmen, including those who have come to prominence during the last thirty years, would contain most of the same names as a list of prominent group members. One source of the group growth comes from incorporating new members into the group. Another source of growth is the establishment of new businesses. Finally, groups expand as a result of the internal growth.

The tendency to grow by acquisition of new members is illustrated in table 9.4, where 90 percent of the respondents indicated that someone had joined the group recently but that no one had left the group. The statement that no one had left the group was puzzling, however, because these answers did not appear to be consistent with the description of certain persons who seemed in the process of leaving one group and moving to another or who were regarded as traitors and renegades. Even Dr. Montealegre's description of how, in a new capital subscription, certain people had been eliminated suggests a form of expulsion from the group.

TABLE 9.4
PERSONS JOINING AND LEAVING GROUPS

Question	*Responses* (25)	
	Yes	No
Have any persons recently joined the groups?	23	2
Have any persons recently left the groups?	3	22
Examples of Persons Recently Joining Groups (23)		
High-level executives	8	
Directors	14	
Subgroups	2	
Gave no example	3	
Examples of Persons Recently Leaving Groups (3)		
Persons in disagreement of personal nature	1	
Bankrupt firm	1	
Director losing influence	1	

A plausible explanation for the apparent inconsistency is that there may be currently more people coming into groups than leaving. Acceptance into the group is also more visible, as is election to the board of directors or an executive appointment. With few exceptions, however, the movement from being a key member to a "marginal" member or an outsider is not so obviously signaled. A person can lose prestige and influence yet continue to be considered a group member.

An important conclusion which might be drawn from the notice-able difficulty which respondents had in providing clear answers to the questions of table 9.4 is that in groups, as in politics, it is the movement toward greater or lesser influence, rather than in and out, which is significant.

Whatever the relative status of people within the groups, new people do enter the group and, even if the group is reluctant to admit it, they also leave. As several of the leading members of one group indicated, attracting new members to the group is a clear objective. This is normally done by offering them shares when capital is augmented by financial institutions (which is frequent given the high dividend payout policy), by offering them a directorship on one of the groups' important financial institutions, or by inviting them in on the ground floor of a new project.

The need for "new blood" was mentioned as a major reason for this policy of attracting new members. For many respondents, the main criterion for selecting new members was personal qualities. Three others indicated that the criterion generally was not capital to invest as much as new business, which these people would bring with them, especially to the financial institutions. Three others stated explicitly that an attempt is made to attract those people who might potentially form a third group. As one put it: "Groups are aware of the danger to themselves of other groups developing or of a significant change in the status quo. They, therefore, take pains to attract those who potentially could form other groups. There is, for example, a recent case of one of the banks wooing a man with a family, a fortune, and a portfolio of investments who might serve as the nucleus of another group."

An interesting, almost paradoxical aspect of the group's recruiting policy is that while it attracts men of considerable wealth to the group, what is sought is rarely the capital. Groups want these men's personal capacity in business and to be associated with their power. This association is important to the group because of the increased power it gives them as well as the potential power it diverts from other groups.

Respondents indicated different degrees of openness among the groups. Several persons felt that present groups tend to be more exclusive than they were in the past. On the other hand, during the time of this study, each group extended a number of tentative invitations. Because of the strong competition between the groups as well as the very real possibility of the formation of new groups, it is my opinion that the doors are open to persons who can contribute to the groups. Nevertheless, the groups are a closed society to those who do not have what the groups want.

In admitting new members, the group leadership finds itself caught in a dilemma. There is, first of all, a natural desire to expand the sphere of the group's activities and influence. To succeed in this, new people must be brought into the group. If this could be done simply by giving a person stock or a membership card, many people could be invited to join the group. Being a member, however, means having influence, being a part of the decision-making apparatus, and sharing in close personal relations with other group members and top executives. Defining membership in terms of influence and personal relationships would then suggest a natural limit to the number of key or influential members which a group can have. If people do not voluntarily leave the group, the group then will face a limited capacity for accepting new members. Ultimately, some mechanism will be needed to replace members who no longer actively contribute to the group.

It was impossible to determine objectively how much of the group's growth is due to new memberships. The list of new key group members seems to represent a significant but not a major portion of group growth, perhaps 10 to 20 percent. Major changes in the composition of the groups are only likely to occur at the death or retirement of an important member or when a major crisis forces the group to make radical adjustments in top level personnel.

Another major means of group expansion is via the creation of new firms. Since 1966, both groups have established *financieras* which issue bonds locally, borrow in the U.S. and other capital markets, and lend or invest this money within the country with more freedom and at higher interest rates than can the commercial banks. The four *financieras* of Nicaragua were all established around 1966. The primary impetus in their formation was probably a change in banking regulations which reduced commercial banks' freedom of investment.

Generalizations can be made about new businesses established by a group. First, a number of the interviewees indicated that groups will not set up firms that compete with existing businesses of group members—in spite of the fact that businesses of group members may already be in competition with one another. Second, new firms begun by the group tend to be complementary to existing firms. Dr. Montealegre mentioned that when the group had met the need for banking services, it turned its attention to other financial needs, establishing institutions to supply them. The bank developed a savings and loan association, later a *financiera*, then acquired an insurance company, and just this past year created a bonded warehouse. One bank has even moved into the cotton brokerage business for foreign exchange purposes.

A member of a construction subgroup described how the firms had gradually expanded from construction into the manufacture of certain building materials, into land development, and even into the sale and production of electrical household furnishings. "When the business the group members or firms are giving to another person or company reaches a large volume, as in, for example, insurance or advertising or financing, they say, 'Why not form a company ourselves and give it our own business? In the process, we will get the profits from this business and the assurance that we have a loyal supplier.' "

The same interviewee mentioned that the group also tends to become involved in businesses which are in financial difficulties, especially those which owe the group's financial institutions money. Sometimes these firms are taken over in an attempt to turn them around. Another interviewee indicated that for this reason one of the groups had gotten into the automobile agency business and into the supermarket business.

If expansion into complementary areas is natural and expansion into firms in financial difficulties is forced, then a third type of expansion might be described as opportune. As the main investment bankers in the private sector, the groups are often approached by local and foreign entrepreneurs with business proposals. In recent years, one of the groups has in this way become involved in a fishing venture and in a lumbering operation. Any venture interests them, especially if it is national, noncompetitive with a group member, and, of course, lucrative. One observer said, "Originally the groups were developed to provide credit, but in recent years their primary purpose is to make new investments." New investments probably represent approximately 30 to 50 percent of the growth of the groups.

A fourth source of group growth is the internal expansion of group firms. While it was not possible to calculate the percentage of group growth attributable to expansion of existing firms, my guess is that approximately 40 to 60 percent of the growth of the last ten years is internal. In the opinion of an overwhelming majority of persons questioned, group firms have grown more rapidly than the average Nicaraguan firm. If this is an accurate opinion, an intriguing question is whether this growth comes from increased market share or whether the groups are in the fastest growing sectors of the economy. The answer seems to be a bit of both. A rough comparison of an industrial firm survey made in 1963 and in 1968 indicates a process of concentration in the industrial sector. Today, in many segments of the business sector there are fewer firms with a much larger average size than there were eight years ago. Many of the group firms are among these larger firms. Professor Nicolás Marín's limited study on the profitability of group firms showed that they had a higher average rate of return on capital than non-group (including foreign) firms. The high variance, the weakness of the underlying data, and the small size of this sample, however, make it unadvisable to put too great an emphasis on these results.

ORGANIZATION OF THE GROUP

In Nicaragua, the *sociedad anónima* is the most commonly chosen legal form for large and medium-size business enterprises, especially when there is more than one owner. Virtually all of the group firms use this corporate form. A separate corporation is generally created for each different business activity. In recent years, several of the groups and subgroups have begun to organize their firms under holding companies.

A *sociedad anónima*, like its counterpart the corporation, generally has a *directiva* or board of directors whose chairman is called the *presidente*. He is the highest ranking officer of the company. Like the board of directors of a U.S. corporation, the *directiva* is elected by shareholders and makes decisions and policies for the company. This board may also delegate some of its responsibilities to an executive committee. The chief operational officer is called the *gerente general*.

265

In some firms, especially the smaller ones, the chairman of the board is actually the chief executive officer who makes virtually all the decisions, signs checks, and involves himself in daily operations. (He plays the role of the owner-manager while his *gerente general*, if he has one, does the work of an assistant executive. In larger firms the *gerente general* has more power and responsibility and serves as the chief executive officer of the firm. This is true in one of the groups whose executives, by virtue of their training, social status, and capacity, are the real leaders of the group.

There is no law in Nicaragua limiting the appointment of one person to multiple directorships. Within the groups and subgroups, this has become common practice. A majority of the interviewees indicated that the principal way in which the group controls and coordinates its different activities is through the use of interlocking directorates.

In 1970, one group published a brochure describing its principal group firms. The brochure had the pictures and names of the ten directors of the bank and separate pictures, names, and titles of seven of the principal executives of the five different financial institutions. Examination revealed that these seventeen men occupied thirty-eight of the top fifty-five positions in the five main group firms and many more director positions in the subsidiary firms.

The usual board of directors has from five to seven men. One interviewee said that the general rule on a five-man board is to appoint four group members and one person who has not yet become a group member, but who is being wooed by the group.

The examination of directorships also revealed that several important group members were not board members and that group status is not necessarily determined by one's formal position in the firms of the group. In practical terms, though, there is a generally high correlation between one's status in the group and one's formal position in group firms. In most groups the person who is given principal responsibility for a firm is then named *presidente* of the board of directors. One interviewee also noted that although personal and social contact among group members is frequent, little communication regarding business decisions of a particular firm takes place among those group members who are not on the firm's board of directors.

266

ROLES WITHIN THE GROUP

There are probably four main types of group members: the leader, members of the inner circle, regular directors, and executives. Each group has a leader, the *manda más*, or godfather, as he is sometimes jokingly called. In the Banco de América, Don Alfredo Pellas is the acknowledged leader; in the Banco Nicaragüense, it is Dr. Eduardo Montealegre; in the Banco Centroamericano Group, General Anastasio Somoza Debayle; and in the AISA/INFISA/La Nacional proto-group, Ing. Roberto Argüello Tefel. In describing these individuals, numerous people made statements to the effect that these persons were the real power in the groups as well as the groups' public representatives.

Further descriptions of this real power indicated that the leader apparently has the right of veto on most important business decisions. One of his roles is to make the strategic decisions, although he acts on the advice of others. As expected, there are differences between the groups. In one group, the leader is said to be an active, aggressive executive who not only makes a great number of the decisions but also originates many of the ideas. In another group, the leader plays a more passive role, approving or vetoing the ideas of others.

Several respondents also mentioned that the leader's role is to serve as referee. One executive put it this way: "Each group has a *manda más*. In our group the leader makes the decisions but does so after consulting with people. At the same time, when there is competition among the institutions he serves as a referee." A member of another group said, "I see our leader as a sort of a traffic cop, channeling people so as to avoid intragroup competition."

A third responsibility of the leader is to maintain group cohesion, to concern himself with the health of the group. Direction and cohesion for a group over a long period of time involves hard decisions, especially personnel decisions. These decisions are not easily made by a board of directors if a realignment of the power of that board is involved. Similarly, a person who is not part of the regular operational machinery may be more perceptive of a need for major changes in the strategy of a group. The leader is expected to initiate these kinds of changes, and it is here that the influence of family and close advisors can be crucial. One interviewee, after noting the real power of the leader, added, "In my group, the key decisions are controlled by the family. For example, key personnel decisions are generally made by the invisible directors. In the area of operational decisions, more and more of the power is delegated to capable executives and the directorates of the various firms. Even this tendency is not without expection, however, when the manager is weak."

Finally, in one of the groups, the leader decides who will be elected to which directorate, although in this matter there is a high degree of participation of the key group members or the inner circle.

Working closely with the leader are a number of the most influential group members. These were described in the interviews as the inner circle, executive committee, or key group members. All of the groups and subgroups have group members who are more active and influential than others. This inner circle coincides closely with the board of directors of the holding companies at the time of their establishment. A key member will generally sit on the board of a large number of firms, often serving as chairman of the board of one of the subsidiaries. A characteristic of most of these men in the inner circle is that each has his own base of power, usually a subgroup where he is the leader. Major decisions are made and coordinated by this inner group. One such key member said, "In our group the leader generally decides who will sit on which board of directors, but the group is really operated by a small number of men whose names are . . . [here he listed four men in addition to the leader]." An executive of the same group told me that the key policy decisions of his group tend to get made by an executive committee and listed the same people. Another indicated that the major orientation of a firm is given to it by the executive committee working closely with the manager.

By law, major powers and responsibilities in a *sociedad anónima* are given to the *junta directiva*. There was some variation in the description of the de facto role of the directors. Some interviewees declared that the director's role was primarily one of giving approval to the decisions which were made by management. Others indicated that the directorate, especially the president, makes most of the operational decisions. In most boards, as perhaps in most social groups, one or two persons gain the most influence, and major responsibilities tend to gravitate to the most active directors. This was demonstrated by the remarks of a junior executive of one of the groups. Comparing two key men in his group, he said, "X uses much less power than he really has, while Y exercises much more power than he really has. I have been in a board meeting in which Y, who holds less than 10 percent of the stock, was virtually the only one to speak when a certain issue was raised for discussion. Before anyone had a chance to say a word he declared, 'This is the decision of the board of directors on that matter . . .' The other directors had not expressed their opinions and no vote was taken. They then went on to another subject."

Full members of a group are normally seated on the directorates of at least one of the group firms, although some members, by their own choice, do not take on this responsibility. When they do not sit as directors, they usually do not play an active role in the decisions of the group. They do, however, keep aware of decisions being made. Both groups are nearly twenty years old and a number of important members are beginning to retire from active roles. The number of members not active in the groups may, therefore, increase.

While the board of directors of a particular firm is not likely to have more than five to seven people, a larger number of people tend to enter the discussion of important decisions. This larger group is consulted both because its contribution to the decision is valued, and because consultations help to maintain a sense of "group-ness." By giving advance information to many members or by seeking out their advice, the key members create a sense of participation in the group decisions among other group members. In reality, however, the person consulted may exercise little or no influence on the final decision.

Just as there are different views on the extent of the power of the board of directors, so there are different views on the role of the executives. Opinions vary in part because in one group the executives are given greater responsibilities, more freedon of action, and a larger share in the profits than in another. The chief executive of a firm, especially of an important firm, is usually regarded as a key member of the group. It is his job to implement most of the operational decisions. He is often the originator of proposals and new projects that come before the board of directors. He may be appointed to the board of other firms which have close ties with his firm or sit on intercompany committees to coordinate activities.

In the period between 1970 and 1975 executives have increasingly been given stock options and equity participation in newly formed enterprises.

DECISION MAKING, CENTRALIZATION, AND OPERATIONAL AUTONOMY

The interplay among the different elements of the group is illustrated in the following descripiton of decision making by one interviewee:

> In the case of a new project for a business, it is probable that the idea would originate with an executive of the group or firm. The idea would then come before the board of directors, which would decide whether or not to study it and if so, start the process in motion . . . . More specifically, an idea for a new business would probably take the following route. X, a member of the group gets an idea. After thinking about it, he would probably share it with those in the group who are his friends of *confinaza* [another mentioned that this would almost always include the leader of the group]. After this, it would be talked about among the group members. Finally, when the idea was sufficiently mature, those outside of the group whom they wish to attract in this or in other projects [via inclusion in this one] would be approached. The basis for being included in the decision-making process is usually the person's capacity. In other words, the person's reputation for good judgment or his contacts or expertise in the area of the project.

Analysis of a number of specific decisions in one group supported the pattern described above, underlining the fact that ideas tend to be developed within a special circle of friends. Only when the idea has been fully developed and the leader is sold on it, if he has not participated in the process, does it reach the formal organization and go before the board of directors.

High-level appointments illustrate the consultative process:

> In the case of an appointment of a chief executive officer for a group firm, the key person in the choice would probably be the president of the board of directors. (1) He would most likely con-

sult with persons on the board and within the group in whom he had absolute confidence. (2) He might also talk in advance with persons on the board who might create opposition or be offended if not consulted, in order to win them over to his choice. (3) He would talk with those who are not members of the group, because they know something about the requisites necessary for the job and they know of promising candidates.

Another interviewee indicated that in personnel appointments within firms, the board of directors generally delegates much of the searching and most of the decision making to the president.

As new investments and high-level appointments are obviously centralized decisions, so are the more operational decisions. Opinions on the degree of centralization among the groups differed, but a clear majority of respondents felt that in all of the groups power is quite centralized, and that the leader or members of the inner group tend to be consulted on most operational decisions of importance.

One of the more perceptive analyses of the decision-making process was made about a subgroup. It is, however, a fairly accurate description of the other groups.

Decision making in the past was very centralized by [the inner circle]. Presently there is a tendency to centralize control and analytical functions in the holding company in order to get better information. The holding company makes recommendations to the managers and discusses these with them. In the future, better organized and trained managers will make the operational decisions—as decentralized as possible—but the supervision of these managers will be considerably better.

The groups are organized legally and administratively to make it possible for each business to operate independently. General policy is that each business stand on its own, as or as one person put it *cada uno tira por su proprio lado* (each shoots in his own direction).

Like all general rules, the rule of autonomous operation requires qualification. One person with knowledge of day-to-day operations indicated that in most of the groups this rule was usually observed but not completely so among financial and construction firms. Another executive in one of the construction subgroups disclosed that one of the obligations of group membership is to look at the overall picture. His particular firm had entered into projects which were not the most profitable for it, but very profitable for sister institutions.

Structural considerations tend to limit the coordination of operations between group firms. Generally the chief executive of each firm is paid a salary plus a percentage of profits. This gives him a strong incentive to maximize the firm's profits and resist unprofitable arrangements. Also the ownership composition of most group firms is not the same. Member X may have a greater interest in one firm than member Y. Those with the greatest interest in a firm are likely to be on the board of directors. They have a clear incentive not to give away profits to another group firm. I would suspect that the role of the leader as referee or traffic cop means not only delineating realms of business but also helping to solve the transfer pricing problems created when group firms work together.

There does not appear to be much integration of firms, however. One economist, who was impressive for the thoughtfulness of his observations, maintained that there was "not much integration of business among the group firms and what there was probably tended to predate the group arrangement."

This conclusion was supported by an analysis of the degree to which firms in a group make use of the same professional personnel. Generally, executive and administrative personnel are not shared, but lawyers and technical persons may be. The more defined the subgroup or the greater the sense of separate identity, however, the greater the likelihood of separate lawyers and accountants.

RELATIONSHIPS WITHIN THE GROUP

As influence appears to be the most important index of the status of a group member, trust and confidence are the key characteristics of the relationships which bind group members. As mentioned earlier, one interviewee stated that the difficulty in establishing a climate of trust was one of the greatest obstacles to the creation of a group.

Interviewees were asked: "What do you consider to be the principal obligation and responsibility of group membership?" While most of the answers to this questions were vague, a frequent answer was loyalty. One person described the principal obligation of membership as respect and the defense of the group. Another felt that it involved "guarding the backs of the others." When asked to explain further, he answered, "It means defending their reputation as serious, competent businessmen." Loyalty, of course, involves more than simple public support of one member by the other. This list of requirements stemming from loyalty is long. Two specific obligations required by loyalty, discussed at some length in the interviews, were giving business to other members of the group and extending financial help to group members in need.

As table 9.5 illustrates, a great majority of the interviewees felt that membership imposes an obligation to give one's business to other group members but at no personal cost. The general rule is *preferencia en circumstancias de igualdad* (preference in equal circumstances). Several mentioned that before doing business with a group member, they make it a point to get other offers. Others indicated that they generally expect to get a discount or a more favorable price from a fellow member. A few felt also that part of the obligation is to recommend to your friends and your associates the wares and services of other group members.

TABLE 9.5
OBLIGATION TO GIVE FELLOW GROUP MEMBERS BUSINESS
(Percentage of 19 Replies)

Yes, even at slight personal disadvantage	16%
Yes, but at no price disadvantage	68%
No obligation	16%
	100%

The obligation to do business with each other extends to doing business with group firms. An interesting additional factor here, alleged by some interviewees and disputed by others, is that the jointly owned group firms are sometimes forced to do business on disadvantageous terms with their constituents. One outsider stated that in a certain group the businesses of the *financiera* "are not operated autonomously but must enter into artificial relationships with each other, often at price disadvantages." Other people indicated that sometimes group firms will use their leverage with customers to force them to make use of other group services. A person taking out a mortgage loan, for example, will be forced to insure his house with the life insurance company of the group. This, however, was denied by one of the group executives, who said that it was true that financial institutions cooperate and refer business to each other but that to date all referrals have not been forced. Although group members give each other considerable amounts of business, the evidence suggests that this business represents only a small fraction, probably less than 5 percent, of the total business of most member firms.

The limited nature of group obligations was also revealed in the attitudes toward rescue work within the group. As table 9.6 reveals, group members are expected to help each other in time of need but, again, not at any risk of personal loss.

TABLE 9.6
HELP FOR A FELLOW MEMBER IN FINANCIAL DIFFICULTIES
(Percentage of 18 Replies)

	Responses
Obligation to help even if it means risking personal loss	0%
Obligation to help but only at no risk of personal loss	83%
No obligation	17%
	100%

As one respondent said, "I am obligated to learn about the matter and help up to that point which my judgment indicates that I should. I would have to check the probability that my help would be successful before I lent any of my personal money or that of the financial institutions." The executive of the financial institutions indicated that the obligation to lend to group members is clearly secondary to that of making good investments and secure loans. One or two interviewees assumed that if the financial institutions would not make the loan, it was already too risky to give personal help.

In another context, one of the interviewees noted that group investments are generally better investments than non-group investments because groups will not let a business venture within the group fail. They will intervene to rehabilitate firms in trouble, especially if they have made loans to these firms. This support, however, is not given altruistically. The terms of the intervention leave the financial institution reaping the major share of any gains should the company be rescued.

274

CONCLUSIONS

The principal objective of this chapter has been to describe major Nicaraguan groups, going beyond a simple listing of the component parts, and to analyze group formation, organization, and obligation.

My interest in business groups stems from a conviction that they are not only dominant economic organizations in their countries, but that they also play a significant role in modernization—a role with economic, political, and social consequences. It is, therefore, important that the dynamics of these groups be better understood. Nicaragua offers an excellent example.

If we are to know more about groups we need more descriptions taken from different cultures and different periods of history. If these descriptions are to be useful, they must be more analytical and they must focus more on how the groups operate internally than simply on their size and external appearance.

Cross-cultural studies require both a more precise definition of business groups and a testable hypothesis. In the introduction to this chapter, I submitted a definition of business group built around the characteristics of diversity of enterprise, pluralism of composition, and fiduciary relationships. In Central America these seem to be the hallmarks of major business groups. I also mentioned two hypotheses which I would recommend for discussion, testing, and refinement by those studying business groups elsewhere.

This first hypothesis is that business groups come into existence and thrive because of the functions or services which they perform for their members. The principal function provided by a business group is one of financial intermediation in which the group facilitates both the making of investments for those members with excess savings and the securing of steady credit for those group members with net capital needs. In addition, groups also help their members maintain a strong market position and provide them with other benefits of concentrated economic power in relation to government agencies, although these group services are of secondary importance. While the association could potentially, and may in fact, provide operational benefits, such as administrative and technical support, and noneconomic benefits, such as social status, these types of group services are not of major importance in the establishment and maintenance of the business group.

The second hypothesis is that business groups begin to appear at the time when a country embarks on the process of industrialization and when financial institutions are being established. In this environment they thrive. Later, in an environment of more sophisticated financial institutions, more reliable markets, and more stable political structures, these groups lose their relative prominence. In short, business groups are an organizational phenomenon which is more suited to and useful in the developing than in developed nations.

10

Barley, Compadres, and Fiestas: Investment and Confidence in a Mexican Regional Elite

GERALD L. GOLD

Department of Anthropology
York University

In recent years, the attention of Latin Americanists has been drawn to the social and cultural importance of agrarian elites. Certainly, land reform in Mexico has led, at least indirectly, to the formation of new regional elites of landowners and merchants (Stavenhagen 1970). But what is usually ignored is that the more recent expansion of the central government and the extension of industry to rural areas has, at the same time, led to the marginality of regional elites in national decision making. This chapter is specifically concerned with the implications of this marginality for the social organization of rancheros in the altiplano of central Mexico.[1] My hypothesis about the rancheros is that their economic and political marginality is minimized by the intraclass cultivation and maintenance of relations of confidence between families and between individuals. Strategies for the management of confidence rely primarily on low-profile and noncorporate dyadic ties that are cemented through affinal relationships, compadrazgo, and feasting. Thus, acquiring and sustaining trust relationships is a form of investment that is deployed by both individuals and groups and that is subject to normative constraints.

277

The diffuse and personal character of these relationships leads them to be both multiplex and ritualized, hence redundant. Nevertheless, my contention is that the repetition of in-group rituals creates the context for mutual prestations and the exchange of valued information. In such an environment, status becomes an asset—a series of indivisible credentials which must be maintained to operate effectively a family enterprise. It follows that, for individuals, the criteria of what is an "investment" include those expenditures that maintain "a life-style which in effect advertises to the world that he is in a position to control significant resources, including informational ones" (Aubey, Kyle, and Strickon 1974:86). The "world" of the rancheros is the altiplano of Los Llanos (a pseudonym) and not the metropole from which state and private economic decisions often emanate.

That investments in noncorporate types of relationships are effective in a situation of strong external dependency is shown clearly in Norman Long's chapter here on rural Peru, in Robert Aubey's work with the plantocracy of El Salvador (1969), and in Schneider, Schneider, and Hansen's use of the term "dependent elite" in the context of their discussion of modernization and development in the western Mediterranean (1972). They suggest a relationship between the dominance of noncorporate groups in regional social structures and the fragmentation of power in some preindustrial societies (Schneider, Schneider, and Hansen 1972:366). An atomistic regional power structure that favors the proliferation of patron-client chains and of multiple coalitions is also an effective substitute for an undependable or underdeveloped state bureaucracy and distribution system as can still be found in some parts of rural Mexico. In a climate of such uncertainty, where economic and political ties are highly personalistic, to prevent sabotage of coalitions and to "build a climate of trust in which future coalitions can be assembled . . . banqueting, impromptu fiesta and other celebrations of friendship, kinship and fictive kinship are common" (Hansen, Hansen, and Schneider 1972:338). Regional political alignments thus cannot be separated from the regional distribution of economic power.

I have shown (Gold 1975) that, in rural Quebec, when an indigenous capitalist elite emerges within an agricultural region, its problems of boundary maintenance involve, first, breaking down the regional particularism and parochialism that benefitted agrarian elites and, second, aligning itself with the agents and the values of national capitalism (Gold 1975). Instead of promoting noncorporate structures, it proceeds to build formal associations that both are internally flexible and present a highly visible corporate face of unanimity to the region and to the nation. I believe it is significant that Mexican and other agrarian elites have been unable to sustain corporate forms of organization without falling back, after threats to their regional power diminish, on fragmented but efficacious noncorporate ties. That is, as a class culture they are more committed to preserving an entrenched position, a preexisting normative consensus, than in seeking a new order of their region based upon national goals. The growth of such a class culture was a logical consequence of the economic changes in southern Hidalgo after the Mexican Revolution. Some explanation of the transformation of the agricultural base of the region is necessary to appreciate its social consequences.

FROM PULQUE TO BARLEY

The town of Los Llanos, *cabacera* of a *municipio* of over fifteen thousand inhabitants, lies at 2,493 meters above sea level at the northeastern extremity of a flat, semiarid, and mountain-girded valley in the southern part of the state of Hidalgo. Only 93.75 rail-kilometers from the national capital, Los Llanos is best known to Mexicans as a center for the production of pulque, the white, syrupy beer that the inhabitants of the valley have made from the fermented sap of the maguey cactus since pre-Columbian times. The completion of the Ferrocarril Mexicano to Los Llanos, in 1868, encouraged the valley's semifeudal haciendas to opt for monoculture of maguey to supply a rapidly increasing demand for pulque from Mexico City (Poggie 1968:38; Simon 1973:38). By 1888, few small holders were left in Los Llanos to coexist with the latifundia and most of the 8,702 people of the *municipio* worked as peons on thirteen haciendas and twenty-one smaller ranchos (Andrade 1910:16–17).

Although the era of the great haciendas is gone, there is an extensive physical record of their wealth and power that no inhabitant of Los Llanos ignores either in stories or in family history. The hacendados lived lavishly with such amenities as immense dining rooms for fiestas, dozens of bedrooms, riding stables, and solaria. The

279

business end of the latifundia was handled by the administrator and his mayordomos who supervised pulque production in the *tinacal;* they "wielded almost unlimited authority over the residents of the hacienda community" (Simon 1973:52) and "did not hesitate to make use of the whipping post and the saber whenever the indolent peon seemed to need such disciplinary measures" (Whetten 1948:101–02).

One Los Llanos administrator, Guillermo Aegis, to whom I will shortly return, was responsible for a *tinacal* that produced and shipped to the capital 250 barrels of pulque per day with the help of over a hundred *tlatchiqueros*, the burro-mounted sap collectors who formed much of the landless proletariat of the region. Even before land reform, Guillermo Aegis identified with the hacendado lifestyle of his patron. During the years of unrest and revolution, however, the patron, like other hacendados of Los Llanos, preferred to remain in the capital, leaving Aegis to mind the "big house." Despite the absence of the owners, the twenty thousand acres of the haciendas (McBeth 1966:11) placed the town and its *fundo legal* of 773 hectares into a status of dependency. The estates were heavily fortified and the hacendados had sufficient political clout in the capital to resist successfully the first land redistributions. It was not until 1932, before the Cardenas régime, that the haciendas of Los Llanos were entirely parceled into ejidos and into small properties of under two hundered hectares of nonirrigated land.

THE RANCHEROS—SONS OF THE REVOLUTION

Most of the newly created private holdings in Los Llanos were sold to the hacienda supervisory class, mayordomos and administrators like Guillermo Aegis, who had the experience of estate management and position and information to enable them to purchase land. Moreover, in the panic selling of the thirties, properties were available for as little as eight thousand pesos, often including the grandiose and deteriorating buildings of the hacienda. The new strata of small holders, the *pequeños proprietarios*, took on a traditional self-identification as rancheros, although they also were "sons of the revolution," with provisions for land tenure under Mexico's new constitution.

Little has been written about the *pequeños preprietarios* for the twenty years that elapsed between land reform and the construction of a planned factory town in the valley. However, in Los Llanos as in the rest of Mexico (Gutelman 1971:223; Stavenhagen 1970: 261–70), reform was met by counterreform and the initial parcellation of the land was followed by a steady accumulation of capital within ejidos and by the emergence nationally of a new class of landholding farmers, *pequeños proprietarios*. Unlike the hacendados, the new landowners could not organize large self-sufficient production units. Instead they became dependent on commercial enterprises of the town, integrating their agriculture into a regional economy and power structure that drew on national corporations for its technology and distribution.

The construction of the factory town in 1952 accelerated the changes that had begun after the revolution. These changes have been extensively documented from the standpoint of the impact of industrialization on the agricultural valley communities (Gold 1968; Miller 1973; Mundale 1973; Poggie 1968; Poggie and Miller 1969; Roufs 1971; Simon 1973; Young and Young 1960a, 1960b, 1962, 1966). Emphasis has been placed on the transition from pulque to heavy industry, but little has been said of the implications for the capitalization in agriculture and the replacement of most maguey cultivation by malt barley as the major cash crop of the valley. Looking retrospectively at pulque, Miller writes: "The image of the product . . . proved increasingly incongruous as Mexico became more modernized . . . . The production of beer rose rapidly as the popularity of pulque fell" (1973:32). Mundale evokes the image of pulque being taken to market in dirty barrels in the back of wheezing, decrepit trucks to be sold in pulquerias, largely owned by Los Llanos producers, in the lower class areas of the capital (1973:32).

Ironically, although the transformation from maguey to barley may be less profitable to the small producer (Mundale:1973:41), it replaces one beer-producing crop with another. Furthermore, this is not a mere substitution; it involves a shift from a labor-intensive undercapitalized system of production to an intensive capitalized agrarian economy.

Harvested every fall rather than every seven years, barley is as land-extensive as maguey, and as amenable to cultivation on a semiarid rainfall-watered plateau. Unlike maguey, though, barley production is sensitive to slight variations in rainfall, sunshine, and

281

temperature. Whereas maguey is labor-intensive and requires little capital on the part of the producer, who must instead furnish his own "cactus plant to drinking glass" vertical control over distribution (Mundale 1973:31), barley lends itself to heavy capital investment in machinery and the vertical integration is provided by Mexican national capitalism in the breweries and the machinery interests (see Aubey in this volume). It is also noteworthy that barley, unlike maguey, is not a staff of life for the peasant, as he does not consume it for food or use its stalks to heat his home in the winter. Finally pulque, unlike barley, is still acceptable as a partial return for peasant labor.

All these factors considered, after the revolution barley became a favored crop for small producers seeking a cash return with a low investment of labor. However, a crucial factor in the transformation is that after the hacendados abandoned the valley, only immigrant Spanish beer and grain merchants had capital to lend to small holders. In the vacuum created by the departure of the hacendados, the barley-seeking Spaniards made clients of the former hacienda administrators who had little of their own capital or of opportunity to control the distribution of pulque. Only a handful of wealthy producers maintained relative independence from the Spaniards by producing both crops. The result has been the development of a barley system in the valley that imposes a constraint on the financial investment of rancheros who control the means of production. Given the ultimate urban control of the barley system, these same landowners do not control the means of distribution. Ranchero wealth has, however, permitted them to control the political machine of the valley and to be identified as a high-status elite group. Even with the dominating presence of the new industrial town, barley growers, together with the wealthiest merchants and factory managers, are given the highest local ranking of prestige (Simon 1973:142–45).

THE RANCHEROS AND THE SPANISH MERCHANTS

As "sons of the revolution" the present-day rancheros are drawn neither from the families of hacendados nor from the ranks of peasantry, as table 10.1 graphically demonstrates. Of forty-three ranchero heads of family surveyed in Los Llanos, twenty-three are

TABLE 10.1
FATHER'S OCCUPATION IN FORTY-THREE RANCHERO MARRIAGES*

	Wife is the daughter of:					
	ranchero	hacendado	campesino	commerciante	empleado	no data	Total
Husband is the son of:							
ranchero	9	1	3	5	3	3	24
hacendado	–	2	–	–	–	–	2
campesino	1	5	1	–	–	–	6
commerciante	1	–	–	–	–	–	2
empleado	–	–	–	–	–	–	–
no data	2	–	–	–	–	7	9
Total	13	8	4	5	3	10	43

*All those who live in the *municipio* of Los Llanos and who own or control more than 200 hectares of land.

the sons of *pequeños proprietarios*, six are descended from campesino families, and only four are sons of hacendados and merchants. It is not surprising, from the data on ranchero family origins, that the generation which is now over sixty years old had to rely heavily on the capital of the Spanish merchants to purchase their land, creating long-term dependencies for the nouveau riche. Whether purchased with one's own capital or with that of a middleman, a large estate was still highly prestigious, both regionally and nationally in the Mexico of the thirties.

The Spanish merchants who financed the ranchero land purchases arrived in Los Llanos just before and slightly after the 1932 repartition. The merchants then widened their clientele by making them dependent on cash advances for their crops. The barley they purchase is sent to national breweries, also controlled by ethnic Spaniards (Lomnitz and Gold 1974). The capital amassed is invested in extensive holdings elsewhere in Mexico and abroad. None of it is invested in pulque. Pulque is grown and marketed by rancheros and controlled by two influential political caciques, each having his own alliance with one of the two families of Spaniards in the barley trade. Through their sons-in-law, the caciques also plant barley. They maintain their economic independence from the Spaniards by consolidating their production and distribution of maguey.

Avoiding traditional economic activities, the merchants forged their major social ties with each other and with other Spanish merchant families outside of the region. They spend most of the year in Mexico City, occasionally visiting Los Llanos to see their employees. Their local ties are thus primarily patron-client relationships which bind them to all of the barley-producing landowners and, indirectly, to every barley producer in the region. These are for the most part oral contracts. A ranchero can enter the store of a Spanish patron and request several thousand pesos on the strength of his reputation. The store manager, one of the owner's kinsman, will record the loan on a scrap of paper and provide cash to his waiting client.

It is important here to note that the entire barley production and distribution in the valley is controlled by the Spaniards.[2] For a generation, grain merchants paid what they wanted to whom they wanted—thus favoring their clients. In the 1970s, however, the Impulsora Agricola, S.A., an urban cartel operated by the breweries, was supposed to have taken over the contracting with farmers and purchased the crop at a uniform price. Even if a seller were to bypass the Impulsora, the prices paid at the brewery gates are similar to those paid by the Impulsora in the countryside. The relationship between ranchero and Spaniard and the role of the cacique–pulque producer is summarized in figure 10.1.

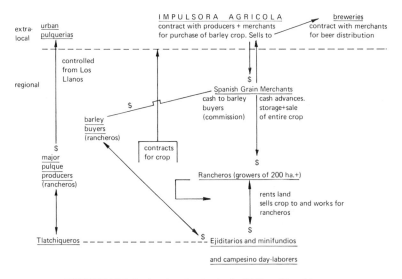

FIGURE 10.1. Barley distribution in the Valley of Los Llanos.

Despite this change, the conditions of production and of distribution assure the continuing dependency of most of the rancheros upon merchants. In the first place, even if their crop is purchased after the harvest, farmers are left with large payments to make for equipment and maintenance, especially after a succession of poor crops. Moreover, bank loans are difficult to negotiate even for property holders. In short, *the climate for producing and distributing barley would be one of uncertainty were the Spaniards not to provide ongoing security for their clients.* The ranchero has a slight advantage in that the Spaniards compete with each other and consequently offer special incentives. Moreover, as the middlemen do not want their position eroded by government intervention, they are not anxious to overextend their hand. Outside of Los Llanos, the distribution system also favors the Spaniards. They have family and social contacts with the brewery operators and with the Impulsora.

The technology of distribution encourages small producers to turn to intermediaries to market their crop.[3] Using a similar arrangement, rancheros purchase the barley of ejiditarios living near their property, taking a commission of one hundred pesos per ton. They then ship all of their grain to the breweries through the intermediary of the merchants. The breweries get exactly what they wish as contracts are issued to large growers at the beginning of the spring planting season by Impulsora agents. During the late fall harvest, they then return to Los Llanos to supervise their interests.

In a good year the centralized purchasing system for barley permits some rancheros to accumulate considerable capital. Nevertheless, long-term increases in output through access to more land and capital are dependent on marital alliances between families, on dyadic contracts of trust between persons, and on the security offered by the political protection of the two ranchero caciques.

The most obvious investment to improve output and income without acquiring more land would be through agricultural technology, and there is some evidence that the use of fertilizers, advanced machinery, and new storage techniques has led to greater yields. But technology explains only part of the ranchero financial success. Many wealthy farmers never fertilize, explaining that the cost is prohibitive and that barley is too unreliable. Others have managed to get high yields using older machinery and piling their harvested barley onto their fields. Agricultural technology also has a universalizing effect in that it is more available, through the implement dealers, than land or political power.

The leasing of Los Llanos machinery has been an important means of accumulating capital, outside the region. Some ejiditarios and rancheros, known as *maquiladores*, purchase combines as a family and then proceed to rent them both locally and, more frequently, to farmers in the north and west of Mexico where the harvests are earlier than in the high Llanos. The money earned is then invested in land when it becomes available during times of threat from peasant movements in the region and throughout Mexico.

In practice, all of the above economic strategies involve some *substitution of factors, with the goal being land that can be put into secure commercial production*. To explain this investment in context, I will turn to the organization of the family holding and the importance of social and political relationships in meeting economic ends.

286

THE FAMILY ESTATE

The first generation of Los Llanos rancheros, the dynastic founders of the thirties and forties, was more concerned with capital accumulation and political security than with an immediate problem of succession. Yet when one considers the high stakes for sons and in-laws, it becomes understandable why primogeniture was rejected by both parties for the transmission of property. In the classic dilemma of patrilineal inheritance in European agrarian societies, the sons' problem of waiting for their father to die is balanced by the father's own interest in having a strong family to protect his security in old age. The structural constraints to investment decisions by sons encourage them to build up alternatives to provide for the contingency of not inheriting the family estate.

Given the closed distribution system for barley, a ranchero who turns to commerce must seek either a different line of commercial activity or turn to local possibilities of capital accumulation in barley. This usually implies seeking ways to incorporate more land into a family enterprise. With a scarcity of land on the open market, however, producers will get their best return by expanding their relationships with other large holders. The rituals of this horizontal integration are highly expressive relationships between status equals that are only instrumental, in a direct economic sense, in the long run. Nevertheless, the rituals of compadrazgo, fiestas, and public political occasions are part of the admission price into the group of rancheros who have run Los Llanos politics since the thirties. To ignore these ties cuts a ranchero off from a vital source of economic and political influence. In putting together a portfolio of relationships, errors in the calculation of social information and in the servicing of transactional relationships can lead to understandable economic consequences. In this situation, obligations that are forfeited can be as disastrous as a skillful investment can be profitable.

Most such decision making is done at the level of the nuclear family where a man will sometimes discuss his possible strategies with his wife or with his most intimate compadres. With few exceptions, a farmer will not make critical decisions with his brothers or with his father. In those few instances where the extended family is united, though, it may take on some corporate characteristics of an *empresa*, family firm, in its unitary dealings with outsiders. The degree of family unity on investment decisions depends upon the father's inheritance policy and the affinal solidarity of in-laws.

Anxious to keep his holdings intact, the father has several possible courses of action. As Guillermo Aegis has done, he could retain nominal or complete control over all farming properties until his death, gradually delegating and dividing authority among his sons and sons-in-law. Or, acting as Rubén Róblez has done, he may subdivide the ownership of his lands in anticipatory inheritance to those sons and sons-in-law with whom he has the strongest relations of *confianza*, trust. He then works together with them and their affines. The father's timing strongly affects the investment possibilities left open to his sons and sons-in-law. A closer examination of these two cases will make this sense of timing more explicit.

THE RÓBLEZ-VELOZ ALLIANCE

The Róblez family illustrates one extreme of the affinal alliances that crosscut the entire class of rancheros. Like several other rancheros of his generation, Rubén Róblez was a mayordomo supervising pulque production in a *tinacal* at the time of the land reform. An employer, anxious to liquidate his properties to avoid possible peasant-sponsored expropriation, sold fifty hectares to Róblez who obtained financing from one of the Spanish merchants in Los Llanos. Róblez and his sons then purchased machinery which they rented to other *maquiladores* to acquire the cash to buy more properties. Róblez then built a home with urban conveniences on his first property, using family labor and only small amounts of his capital at any one time. This *rancho nuevo* was given the name La Magdalena, an important symbolic action that elevated his property from the status of an expanded ejido to that of an estate, in the tradition of the hacienda.

Significantly, after the age of sixty, Don Rubén turned over most of his land to of his married or engaged sons who in turn established their own ranchos next to La Magdalena. The combined holdings of the family then included over three hundred hectares, nine combines, and other agricultural implements and machinery. With all of this property, Don Rubén and his sons were one of the wealthiest families in Los Llanos, but they had still to complete their unit of production through alliance with the neighboring Veloz family, an equally influential group of landowners whose founder was also an ex-mayordomo.

The alliance was consummated by the marriage of one of Róblez's daughters to a son of the Veloz family (marriage a in fig. 10.2). The subsequent marriage of two Róblez males to Veloz females solidified the alliance (marriages b and c in fig. 10.2).

The resulting alliance is now identifiable to other rancheros, although the families keep a low profile to outsiders. It is operated by the two founding fathers, whose sons and sons-in-law work under their guidance rather than under their authority. A common pool of machinery is shared by producers from both families and much of it is housed in a single concrete barn at La Magdalena. When there is no harvest in Los Llanos, the machinery and several of the brothers-in-law travel to northern Mexico to keep their capital working.

Those brothers and in-laws within the alliance (some have moved to the cities) exchange farm labor, fodder, animals, and sometimes automobiles. They hold common fiestas to which each family contributes food and alcohol, and every month there is a family mass and supper at a private chapel. Significantly, the holdings of the alliance form a single, defendable, rectangular block on the altiplano, a spatial arrangement that increases the opportunities for intragroup contacts.

Despite this cooperation, the alliance lacks a legal identity or a corporate organization. Each family is still a separate producing unit, selling its own crops and paying nominal rents to use the machinery of relatives. Each has its own *rancho nuevo* and private automobile. Each family head makes his own private arrangements to rent ejidal lands. Finally, some sons have opted for noninvolvement in family interests, making their own alliances elsewhere, especially with commercial interests in the town.

In sharp contrast to the Róblez-Veloz families and others like them, the Aegis family's internal differentiation is largely a product of their involvement in the new factory town and in Mexico City. It has led to friction within the family, a conflict that is aggravated by Don Guillermo's tenacious refusal, at eighty-four, to bequeath more than a few urban properties in any form of anticipatory inheritance.

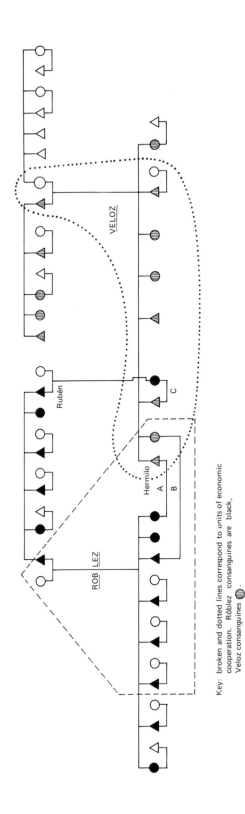

Key: broken and dotted lines correspond to units of economic cooperation. Róblez consanguines are black, Veloz consanguines ⊕.

FIGURE 10.2. Róblez-Veloz marital and economic alliances.

THE AEGIS FAMILY–URBAN RANCHEROS

Unlike the Róblez and Veloz families, the Aegises have never been campesinos. Don Guillermo Aegis, once the administrator of Espejel, an important pulque and barley hacienda at the edge of town, was the first patron to hire Róblez as a mayordomo, but the years have led them along different mobility routes. Aegis purchased the small ex-hacienda of Yerba Buena in 1947 with the help of one of the Spanish merchants who contracted for his barley crop. Several years later, Aegis's machines were used to prepare the land for the industrial city while he housed the automobile factory's temporary offices in an apartment that is part of a house he purchased facing the *presidencia* in Los Llanos. Don Guillermo and two of his sons moved back to Los Llanos several years after purchasing their estate. Francisco, the oldest son, was able to get a minor executive post through the family's connections with the automobile factory in Ciudad Industrial. Xavier, the other urban son, managed the ranch for his ailing father, while a younger son, Jaime, who married the daughter of a wealthy ejiditario, has been asked to remain on the rancho. He is considered by the others, to be the least competent of the family and, furthermore, lost favor with his father when he married the daughter of a campesino.

The significant differences between the Aegis family and the Róblez-Veloz family are summarized in tables 10.2 and 10.3. The Aegis family is clearly more involved in urban occupations, mainly in the managerial upper middle class. None of their relatives is a campesino, but two males in their early twenties are working in the automobile factory as semiskilled laborers. Although both families have urban kin, the Aegis contingent in Mexico City is, relatively speaking, as large as the Róblez-Veloz concentration on the altiplano. These residential and occupational differences do not alter their regional identity as ranchero families and the three family groups are of approximately equal wealth in land in assets. A crucial difference lies in the investment decisions of the family. Whereas the Róblez and Veloz families are expanding their farms and building on their status as members of a regional agrarian elite, the Aegis family has gradually rejected its local status where possible and opted for associations with the new urban middle class. This, however, is not without bitter conflict that is splitting the family.

291

TABLE 10.2
OCCUPATIONAL COMPARISON OF THE RÓBLEZ-VELOZ
AND AEGIS FAMILIES*

| | Aegis | | Róblez-Veloz | | |
	number	%	number	%	Total
Ranchero	3	12.5	19	34.5	22
Campesino	0	–	11	20.0	11
Worker	2	8.3	11	20.0	13
Employee	9	37.5	4	7.2	13
Commerce	2	8.3	4	7.2	6
Professional–white collar	8	33.3	1	1.8	9
No data	0	–	5	9.0	5
Totals	24	100.0	55	100.0	79

*Calculated for all consanguines as head of household or husband's occupation if female consanguine is not employed. For Róblez-Veloz the calculations begin with the two youngest of three living generations; for Aegis, they begin with the oldest living generation and then the next two younger generations.

TABLE 10.3
RESIDENTIAL COMPARISON OF RÓBLEZ-VELOZ AND
AEGIS FAMILIES*

| | Aegis | | Roblez-Veloz | | |
	number	%	number	%	Total
Los Llanos—rural	1	4.2	23	41.8	24
Los Llanos—urban	11	45.8	15	27.3	26
Ciudad Industrial	0	–	6	10.9	6
Districto Federal	9	37.5	6	10.9	15
Other	3	12.5	5	9.1	8
	24	100.0	55	100.0	79

*Four of eight white collar members of the Aegis family work as executives or as engineers in the car factory at Ciudad Industrial. Three of the four married into the family.

The three Aegis brothers see each other several times a week, but they have little to say to each other. White collar Francisco is the most isolated from ranchero subculture. By his own choice as well as the decision of others, he is excluded from the fiestas and the ranchero network of compadrazgo. However, Francisco seeks to become the inheriting son, kissing his father's hand at least once a day, running his errands, wearing a charro uniform every other

Sunday to remind his father of his claims to Yerba Buena. His sisters-in-law may not be the first to notice Francisco's behavior, but they gossip about it and extend their animosities to Francisco's wife whom they feel is behind his pretentions to high class.

The conflict within the Aegis family points to the mounting incongruity and conflict between the old and the new rural national middle class. It follows that ranchero Xavier Aegis would invest more than his bureaucrat-brother Francisco in ranchero networks. Compadrazgo, important to all rancheros, is even more essential to the urban ranchero like Xavier Aegis who lacks family alliances of the Róblez-Veloz variety. Thus Xavier Aegis uses compadrazgo to give permanence and security to his ties with the merchants and caciques of town. In seeking maximum horizontal solidarity, all three families extend the institution of ritual co-parenthood beyond its original meaning of godparenthood (Mintz and Wolf 1950). For it marks and controls boundaries of trust and reciprocal obligation that can then be manipulated to personal advantage.

COMPADRAZGO AND FIESTAS

Beyond the arena of the family, sociability and reciprocal obligations are assured through ritual kin relationships. Moreover, the occasion for constructing a compadrazgo relationship with another family may thus be of much less importance than the goal of the alliance. A confirmation, a graduation, a new house or office, a new tractor, a car, a stereo set, or the *noche buena* (Christmas Eve)—all serve as occasions for some of the most important compadrazgo relationships. Therefore, although having many *ahijados*, godchildren, may be of long-term political utility, it is not the short-run objective of rancheros who manage and plan their repertoire of compadres as a reserve of secured extrafamilial relationships.

In this wider sense, compadrazgo is a relationship that crosscuts the elite families of the region. It unites rancheros and merchants and defines a wide net of *buena gente* who are acceptable participants in fiestas (Lomnitz and Gold 1974). Significantly, this wide net is bypassed by the town's several doctors, who refuse to become *padrinos* of locals, and by about twenty nonresident landowners who

293

maintain lavishly appointed ex-haciendas in Los Llanos as country estates. Their hired administrators, however, are part of the wide net of fiesta personnel. Also excluded, for the most part, are factory executives from the industrial town who rarely attend ranchero fiestas and whose compadrazgo ties are not part of the ranchero compadrazgo and fiesta networks.

Most rancheros have several vertical compadrazgo ties with peasants, mostly with their own workers who seek protection for themselves and for their children. These are not intra-class ties and are accompanied by little sociability or exchange of information. In this context, with the emphasis on horizontal intra-class links, ranchero compadrazgo is similar to what Lomnitz (1971) finds in the Chilean middle class. *Confianza*, trust, is stretched to its class limits, and the flow of prestations between families is regularized when this is seen as desirable, providing an assured framework for behavioral responses from transacting partners. In the few cases of vertical compadrazgo in which the rancheros solicit a *padrino*, it is with the most influential ranchero politicians, who nonetheless treat other rancheros as status equals in interpersonal relations. Similarly, it is the cacique and those who aspire to political power who will accumulate a cadre of *ahijados*, godchildren, for political supporters.

To see how compadrazgo is managed, it is instructive to look at how Xavier Aegis became a compadre of Hermilo Veloz, son-in-law of Don Rubén Róblez. A member of an established town family, Aegis already had more compadres than he could remember. Despite the eighteen families whom he "treats regularly," Aegis wanted compadres in the influential Róblez-Veloz alliance whose fiestas he had started to attend as the elections drew near in 1972. The events unraveled as follows:

1. The Róblez-Veloz family holds a fiesta, and a wide cross section of rancheros is present. Xavier Aegis is invited by a friend of a friend and he decides to profit from the occasion by asking Hermilo Róblez to be the *padrino* of Xavier's daughter's graduation.

2. This would make the two men compadres and their wives comadres. They immediately begin to use ritual kin terminology of compadre/comadre. Xavier then invites Hermilo and family to a fiesta at the family home in Los Llanos. Hermilo accepts, as it is an obligation of the *padrino* to sponsor the first fiesta.

3. Xavier serves an elaborate supper and during the drinking, he is

invited to Hermilo's rancho. Although Xavier is too inebriated to remember, the wives take note of the invitation.

4. A longer, larger, and more costly fiesta is given by Hermilo who publicly and aggressively denigrates his own hospitality, boasting of the wealth and power of his guest. The new compadres proceed to exchange private visits and favors.

Once the relationship was established, it had to be serviced, that is, sustained by an ongoing exchange of food and alcohol through fiesta invitations. Both partners availed themselves of these opportunities to widen their contacts with the kin of their compadres. Should these contacts continue on a frequent basis, the partners become *cuates* or intimates. This would be both advantageous for the intimacy and trust that *cuatismo* affords and disadvantageous to the extent that it would prevent either party from dropping the relationship or circulating freely through chosen sets of the wide network of rancheros. A conscious attempt is thus made to be free to develop new relationships and the obligations that accompany them. The compadre is ideally someone to whom one is "to give everything," but the restrictions on giving are dependent on what can be gotten in return.

Cuates are usually also compadres and, on occasion, in-laws may be both compadres and *cuates*, especially in strongly united kin groups such as the Róblez-Veloz family, isolated from the town and in frequent contact with one other. *Cuates* may also share scarce agricultural machinery or provide each other with political support, as in the jockeying for power that takes place immediately before the triannual municipal elections. The relationship between the *comadres* is here equally or more important than that between compadres. Seeing each other privately during the day, the women make arrangements and provide information that sustains the relationship.

In trying to outdo each other, hospitality may become aggressive, with each party taunting the other about his wealth. For example, host Hermilo Róblez repeatedly offered his new compadre, Xavier Aegis, costly cuts of roast lamb as "a morsel of dog meat [or pigeon, or whatever] from a poor man." This intensity of the relationship, among both males and females, leads to disagreements. The rancheros that I knew during my first field trip to Los Llanos in 1967 had redefined their group of intimates by 1972. The former *cuates* were still compadres, but the relationship had been put on ice.

295

COMPADRAZGO AS INVESTMENT

A study of the occasions for compadrazgo (in tables 10.4 and 10.5) and the occupations of those who choose, as well as of those who are chosen, tells us a great deal about the elite of Los Llanos and about their calculation of relationships. Xavier Aegis, at fifty-five, provides a good example of how an urban ranchero of the old political elite of Los Llanos compares with the entrepreneurial strategies of upwardly mobile merchants such as Enrique López, an agricultural machinery vendor in his mid-thirties. Both men have many more *compadres* than are in the group indicated in tables 10.4 and 10.5 as "current and remembered." Furthermore, both have balanced the number of active compadres between those they have chosen as *padrinos* for their children (about one-third) and the relationships they maintain as *padrinos* for other families (about two-thirds). Neither man listed as comparable his compadrazgo relations with peasants, for these are seen as having a very different content.

TABLE 10.4
RANCHERO-MERCHANT COMPADRAZGO: OCCASIONS AND OCCUPATIONAL CONTACTS—A COMPARISON OF CURRENT AND REMEMBERED RELATIONSHIPS

Occasion	Xavier Aegis			Enrique López		
	as C[a]	*as P[b]*	*Total*	*as C[a]*	*as P[b]*	*Total*
Baptism	1	8	9	4	0	4
Communion	no data		—	2	1	3
Confirmation	3	0	3	0	3	3
Wedding	0	0	0	0	1	1
Graduation	2	3	5	0	0	0
Niño Dios	0	0	0	1	1	2
House/office	0	0	0	0	2	2
Machinery	0	1	1	0	6	6
De mentiras	0	1	1	0	0	0
Total	6	13	19	7	14	21

[a]As compadre, relationships solicited with other families.

[b]As *padrino*, relationships accepted after being solicited by another as a sponsor.

The differences in the two men's strategies appear with the occupations of their compadres and with the occasions for seeking compadrazgo relationships. Enrique López relies on rancheros for almost all of his sales of large and costly agricultural machinery. Appropriately, all but one of the seven compadres whom he has solicited are rancheros. Three of these men are also associate owners of López's machinery agency. The same tendency holds for the relationships that López has acccepted at the request of others. Nine of fourteen are with rancheros, and of this number, four are members of the Róblez-Veloz alliance who asked him to be the *padrino* of new combines or of other large machinery purchased at his agency. Besides assuring Enrique of a costly fiesta but a satisfied client, this practice permits Róblez-Veloz to get constant attention for their mechanical and technical difficulties.

TABLE 10.5
COMPADRAZGO AND OCCUPATION

Occupation of Compadre-Padrino	Xavier Aegis			Enrique López		
	as C[a]	as P[b]	Total	as C[a]	as P[b]	Total
Merchant	1	5	6	1	4	5
Ranchero	3	6	9	6	9	15
Other	2	2	4	0	2	2
Total	6	13	19	7	15	22

[a]As compadre, relationships solicited with other families.
[b]As *padrino*, relationships accepted after being solicited by another as a sponsor.

López's office is one of the daily ranchero meeting grounds in Los Llanos. Standing on his doorstep, one would have little difficulty meeting more than half of the large landowners in any given week during the late fall harvest. Those who do not come for machinery (compadre Xavier Aegis, for example, buys a different make of machinery) come for information, tires, oil, and mechanical work, or simply for the possibility of meeting others on a similar mission. The only other place where so many rancheros congregate during harvest is in the stores and warehouses of the Spanish grain buyers.

In comparison to the merchant López, the ranchero Aegis accepts the overtures of potential compadres who are merchants or top-level employees of the Spaniard to whom he sells his crop. These include a warehouse manager and a garage foreman who work for the Spaniard, a clothing merchant (influential in P.R.I.), a construction material merchant, a trucker, and a furniture dealer (who was municipal treasurer when the relationship began and out of office when it tapered off). Xavier Aegis uses different occasions from those Enrique López uses as the pretext for his relationships and places more importance on baptisms and life-cycle events. Aegis, whose family has more status and more land than the López family, does not need local clients for his merchandise and he can afford to wait for a more intrinsic context in which to make his important political friendships. Thus he is a compadre of one of López's tractor agency partners, but in name only, *de mentiras*. Finally, Aegis is also a compadre of the merchant López (*padrino* at his eldest child's baptism), and both share a common and recent bond with Hermilo Veloz of the Róblez-Veloz alliance. This is one of many examples of the machinery merchant's role as a "weak bridge" (Granovetter 1973) in bringing rancheros from different families and factions together as a single occupational group.

This brief look at compadrazgo has tied the barley system and family organization to social exchanges. However, the relationship will not be complete until it is placed into the context of fiesta networks and political and regional organization.

ASSOCIATIONS AND FIESTAS

Feasting and the combination of fiesta sets (the personnel of a fiesta) are more instrumental than associations to a ranchero's investment strategy. Not surprisingly, no rancheros joined the Leones (Lion's Club) when local teachers and professionals established a Los Llanos chapter in 1973. One of many rancheros who were invited to organizational dinners could not fathom why the Leones had to fabricate complicated rules for interacting with each other as friends at a large dinner. Yet a half-dozen rancheros, all of whom are involved in town businesses, do participate in the less ritual-oriented Rotarios, Rotary Club. Rotario meetings are frequented by the merchant elite of the town and, until recently, by the presidente, a merchant, who redecorated and refurbished the Cabildos meeting hall expressly for club meetings. Although the businessman or professional can use service clubs as an entree into an urban and national network, in Los Llanos, these clubs are still not a stage for important information exchange as is the case among regional commercial-industrial elites elsewhere (Gold 1975:147). In the Rotarios, for example, many of the members are already compadres and frequent participants in the same fiesta sets. They do not need the formal ties of a club to maintain their relationships. The Rotary Club president, faced with several earlier failures of his organization, must continually exhort members to participate in the club's Red Cross service activities.

Fiestas, with their constantly changing personnel, serve as the arenas for intragroup information exchange and reaffirmation of common values (Gold 1974). When compadres feast together, information exchange gives way to more expressive collective rituals of commensalism and ritual drinking, the kind of behavior that Madsen and Madsen (1975:449), incorrectly, I think, set aside as "inconspicuous intoxication." In many ways, however, ranchero fiesta drinking conforms to the Indian model of "peaceful integration among individuals who identify themselves as a unit functioning in a homogeneous and predictable social environment" (Madsen and Madsen 1975:443). Furthermore, a ranchero's fiesta network is his major source of in-group information. Thus, in 1972, after peasant land invasions in nearby Tlaxcala, rancheros became interested in the creation of a National Confederation of Small Holders. In practice, though, their response to peasant and governmental threats followed in the channels of family alliances, compadrazgo and fiesta networks, rather than in the establishment of an association for protection.

This instrumental side of fiesta attendance is not visible at even the largest of ranchero fiestas where as many as six freshly slaughtered pigs (1973 market value of over 7,000 pesos) and much pulque and imported liquors are served to as many as several hundred guests. These large fiestas are infrequent and reserved mainly for the weathiest families to sponsor. Most fiestas, with fewer than twenty families present, are in favply ritualized events, where drinking is paced and guest-host relationships are paramount. In a series of arm-linked toasts—cruzados done in the proper manner—the men drink through the late afertnoon and evening, while the women sit separately and monitor their husbands' behavior.

Each cruzado is followed by an individual abrazo in which each man in the toast privately embraces all of the others. Shaking hands, with glass in the left hand, the rancheros exchange intimate remarks. These may be comments on the character of their friendship or private invitations to visit later in the week. This is an essential moment in managing one's network. If the two men are not

299

compadres, the cruzados may be a first step in establishing the *confianza* that is a prelude to a compradazgo relationship.

These compadrazgo relationships are far from randomly contracted throughout the ranchero community, as they are influenced by the relationship of individual families with the pulque-producing caciques. These two men hold the largest fiestas that are attended by their core group of supporters and by representatives from most other major families. Anyone associated with them, even indirectly, is expected to attend, and with the fiesta so lavish, the obligation is hardly a burden. Not to attend these fiestas, however, would be a tactical error—even if the host is not particularly close to the guest. When one needs political support in matters relating to land, taxes, or crops, the invitation is not to be ignored. In a number of instances, those who are not "proper"—being lewd or overly drunk or refusing invitations without due cause—have been passed over for political office, denied political favors, or, as in one case I documented, encouraged to sell their land and depart.

The fiestas of the caciques should not be confused with those large fiestas that are publicly held for special occasions. These are overtly political gatherings: dances, feast days, political rallies, the visit of a politician or a bishop. The entire ranchero and merchant elite of the town, as well as dignitaries from other communities, are always in attendance. The fiestas are public and shorter in duration than the private gatherings. They are also, as might be expected, less important as a means of establishing relationships. At a private fiesta one does not leave without the permission of the host— something unnecessary at public occasions where one goes to be seen rather than to seek and sustain relationships.

RANCHERO POLITICAL POWER

Until 1972, the rancheros and their merchant allies occupied all offices of importance in the *municipio* as well as the posts of state and federal deputies. A number of small coalitions were grouped into two factions, each associated with one of the two caciques and their core of supporters. These groups were not openly opposed to each other, and crisscrossing allegiances and friendships led to overlapping attendance at fiestas and ties of marriage and compadrazgo linking the two factions. These bridging ties (Granovetter 1973) extend as far as the two caciques and the Spanish merchants. The caciques have alternated in their control of major political offices, especially *presidente*, *jefe de hacienda*, and *administrador del rentas*, the latter two being lucrative offices in charge of federal and state tax collection. As each of the caciques is associated commercially and socially with at least one of the Spanish grain merchants, the merchants are given an indirect representation in the *presidencia* without actual participation in local politics. This relationship between political control, economic control, and sociability has been found elsewhere in rural Mexico, although the structural aspects of relationships within the agrarian elite have not been widely explored.

Of direct relevance to the case of the rancheros of Los Llanos is the erosion of the regional power base of agrarian elites that began in the 1960s. The immediate threats to the rancheros were exogenous to the valley, but there was considerable public dissatisfaction with the regional government stemming from inadequate water supply, run-down municipal services, and an insufficient budget for the *presidencia* (about 100,000 pesos in 1973). The dissatisfaction was voiced by the approximately 20 percent of the townspeople who worked in the industrial city, men like Francisco Aegis of the white-collar middle class, who are not part of ranchero fiesta sets or the controlling political coalitions in P.R.I.

With similar discontent occurring elsewhere in his state, Governor Sánchez Vite, in 1972, turned down the ranchero candidate for *presidente* chosen in the usual compromise by the local P.R.I. committee. In his place, the governor selected a *preparado*, an educated man, a respected doctor who was a close acquaintance (but not compadre!) of many rancheros. The interest that this *presidente*, himself an outsider to Los Llanos, encouraged in urbanism and in urban administration began a regional political process in which the rancheros, who always had a minimal stake in town life, were discouraged from engagements in town politics. Not coincidentally, similar conflict and erosion of ranchero and cacique power had surfaced earlier in the neighboring *cabacera*, which borders directly on the industrial city, itself part of the older *municipio* boundaries. In both instances, changes in the rules of the political game of the cultivation of confidence were introduced by agents who were out-

301

side of the regional elite and who were sympathetic to the goals of the urban middle class.

The personnel of the ranchero class is also changing. Some ejidatarios, particularly those in outlying villages, have been able to accumulate enough capital in land and in machinery to become rancheros in their own right. One of these upwardly mobile men, selected as local president of P.R.I., was offered a fifth share in the López tractor agency without any appreciable investment on his part. When squatters invaded the Tlaxcalan border area, he not only was the liaison with the new National Confederation of Small Holders (C.N.P.P.) but also participated in forming a vigilante army to evict the invaders. Only a few months earlier, however, he and his brother had purchased land from a frightened landlord in the same area. Another man at the same time acquired land through his role as *comisario* in the ejido of Los Llanos. Both these new landowners are associates in the tractor agency, compadres, and *cuates*; they are also the only farmers to belong to the Rotary Club. As new rancheros and the potential core of a new municipal political coalition, they represent upwardly mobile interests as opposed to the ruling group of post-land-reform "sons of the revolution." Nevertheless, their behavior does not represent a threat to the rancheros as a group. The failure of the class to reproduce itself, to place its children successfully within its own activities, is a more significant turn of events.

MIDDLE CLASS OR REGIONAL ELITE?

In many ranchero families children have been given little encouragement to become farmers, and many have been absorbed into urban middle-class occupations (see tables 10.2 and 10.3). A case that is not atypical is the only son of ranchero Xavier Aegis. This son was deliberately kept away from the family rancho even though he repeatedly told his parents that he wanted to become a ranchero like his father. His parents sent him away to a private school where he did not fare well. They did not then discourage him from taking factory work even though Aegis was without a male heir to his operations. Finally, his two daughters married automobile factory executives from the new industrial town.

302

In a more striking example, the *padrino* of the Aegis children, one of Aegis's brothers-in-law, has five daughters, of whom three have turned away ranchero suitors even though they are approaching thirty. The other two have married automobile factory executives. Clothed in a high traditional status, these and other ranchero daughters are encouraged to marry urban middle-class males. The sons, however, are in a more delicate position should they not do well in their studies.

These examples emphasize the declining status of the rancheros, both in their region as an elite and in the nation as an element of the national upper middle class. Of the children who are encouraged to leave the Llanos, sons, in particular, are at a disadvantage once they have left the security of ranchero culture and its wide network of reciprocities. Furthermore, within that wide network, the alliances of individuals and of their families have come to include more formal commitments to associations and to urban-capitalist enterprise. The former political maneuverability of rancheros is also now severely limited by exogenous variables. The rules of the game are redefined and the criteria for managing confidence and trust are also changing. This redefinition may be symptomatic of the disappearance of the rancheros as an agrarian regional elite and perhaps as a rural social class.

NOTES

1. Research for this paper was conducted in three field trips during 1967, 1972, and 1973–74. Financing came from the University of Minnesota Occupations and Ecosystems Project and York University minor research grants. My special thanks to members of the Santa Fe seminar and Frank C. Miller, Pertti Pelto, Robert Paine, Philip Gulliver, Allan Simmons, Larissa Lomnitz, Robert Hunt, Ina Dinerman, and Kenneth Westhues for their helpful comments and suggestions.

2. The role of merchants in the monopoly purchase of cash crops has been well described in rural Mexico by Durand (1974), who deals with isolated regions of Puebla, and by Hunt (1965), who has clarified the developmental cycle of general stores that purchase grain crops and distribute beer.

3. To accommodate grain shipments, the Spaniards operate costly cleaning machines, sizable warehouses, and large trucking fleets. They store thousands of tons of barley until they can arrange shipment to the breweries. Some box cars are shipped to a scale and a railroad spur in the countryside where barley is graded, weighed, and sold directly to a ranchero who acts as a commission agent for the Spaniards.

11
Family Firms and Firm Families: A Comparison of Indian, Chinese, and Creole Firms in Seychelles[1]

BURTON BENEDICT

Department of Anthropology
University of California, Berkeley

In 1960 in a small village on Mahé, the principal island of Seychelles, there were three Chinese shops and half a dozen small shacks and vegetable stands run by Creoles of mixed African and European descent. In 1975 there were two Chinese shops and eight smaller shops run by Creoles. These Chinese shops were the same ones that had existed fifteen years earlier. Only one of the Creole shops was run by a man who had been a vegetable seller in 1960. The rest were new; the oldest had been in existence for only five years. The third Chinese shop had existed until a few months before my arrival when it had burned down. Its owner still had interests in the village and a shop in a neighboring village.

Why, on the whole, had the Chinese been successful and the Creoles not? Village shops are family firms. The structure of the family and the relations among its members have much to do with success or failure in business. Is there something about the Chinese family that conduces to such success? Conversely, is there something about the Creole family that is inimical to business success? In this paper I propose to examine these questions regarding Seychelles, where I did fieldwork in both 1960 for six months (Benedict 1966) and 1975 for five months.

SEYCHELLES

Seychelles is an archipelago of more than ninety islands scattered across 400,000 square miles of the western Indian Ocean. The chief island, Mahé, lies about 1,000 miles east of Mombassa. It is 17 miles long and 3 to 5 miles wide. On it are crammed over 85 percent of the islands' 62,000 people, that is, more than 1,000 people per square mile. The Seychelles were uninhabited when discovered by the Portuguese early in the sixteenth century. They remained uninhabited until the middle of the eighteenth century when they were colonized by the French who brought in slaves from Madagascar and the African mainland. After the Napoleonic wars, the islands were ceded to Britain in 1814. Africans continued to be imported into Seychelles even after the abolition of slavery in the British Empire in 1835. In the 1860s and 1870s several thousand "liberated Africans" were deposited in the islands by British ships that had taken them from Arab dhows operating in the Zanzibar waters. They were indentured to planters and the government. Also in the nineteenth century small numbers of Indian and Chinese traders arrived in Seychelles. Miscegenation was common, especially between Europeans and Africans and, to a lesser extent, between Europeans and Chinese. Today the population consists of a small number of Europeans of French descent, a few British settlers and a larger number of British administrators, a few Indian and Chinese merchants, and a large number of Creoles of mixed African and European descent. English is taught in the schools, but the vast majority of the population speaks Creole, a French patois. In 1976, Seychelles achieved independence.

In 1960, when I did my first fieldwork, the Seychelles economy was based primarily on copra and secondarily on cinnamon and vanilla. Unemployment and underemployment were rife. Laborers supplemented their small wages with locally grown foodstuffs and freshly caught fish. Fifty-six proprietors held two-thirds of the commercial agricultural land. These proprietors and the government were the major employers. They drew on a labor force much larger than was required. The result was low wages and minimal job security. In fact the colony could only maintain itself through periodic subventions from Britain. This situation changed radically in 1971 with the completion of an airport. In 1960 there had been two ships a month from Mombassa and Bombay. In 1975 there were twenty planes a week from all parts of the world. The number of tourists visiting the Seychelles in 1960 was 490 (Seychelles Report 1959–60:39); in 1975 there were 37,321 (*Seychelles Handbook* 1976:79). The construction of hotels and restaurants needed to accommodate these tourists brought full employment to the islands between 1971 and 1974. Construction companies, paying higher wages than Seychellois had ever seen, became the chief employers. By 1975 this panic pace had slowed, and there were fears that the world recession would cut into the tourist industry on which the islands were now dependent. Inflation diminished the buying power of the rupee, one rupee equaling about 20 U.S. cents in 1974-75. Today Seychelles imports nearly all its necessities, including most of its food.

CHINESE AND INDIAN FAMILY FIRMS

One Chinese shop in the village where I did fieldwork was founded by a Cantonese who came to the Seychelles in 1928 at the age of eleven. He worked for a kinsman in a large Chinese shop in the town for three years. He then returned to China where he remained with his family for five years. In 1936 he came back to the Seychelles with the wife his family had chosen for him and again worked for his kinsman. With this kinsman's help he set up his own shop which he ran through World War II. He again returned to China where his mother and sister still lived. In 1951 he came back to Seychelles for a third time and rented shop premises in the village. He built up his business both as a retailer and a dealer in copra, renting land to build a copra dryer and store from the same local resident from whom he rented his shop premises. He acquired coconuts from the local populace in return for credit at his shop. In the middle fifties he retired to Hong Kong, where he subsequently died. He and his wife were childless but the business was passed to a brother's son who had been brought up in Malaysia, where he had married. In running their business, both uncle and nephew were

307

greatly assisted by their wives, who took charge of the shop while their husbands purchased supplies or managed the buying and processing of copra and cinnamon. The wives knew prices, kept the books, and managed clerks and laborers in the shop. They were, in effect, unsalaried comanagers. The nephew has a small son who has been sent to Hong Kong for his education. The control of the business remains strictly within the family. Its connections extend to the Chinese community within Seychelles and overseas to Hong Kong, Malaysia, and elsewhere. Family ties and business ties reinforce one another and control is vested in the hands of fathers who are the managers. As yet, the business is fairly small, and outsiders are only employed as clerks and laborers.

A more developed example can be seen in a large Indian firm in the town. The founder arrived in Seychelles about the turn of the century from Gujarat with capital derived from the sale of family jewels. He began as a hawker of cloth, but soon set up a shop over which his family lived. He was joined by his elder brother and his son. The elder brother soon died, but the son continued the business and with his sons formed what is today a flourishing shop of general merchandise. The founder of the firm had six sons and four daughters. His business expanded into the buying and selling of copra. Arrangements were made with a large Indian shipping company so that the firm became the agents for virtually all shipments to and from the subcontinent. The firm also obtained franchises from various British companies for the sale of packaged foodstuffs, radios, and manufactured goods. More recently franchises have been obtained from German and Japanese companies. The growth of the firm and the pattern of interactions between its managers—all members the same family—closely paralled the growth of the Indian firm in East Africa which I have described elsewhere (Benedict 1968). Early in its history there was a split between the founder and his deceased brother's son. The assets were divided equally, and the two firms thereafter developed separately.

When the founder died in 1942, he was succeeded by his eldest son. The several functions of the business were distributed among his brothers. The eldest concerned himself chiefly with shipping, the second brother with commerce, and the fourth brother with accounting. The third brother went to England, where he became a surgeon and married an English woman. The fifth brother also went to England, where he qualified as an engineer and took a Danish wife; he now practices in Denmark. The sixth brother returned to India, where he became a commercial produce farmer and founded a printing and dyeing works for cloth in Hyderabad. The daughters have all left Seychelles.[2]

The eldest brother has three sons and two daughters. His eldest son is an architect who works in Hyderabad at the printing and dyeing works founded by his uncle. The second son is a doctor practicing in Seychelles. The third son is an engineer and runs a car-hiring service in Seychelles. The second brother has three sons and three daughters. His eldest son works on his uncle's farm in Hyderabad. The second is a textile technologist working in the U.K. The third son is an automotive engineer trained in the U.K. and Japan. The fourth brother has a single son who has been sent to university in India to train in commerce. The third brother who married an English woman died; his two children have remained in England and are no longer in contact with the family. The children of the other two brothers are still young. All the daughters in this second generation left Seychelles, after completing their secondary education.[3]

The founder of the firm supervised his sons closely. They were given specific tasks in the business, and he often struck them when they performed badly. He imported instructors from India to teach them mathematics and Gujarati. He taught them never to waste anything. He forbade them to mix with Seychellois except for business or matters promoting business. He paid enormous attention to them, for on them both his family and his business rested. The women of his family played no part in the business. They never served in the shop. They ran the household. Daughters married out. Sons-in-law were not brought into the business. When the founder died, his eldest son assumed the authoritarian paternal role, supervising both his brothers and his own children. Over time his authority has come to be disputed, and some of the brothers have struck out on their own, as related above. Even those remaining with the eldest brother in the Seychelles firm have wanted increasingly to act independently. A source of friction has been arguments between the brothers' wives. They argue about household management, the authority of their husbands in the business, and the shares their children will receive. It is difficult to say how much of this friction is instigated by the men who can complain to their wives in a way they cannot complain to their brothers, or how much is due to jealousy between wives. The men can conveniently blame their wives and thus avoid direct confrontation with their brothers.

As I noted in the 1968 article, family firms face two major crises: the passing of authority from fathers to sons and the incorporation of outsiders. When the founder died, his eldest son was thirty-three and able both to take over the business and to manage his younger brothers. As they grew older, some of the tensions were resolved when two of the sons entered professions and went to the U.K. while a third established himself as a farmer, printer, and dyer in India. His success has enabled him to employ two of his nephews. It has also given an outlet to the fourth brother, who is entering into partnership with him. The crisis in family authority appears headed toward a split of the family firm into several new firms just as the founder and his elder brother's son split the original firm. There is still cooperation but no overall leader.

The family firm has brought in no outsiders and has thus staved off a second crisis. The family has been well supplied with sons and sons of sons, and they have specialized as a textile technologist, an automotive engineer, and so on. Some sons have been lost to the firm by entering professions, but to date the firm has not suffered from lack of qualified personnel. If the firm is to expand, however, it cannot avoid bringing in outsiders.

The political climate of the Seychelles may hasten this process. Independence having arrived, politicians are eagerly looking for popular issues on which to build a following. Rampant inflation and rising prices have led to accusations that shopkeepers make excessive profits. With the vast majority of shopkeepers Indians and Chinese who remit some of their profits overseas, a Uganda-like purge of them is not impossible. As a result, shopkeepers have begun to see the advantage of bringing Creole Seychellois into their firms. In some cases, Creole apprentices have even been incorporated into the family.

The principal differences between the Chinese and Indians in Seychelles are that Chinese wives play a more active role in running the business and that Chinese have a greater tendency to intermarry with Creoles.

In both Chinese and Indian families, interaction between father and sons is close and constant, with the father always in the superordinate position. Serving as the major role model, he regulates nearly every aspect of his sons' lives. As place of residence and place of business are on the same premises, the roles of father and business head are merged as are the roles of son and business subordinate. Sons are expected to work hard at the business. Fathers continually train and test them and assign them more responsibility as they prove their worth, which sons may accept or reject.[4] As contact with outsiders is discouraged—and there would be little time for that anyway—their social interactions are mainly with members of their own family. For family members, who form a closed unit, can be trusted, as opposed to outsiders, who are generically untrustworthy—a notion reinforced by culture and religion.

Paternal authority receives strong support from the traditions of China and northern India. In both, the patrilineal joint family with patrilocal residence is the standard. In both, there is the idea that a son's status derives from his father, although strictly speaking, in the joint family sons are frequently joint heirs with their father (see Madan 1965; Fei 1946; Freedman 1958; Lang 1946). All this, however, is not to deny that tensions are produced by such paternal authority and that the family firm, like the joint family, breaks up.

The ideals of the patriarchal family can also be attributed to Hinduism, Islam, and Confucianism, but religion does not seem a crucial factor, for these same ideals are also a part of Christianity and Judaism. One Indian informant stressed that it was not religion per se that made for success in family firms but general culture.[5] He cited the success of nonreligious Jews in various counties and of the Chinese in Seychelles, many of whom have converted to Christianity. For them, he maintained, religion was a matter of convenience. (In Mauritius, I encountered Chinese families who were Roman Catholic, Anglican, Seventh Day Adventist, Confucian, and Buddhist.)

CREOLE CULTURE

Creole culture in Seychelles presents a marked contrast to the Chinese and Indian. It is characterized by what Smith (1956) has called the matrifocal or matricentric family. The core of the household is a woman and her children, while the male is peripheral, providing money for the maintenance of the household through wage earning, rather than working with his wife and children. Many Creole couples are not married and the illegitimacy rate is 56 percent. Children are brought up almost exclusively by women, usually by the mother but sometimes by the mother's mother or mother's sister. Fathers take little interest in their children's education. It is left to the mother to find out how the child is doing in school.

The position of the male in the home was clearly evident when I visited households on Sundays or holidays. The woman was always in or near the house with her children. The man, if he was there at all, sat at some distance in the yard, drinking or playing dominoes with male friends.

In Seychelles a man is a male with money. A male without money is not a man. He shows he has money by spending it, not by saving or investing it. As a result, the male Creole role model is not an authoritarian father who closely supervises his family, but a carefree big earner and big spender who attempts to avoid entanglements.

Children are close to their mother and almost invariably take their mother's part against their father or the man with whom the mother is living. When the child is old enough to begin to earn, the child is expected to give the mother all his earnings. The threat to this is the son's marriage or cohabitation. Mothers rarely approve of the girls with whom their sons take up, but know that they can equally rarely keep a son at home beyond his early twenties. In his late teens the boy begins to consort with his age-mates and older men who tease him about his attachment to his mother. They expect him to buy them drinks and this takes part of his earnings. He begins to make sexual conquests and this too costs money, as do expensive clothes and consumer goods. Eventually he moves out of the home, and sets up with a woman *en menage*, as Seychellois put it.

Daughters too leave the maternal home to set up with a man. Sometimes they return, bringing their babies with them. The mother can then care for the babies while her daughter works.

SOME CREOLE ENTREPRENEURS

Despite this pattern there are some Creoles who attempt to go into business for themselves. There are eight Creole shops in the village. One has been in existence for five years, two for three years, one for one year, and four for less than a year.

Georges Cloche[6] is a young man of twenty-four. His mother has had children by three men. Her father's sister's daughter was married to a local Chinese shopkeeper, and Georges was able to get a job working in the shop. He set up a rather unstable menage with the Chinese shopkeeper's daughter when she was only fifteen, and this had led to friction, particularly with her brothers, who attempted to beat him up. Nonetheless, he saved his money until he had about 1,000 rupees and he rented for 25 rupees per month a piece of land near the road where he started a small shop in 1971. Later he was able to buy a secondhand refrigerator for cold drinks. He stocks a small range of goods in his shop (see appendix 1), and clients owe him about 2,200 rupees. He gives credit to only twelve regular clients.

As regards the shop, Georges must do everything himself. The shop is only open when he is there. He cannot often afford to go into town to buy supplies and so must rely on the traveling vans which the large town shopkeepers send into the countryside to supply small shops like his. This means that the range of goods offered him is limited and basically the choice of the town shopkeepers. Prices are fixed the same as in town, with a markup of about 10 percent. His position as a shopkeeper is vulnerable. His is a one-man business with no support from family members and too small to hire assistants. The stock is small. The margin of profit is low. He must pay cash for all his supplies. The likelihood of continuing success is small.

Another small shop in the village sells mostly drinks. Its owner is a man married to a schoolteacher, and the shop is located on her land. Neither she nor her children take any part in running the shop. The owner has hired a woman in the village to manage the shop, as his principal income derives from hauling—done with a truck he owns. Husband and wife keep their money separate. The husband buys food for the household and his own clothing. The wife has her salary which is deposited directly into a bank. Earning extra income from raising pigs and from the sale of *bacca* (fermented sugarcane juice), she buys her own clothes and those of her children. They have four sons and a daughter, all of whom go to fee-paying schools. The wife pays the daughter's fees; the husband pays the fees for his sons. Husband and wife frequently squabble over money, for example, who should pay the electricity bill. Their work and the management of their incomes continually pull them apart. As the shop is not a family enterprise, it would be unlikely to survive the breakup of the marriage.

The proprietor of the eighth Creole shop in the village was a vegetable seller in 1960 who displayed his produce at the side of the road. His parents died when he was eighteen, and he took responsibility for raising his three younger brothers. The small piece of land his family owned was a help. He worked hard at selling, saved his money, and was at last able to rent a small shop. In 1969 he bought the small plot of land—about eighty square feet—on which his shop stood. He planted it intensively and sold the produce in his shop which he also stocked with packaged foods, drinks, and toiletries. He buys from the traveling vans, but he also goes into town once a week to purchase supplies. About 40 percent of his supplies he imports directly from overseas at a lower cost.

Like Georges, he operates entirely on his own. When he goes to town, he must shut his shop, thus losing business. He lives *en menage* with a woman twelve years younger than he, and they have three small children, their living quarters adjoining the shop. The shop, which it took him fifteen years to get, is larger and more fully stocked than the other Creole shops (the shop which has been in existence for five years is the next largest), but it cannot compare with the Chinese shops. He has about forty regular clients to whom he gives credit, but he must supervise this very carefully, paying particular attention to their jobs, salaries, and general character. If a man earns 200 rupees per month, for example, he can give 125–150 rupees credit, but only for necessities and not for drink, which is sold strictly on a cash basis. His profit is only about 400–500 rupees monthly. Despite his energy and enterprise, he is in a vulnerable position as he lacks anyone with whom to share responsibilities.

The successful Creole entrepreneur is very much a man working on his own. Two of the most successful farmers in the village have thrown out their wives and manage their small properties—about five acres—entirely on their own, hiring casual labor when necessary. In these enterprises it is the individual, not the family which is involved.

There are many instances of failure. One man started a shop three times and each time went bankrupt. A chief reason for failure is the difficulty in handling credit relationships with clients. Shopkeepers advance credit to friends and relatives who are unable to pay. As I have pointed out elsewhere (Benedict 1964), when the shopkeeper belongs to a different ethnic group, it is easier for him to be an impersonal creditor. The indigenous village shopkeeper surrounded by his friends and relatives is under heavy social pressure to advance them credit, based not on their ability to pay but on his relationship to them. If this general proposition is added to the male ethic of being a big spender, it becomes easy to understand why so many Creole shopkeepers fail. It is also true, of course, that Creole shops tend to be undercapitalized and that their proprietors do not have credit from their suppliers. Further, the fact that the shopkeeper works alone militates heavily against his success.

Two other instances of success are worth examination here. One is the Chinese shopkeeper for whom Georges Cloche worked. The shopkeeper married a Creole woman whose mother has had eight children by five men, none of whom she married. Her daughter, however, has been married to the shopkeeper for twenty-eight years. She has been trained by him to work in the shop which she is capable of managing in his absence. They have nine children who also frequently help in the shop. They receive wages for their work which go toward their school fees. The eldest son is in the police force; the second son works in town; the third and fifth work in the shop. The fourth is in England taking a course in telegraphy. The eldest daughter is a teacher; the second daughter lives with Georges Cloche, a detail related earlier, and there are a son and daughter still in school. The family pattern is Chinese not Creole.

The second instance of success is that of a Creole family who runs a bakery in the town. The head of the family is Jean-Paul,[7] and the business was started by his father. His father and mother were married in 1925 when they were twenty-five and nineteen and remained married throughout their lives. They had three children—Jean-Paul and his two sisters. Even after the three children married, they all lived on the family property which had belonged to the mother's mother, each sibling setting up his or her own household. Jean-Paul married when he was twenty-seven and his bride twenty-one. The bakery was on the family property, and in 1960 Jean-Paul would bake from 6 A.M. to midnight, each day producing between two thousand and three thousand loaves and small cakes. These were sold to shops in town as well as to a number of hawkers. His wife assisted Jean-Paul when she could, but most of her time was spent tending their six children who were of school age. His mother also helped with the children. In addition to the bakery business, he raised fruit trees and vanilla vines and kept poultry. He also had several palm trees which he tapped for toddy to sell locally. Sometimes he earned additional money by working as a mason.

In 1975 the bakery still flourished. Jean-Paul had rebuilt his house in concrete blocks. He had an electric stove, a refrigerator, two radios, and a casette recorder. His eldest son was in the U.K. where he had worked for eight years as a fitter. His second son operated a minibus which he owned. His third son owned a pickup truck and delivered bakery products, hawkers having virtually disappeared except at public holiday gatherings. He was not, however, closely tied to the bakery, and his major earnings came from driving his van for other employers. Jean-Paul's fourth son was paralyzed and had to remain at home. His eldest daughter had been married for twelve years and lived with her husband, a Seychellois, in the U.K. The second daughter lived next door in a house on the family property which her husband had built. She made dresses which were sold to tourists at a shop in the port, and her husband drove an airport bus. Together they earned more than 1,200 rupees per month. Jean-Paul had three employees in the bakery. None of the sons, the eldest of whom is twenty-six, is yet married, nor are they living *en menage*.

These two cases demonstrate how success in Seychelles is apt to be correlated with stable marriage and a patriarchal family structure. In the former instance, the Creole wife assimilated into a Chinese pattern despite the fact that she had been raised in a family in which the Creole pattern predominated. Her children were brought up under their father's control and worked with him in the shop. Yet one daughter has chosen the Creole pattern by going to live with Georges Cloche. Her family disapproves strongly and her brothers have tried to intervene—an unlikely occurrence in a Creole family.

Jean-Paul was trained by his father who was a baker before him. He has maintained control of the family and educated his children who have good jobs, but, except for the son who uses his van to deliver bread, none has entered into the bakery business, nor has it expanded.

In general, Creoles do not see financial success in terms of family cooperation in a business venture but rather in terms of individual wage earning or perhaps fishing or running a truck with a few friends. Family patterns conduce to this choice, but it is also reinforced by the occupational structure of Seychelles, which has few large employers on plantations or in the tourist industry and a long history of casual day labor.

THE EDUCATION OF SONS

A striking factor in the successful firms, whether Indian, Chinese, or Creole, is investment in the education of sons and, to a lesser extent, daughters. The founder of the Indian firm imported teachers from India to instruct his sons. Later he sent his sons overseas to be educated in the U.K., India, or Japan. The Chinese sent their children to Hong Kong or Malaysia. The Creole baker invested large amounts of money in giving his children the best education Seychelles could offer and later sent one son to the U.K. In the Indian and Chinese examples, this pattern ties the sons to the firm. They are obligated to their father to return to work for the family business. Further, in the cases where the son is sent back to the country of origin, kinship ties with relatives there are strengthened. The fourth brother in the Indian firm, for example, has sent his son to an Indian university near the dyeing works and farm of his brother. This son will be under his uncle's supervision. Moreover, this fourth brother and the younger brother in India are forming a partnership, and the son is being groomed to play an important part in this. Thus business obligations and family obligations coincide. The loyalty engendered is to the family and the family is the firm.

As I have written elsewhere (Benedict 1968), it is the kind of obligation which governments cannot hope to emulate when they give scholarships for training overseas. Of twelve women sent to the U.K. recently by the Seychelles government for nurses' training, only one has returned. The government now requires the recipients of overseas scholarships to sign a statement that binds them to return to Seychelles for a minimum of two years. In a developing economy, therefore, family firms represent an important growth potential because they commit trained personnel to return to home country, for kinship obligations are stronger than the obligations of patriotism.

In the case of the Creole baker, however, though his sons were educated, they were not tied to the bakery. They have set up on their own, and the son in the U.K. has not returned. The obligation to the family and the firm is not felt. The bakery has probably reached its maximum point of expansion, as a large commercial bakery has been successfully established in Seychelles using overseas capital. Jean-Paul has not expanded in other directions and he sees success for his sons not in terms of entering the family business but of getting good jobs at home or overseas. Indeed, this has been the goal of their education.

A COMPARISON OF FAMILY STRUCTURES AND THEIR UNDERLYING VALUES

The differences in family structure between Creoles, on the one hand, and Indians and Chinese, on the other, are correlated with differences in attitudes to many aspects of life—to time, to work, to the future and how one plans for it, to recreation, to marriage and what one expects from it, to children. A Cambridge economist, J. W. F. Rowe wrote concerning the Creoles: "As individuals they conclude that the best thing they can do is to try and ensure that things will not get too difficult for themselves in their lifetime . . . . As a community their attitude is to live for the present and ignore the future" (1959:2). Since then, there has been massive economic development, but the attitude which Rowe described, though not universal, prevails. The working-class Creole male, in general, sees his job as a means of earning money which is to be used for immediate gratification. He spends it on drink, on women, and on consumer goods. He has little interest in his work per se. During the period of full employment, men continually changed jobs, not only in search for higher pay, but also because of a dispute with a foreman or a fellow worker. The Creoles evinced very little interest in working their way up to a better position with the same employer. This may be understood in view of the Creole's strong dislike of being bossed. A term of opprobrium is *domineur*, and *esclave* (slave) is the reciprocal. Men talk of women as *domineurs* when they try to boss them or create a scene. In jobs, this dislike of being dominated makes for poor employees and even poor team workers. Fishing partnerships frequently dissolve because a man believes one of his partners is behaving as a *domineur*.

These attitudes seem to have their roots both in the family situation of Creoles and in the employment situation of casual labor. A boy is dependent on his mother. She supervises him closely, bosses him about, and often gets him his first job. As indicated, she tries to keep him bound to her. He only feels he is a man when he quits his job or gets drunk. It is his way of freeing himself from his mother, of asserting himself as a man. This relation repeats itself from generation to generation.

Reinforcing this attitude was the employment situation of casual labor. On coconut plantations most work was paid by the task, and many men were able to complete their tasks by working from seven to eleven in the morning. On days on which men had money or were not inclined to work, they did not show up. In the boom period in the 1970s absenteeism was a major problem for employers. It may be that after the emancipation of slaves, regular employment was associated with slavery. Employers encouraged this attitude as well. Their products—cotton at that time—were doing badly in world markets, and, unable to pay regular salaries, they would hire only casual labor which was always available. Up until the construction boom, agricultural employment was on the decline. During 1975 when employment was again dropping off, I found many men making their living by fishing or doing odd jobs. A great variety of such jobs exists (see appendix 2), and men hear about them through friends and former employers. In fact, there is a whole network of informal job getting outside the control of government and major employers.

For the money he earns, a man has many demands on him: from his wife, from his mother, from other women by whom he has had children, from his friends who wish to borrow and from whom he will have to borrow in the future, from other women for sexual favors in return for gifts. He can buy drinks or go to a dance or buy a radio. Saving and investing do not figure in this list. Yet some do manage to save, usually cutting themselves off from social relationships and living alone, as in the instance of the two Creole farmers mentioned above.

319

A nonworking Creole woman is dependent on a man for her necessities. She waits at home with her children for the man to bring money or the food he has bought with it. If he returns late, drunk and with nothing, she has two choices. She can accept him and hope that he will do better tomorrow, or she can berate him (that is, be a *domineur*) and perhaps cause a public scene which men find acutely embarrassing. In either case, the conjugal bond is weakened. If a woman berates the man, she may diminish the chances of his coming home tomorrow. There are other women waiting to take up with him in return for support. She, too, may begin to look for another man. In this way there is enormous tension and animosity built up between Creole men and women.

In families where both the man and the woman work, it is usual for the man to provide food for the household. The woman uses her earnings to clothe herself and her children. The man buys his own clothes. Again there is a separation with the man on one side and the woman and her children on the other. As a result, it is not difficult for such households to split up. An unemployed woman tries to get her man to give her his entire wage. If she is clever, she then gives him back a small amount to spend on drinks and entertainment. She buys all the family's clothes, including his. If she attempts to keep all the money, she increases the possibility that the man will hold back some of his earnings and increases the likelihood of a breakup. Men who play along and give their wives all their earnings become known among their peers as men with little to spend, and they can blame their wives for this situation. Some isolation from male society results, but the family is more likely to be able to save.

Enough has been said to show that the working-class Creole is not oriented toward the future. He earns today to spend today. The kinds of relationships he has with his wife or *menagère* and other members of his family do not encourage him to invest in them. As mentioned, he takes little part in the education of his children, and he does not expect much in return from them. I frequently found old men living alone, with little hope of help from their children. The women, on the other hand, are more future-oriented and expect that their children will support them. Old women are rarely alone. They have a child or grandchild to look after. Women would be unable to work in hotels or go overseas in domestic service if their mothers or sisters did not care for their children.

Family Firms and Firm Families

Males seek recreations with other men outside the home. It is a commonplace for married men to go to dances to meet women. Men not interested in sexual exploits often spend their time drinking. (Drunkenness is rampant in the islands and has long been considered a serious problem.) Women seek recreation with their children and other women. Some find it in the milieu of the Church (96 percent of the population is Roman Catholic), others in exchanging visits with neighbors and relatives. Again the emphasis is on the separate spheres of men and women. The woman's domain is the house and the neighborhood. The man's is the shop, the roadway, and the toddy sellers.

The only woman a Creole man is close to is his mother or mother-surrogate. A man can always return to his mother's house, and this is another factor which works against a marriage or menage. Some men never break this bond with their mothers, remaining in or near the mother's house all their lives. They frequently become drunkards. One man stated, "My wife is my bottle." Usually, however, friction develops between mother and son when he takes up with a woman.

In contrast, life for the Indian and Chinese male centers on the family. He spends most of his time in the household, supervising and working with his children. The idea is to build for the future. He attempts to teach notions of thrift and saving.

Arranged marriages are common with most Chinese and Indians in Seychelles. Wives were imported by the Indian family firm from the same caste and area in India which it came from originally. The wife became a part of the family home, as was the case with the Chinese. In both instances, an Indian or Chinese man does not leave his mother; rather, he brings his wife to her.

The Indian and Chinese work for the future, and they work nearly all the time. They will keep the shop open for a late client. They will go to enormous trouble to find a special item for a client. They will provide services to attract more clients. All this time, they are building up the business for themselves, their sons, and their sons' sons. The whole family is involved in this enterprise, and it comes before everything else. There are no hours, no paid task work for family members, no salaries. All invest their time and labor to make the enterprise succeed. In place of salaries, sons expect to get education and a share of the business which will yield them profits later. Their status depends almost entirely on their membership in the family and hence the firm. In contrast, the status of the Creole is a matter of his individual achievement even when he is a shop-keeper.

Recreation in the Indian and Chinese family takes place largely within the home in eating or listening to the radio or in preparing for the next day's business. When men do go out, it is usually with family members or people in the business community. Women may visit each other but the visits are to relatives or to the wives of men in the business community.

A man expects subordination and cooperation from his wife. She may assist him in the shop, as in the Chinese case, or be in charge of the household, as in the Indian case, but she is not independent or free to come and go as she pleases. Similarly the children are under the authority of their parents. They are expected not only to work in the business but also to get good marks at school. A poor school report is not met with indifference as it might be in a Creole household, but with enormous concern and a visit to the school.

An Indian or Chinese man supports his family. He may have a mistress, but he will not consider leaving his wife for her. Rather than spending his income, he will invest a significant part of it in the firm. The demands on his money, thus, are internal, directed toward the maintenance of his family, which is also his work force. The woman can only look to her husband and her children for support. She cannot easily leave her man. Coming from overseas, she has no alternative but to stay with her husband and family.

The foregoing contrast of Creoles with Indians and Chinese in Seychelles has been presented in terms of ideal types or models. There are, of course, many variations. For example, since 1960 a Creole middle class has begun to emerge. It is made up of higher civil servants and entrepreneurs, such as contractors, and those who have entered tourist-related businesses. Some Creoles who had left for East Africa ten to twenty years before have returned with suffi-cient capital to set up small businesses. These people, on the whole, are married, and often both husband and wife work. They pool their earnings in the hope of buying property or establishing or expanding a business. Future-oriented, they save and invest their money and pay a great deal of attention to the education of their children. They send them to better schools, and often a child will go overseas for his higher education. On the other hand, the children of some Indian and Chinese merchants have married Creoles, and some have followed the Creole pattern by having a series of menages and taking to drink.

Throughout this discussion I have stressed the importance of the structure of the family to the neglect of the more traditional economic factors such as the availability of capital and credit. The Indian and Chinese firms were capitalized and had sources of credit which were not available to the Creole entrepreneurs. The Indan merchant brought capital with him to Seychelles and, when he began to deal in copra, he was able to negotiate loans both within Seychelles and overseas. The Chinese shopkeeper was financed by a wealthy kinsmen who already had a large shop in Seychelles. By contrast, the Creole shopkeepers started with only their own savings. By and large, they have been unable to obtain loans, nor have their suppliers advanced them credit. I do not wish to underestimate these factors. Yet, even if those economic differences are set aside, the fact that Creoles are not usually able to mobilize family support militates against their success in business. It may even be that the lack of this support influences creditors and suppliers against them.

CONCLUSION

In 1968 I concluded an article on family firms with the following plea:

> We need to know what types of family structure are best suited for the development of family firms and what types of enterprises family firms can best engage in. A much closer examination of the factors making for success or failure of the family firm is required. This necessitates both historical analysis of family firms in a wide variety of societies and intensive field work on family firms in developing societies (1968:18).

This paper has attempted to go further along these lines. It deals with a very small kind of firm, the retail shop, though these shops have sometimes expanded into larger and more diversified enterprises. It treats two contrasting types of family structure: the patriarchal family with a patrilocal joint family ideology and the conjugal family with a neolocal nuclear family ideology. The patriarchal type

323

was represented chiefly by the Indians and Chinese; the conjugal type by the Creoles. These types are, of course, polar models, and there were variants in each ethnic category. Historical perspective was attempted through the collection of the history of the firms from informants and by the fifteen-year interval in my fieldwork in Seychelles from 1960 to 1975. The data are not nearly as complete as I would like.

My contention is that the growth and success of a family firm is highly dependent on a strong and authoritarian father and a closely knit cooperative family. The reciprocal of this is wives and sons willing to submit to the father's rule. This is accompanied by an ideology which stresses loyalty to the family and hence the firm. Such an ideology is fostered particularly if the family is somewhat isolated from the surrounding social milieu. I do not contend that only a strong patriarchal family is required for a successful family firm but that without it the firm is likely to fail. I argue from a few cases, and this is a weakness of the chapter. They were all I was able to collect. More cases are needed. Therefore I renew my plea.

APPENDIX 1: THE STOCK OF GEORGES CLOCHE'S SHOP

Alcoholic drinks
  Guiness Stout
  *Seybrew beer
  Scotch whiskey (half-pint bottles)

Soft drinks
  Orange drinks (4 brands)
  *Seypearl soft drinks

Beverages
  Cocoa
  Imported tea
  *Island tea
  Tinned coffee (2 brands)

Tinned foods
  Apricots
  Baby foods (2 brands)
  Baked beans
  Carrots (2 brands)
  Cheese
  Custard powder
  Fruit jams
  Marmalade
  Milk powder

Breads, cereals, etc.
  *Bread loaves and rolls
  Biscuits (3 brands)
  Noodles
  Oat cereal
  Rice

Cooking oils
  *Coconut oil
  Cooking oil
  Ghee
  Margarine

Sauces and condiments
  Catsup
  Chili sauce (3 brands)
  Hot chili sauce
  Salt
  Soy sauce
  Tomato sauce
  *Vinegar

Cleaning products
  Bar soap

324

Floor polish
Scouring powder
Shoe polish

Toiletries
  Baby powder
  Razor blades
  Sanitary pads
  Toilet paper (2 brands)
  Toothpaste

Sundries
  Airmail envelopes
  *Cigarettes

Cigarette papers
Dress material (12 lengths)
Flashlight batteries
Matches
Rubber sandals
Straws
Women's panties

Miscellaneous
  Garlic
  Onions
  *Salt fish
  Kerosene for fuel

---

*Seychelles products. All others are imported, though salt and rice are packaged in Seychelles.

He stocks only six to twelve each of the above items except razor blades, onions, bread and rolls, matches, beer, and soft drinks. In addition, he sells lottery tickets and has a pinball machine from which he gets 25% of the take.

APPENDIX 2: SOME ODD JOBS FOR MALES

	Pay per day in rupees
Unloading truck	8–10
Gathering cinnamon leaves	8
Gathering coconuts	10
Loading sand from beach	10
Helping move house	5–10
Clearing ground	5
Clearing banana trees	5
Digging trench for rubbish	6–7
Fishing with handline	depends on catch
Planting	5
Breaking rocks	10
Making charcoal	25 per two days
Crushing rock for concrete	13
Cutting grass with scythe	10
Cutting fodder for cows	4
Substitute driving of truck	10
Night watchman	8
Sweeping school playground	8
Preparing land for planting cassava or sweet potatoes	5
Crushing sugar cane to make *bacca*, a fermented drink	10
Collecting empty bottles	6
Picking breadfruit	5
Cutting latanier leaves for thatching	7–8
Husking coconuts	15
Making a chicken pen	10
Selling vegetables	commission
Butchering a pig	some of the meat
Tapping palm trees for toddy	15 per week
Making bamboo fish traps	20

NOTES

1. For suggesting the title I thank Professor Gerald Berreman. For helpful comments and criticism I thank the contributors to this volume and my colleagues in the Department of Anthropology at Berkeley especially Professors Elizabeth Colson, Jack Potter, and William Shack. My most profound thanks go to my wife and co-worker, Marion S. Benedict, and to those Seychellois who patiently and good-humoredly submitted to my questions. Opinions expressed in this article are those of the author and not of any government authority.

2. The eldest daughter became a doctor of medicine and married in India where she practices. The second daughter became a tourist specialist in India. She married a doctor there. The third daughter became a professor of radio-therapeutic medicine in Canada. The fourth daughter is an obstetrician-gynecologist who practices in the U.S. where she is married to a doctor.

3. The elder daughter of the oldest brother is a doctor practicing in the U.S. The eldest daughter of the second brother is married to a jeweller in South India. The second is in the U.K. and the third is at a university in India. The others are still at school in Seychelles.

4. For a fuller treatment of this aspect, see Benedict 1968.

This point receives support from the work of Brian Foster who shows how the Mons of Thailand, who are mostly in commerce, have maintained a separate ethnic identity "though they have no ascertainable Mon identity except their ancestry" (1974:439).

6. The name is fictitious.

7. The name is fictitious.

PART 4

New Directions

12

Entrepreneurship and Social Change: Toward a Populational, Decision-Making Approach

SIDNEY M. GREENFIELD

Department of Anthropology
University of Wisconsin–Milwaukee

ARNOLD STRICKON

Department of Anthropology
University of Wisconsin–Madison

In the first major work in which it occupied a central place, entrepreneurship—as noted in the introduction to this volume—was viewed as the putting together, by "creative" individuals, of "new combinations" of materials and resources that resulted in changes in the equilibrium states of social and economic systems (Schumpeter 1949, original 1934). From its beginnings, then, students of entrepreneurship have been interested in the effect of the behavior of the individual on the institutionalized patterns of society. Unfortunately, as William P. Glade (1967) has observed, research has not shown us how the behavior of individuals effects social change. Instead, Glade argues, what emerges from the studies of entrepreneurship conducted thus far is a series of economic, social, and psychological variables that may be grouped in the form of two contrasting models. "The one, a sort of pre-development model," he writes, "describes relationships which obtain in an economy in which growth has not yet occurred. The other model is descriptive of an economy in which growth is already present and in which the growth experience has provided conditions which tend to support entrepreneurial endeavor." The two models, represent *au fond*, an approach which could best be described as one based on comparative statics. Still missing, Glade concludes, "is a model of a transitional type of system, a theory of change which explains the transition from the state of affairs depicted by the 'underdeveloped economy' model to that represented by the 'developed economy' model" (1967:246).

The objective of this essay is to outline a theory of social change—and social persistence—that will resolve the dilemma of the relationship between the individual and the institutionalized segments of society in a new way. We shall argue that present theories of continuity and change both do not, and cannot, see the individual as an active agent in the social process, be it persistence or change. The reason for this, we maintain, is that the theories that inform most of the work that has been done in the social sciences are based upon a view of the world that, following Popper (1950) and Mayr (1976), we call essentialism. According to this view of the world, societies, or cultures, are seen as entities attributed ontological reality in their own right. Based ultimately on Plato's famous parable of the cave, the apparent assumption is that there are entities such as society, made up of parts—for example, economy, religion, social stratification—that exist but are not amenable to direct human sense perception. What men see instead are but manifestations of these realities, very much like the flickerings and shadows of reality seen by Plato's hypothetical prisoners on their cave wall. What is real in this view are the categories that have properties and characteristics which are taken to be immutable. Since the entities that constitute reality are not amenable to sense perception, they can be learned about and understood only by working backward from the incomplete shadows they cast on the cave wall. The observable world in which men live in this view represents only an aspect of reality, not reality itself. The theories of scholars as diverse as Joseph Schumpeter, David McClelland, Everett Hagen, Talcott Parsons, Auguste Comte, Lewis Henry Morgan, Karl Marx, A. R. Radcliffe-Brown, and Leslie A. White, we maintain, share this view of the world.

Theories of society rooted in the essentialist world view, we

330

contend, cannot account for the individual, either as an agent of change or as the maintainer of equilibrium. Furthermore, previous attempts to include the individual as a part of the social process within the essentialist framework have been singularly unsuccessful.

To resolve the dilemma and to provide a theory of society that can incorporate the behavior of individuals in accounting for both equilibrium states (persistence) and change, we propose a view of the world other than the one that reflects essentialism.[1] On the basis of contributions by Charles Darwin and his followers in the biological sciences, we propose for application in the social sciences the position referred to as "populationism" (Popper 1950; Mayr 1976). In brief, we maintain that reality is nothing more nor less than the behavior of the individuals that form the populations or communities that inhabit the earth. Society, economy, religion, family, stratification, and so on all in this view become but abstractions based on the statistics of variation, epiphenomena of the behavior of individuals. Using the imagery of the Darwinian scheme as it has been applied in biology as a metaphor for looking at social and cultural phenomena, we elaborate in the following pages a view of the world and a theory of social process to account for both social patterns (or equilibrium states) and change.[2]

STEPS TOWARD THE NEW IMAGERY

In his 1967 article Glade made two contributions to advance entrepreneurial studies and the study of social change. First, he reminded us that studies of economic growth and development, of which entrepreneurial studies are a part, are rooted in an evolutionary perspective. The use of terms such as stages, social statics, and social dynamics call forth the imageries and presentations of the giants of the past century—Comte, Spencer, Morgan, Tylor, Marx, to mention a few—who provided us with the framework within which many of today's social scientists view social reality. But as Glade pointed out, the stages, both in the schemes of the evolutionists of the past century and for students of development of the present, are static.

In his effort to do what generations of evolutionists and students of development, and entrepreneurship, had been unable to do—to show

331

how societies move from one stage or type to another—Glade made his second contribution. He directed us to the individual as the maker of decisions and choices in social situations. After presenting a model of decision making at the level of the individual—a model which at the time was gaining popularity in several of the disciplines that constitute the social sciences—he was compelled to invoke what may be thought of as a deus ex machina in order to relate the choices and decisions of individuals to the stages of the developmental schema. The external factors he referred to as the "opportunity structure." Individuals, he contended (1967:251), must take advantage of opportunities or lose out to others who will.

"What emerges" for Glade, then, "as integral features of any given situation are both an 'objective' structure of economic opportunity and a structure of differential advantage in the capacity of the system's participants to perceive and act upon such opportunities" (1967:251). Those who act upon the opportunities, of course, are in Glade's view the entrepreneurs who move economy and society to new stages in their developmental growth.

Approximately a quarter of a century before Glade tried to make a place for the individual in developmentally oriented studies of entrepreneurship, Raymond Firth, writing in the tradition of British structural-functionalism—a competing alternative to evolutionism within the essentialist framework—came to a similar position in an effort to conceptualize social change. He also focused on the individual as the maker of decision and choices in social contexts.

The place of the individual in the social and cultural process had been raised previously at several junctures in the development of anthropology as a discipline. Evolutionists, for example, had dealt with it in discussions of the place of "the great man" (White 1949). Historicists, in the tradition of Frans Boas and American cultural— as opposed to British social—anthropology, also had addressed themselves to the place of the great man (Kroeber 1948). Then some went further, specifically with the development of the subfield of culture and personality. Unfortunately, as with other efforts to conceptualize the individual as an element in the social process, culture and personality theory was to be a one-way street. That is, culture, the reality, was seen to act or to have an effect upon the development and behavior of the individual, which was conceptualized as a phenomenon with an attribute called personality. Culture was thought to create a personality type that fit with the demands and characteristics of the culture (Kardiner 1939; Linton 1945). The fit was obtained by means of a system, (another entity?), called child rearing, or enculturation, which inculcated in each youngster the appropriate behavioral patterns constituting the personality that went with the cultural type (Mead 1939; Whiting 1963). In complex cultures, it should be noted, social and cultural subsegments such as classes, regions, and subcultures each were assumed to produce their own personality types. As was the case in the study of entrepreneurship and of great men, there was in this formulation no way to analyze or model the effect of the individual on the society or culture.

Although fully aware of the variability of individuals and their behaviors, essentialist social science could not deal with such variability on the theoretical and conceptual level. Empirical differences, therefore, had to be left out of the analysis, or, as in the case of most functionalists, treated as deviance. Individuals, for theoretical purposes, were thus classified into dichotomous categories—the one composed of those whose behaviors conformed to the patterns of the cultural systems or social institutions, and the other of those who did not. Those in the first category presented no problem to functionalists, to historicists, or to evolutionists, since their behavior was what each theory in its own way predicted. Those in the second category, however, posed a problem.

Radcliffe-Brown, who more than any other scholar has been responsible for introducing structural-functionalism into anthropology, approached deviance by looking at the sanctions such behaviors evoked from representatives of society. Sanctions, he wrote,

> constitute motives in the individual for the regulation of his conduct in conformity with usage. [Sanctions] are effective, first, through the desire of the individual to obtain the approbation and to avoid the disapprobation of his fellows, to win such rewards or to avoid such punishment as the community offers or threatens; and second, through the fact that the individual learns to react to particular modes of behavior with judgements of approval and disapproval in the same way as do his fellows, and therefore measures his own behavior both in anticipation and retrospect by standards which conform more or less closely to those prevalent in the community to which he belongs. What is called conscience is thus in the widest sense the reflex in the individual of the sanctions of society. (1933:531)

Society, then, is thought to respond to the deviant by bringing him "into line" or by disposing of him. The assumption here, of course, is that the individual is unable to change society. Furthermore, society itself appears to be unchangeable. The empirical fact of social change, as critics of structural-functionalism have pointed out, cannot be accounted for by the theory, at least as formulated by Radcliffe-Brown. The possibility, for example, that deviance in some cases might be rewarded and copied by others was inconceivable. That the individual could in some way affect society, causing it to change, was an empirical possibility rejected on theoretical grounds, in the same way that the possibility of the great man making "history" was rejected by evolutionist and historicist theory.

Firth responded to this theoretical blind spot in functional theory by introducing his now classic distinction between social organization and social structure. "Social organization," he wrote,

has usually been taken as a synonym for social structure. In my view it is time to distinguish between them. The more one thinks of the structure of a society in abstract terms, as of group relations or ideal patterns, the more necessary it is to think separately of social organization in terms of concrete activity. Generally, the idea of organization is that of people getting things done by planned action. This is a special process, the arrangement of action in sequences in conformity with selected social ends. These ends must have some elements of common significance for the set of persons concerned in the action. The significance need not be identical, or even similar, for all persons, it may be opposed as between some of them. The processes of social organization may consist in part in the resolution of such opposition by action which allows one or other element to come to final expression. Social organization implies some degree of unification, a putting together of diverse elements into common relation. To do this, advantage may be taken of existing structural principles, or variant procedures may be adopted. This involves the exercise of choice, the making of decisions. As such, this rests on personal evaluations, which are the translation of general ends or values of group range into terms which are significant for the individual. (1964:35–36, original 1951)

The emphasis on social structure alone, Firth recognized, leaves us without a theory of change. "A structural analysis alone cannot interpret social change" (1964:35). It leads instead to classification and a taxonomy of social types. "A social taxonomy," he added "could become as arid as classification of species in some branches of biology. Analysis of the organizational aspects of social action is the necessary complement to analysis of the structural aspect" (1964:35).

Firth's recommendation, then, was to incorporate the organizational as a theoretical and conceptual dimension equivalent to structure within structural-functional theory, much the way statics and dynamics had been treated as separate but equivalent dimensions of reality in evolutionary theory. Organization for Firth rested on the choices and decisions made by individuals, just as did dynamics in the developmental view for Glade. As evolutionary theory was to have no place for the individual in affecting society, culture, and institutions, so structural-functionalism was to be unable to incorporate a dynamic, decision-making individual into its view of society. The individual in the structural-functional view of the world, we must emphasize, is conceived of as an actor playing roles within an ordered system. Consequently, instead of a world view that sees individuals making choices and decisions that have an impact on institutions, we have one that sees a collection of social and psychological attributes the content of which is determined by aspects of the social structure. Notions of choice, alternative, and variation have no place in the imagery on which structural-functionalism rests. What Firth has given us with his idea of social organization is not a complementary dimension equivalent to structure within a structural-functional perspective, but rather the seeds of an alternative view of the world that contradicts structural-functionalism. Firth and his students, however, have not confronted the implications of his suggestion.

The most significant elaboration of the view implicit in Firth's concept of social organization has been made by the Norwegian anthropologist Frederik Barth. Building on the imagery of the individual as the maker of choices and decisions, who follows strategies to attain ends, and who transacts with others to achieve those ends, Barth (1966) has developed models of social process that, as he puts it, may be used to generate the social forms that are the subject of anthropological investigation. We have incorporated much of Barth's thinking into the theory of society and social change presented in this essay, and for this we acknowledge our debt to him.[3] Nonetheless, it seems to us that Barth never grasped the full implications of his revolutionary position, a limitation that has been the basis for much of the recent criticism directed his way (Paine 1974;

Evans 1977). In his published works at least, Barth appears not to realize that the view of the world on which his generative models rest both differs from and challenges those on which structural-functionalism, historicism, and evolutionism depend. Barth's models, like Firth's concept of social organization—and Glade's decision-making perspective—have as their basic elements the individual, choice, alternative, and variation. These are concepts that have no place in theories of society rooted in an essentialist view of the world. Instead, they contain the seeds of what we refer to as a populational view of social reality. That Barth himself has not grasped these implications is evident in his persistent application of structuralist-essentialist images when he turns in his analysis from the individual to the community. In his work on entrepreneurship with his colleagues at the University of Bergen (1963), for example, in spite of selecting the subject because, as he (1967:664) later put it, "they [entrepreneurs] make innovations that affect the community in which they are active," he makes no attempt to develop a model to analyze how entrepreneurial activity affects the community in which it occurs (1963:14-18). In his seminal work on *Ethnic Groups and Boundaries*, he speaks of ethnic groups in several places as if they were entities in the structuralist-functionalist mode with their own reality (1967:17, 18, 27, 28, 38). In his paper on "Analytical Dimensions in the Comparison of Social Organization" (1972) he reverts to the kind of classification Firth feared emphasis on social structure alone could result in.

THE METAPHOR OF A DARWINIAN POPULATION[4]

In place of essentialism, we turn to a view of the world that has its basis in the populational thinking introduced into science more than a century ago by Charles Darwin. We suggest that Darwinian notions enable us more satisfactorily to develop the theory of social change implicit in the works of Firth, Barth, Glade, and others and to apply what has been called a decision-making approach to the study of social phenomena.

The title of Darwin's masterpiece, it should be remembered, was *On the Origin of Species*. In the thinking of his times species were

336

defined by the physical, or structural, characteristics of an ideal representation. Yet the actual plants and animals that made up the several species, Darwin observed, showed a considerable range of variation away from the characteristics used to define the types or species. One of Darwin's great contributions to biological science was to focus attention away from the typological categories, the species, and onto specific characteristics of the organisms whose variation was the stuff upon which his theory rested. These variations appeared in a unit that we now call a breeding population. It consists of a group of individual animals in sufficient contact with each other so that the probability is greater that they will mate with each other than with other animals of the same type. The unit of reality for Darwin, then, was the population and not the type or species. The consequence of this emphasis on populations and the variation of individuals within them was a rejection of the Aristotelian and Linnean typological and essentialist view of the world.

Darwinian populations consist of individuals that vary from each other in specific characteristics.[5] The follower of Darwin today, as Mayr states,

> stresses the uniqueness of everything in the organic world. What is true for the human species—that no two individuals are alike—is equally true for all other species of animals and plants. Indeed, even the same individual changes continuously throughout its lifetime and when placed in different environments. All organisms and organic phenomena are composed of unique features and can be described collectively only in statistical terms. Individuals, or any kind of organic entities, form populations of which we can determine only the arithmetic mean and the statistics of variation. Averages are merely statistical abstractions; *only the individuals of which the populations are composed have reality* (1976:27, 28, emphasis added).

Among the varied individuals that constitute any breeding population, Darwin noted, some are better able to utilize the resources of their environment than others. Those better able to utilize resources produce more offspring relative to the other members of the population. Over time, however, this differential reproduction results in a shift in the average characteristics of the population. This is the process of evolution. In genetic terms this would be expressed as the increased frequency in the gene pool of the genes of more successful breeders at the expense of the less successful.

337

In the long run this process of modification in characteristics of the population occurring in each generation resulted in better resource acquisition by following generations. It was also believed to produce a closer fit between the individuals that made up the population and the environment from which they obtain their sustenance. The environment included not only the geographical and geological features of the habitat but also other living organisms. The improved fit was to what we would call today an ecological system. This total process of variation, differential reproduction, and more effective use of an environment was termed natural selection, the process by which evolution occurred. It should be kept in mind, however, that natural selection could result in stagnation or extinction as well as in improved adaptation.

Darwin's view of the world was of populations of individual organisms adapting to environmental settings. As the result of this adaptive process, the average characteristics of populations changed with the passage of time, ultimately giving rise to groups of animals with characteristics that were sufficiently different from those of their ancestor so as to constitute a new species. Exactly when a new species emerged was difficult to discern—a question which appears to have been of little interest to Darwin. It was the process of evolution which concerned him, not its structural/typological outcomes. This emphasis on the process as opposed to its specific outcomes characterizes the work of most present-day students of biology, genetics, and ecology.

In the Darwinian view here summarized, with its emphasis on populations of individual organisms in an environmental setting, the individual organism is assumed to be goal-directed as it strives to acquire resources and to reproduce. Higher level units, such as populations and species, are not assumed to have goals. Teleological processes are postulated for the individual only (Richerson 1977: 14, 21).

The view of social phenomena we propose in place of essentialism follows Darwin in its populational rather than typological concerns. But we also propose to use the Darwinian model metaphorically. That is, in our view of the world, social phenomena are assumed to be the result of processes similar to the one described by Darwin for biological phenomena. Although we clearly recognize that biological and social phenomena are not the same, we propose to think of the

338

social *as if it were like* the biological (Turbayne 1971:12, 13). Thus we use Darwin's model of evolutionary process as the metaphor for ways in which social phenomena are produced.

Our objective is to examine and explain social phenomena. By the term "social phenomena" we mean the same things our colleagues have meant for centuries. We refer to society, culture, and institutions such as religion, politics, and economics. Following the Darwinian lead, however, we do not see society, culture, religion, politics, and economics as entities with a reality of their own. Rather, they exist as statistical patterns abstracted from the variable behaviors of members of specific populations. Furthermore, also like Darwin, we see them as the result of a more fundamental process that generates both the patterned regularities that are social institutions and the changes that transform those patterns and institutions. It is to this process that we now turn.

To begin with, we see the world of which social phenomena are a part as composed of individuals who are assumed to be goal directed. These human individuals, like all animals, are assumed to live in groups, the members of which have sufficient contact with each other so that the probability is greater that they will interact with one another than with members of other populations. We refer to such human populations as communities.

In striving to attain their goals, members of specific communities perform a variety of behaviors. At any specific time, however, the sum total of a specific kind of behaviors performed may be averaged statistically to produce a pattern. The results of the statistical manipulation of behaviors performed provide us with patterned regularities that proponents of the paradigm we have rejected refer to as institutions.

It must be remembered, that for any regularities in behavior that might be referred to as "the pattern" for a given population at a given time, there will in fact be a variety of behaviors actually performed. In conventional kinship-based societies, for example, the actual relations among the members of some families may in fact be weak; in agrarian states, some commoners may be wealthier and more powerful than some aristocrats; in authoritarian societies some people may reject authority; in tradition-bound societies some individuals may develop new ways of getting things done. As Darwin did in biology, we propose to emphasize the variation in behavior performed by individuals rather than the statistical regularities that may be abstracted from the behavior.

Darwin saw the variability of characteristics in the individual members of a population as related to the competition for resources. That is, in striving to achieve their goals—which is to say to obtain resources—within a given environment, individuals with certain characteristics held an advantage vis-à-vis others in the population. Those individuals with the more successful traits were then able to produce more offspring than others, thereby increasing the probability of the more adaptive characteristics appearing in succeeding generations. By analogy we maintain that some of the varying behaviors performed by some of the members of a human community will enable them to obtain more resources—more of their goals—than will the behaviors performed by others. These behaviors, in the context of the specific environment, could be viewed as more adaptive to the individuals who perform them than behaviors that obtain fewer resources. It would follow, by extending the analogy, that those behaviors in the social world that result in the acquisition of relatively larger amounts of available resources for those who perform them may be considered more adaptive than their alternatives. The more successful variants of behavior, then, could be expected to be found in increased frequency at later periods of time. The result would be a process comparable to Darwin's theory of natural selection. Whereas in biological evolution the effects of natural selection are transmitted by genetic means, in the model of social reality we are proposing the effects are transmitted by means of learning.

By learning, we refer not merely to the acquisition of behavioral repertories by the young. Persons of all ages learn and continue to do so throughout the course of their lives. By learning, we thus refer to the continuous process by which new behaviors are added to the repertories of the individuals constituting a population or community. As new behaviors are learned and added, others previously performed may be discarded.

Learning also can occur across the boundaries of a given population; that is, information can be obtained, accurately or with unintended modification, from members of other communities. Consequently, as Richerson has observed, human behavioral phenomena include "the Lamarckian possibility of transmitting acquired information . . ." (1977:11). Information acquired by any one member of a population, from within or without, can be translated into behavior and transmitted to others across generations.

We have stated above that we are using the Darwinian imagery metaphorically and not literally. Assumptions and definitions not to be found in evolutionary biology therefore now can be added. In the Darwinian model the rewards are simple material goals such as food and protection. In the social context, however, they are more complex. What would be a goal worth achieving to a member of one human community, for example, might be unimportant to a member of another population. Human goals, we must emphasize, are the result of the ability of the organism to use, receive, and transmit symbols. The emergence of the unique and distinctive ability to symbolize has long been recognized as the crucial event in the evolutionary development of the species *Homo sapiens*. Human beings, therefore, are able to attach symbolic meaning and hence value to events, objects, and activities that go beyond the satisfaction of biological imperatives. Likewise, biological imperatives themselves can acquire additional meanings. As such, human symbols stand between the organism and its environment. The actual environment of a human population is consequently mediated by the symbols used by the individuals who occupy it.

Given the arbitrary relationship between the physical representations of symbols and their referents, symbol systems, if they are to be used by individuals, must be shared. Those individuals who share common definitions and symbols then constitute the population or community from whose behavior we abstract the patterns that are the institutions of society.

In the transactions and exchanges that make up the complex interactions by which symbols come to be shared by the members of a population, individuals learn what they can and cannot expect from others. They also come to agree on rules for proper conduct, along with rules for exchanges and obligations among themselves. Those agreements manifest themselves behaviorally in expectations of rights and obligations, what structuralist-functionalists and others have called social status and roles.

Symbolic ability, of which language is the prime example, makes it possible for human beings to contemplate events and situations other than the ones they experience directly. As a result, they can

341

invent situations and the behaviors to perform in them. They also can define symbolically what for them will be rewards. Furthermore, they can conceptualize what may be thought of as sets of alternative means for the attainment of goals. They can select from the range of alternative possibilities, given the information and knowledge they have, what in their judgment and evaluation will enable them to achieve their goal—a process which is called decision making (Barth 1966; Bennett 1976a, 1976b; Keesing 1967).

The founders of decision-making theory in anthropology, such as Firth and Barth, unfortunately have placed their work within the tradition of social anthropology and its essentialist view of the world. It should be clear, however, that the imagery and assumptions of decision theory are not inconsistent with the populational view of the world we propose. More than this, we maintain that the decision-making perspective becomes an even more powerful tool of analysis when freed from the limiting assumptions of essentialism and reformulated in populational terms.[6]

For example, students of decision making generally see individuals as striving to obtain goals and rewards. However, they see this striving in social contexts in which individuals interact with (1) material and biological things in the environment, (2) other members of their communities, and (3) the symbolic abstractions and definitions they have come to share with specific others. In social settings, cooperative interaction may occur in terms of the shared definitions of meaning that characterize the members of a given community. Individuals, therefore, are assumed to strive to obtain rewards that at times require their cooperation with fellow members of their community. Each individual, it is further assumed, not only strives to obtain rewards but also to maximize what he might obtain relative to the amount of time, energy, and other resources applied in the effort.

The focus of the decision-making approach, then, is on the manner in which individuals allocate the resources available to them while striving to obtain the ends they seek. The means used to obtain their goals may be of several different kinds, such as material goods and services, symbols, or other members of the population.

Individuals soon learn that not all choices of action obtain for them the goals they desire. Sometimes, they miscalculate, either because they have faulty or insufficient information or because they have misjudged the situation. Courses of action that do not obtain rewards, again in terms of learning theory, will not be reinforced in that they will not be selected again from the range of possibilities available to the individual. Furthermore, they will not be learned and copied by others also interested in obtaining the specific goal. Unless the goal is abandoned, other behavioral alternatives will be tried until one successfully obtains for the individual the goal he desires. Then it will be repeated, and perhaps learned and copied by others. On occasion, a behavior that attains a desired end also might bring undesired consequences. Before selecting it again, the decision maker will have to evaluate the reward obtained in terms of the unanticipated, possibly negative consequences.[7] The behavior then will be repeated or rejected by the innovator and others copying him, depending upon the relative weights assigned to each. One should be cautioned that the patterns to emerge are *not* the result of the choices and decisions of the individuals; instead they are the result of the interaction of those choices and factors in the environment that reinforce some and not other behaviors.

We see the social world then as made up of populations of human individuals, or communities. Each community we see as composed of individuals each seeking to maximize their own goals and rewards. The actors in the model are assumed to be able to learn new behaviors. By means of their symbols, they interact with each other, thereby coming to share meanings and definitions of value. One result of this may be, and often is, cooperation between individuals. Therefore, although in one sense our emphasis is on individuals striving for goals, the imagery makes possible the analysis of cooperative and even collective behavior.

Within any population, then, we assume that there are numerous individuals each striving to obtain goals. The goals also may be desired by a relatively large number of the members of the community. Consequently, many of the choices and decisions to be made by individuals within a population are aimed at obtaining goals and rewards also sought by others. In what becomes a competition for the often limited rewards, each individual may be thought to search for means that will give him a competitive advantage. Each, in thinking through the alternatives, will try to invent conceptually new means, while also incorporating actions that have proved successful for others. In each situation and at each step, the individual seeks strategies that, given the information and knowledge available to

343

him, he believes are most likely to bring him success. Each individual chooses a line of action or behavior in the hope of obtaining these rewards. Some choices, as we have seen, lead to success, while others do not. Successful strategies, however, need not necessarily be, and often are not, ones in which an individual privately reaps the benefits of his planning. A successful strategy in some situations, for example, may be one where security is emphasized over private gain, or where benefits, and risks, are shared with one's fellows.

With the passage of time more and more members of the population learn the strategies and behaviors that have proven successful for others. These choices of behavior then will be selected and performed with increased frequency within the population at large (see Barth 1967). Rarely, if at all, will they be the only behavior selected in the situation. Some individuals will continue to experiment with new alternatives, while others might step back to redefine the goals and rewards so that new strategies and behaviors to attain them will be called for. Variation in goals, strategies, and behaviors, therefore, can always be found in a given population.

At any point in time, we may, if we so desire, stop the flow of action and make statistical summaries of the behaviors selected and performed in given situations by the members of a community. This will provide us with the relative frequencies of the various behaviors actually being selected and performed. Those with the greatest frequency distributions, of course, are the patterned regularities described and analyzed by social scientists. They also serve as the empirical referent for essentialist discussions and analyses of institutions and other higher level abstractions. The continuing presence of variation in the behavior of the members of a community, however, provides the potential for change in the static picture that results when we engage in the clock-stopping exercise to take statistical averages.

Within a given population the frequency of what, in the Darwinian metaphor, would be thought of as behavioral variants might remain relatively constant over a period of time. From the essentialist point of view, such a situation would result in the persistence of the patterns and institutions—in a static society. From our point of view, however, the persistence of a high frequency of some given behavior reflects continuing reinforcement and selection by individuals in their decision making, and hence the success of the variant vis-à-vis others. When, on the other hand, we observe a change in the relative frequency of behaviors, we have social change.

In the Darwinian/populational view proposed here, change in frequencies is due to changes in the distribution of behavioral variants which are being rewarded. That is, new or different behaviors at times may enable members of a community to obtain resources not previously obtainable, or obtainable in inefficient ways. The new behaviors will increase in the frequency of their appearance with respect to the appearance of other forms. As we see it, this process is directly analogous to the manner in which some organisms, through the process of natural selection, contribute their genes disproportionately to the gene pool of the breeding group of which they are a part. Successful new behavior will be copied and transmitted at the expense of older, now less effective forms. The more rewarded variants then will become preponderant statistically with the passage of time, assuming that selective pressures remain constant.

What we find particularly interesting in all of this is that where the essentialist must appeal to separate models of social statics and social dynamics (Glade 1967), or social structure and social organization (Firth 1964), the populationist needs only one. The only difference between statics and dynamics or structure and organization is the characteristics of the selective pressures which lead to the maintenance of a given frequency distribution of variant forms as opposed to selective pressures favoring a change. We assume that all populations, social and biological, change; but they do so at differing rates. The evolutionary biologist, for example, does not need one theory to analyze the shark, essentially unchanged over eons of time, and another for virus and bacteria which are changing almost visibly in response to antibiotics pumped into their habitats.

Can general statements be made about selective pressures? If we turn to the studies from which our imagery is taken, we would be led to anticipate that any generalization about selective pressures would be difficult to make. As the biologist Stebbins writes,

.... the fact was brought out that populations evolve new characteristics largely as a result of changes in the organism-environment relationship, acting through the medium of natural selection. Since environments are very diverse and complex in both space and time, organism-environment relationships are always different for related populations living in different parts of the earth, and are perpetually changing as the earth's environments are altered in various ways. Changes in climate, in the distribution of land and sea, elevation and degradation of mountain systems, and particularly the increase, decrease, and extinction of different kinds of animals and plants all interact to produce changes in organism-environment relationships . . . these changes affect the nature, course, and rate of evolution. (1966:85)

Stebbins, in effect, is saying that everything that affects a population may contribute to its potential change, which is to say to its evolution. We can safely assume that the factors that affect the selection of one or another form of human behavior in a community must be at least as complex as those impinging on the biological characteristics of a population.

There is one further point about the process of natural selection discussed by Stebbins that is of importance to us. It is that, potentially at least, everything with which an organism interacts may have an effect on its future states and that of the population of which it is a member. Stebbins does not exclude from his analysis the unique or accidental in the organism-environment relationship. In sum, the evolution of a population is viewed as the consequence of the history of the organisms that constitute it. The essentialist position in the social sciences, by contrast, seeks to factor out chance along with idiosyncratic events. To do this, it focuses on elements that appear across a range of societal settings. Consequently, history and those who study it have been placed outside the social sciences as practitioners of a separate, only tangentially related endeavor. The populationist, however, sees no difference between history and science. The regularities with which science must deal, he would maintain, are neither in the events to be described nor in the generalizations abstracted from them. The regularities instead lie in the process of selection and adaptation rather than in the outcomes of the process. The rejoining of history and science that this view leads to is but one of the advantages of the position we advocate.

A NEW FRAMEWORK FOR ENTREPRENEURIAL STUDIES

Having presented in broad strokes our alternative populational view of the world based on the metaphor of the Darwinian biological system, and having shown that we are able to generate from it both social regularities or patterns and changes in the statistical frequencies that constitute the patterns, we now return to entrepreneurship and entrepreneurial behavior.

According to Schumpeter (1949:74), who, as has been indicated in the introductory chapter, was the first scholar to treat the subject in a major theoretical work, enterprise is the "carrying out of new combinations. . . ." The individuals who carry them out he defined as entrepreneurs. Schumpeter and those to follow in the tradition he started, however, proceeded to place the subject in the essentialist framework. This is why the scholars, whose work Alexander (1967) summarized and which Glade (1967) rightly criticized, were looking for features that characterized entrepreneurs, with entrepreneur as a typological construct.

For Schumpeter the entrepreneur also was the key to social and economic change. In the evolutionary or developmental variant of the essentialist framework, this could only mean that entrepreneurs moved economies and societies—which were real entities and, according to the metaphor of organic growth, grew in stages (Nisbet 1969)—from one typological state or stage to the next.

Having rejected the essentialist framework, however, we can now place Schumpeter's definition of entrepreneur in our framework of the individual members of a community making decisions and choices and acting in terms of them. Entrepreneurship can still be defined as the carrying out of new combinations, but the role of the entrepreneur in the social process must be reconsidered.

An entrepreneur carries out new combinations, which is to say makes decisions and behaves in ways that differ from the behavior of others in his community. This new behavior, on occasion, may enable him to obtain the goals and rewards he desires. On other occasions it may not. The new combinations themselves are neither good nor bad, advantageous nor disadvantageous. They are simply additional variants to the range of behaviors already present in the population.

At certain times, for reasons related to the unique history of the community, some innovative, entrepreneurial behavior may bring to the individual the ends he desires, which also may be sought by a large number of others in the population. In the competition among individuals for specific goals, the new variant is considered successful. Others also desiring the goal may learn and copy the new behavior, selecting it from among alternatives, if it is within the constraints of the situation, as they think through and choose the means to obtain their ends.

As individuals reach the conclusion that the selection of the new variant, if feasible, increases the probability of their also obtaining a desired goal, the frequency of occurrence of the new behavior will increase. In time that increase, relative to the occurrence of alternatives, may be so great that in the statistical analysis of patterns it will replace the previously most widely practiced form. The behavior most often selected and performed in a community is the patterned regularity described by the ethnographer. But as more people choose a variant that now appears to offer them a greater probability of success, the pattern for the population will be altered. In the imagery of the Darwinian metaphor, the new pattern, in this case introduced by the entrepreneur, may be said to have been selected over the one that had been preponderant previously.

The selection of a variant introduced by an entrepreneur into a population may be more or less significant for that population. In some cases, the new behavior may lead to additional alternatives and changes in the alignment of selective features so that the secondary effects of the entrepreneurial activity may be far more profound than the original variation.

The consequences of some changes, we also should note, may not always be viewed as beneficial by all members of the community in which they occur. In fact, from the perspective of the values and definitions of the members of a given population, they may even result in reduced access to resources by some, perhaps as a consequence of new and increased constraints. In such cases the innovation could be considered harmful by some members of the community.

But we have gone far beyond a discussion of entrepreneurship. In our populational view of the world we are able to treat entrepreneurship as one source of variation among many in a population. Without slipping out of the populational decision-making framework, we are able to see that an appreciation of the role of the entrepreneur requires that we seek the selective factors that determine the fate of entrepreneurial innovations. In the framework of the new metaphor, the entrepreneur introduces variant behavior

348

into a community; but the ultimate historical significance of his activities is the result of the selective process. It is only if an innovative act is copied, and its frequency increased, or has secondary effects, that it appears as a patterned regularity, or institution in the community.

Previous social science studies of entrepreneurship have taken as their subjects the successful, that is, they have been studies of individuals whose innovative decisions and behaviors were selected positively within their community. Failures, on the other hand, to the extent that they have been considered at all, have appeared as deviants. In the populationist view, of course, deviants and failures are but the other half of the coin to innovators and entrepreneurs. They are but individuals whose innovative contributions have not been copied by others, and instead have been negatively selected for. In the populationist view, both successes and failures can be viewed as individuals seeking new or modified ways to obtain goals. Theoretically they are the source of both social pattern and its change.

NOTES

1. Limitations of space prevent us from presenting the philosophical and theoretical arguments that have led us to reject essentialism in all of its varieties, that is, evolutionism or developmentalism, historicism and structural-functionalism. We direct the interested reader to the following sources that have been critical to our thinking: Thomas Kuhn (1970), Colin Turbayne (1971), and Robert Nisbet (1969).

2. Limitations of space also force us but to outline in very broad strokes the main features of the position we are advocating. A more detailed statement will be forthcoming in a later publication.

3. We are equally indebted to the work of John Bennett (1969, 1976a, 1976b) who, like Barth, however, has not projected his critical insights and conceptual reformulation beyond the microlevel.

4. Our summary of the Darwinian view follows the writing not only of Darwin (1909, original 1859) himself, but of contemporary biologists and geneticists such as Dobzhansky (1962), Mayr (1976), Simpson (1949), Stebbins (1966), and Volpe (1967).

5. Darwin himself did not know the causes of the variation in the populations he studied. They were learned only later, with the development of the science of genetics. Although the knowledge and understanding contributed by genetics strengthened and added to Darwin's theory, it did not change its essential features.

6. The decision-making framework has long been used by microeconomists and planners. There is at least one significant difference, however, between the way in which they have used it and what we propose. That difference relates to the contrast between the essentialist world view to which they are wedded and the populational one we are developing.

In using the decision-making model economists and planners generally assume that for each decision, there is an optimal or right choice from among the alternative possibilities. This right selection represents what in their view would be the rational decision that should be made by the person faced with the choice. Its selection, it is maintained, would maximize for the individual the probabilities of obtaining the goal assumed by the analyst to be desired.

The clear implication is that there is a right choice. This premise, however, rests upon the further assumption that the analyst knows the goals which are sought not only by the individual in question, but also by all potential individuals that may be faced with the decision. The implication is that there is an objective truth out there and the role of the analyst is to advise and help individuals to obtain it.

Our view of the world emphasizes diversity as opposed to a belief in the existence of true forms whose essences are to be sought in the conduct of research. Consequently, we propose to be more ethnographic in our assumptions than the economists and planners have been. Since we have assumed that the world of social phenomena rests on symbols, and symbols are arbitrary and subject to redefinition and change, we do not dare to assume that we know the goals sought by individual actors, before the fact. Instead, the goals and rewards desired by the people we study are to be determined by us in the conduct of research. And since we assume the individuals know what they want while we do not, we further assume that they are in a better position than we are to evaluate the means by which they may obtain those goals. Consequently, we eschew the idea that the role of the analyst in our use of the decision-making framework is to help actors make more rational decisions. Instead, we wish to understand the choices and decisions made, along with the reasoning on which they are based. We then wish to separate those choices that result in success—obtaining the goals of the individual—and investigate the ways in which they are learned and copied by others. Therefore, although our approach at first glance is similar to that employed for some time by economists and planners, when qualified by the assumptions derived from the populational view of the world, the differences and their implications become clear.

7. These possible negative consequences, or costs, are what the microeconomist refers to as constraints.

References

ADAMS, RICHARD N.

1959 "A Community in the Andes: Problems and Progress in Muquiyauyo," in *Proceedings of the American Ethnological Society* (Seattle: University of Washington Press).

1970 "Brokers and Career Mobility Systems in the Structure of Complex Societies," *Southwestern Journal of Anthropology* 26:315–27.

AITKEN, HUGH G. J.

1967 "Entrepreneurial Research: The History of Intellectual Innovation," in *Explorations in Enterprise*, ed. Hugh G. J. Aitken (Cambridge, Mass.: Harvard University Press).

ALDERSON-SMITH, G.

1975 "The Social Basis of Peasant Political Activity" (Ph.D. diss., University of Sussex).

ALEXANDER, ALEC

1967 "The Supply of Industrial Entrepreneurship," *Explorations in Entrepreneurial History*, 2d series, 4:136–49.

ALISKY, MARVIN

1973 "CONASUPO: A Mexican Agency Which Makes Low-Income Workers Feel Their Government Cares," *Inter-American Economic Affairs* 27:47–59.

ALLEN, T. J. AND S. T. COHEN

1969 "Information Flow in Research and Development Laboratories," *Administrative Science Quarterly* 14:12–15.

ALLISON, GRAHAM T.

1969 "Conceptual Models and the Cuban Missile Crisis," *American Political Science Review* 63:689–718.

ALLISON, GRAHAM T., AND M. H. HALPERIN

1972 "Bureaucratic Politics: A Paradigm and Some Policy Implications," in *Theory and Policy in International Relations*, ed. Richard H. Ullman and R. Tanter (Princeton: Princeton University Press).

ANDRADE, V. DE P.
1910 *Estudio sobre la Ciudad de Apan, E. de Hidalgo* (Mexico City: El Tiempo).
ANSOFF, H. I.
1965 *Corporate Strategy* (Harmondsworth, U.K.: Penguin Books).
ARONSON, D. R. (ED.)
1970 "Social Networks," a symposium, *Canadian Review of Sociology and Anthropology* 7.
AUBEY, ROBERT T.
1969 "Entrepreneurial Formation in El Salvador," *Explorations in Entrepreneurial History* 6:268–85.
1970 "Private-Sector Capital Mobilization and Industrialization in Latin America," *Journal of Interamerican Studies and World Affairs* 12:583–601.
AUBEY, ROBERT T., JOHN KYLE, AND ARNOLD STRICKON
1974 "Investment Behavior and Elite Social Structure in Latin America," *Journal of Interamerican Studies and World Affairs* 16:71–95.
BARNEY, WILLIAM L.
1974 *The Secessionist Impulse: Alabama and Mississippi in 1860* (Princeton: Princeton University Press).
BARTH, FREDERIK
1963 *The Role of the Entrepreneur in Social Change in Northern Norway* (Bergen: Universitetsfoklaget).
1966 *Models of Social Organization*, Occasional Papers of the Royal Anthropological Institute of Great Britain and Ireland, no. 23.
1967 "On the Study of Social Change," *American Anthropologist* 69:661–69.
1969 "Introduction," in *Ethnic Groups and Boundaries*, ed. Frederik Barth (Boston: Little, Brown and Co.).
1972 "Analytical Dimensions in the Comparison of Social Organization," *American Anthropologist* 74:207–20.
BAILEY, F. G.
1957 *Caste and the Economic Frontier* (Manchester: Manchester University Press).
BASCH, ANTONÍN
1968 *El mercado de capital en México* (Mexico City: Centro de Estudios Monetarios Latinoamericanos).
BENEDICT, BURTON
1964 "Capital, Savings and Credit Among Mauritian Indians," in *Capital Savings and Credit in Peasant Societies*, ed. R. Firth and B. S. Yamey (London: George Allen and Unwin).
1966 *People of the Seychelles* (London: Her Majesty's Stationer's Office).
1968 "Family Firms and Economic Development," *Southwestern Journal of Anthropology* 24:1–19.
BENNETT, JOHN W.
1969 *Northern Plainsmen: Adaptive Strategy and Agrarian Life* (Chicago: Aldine Publishing Co.).
1976a "Anticipation, Adaptation and the Concept of Culture in Anthropology," *Science* 192:847–53.
1976b *The Ecological Transition: Cultural Anthropology and Human Adaptation* (New York: Pergamon Press).
BENTLEY, MARVIN
1973 "Incorporated Banks and the Economic Development of Mississippi, 1829–1837," *Journal of Mississippi History* 35:381–401.

352

References

BERMÚDEZ, ANTONIO J.
1963   *The Mexican National Petroleum Industry: A Case Study of Nationalization* (Stanford, Calif.: Institute of Hispanic American and Luso-Brazilian Studies, Stanford University).

BLAINE, JOHN EWING
1920   *The Blaine Family* (Cincinnati: Ebbert and Richardson).

BLAU, PETTER M., AND M. W. MEYER
1971   *Bureaucracy in Modern Society* (New York: Random House).

BOISSEVAIN, J.
1974   *Friends of Friends: Networks, Manipulators and Coalitions* (Oxford: Basil Blackwell, Pavilion Series).

BONEY, F. N.
1974   "Nathaniel Francis, Representative Antebellum Southerner," *Proceedings of the American Philosophical Society* 118:449–58.

BOTT, E.
1957   *Family and Social Network* (London: Tavistock Publications).

BOXER, C. R.
1949   "Padre Antonio Viera, S.J., and the Institution of the Brazil Co.," *Hispanic American Historical Review* 29:474–97.
1952   *Salvador de Sa and the Struggle for Brazil and Angola, 1602–1686* (London: Athlone Press).
1969   *The Portuguese Seaborne Empire, 1415–1825* (New York: Alfred A. Knopf).

BRANDENBURG, FRANK R.
1962   "A Contribution to the Theory of Entrepreneurship of the Developing Areas: The Case of Mexico," *Inter-American Economic Affairs* 16:3–23.
1964a   *The Development of Latin American Private Enterprise* (Washington, D.C.: National Planning Association).
1964b   *The Making of Modern Mexico* (Englewood Cliffs, N.J.: Prentice-Hall).

BRAZÃO, EDUARDO (ED.)
1940   *Dom Affonso VI Segundo Um Manuscrito da Biblioteca de Ajuda, Sobre Seu Reinado* (Pôrto, Portugal: Livraria Civilzaçao).

BUTLER, PIERCE
1948   *The Unhurried Years: Memories of the old Natchez Region* (Baton Rouge: Louisiana State University Press).
1954   *Laurel Hill and Later* (New Orleans).

CALHOUN, ROBERT D.
1932   "A History of Concordia Parish, Louisiana," *Louisiana Historical Quarterly* 15:620–32.

CAMPBELL, RANDOLPH B.
1974   "Planters and Plain Folk: Harrison County, Texas, as a Test Case, 1850–1860," *Journal of Southern History* 40:369–93.

CARDOZA, MANUEL
1950   "Notes for a Biography of Salvador Correia de Sá e Benavides, 1594–1688," *The Americas* 7:135–70.

CAREY, RITA K.
1947   "Samuel Jarvis Peters," *Louisiana Historical Quarterly* 30:442–75.

CARTER, HODDING, AND BETTY W. CARTER
1955   *So Great a Good* (Sewanee, Tenn.: Sewanee University Press).

CARVALHO, FRANCO
1941   *Os Correia do sa na Historia das Minas de São Paulo, 1578–1662* (São Paulo: Estado de São Paulo).

CHISHOLM, J. JULIAN
1972   *History of the First Presbyterian Church of Natchez* (Natchez: McDonald's Printers).
1975   *The Civil War Tax in Louisiana: 1865; based on direct tax assessment of Louisianans* (New Orleans: Polyanthos).

CLAIBORNE, F.
1803   "A List of the Gentlemen Little Nabobs of the Mississippi Territory," in Miscellaneous Collections of the American Philosophical Soceity, Philadelphia.

CLAIBORNE, J. F. H.
1880   *Mississippi, as a Province, Territory and State* (Jackson).

CLEAVES, PETER S.
1974   *Bureaucratic Politics and Administration in Chile* (Berkeley and Los Angeles: University of California Press).

COARCY, VIVALDO
1965   *O Rio de Janeiro no Seculo 17* (Rio de Janeiro: José Olympio Editora).

COBB, GWENDOLYN B.
1949   "Supply and Transportation for the Potosí Mines, 1540–1640," *Hispanic American Historical Review* 29:25–45.

COCHRAN, THOMAS C.
1960   "Cultural Factors in Economic Growth," *Journal of Economic History* 20:515–30.
1964   *The Inner Revolution: Essays on the Social Sciences in History* (New York: Harper & Row).

COHN, DAVID L.
1940   "Natchez Was a Lady," *Atlantic Monthly* 165:13–19.

DARWIN, CHARLES ROBERT
1909   *The Origin of Species* (1859; New York: P. F. Collier & Sons).

DAVID, PAUL, HERBERT E. GUTMAN, RICHARD SUTCH, PETER TEMIN, AND GAVIN WRIGHT
1976   *Reckoning with Slavery* (New York: Oxford University Press).

DAVIDSON, CHALMER G.
1971   *The Last Foray: The South Carolina Planters of 1850: A Sociological Study* (Columbia: University of South Carolina Press).

DAWES, EMMA L. M.
1953   "Judge Thomas Butler of Louisiana: A Biographical Study of an Ante-Bellum Jurist and Planter" (M.A. thesis, Louisiana State University).

DE FOREST, EMILY JOHNSTON
1926   *James Colles, 1788–1883* (New York: privately printed).

DEGLER, CARL
1974   *The Other South* (New York: Harper & Row).

DeGRUMMOND, JEWELL L.
1948   "A Social History of St. Mary Parish" (M.A. thesis, Louisiana State University).

D'ELIA, DONALD J.
1967   "Dr. Benjamin Rush and the Negro," *Journal of the History of Ideas* 30:413–22.

DEROSSI, FLAVIA
1971   *The Mexican Entrepreneur* (Paris: Development Center of the Organization for Economic Cooperation and Development).

References

DOBZHANSKY, THEODOSIUS
1962   *Mankind Evolving: The Evolution of the Human Species* (New Haven: Yale University Press).
DOMETT, HENRY W.
1884   *A History of the Bank of New York, 1784–1884 (New York: privately printed)*.
DOUGHTY, P. L.
1970   "Behind the Back of the City: Provincial Life in Lima, Peru," in *Peasants in Cities*, ed. W. Mangin (Boston: Houghton Mifflin Co.).
DOUGLASS, W. A.
1971   "Peasant Emigrants: Reactors or Actors," in *Migration and Anthropology*, Proceedings of the American Ethnological Society (Seattle: University of Washington Press).
DOWNS, ANTHONY
1967   *Inside Bureaucracy* (Boston: Little, Brown and Co.).
DURAND, PIERRE
1974   "Anthropologie politique des communautés paysannes de la sierra Norte de Puebla (Mexique): Deux villages de basse montagne," *Anthropologica* 16:205–32.
ECKSTEIN, ALEXANDER
1958   "Individualism and the Role of the State in Economic Growth," *Economic Development and Cultural Change* 2:81–87.
ELLIS, HOWARD S.
1964   *Industrial Capital in Greek Development* (Athens: Center of Economic Research).
ENGERMAN, STANLEY L.
1975   "A Reconsideration of Southern Economic Growth, 1770–1860," *Agricultural History* 49:343–61.
EPSTEIN, A. L.
1963   "The Network and Urban Social Organization," *Rhodes-Livingstone Journal* 29:29–62.
EVANS, T. M. S.
1977   "The Prediction of the Individual in Anthropological Interactionism," *American Anthropologist* 79:579–97.
FEI HSIAO-TUNG
1946   *Peasant Life in China* (New York: O.V.P.).
FERNÁNDEZ Y FERNÁNDEZ, RAMÓN, AND RICARDO ACOSTA
1969   *Política Agrícola* (Mexico City: Fondo de Cultura Económica).
FEYDIT, JULIO
1900   *Subsidios Para a Historia dos Campos dos Coytacazes Campos* (Rio de Janeiro: J. Alvarenga).
FILLOL, TOMÁS R.
1961   *Social Factors in Economic Development: The Argentinian Case* (Cambridge, Mass.: M.I.T. Press).
FINANCIAL TIMES SURVEY
1975   "Seychelles," May 17 (London).
FIRTH, RAYMOND
1964   *Elements of Social Organization* (Boston: Beacon Press).
FOGEL, ROBERT W., AND STANLEY L. ENGERMAN
1974   *Time on the Cross* (Boston: Little, Brown and Co.).
FOLSOM, BURTON W., II
1973   "The Politics of Elites: Prominence and Party in Davidson County, Tennessee, 1835–1861," *Journal of Southern History* 39:359–78.

FOSTER, B. L.
1974   "Ethnicity and Commerce," *American Ethnologist* 1:437–48.
FOUST, JAMES D.
1967   "The Yeoman Farmer and Westward Expansion of U.S. Cotton Production" (Ph.D. diss., University of North Carolina).
FREEDMAN, M.
1958   *Lineage Organization in Southeastern China*, London School of Economics Monographs in Social Anthropology (London: Athlone Press).
FRIEDRICHS, ROBERT
1970   *A Sociology of Sociology* (New York: Free Press).
GALBRAITH, JOHN KENNETH
1973   *Economics and the Public Purpose* (Boston: Houghton Mifflin Co.).
GALLMAN, ROBERT E., AND RALPH V. ANDERSON
1977   "Slaves as Fixed Capital: Slave Labor and Southern Economic Development," *Journal of American History* 64:24–46.
GATES, PAUL W.
1960   *The Farmer's Age: Agriculture, 1815–1860* (New York: Holt, Rinehart).
GEERTZ, CLIFFORD
1963   *Peddlers and Princes: Social Change and Economic Modernization in Two Indonesian Towns* (Chicago: University of Chicago Press).
GENOVESE, EUGENE D.
1974   *Roll, Jordan, Roll: The World the Slaves Made* (New York: Pantheon Books).
GHENT, JOYCE MAYNARD, AND FREDERIC C. JAHER
1976   "The Chicago Business Elite: 1830–1930: A Collective Biography," *Business History Review* 50:288–328.
GLADE, WILLIAM P., AND CHARLES W. ANDERSON
1963   *The Political Economy of Mexico* (Madison: University of Wisconsin Press).
GLADE, WILLIAM P.
1967   "Approaches to a Theory of Entrepreneurial Formation," *Explorations in Entrepreneurial History*, 2d series, 4:245–59.
GOLD, GERALD L.
1968   "The Commercial Complexity and Development of a Mexican Region" (M.A. thesis, University of Minnesota).
1974   "Structural Constraints to Sociability in Two Regional Elites," paper presented at the Annual Meeting of the Northeastern Anthropological Association, Burlington, Vermont.
1975   *Saint Pascal: Changing Leadership and Social Organization in a Quebec Town* (Toronto: Holt, Rinehart and Winston of Canada).
GOODSTEIN, ANITA S.
1976   "Leadership on the Nashville Frontier, 1780–1800," *Tennessee Historical Quarterly* 35:175–98.
GRANOVETTER, M.
1973   "The Strength of Weak Ties," *American Journal of Sociology* 78:1360–80.
GREENFIELD, SIDNEY M.
1966   *English Rustics in Black Skin: A Study of Modern Family Forms in a Pre-Industrial Society* (New Haven: College and University Press).
1977   "Madeira and the Beginnings of New World Sugar Cane Cultivation and Plantation Slavery: A Study in Institution Building," in *Comparative Perspectives on Slavery in New World Plantation Societies*, ed. Vera Rubin and Arthur Tuden (New York: New York Academy of Science).
GRUHLKE, VERNA KING
1971   *Small Town Wisconsin* (Madison: Wisconsin House).

References

GUTELMAN, MICHEL
1971   *Réforme et mystification agraire au Mexique* (Paris: Maspéro).
GUTMAN, HERBERT G.
1976   *The Black Family in Slavery and Freedom, 1750–1925* (New York: Pantheon Books).
HAGEN, EVERETT E.
1957   "The Process of Economic Development," *Economic Development and Cultural Change* 5:198.
1962   *On the Theory of Social Change* (Homewood, Ill.: Dorsey Press).
1968   *The Economics of Development* (Homewood, Ill.: Richard D. Irwin).
HAMBURGER, PHILIP
1963   "Notes for a Gazetteer: XL—Natchez, Miss.," *The New Yorker*, March 2, pp. 110–14.
HAMILTON, WILLIAM B.
1944   "The Southwestern Frontier, 1795–1817: An Essay in Social History," *Journal of Southern History* 10:389–403.
1948   "Politics in the Mississippi Territory," *Huntington Library Quarterly* 11:227–91.
HARBISON, F. H.
1956   "Entrepreneurship Organization as a Factor in Economic Development," *Quarterly Journal of Economics* 70:364–79.
HARRISON, WILLIAM F.
n.d.   "A Struggle for Land in Colonial Brazil: The Private Captaincy of Paraiba do Sul, 1553–1753" (unpublished manuscript).
HAYNES, ROBERT V.
1965   "The Formation of the Territory," in *A History of Mississippi*, ed. R. A. McLemore (Baton Rouge: Louisiana State University Press).
1976   *The Natchez District and the American Revolution* (Jackson: University Press of Mississippi).
HAZARI, R. K.
1966   *The Structure of the Corporate Private Sector: A Study of Concentration, Ownership, and Control* (London: Asia Publishing House).
HILGER, MARYE THARPE
1976   "Consumer Perceptions of a Public Marketer: The Case of Conasupo in Monterrey, Mexico" (Ph.D. diss., The University of Texas at Austin).
HIRSCHMAN, ALBERT O.
1963   *Journeys Toward Progress* (New York: Twentieth Century Fund).
HOFFMAN, FREDERICK L.
1900   *History of the Prudential Insurance Company of America (Industrial Insurance), 1875–1900* (Newark: Prudential Press).
HOLE, F. D., R. D. SALE, H. T. BEATTY, C. J. MILFRED, G. B. LEE, A. J. KLINGENHORTS, AND J. T. LIU
1968   *Overlay Soil Map of Wisconsin 1:250,000* (for use with the U.S. Geological Survey 1:250,000 Topographic Map) (Madison: University of Wisconsin Geological and Natural History Survey).
HOLMES, JACK D. L.
1965a   *Gayso: The Life of a Spanish Governor in Mississippi 1789–1799* (Baton Rouge: Louisiana State University Press).
1965b   "A Spanish Province," in *A History of Mississippi*, ed. R. A. McLemore (Baton Rouge: Louisiana State University Press).
HOLZMAN, JAMES M.
1926   *The Nabobs in England: A Study of the Returned Anglo-Indian, 1760–1785* (New York: privately printed).

357

HOMANS, GEORGE C.
1961   *Social Behavior: Its Elementary Forms* (New York: Harcourt, Brace and World).
HOSELITZ, BERT F.
1963   "Entrepreneurship and Traditional Elites," *Explorations in Entrepreneurial History* 1:36–49.
HUNT, ROBERT
1965   "The Developmental Cycle of the Family Business in Rural Mexico," in *Essays in Economic Anthropology*, ed. June Helm, 1965 Proceedings of the American Ethnological Society (Seattle: University of Washington Press).
IBARRA, ROBERT
1976   "Ethnicity, Genuine and Spurious" (Ph.D. diss., University of Wisconsin).
IRVINE, W.
1907   *Storia de Magor, or Mogul India, 1653–1708, by Niccolao Manucci, Venetian* (London).
JAMES, D. CLAYTON
1968   *Antebellum Natchez* (Baton Rouge: Louisiana State University Press).
JAMES, MARQUIS
1947   *The Metropolitan Life: A Study in Business Growth* (New York: Viking Press).
JOHNSON, HARRY
1967   *Economic Nationalism in Old and New States* (Chicago: University of Chicago Press).
JOHNSON, KENNETH
1971   *Mexican Democracy: A Critical View* (Boston: Allyn and Bacon).
KANE, HARNETT
1890   *Biographical and Historical Memoirs of Mississippi*, vol. 2 (Chicago).
1947   *Natchez on the Mississippi* (New York: Bonanza Books).
KARDINER, ABRAM
1939   *The Individual and His Society: The Psychodynamics of Primitive Social Organization* (New York: Columbia University Press).
KARDINER, ABRAM, RALPH LINTON, CORA DU BOIS, AND JAMES WEST
1945   *The Psychological Frontiers of Society* (New York: Columbia University Press).
KEESING, ROGER
1967   "Statistical and Decision Models of Social Structure: A Kwaio Case," *Ethnology* 6:1–16.
KHALAF, SAMIR, AND EMILIKE SHWAYRI
1966   "Family Firms and Industrial Development: The Lebanese Case," *Economic Development and Culture Change* 15:59–69.
KNIGHT, LUCIAN L.
1930   *History of Fulton County, Georgia, Narrative and Biographical* (Atlanta: A. H. Cawston).
KROEBER, A. L.
1944   *Configurations of Culture Growth* (Berkeley and Los Angeles: University of California Press).
1948   *Anthropology* (New York: Harcourt, Brace).
KUHN, THOMAS S.
1970   *The Structure of Scientific Revolutions* (Chicago: University of Chicago Press).

References

KULP, D. H.
1925   *Country Life in South China* (New York: Columbia University).

LAGOS, RICHARD
1962   *La concentración del poder económico: Su teoría, realidad chilena* (Santiago: Editorial del Pacífico).

LAITE, J.
1975   "Migration and the Development of Rural Entrepreneurship in the Peruvian Central Sierra" (mimeo).

LAMEGO, ALBERTO
1913–25 *A Terra Goytaca a Luz de Documentos Ineditos*, 3 vols. (Brussels and Rio de Janeiro).

LANDRY, STUART O.
1938   *History of the Boston Club* (New Orleans: Pelican Publishing Co.).

LANG, O.
1946   *Chinese Family and Society* (New Haven: Yale University Press).

LA PALOMBARA, JOSEPH (ED.)
1963   *Bureaucracy and Political Development* (Princeton: Princeton University Press).
1964   *Interest Groups in Italian Politics* (Princeton: Princeton University Press).

LARSON, HENRIETTA
1964   *Guide to Business History* (Boston: J. J. Canner & Co.).

LEE, SUSAN PREVIANT
1975   "The Westward Movement of the Cotton Economy, 1840–1860: Perceived Interests and Economic Realities" (Ph.D. diss, Columbia University).

LEEDS, A.
1964   "Brazilian Careers and Social Structure: An Evolutionary Model and Case History," *American Anthropologist* 66:1321–47.

LEIBENSTEIN, HARVEY
1957   *Economic Backwardness and Economic Growth* (New York: John Wiley & Sons).

LEITE, SERAFIM, S. J.
1938–50 *Historia de Comanhia de Jesus no Brasil*, 10 vols. (Rio de Janeiro).

LINTON, RALPH
1945   *The Cultural Background of Personality* (New York: D. Appleton-Century).

LIPMAN, AARON
1969   *The Colombian Entrepreneur in Bogotá* (Coral Gables, Fla.: University of Miami Press).

LIZONADO BORDA, M. (ED.)
1936–38 *Documentos coloniales relativos a San Miguel de Tucumán y la Gobernación del Tucumán*, ser. 1, 3 vols. (Tucumán, Argentina: Publicaciones de la Junta Conservadora del Archivo de Tucumán.).

LODAHL, JANICE BEYER, AND GERALD GORDON
1972   "The Structure of Scientific Fields and the Functioning of University Graduate Departments," *American Sociological Review* 37:57–72.

LOMNITZ, LARISSA
1971   "The Reciprocity of Favors in Urban Middle Class Chile," in *Studies in Economic Anthropology*, ed. George Dalton, American Anthropological Studies, no. 7 (Washington, D.C.: American Anthropological Association).

LOMNITZ, LARISSA, AND GERALD L. GOLD
1974   "From Net to Set: The Changing Reciprocity of Favors in the Mexican Upper Strata," paper presented at the Seventy-third Annual Meeting of the American Anthropological Association, Mexico City.

LONG, NORMAN
1972   "Kinship and Associational Networks Among Transporters in Rural Peru: The Problem of the 'Local' and the 'Cosmopolitan' Entrepreneur," in *Kinship and Social Networks* (London: Institute of Latin American Studies).
1973a   "Commerce and Kinship in the Peruvian Highlands," paper presented to the Seventy-second Annual Meeting of the American Anthropological Association, Toronto.
1973b   "The Role of Regional Associations in Peru," in *The Process of Urbanization* (Bletchley, U.K.: Open University Press).

LONG, N. AND B. ROBERTS
1975   "Regional Structure and Entrepreneurial Activity in a Peruvian Valley," final report for Social Science Research Council of the United Kingdom, deposited in the British Lending Library.

LONG, N., AND D. WINDER
1975   "From Peasant Community to Production Cooperative: An Analysis of Recent Government Policy in Peru," *Journal of Development Studies* 12:75-94.

LOVOLL, ODD SVERRE
1975   *A Folk Epic: The Bygdelag in America* (Boston: Twayne Publishers).

McBETH, MICHAEL C.
1966   "The Agrarian Revolution in Apan" (unpublished manuscript).

McCLELLAND, DAVID S.
1961   *The Achieving Society* (Princeton: D. Van Nostrand).

McELREATH, WALTER
1935   *History of the Industrial Life and Health Insurance Company* (Atlanta: Lyon-Young Printing Company).

MADAN, T. N.
1965   *Family and Kinship: A Study of the Pandits of Rural Kashmir* (London: Asia Publishing House).

MADSEN, WILLIAM, AND CLAUDIA MADSEN
1975   "The Cultural Structure of Mexican Drinking Behavior," in *Contemporary Cultures and Societies of Latin America*, ed. Dwight B. Heath, 2d ed. (New York: Random House).

MANGIN, W. P.
1959   "The Role of Regional Associations in the Adaptation of Rural Population in Peru," *Sociologus* 9:23-35.

MANNERS, GEORGE E., SR.
1959   "History of Life Insurance Company of Georgia, 1891-1955" (Ph.D. diss., Emory University).

MARÍN, JOSÉ NICOLÁS
1971   "Industrial Finance in Nicaragua" (Ph.D. diss., Harvard Business School).

MARK, LEONARD J.
1959   "The Favored Status of the State Entrepreneur in Economic Development Programs," *Economic Development and Cultural Change* 7:422-30.

MARSHALL, THEODORA B., AND GLADYS C. EVANS
1940   *They Found It in Natchez* (New Orleans).

MARTIN, LAWRENCE
1974   *The Physical Geography of Wisconsin* (Madison: University of Wisconsin Press).

MASSELMAN, GEORGE
1963   *The Cradle of Colonialism* (New Haven: Yale University Press).

References

MASTERMAN, MARGARET
1970   "The Nature of Paradigm," in *Criticism and the Growth of Knowledge*, ed. Imre Lakatos and Alan Musgrave (Cambridge: Cambridge University Press).

MAYR, ERNST
1976   *Evolution and the Diversity of Life* (Cambridge, Mass.: Harvard University Press, Belknap Press).

MEAD, MARGARET
1939   *From the South Seas: Studies of Adolescence and Sex in Primitive Societies* (New York: William Morrow).

MENN, JOSEPH K.
1964   "The Large Slaveholders of the Deep South, 1860" (Ph.D. diss., University of Texas).

MEYERS, MARGARET G.
1954   "Mexico," in *Banking Systems*, ed. Benjamin H. Beckhart (New York: Columbia University Press).

MILLER, ELINOR, AND E. D. GENOVESE (EDS.)
1974   *Plantation, Town, and County: Essays on the Local History of American Slave Society* (Urbana: University of Illinois Press).

MILLER, FRANK C.
1973   *Old Villages and a New Town: Industrialization in Mexico* (Menlo Park, Calif.: Cummings Publishing).

MINTZ, SIDNEY W., AND ERIC R. WOLF
1950   "An Analysis of Ritual Co-parenthood (Compadrazgo)," *Southwestern Journal of Anthropology* 6:341–68.

MOHR, CLARENCE L.
1972   "Slavery in Oglethorpe County, Georgia, 1773–1865," *Phylon* 33:4–12.

MOORE, JOHN HEBRON
1967   *Andrew Brown and Cypress Lumbering in the Old Southwest* (Baton Rouge: Louisiana State University Press).

MUNCH, PETER A.
1949   "Social Adjustment Among Wisconsin Norwegians," *American Sociological Review* 14:780–87.

MUNDALE, CHARLES I.
1973   "Local Politics, Integration, and National Stability in Mexico" (Ph.D. diss., University of Minnesota).

NESBIT, ROBERT C.
1973   *Wisconsin: A History* (Madison: University of Wisconsin Press).

NISBET, ROBERT A.
1969   *Social Change and History* (London: Oxford University Press).

NORTON, LUIS
1943   *A Dinastia dos Sas no Brasil, 1558–1662* (Lisbon: Agência Geraldas Colónias. Divisão de Publicaçoes e Biblioteca).

OLIVEIRA MARQUES, A. H. DE
1972   *History of Portugal*, 2 vols. (New York: Columbia University Press).

ORTIZ, S.
1967   "The Structure of Decision Making Among Indians of Colombia," in *Themes in Economic Anthropology*, ed. R. Firth (London: Tavistock Publications).

PAINE, ROBERT
1974   *Second Thoughts About Barth's Models*, Royal Anthropological Institute Occasional Paper, no. 32.

PARKER, WILLIAM N.
1970   "The Structure of the Cotton Economy of the Antebellum South,"
        Agricultural History 44:149–65.
1973   "Through Growth and Beyond," in *Business Enterprise and Economic Change*,
        ed. Louis P. Cain and Paul J. Uselding (Kent, O.: Kent State University Press).
PHILLIPS, ULRICH B. (ED.)
1909   *Plantation and Frontier: Documentary History of American Industrial Society*,
        vols. 1 and 2 (Cleveland, O.: Arthur H. Clark Co.).
1966   *American Negro Slavery* (Baton Rouge: Louisiana State University Press).
PILKINGTON, JOHN (ED.)
1975   *Stark Young: A Life in the Arts: Letters, 1900–1962*, vol. 2 (Baton Rouge:
        Louisiana State University Press).
PIZZARO E ARAUJO, JOSÉ DE SOUSA DE AZEVEDO
1820–22 *Memorias Historicas da Provincia de Rio de Janeiro*, 9 vols. (Rio de Janeiro).
POGGIE, JOHN J., JR.
1968   "The Impact of Industrialization on a Mexican Intervillage Network" (Ph.D.
        diss., University of Minnesota).
1972   "Ciudad Industrial: A New City in Rural Mexico," in *Technology and Social
        Change*, ed. H. Russell Bernard and Pertti J. Pelto (New York: Macmillan Co.).
POGGIE, JOHN J., JR., AND FRANK C. MILLER
1969   "Contact, Change and Industrialization in a Network of Mexican Villages,"
        Human Organization 28:190–98.
POPPER, KARL
1950   "The Open Society and Its Enemies," in *Spell of Plato*, vol. 1 (London:
        Routledge and Kegan Paul).
POSADA, ANTONIO J., AND JEANNE DE POSADA
1966   *The CVC: Challenge to Underdevelopment and Traditionalism* (Bogotá:
        Ediciones Tercer Mundo).
PUCKETT, NEWBELL N.
1926   *Folk Beliefs of the Southern Negro* (Chapel Hill: University of North Carolina
        Press).
RADCLIFFE-BROWN, A. R.
1933   "Social Sanctions," in *Encyclopedia of the Social Sciences*, vol. 13 (New York:
        Macmillan Co.).
1952   *Structure and Function of Primitive Society* (London: Cohen & West).
RADY, DONALD E.
1973   *Volta Redonda: A Steel Mill Comes to a Brazilian Coffee Plantation*
        (Albuquerque, N.M.: Rio Grande Publishing Co.).
REED, GEORGE L. (ED.)
1905   *Alumni Record*, Dickinson College, Carlisle, Pa.
REVIEWS IN AMERICAN HISTORY
1974   "The Econometrics of Slavery: A Symposium" (pp. 457–87).
RIBEIRO DE LESSA, CLADO
1940   *Salvador Correia de Sá e Benavides: Vida e Feitos* (Brasil-Lisbon:
        Principalmente).
RICHERSON, PETER J.
1977   "Ecology and Human Ecology: A Comparison of Theories in the Biological and
        Social Sciences," *American Ethnologist* 4:1–26.

362

References

RITZER, GEORGE
1975　*Sociology, a Multiple Paradigm Science* (Boston: Allyn and Bacon).

ROGERS, TOMMY W.
1971　"D. R. Hundley: A Multi-Class Thesis of Social Stratification in the Antebellum South," *Proceedings of the Southern Anthropological Society* 5:76–87.

ROSENBERG, CHARLES E. (ED.)
1975　*The Family in History* (Philadelphia: University of Pennsylvania Press).

ROTHSTEIN, MORTON
1968　"Sugar and Secession: A New York Firm in Ante-bellum Louisiana," *Explorations in Entrepreneurial History*, 2d series, 5:115–31.
1977　"The Natchez Nabobs: Kinship and Friendship in an Economic Elite," in *Toward a New View of America: Essays in Honor of Arthur C. Cole.* ed. Hans L. Trefousse (New York: Burt Franklin & Co.).

ROUFS, TIMOTHY G.
1971　"Education and Occupational Aspirations in a Changing Society" (Ph.D. diss., University of Minnesota).

ROURKE, FRANCIS E.
1969　*Bureaucracy, Politics, and Public Policy* (Boston: Little, Brown and Co.).

ROWE, J. W. F.
1959　*The Economy of the Seychelles and Its Future Development* (Seychelles: Government Printer).

RYLE, GILBERT
1949　*The Concept of Mind* (London: Hutchinson's University Library).

SAVETH, EDWARD N.
1966　"The American Patrician Class: A Field of Research," in *Kinship and Family Organization*, ed. Bernard Farber (New York: John Wiley and Sons).

SCARBOROUGH, WILLIAM K.
1973　"Heartland of the Cotton Kingdom," in *A History of Mississippi*, ed. R. A. McLemore, 2 vols. (Jackson: University and College Press of Mississippi).

SCHNEIDER, PETER, JANE SCHNEIDER, AND EDWARD HANSEN
1972　"Modernization and Development: The Role of Non-corporate Groups in the European Mediterranean," *Comparative Studies in Society and History* 14:338–50.

SCHUMPETER, JOSEPH A.
1934　*The Theory of Economic Development* (Cambridge, Mass.: Harvard University Press).
1939　*Business Cycles* (New York: McGraw-Hill).
1942　*Capitalism, Socialism, and Democracy* (New York: Harper & Bros.).
1949　*The Theory of Economic Development* (Cambridge, Mass.: Harvard University Press).
1954　*A History of Economic Analysis* (New York: Oxford University Press).

SEEBOLD, HERMAN DE BACHELLE
1941　"Butler Dynasty," in *Old Louisiana Plantation Homes and Family Trees*, 2 vols. (New Orleans: privately printed).

SELLARS, CHARLES C.
1973　*Dickinson College: A History* (Middleton, Conn.: Wesleyan University Press).

SEYCHELLES HANDBOOK
1976　(Victoria, Seychelles)

SEYCHELLES REPORT
1959–60 (London: Her Majesty's Stationer's Office)
SHATER, ROBERT
1966   *Mexico: Mutual Adjustment Planning* (Syracuse, N.Y.: Syracuse University Press).
SHENTON, JAMES P.
1961   *Robert John Walker* (New York: Columbia University Press).
SHEPPARD, JOHN H.
1871   *Reminiscences of Lucius Manlius Sargent* (Boston: David Clapp & Son).
SHIRLEY, R. W.
1971   *The End of A Tradition: Culture Change and Development in the Município of Cunha, São Paulo, Brazil* (New York: Columbia University Press).
SIMON, BARBARA
1973   "Power, Privilege, and Prestige in a Mexican Town: The Impact of Industry on Social Organization" (Ph.D. diss., University of Minnesota).
SIMPSON, GEORGE GAYLORD
1949   *The Meaning of Evolution* (New Haven: Yale University Press).
1955   *The Major Features of Evolution* (New York: Columbia University Press).
SITTERSON, J. CARLYLE
1943   "The William J. Minor Plantations: A Study in Ante-bellum Absentee Ownership," *Journal of Southern History* 9:59–74.
SMITH, ADAM
1937   *An Inquiry into the Nature and Causes of the Wealth of Nations* (1776; New York: Modern Library).
SMITH, DANIEL S.
1970   "Cyclical, Secular, and Structural Change in American Elite Composition," *Perspectives in American History* 9:351–74
SMITH, J. FRAZER
1941   *White Pillars: Early Life and Architecture of the Lower Mississippi Valley Country* (New York: W. Helburn).
SMITH, KATHERINE D.
1928   *The Story of Thomas Duncan and His Six Sons* (New York: T. A. Wright).
SMITH, PETER
1975   "La Movilidad Política en el México Contemporaneo," *Foro Internacional* 15:379–413.
SMITH, R. T.
1956   *The Negro Family in British Guiana* (London: Kegan Paul).
SMITH, W. WAYNE
1968   "Jacksonian Democracy on the Chesapeake: Class, Kinship, and Politics," *Maryland Historical Magazine* 63:55–67.
SOLTOW, LEE
1971   *Patterns of Wealthholding in Wisconsin Since 1850* (Madison: University of Wisconsin Press).
1975   *Men and Wealth in the United States, 1850–70* (New Haven: Yale University Press).
SOUTHERN WORKMAN
1897   "Beliefs and Customs Connected with Death and Burial," *Southern Workman* (Hampton Institute) 26:18–19.

References

STAVENHAGEN, RODOLFO
1970   "Social Aspects of Agrarian Structure in Mexico," in *Agrarian Problems and Peasant Movements in Latin America*, ed. Rodolfo Stavenhagen (New York: Anchor Books).

STEBBINS, G. LEDYARD
1966   *Process of Organic Evolution* (Englewood Cliffs, N.J.: Prentice-Hall).

STEITENROTH, CHARLES
1922   *One Hundred Years with "Old Trinity" Church* (Natchez).

STEPHENSON, WENDELL H.
1934   *Alexander Porter: Whig Planter of the Old South* (Baton Rouge: Louisiana State University Press).

STRACHAN, HARRY W.
1972   "The Role of Business Groups in Economic Development: The Case of Nicaragua" (Ph.D. diss., Harvard Business School).

STRATTON, REV. JOSEPH B.
1869   *Memorial of a Quarter-Century's Pastorate* (Philadelphia: T. B. Lippincott & Co.).

SYDNOR, CHARLES S.
1938   *A Gentleman of the Old Natchez Region: Benjamin L. C. Wailes* (Durham, N.C.: Duke University Press).

1966   *Slavery in Mississippi* (Baton Rouge: Reprinted by Louisiana State University Press).

TOWNSEND, REGINALD T.
1936   *Mother of Clubs: Being the History of the First Hundred Years of the Union Club of the City of New York, 1836–1936* (New York: privately printed).

TURBAYNE, COLIN M.
1971   *The Myth of Metaphor* (Columbia: University of South Carolina Press).

UGALDE, ANTONIO
1973   "A Decision Model for the Study of Public Bureaucracies," *Policy Sciences* 4:75–84.

VAN COURT, CATHERINE
1938   *In Old Natchez* (New York: Doubleday, Doran & Co.).

VARNHAGEN, FRANCISCO ADOLFO, BARAO DE PORTO SEGURO
1927–36 *Historia Geral de Brasil Antes Sua Separacão e Independencia de Portugal*, 3d ed. with additional notes by Capistrano de Abreu and Rodolfo Garcia, 5 vols. (São Paulo: Companhia Melhoramentos de São Paulo).

VERLINDEN, CHARLES
1954   *Precedents medievaux de la colonie en Amerique, Publicación num. 177 del Instituto Panamericano de Geografía e Historia* (Mexico City).

1966   *Les Origines de la civilisation Atlantique* (Paris: A. Michel. Neuchatel: La Bacconière).

1970   *The Beginnings of Modern Colonization* (Ithaca: Cornell University Press).

VOLPE, E. PETER
1967   *Understanding Evolution* (Dubuque, Iowa: Wm. C. Brown).

1977   *Understanding Evolution*, 3d ed. (Dubuque, Iowa: Wm. C. Brown).

VOTAW, DOW
1964   *The Six-Legged Dog; Mattei and ENI—A Study in Power* (Berkeley and Los Angeles: University of California Press).

WAINWRIGHT, NICHOLAS B.
1964   *The Irvine Story* (Philadelphia: Pennsylvania Historical Society).

365

WARMOTH, H. C.
1930   *War, Politics and Reconstruction: Stormy Days in Louisiana* (New York: Macmillan Co.).
WEAVER, GUSTINE C.
1929   *The Gustine Compendium* (Cincinnati: Powell & White).
WEBER, MAX
1930   *The Protestant Ethic and the Spirit of Capitalism*, trans. Talcott Parsons (London: George Allen and Unwin).
WEEMS, ROBERT C., JR.
1953   "The Makers of the Bank of Mississippi," *Journal of Mississippi History* 15:137–54.
WHETTEN, NATHAN L.
1948   *Rural Mexico* (Chicago: University of Chicago Press).
WHITE, LESLIE A.
1949   *The Science of Culture* (New York: Grove Press).
WHITING, BEATRICE B. (ED.)
1963   *Six Culture Studies of Child Rearing* (New York: John Wiley & Sons).
WILBURN, JEAN A.
1967   *Biddle's Bank: The Crucial Years* (New York: Columbia University Press).
WINDER, D.
1974   "The Effect of the 1970 Reform on the 'Peasant Communities' and on the Community Development Process in an Area of Peru" (M. Ed. thesis, Manchester University).
WINGFIELD, CHARLES L.
1950   "The Sugar Plantations of William J. Minor, 1830–1860" (M.A. thesis, Louisiana State University).
WIRTH, JOHN D.
1970   *The Politics of Brazilian Development, 1930–1954 (Stanford, Calif.: Stanford University Press).*
WYNIA, GARY W.
1972   *Politics and Planners: Economic Development Policy in Central America* (Madison: University of Wisconsin Press).
YOUNG, FRANK W., AND RUTH C. YOUNG
1960a   "Two Determinants of Community Reaction to Industrialization in Rural Mexico," *Economic Development and Cultural Change* 8:257–64.
1960b   "Social Integration and Change in Twenty-four Mexican Villages," *Economic Development and Cultural Change* 8:366–77.
1962   "Occupational Role Perceptions in Rural Mexico," *Rural Sociology* 27:42–52.
1966   "Individual Commitment to Industrialization in Rural Mexico," *American Journal of Sociology* 31:373–83.

Index

Index

Index

Index